ORTHO'S COMPLETE GUIDE TO Successful Houseplants

ORTHO'S
COMPLETE
GUIDE TO

Successful Houseplants

Editor   Marianne Lipanovich

Writers   Larry Hodgson, Dr. Charles C. Powell

Additional Writing by   Donald M. Vining

Ortho Books

Publisher
Richard E. Pile, Jr.

Editorial Director
Christine Jordan

Production Director
Ernie S. Tasaki

Managing Editors
Robert J. Beckstrom
Michael D. Smith
Sally W. Smith

System Manager
Linda M. Bouchard

Marketing Specialist
Daniel Stage

Distribution Specialist
Barbara F. Steadham

Sales Manager
Thomas J. Leahy

Technical Consultant
J. A. Crozier, Jr., Ph.D.

Address all inquiries to:
Ortho Books
Chevron Chemical Company
Consumer Products Division
Box 5047
San Ramon, CA 94583

Copyright © 1984, 1992
Chevron Chemical Company
All rights reserved under international and Pan-American copyright conventions.

1 2 3 4 5 6 7 8 9
92 93 94 95 96 97

ISBN 0-89721-249-5
Library of Congress Catalog Card
Number 92-70582

Chevron Chemical Company
6001 Bollinger Canyon Road
San Ramon, CA 94583

Contributing Editors
Tom Bass
Barbara Helfman

Writing Stylist
Naomi Wise

Illustrators
Kirk Caldwell: 77
Ron Hildebrand: 58, 59, 74, 81,
109, 165, 171

Design Consultant
JIL Design Group, Inc., Carmichael, Calif.

Photo Editor
Pamela K. Peirce

Editorial Coordinator
Cass Dempsey

Copyeditor
Hazel White

Proofreader
David Sweet

Indexer
Trisha Feuerstein

Layout by
Nancy Patton Wilson

Composition by
Laurie A. Steele

Associate Editor
Sara Shopkow

Editorial Assistant
Deborah Bruner

Production by
Studio 165

Separations by
Color Tech Corp.

Lithographed in the USA by
Webcrafters, Inc.

Designers
Carolina West Designs, San Francisco: 139
CoClico & Co. Inc., Interior and Exterior Landscape Design, San Francisco: 46, 51, 102T
Cois Pacoe Design, Sausalito, Calif.: 28, 138, 146
Trudi Copeland, Alamo, Calif.: 34–35
Helen Craddick, John Wheatman & Associates Inc., San Francisco: 32–33, 37
Craig Dinsdale, San Francisco: 162
Nancy Doolittle Residential Design, Palo Alto, Calif.: 56–57, 157
Nancy Glenn Design, Sausalito, Calif.: 38, 48–49
The Kreiss Collection, San Francisco: 139, 148
Gary Millar, Oakland, Calif.: 162–163
Ruth Livingston, Tiburon, Calif.: 12, 22, 23, 26–27, 54–55
Mary C. Peck Interiors, Menlo Park, Calif.: 17, 161, 169
Myra Posert, Laura Ashley Interior Design Service, San Francisco: 15
Nan C. Rosenblatt/Gabrielle Whitney, San Francisco: 20
Carlos Sanchez, Sanchez-Ruschmeyer Interior Design, San Francisco: 184–185, 198–199
Ruth Soforenko Associates, Palo Alto, Calif.: 1, 2–3, 8–9, 53, 82, 103L, 129, 143, 144, 159
Jonathan Straley, John Wheatman & Associates Inc., San Francisco: 105, 107
Van Fleet Construction, Ashland, Oreg.: 105, 107
John Wheatman, John Wheatman & Associates Inc., San Francisco: 30, 41, 79, 114–115, 118, 136–137

Photographic Plant Stylists
Milana Hames
Jo Ann Masaoka Van Atta

Photographic Credits Appear on Page 320.

Manufacturers of Self-Watering Planters
Decor America Incorporated, 250 West Artesia Boulevard, Compton, CA 90220
J & J Swift (for African violets), P.O. Box 28012, Dallas, TX 75228
Jardinier Planter Systems, Inc., P.O. Box 2368, La Habra, CA 90632
Natural Spring, Planter Technology, 999 Independence Avenue, Mountain View, CA 94043

Special Thanks to
Pamela Bain, Gary Beck, Judith Becker, Nathan Bennett, Jane Birge, Mr. & Mrs. Jonathan W. B. Cosby, John Demergasso, Jon Dixon, William D. Ewing, Geoffrey A. Gatz, Dorothy Gawienowski, Lynn Hansen, Jay Kilbourn, Alan Krosnick, Kenneth and Marilyn Lavezzo, Eli Lew, Janet Lennox Moyer, Harold & Susan Muller, Marina Ricciardi, Wes & Laurie Rose, Tralelia Twitty, Bruce Alan Van Natta, Charlotte Vrooman, Jacqueline Young; Adachi Florists and Nursery, El Cerrito, Calif.; American Plant Life Society, San Diego, Calif.; American Rose Society, Shreveport, LA; Benefit Guild of the East Bay, Piedmont, Calif.; Berkeley Horticultural Nursery, Berkeley, Calif.; Cactus Gems, Cupertino, Calif.; Conservatory of Flowers, Golden Gate Park, San Francisco; East Bay Nursery, Berkeley, Calif.; Floorcraft, San Francisco; Living Green, Plantscape Design, San Francisco; Magic Gardens, Berkeley, Calif.; Marie's Adoptable Violets, Healdsburg, Calif.; Ornamental Horticulture Department of City College of San Francisco; Plants Unlimited Inc.; San Lorenzo, Calif.; Rainbow Garden Nursery & Bookshop, Vista, Calif.; Red Desert Cactus, San Francisco; Shelldance, Pacifica, Calif.; Sloat Nursery (Wawona St. Store), San Francisco; Strybing Arboretum Society, San Francisco; Phyllis Sutton, San Francisco Decorator's Showcase; Tommy's Plants, San Francisco; Barbara Waldman, Designer Preview, San Francisco.

Front Cover
Flowering and foliage plants blend in this indoor garden. A lacy-tree philodendron (Philodendron selloum) nestles between the couch and table while the blue and white cachepot highlights the mother fern (Asplenium bulbiferum). On the coffee table, a peace-lily (Spathiphyllum), mistletoe fig (Ficus deltoidea) and blooming cymbidium orchid add color to the scene.

Title Page
Baskets, Hiemalis begonias (Begonia × hiemalis), and wax fruit form a three-dimensional still life on the shelf of an etagere.

Pages 2–3
Two weeping figs (Ficus benjamina) stand as sentinels along one wall of this formal dining room while a mother fern (Aspenium bulbiferum) and moth-orchids (Phalaenopsis) share the table with a prized collection of blue and white china. In the window, a maidenhair fern (Adiantum) benefits from the natural sunlight.

Back Cover
Top left: *Aechmea fasciata*
Top right: *Saintpaulia ionantha*
Bottom left: *Ficus benjamina*
Bottom right: *Crassula argentea*

Contents

Why do we have a fondness for plants in our homes? If all we're looking for is a particular shape, texture, or color, wouldn't something else—a piece of furniture, an urn, or a basket—do as well? The answer is a resounding no. In this technological age, there is a need to stay in touch with nature—a desire to have living, growing things around us. A happy, healthy plant fulfills these needs and supplies a sense of accomplishment.

The successful indoor gardener is someone who does more than merely garden indoors. Obviously, indoor and outdoor conditions are very different and what you grow is also different. But beyond the practical limitations, there is a different philosophy attached to indoor gardening. A houseplant on display has to look good at all times of the year. It must enhance and coordinate with other furnishings in your home—inanimate objects—whereas the outdoor plant is surrounded by its own kind.

"Designing With Houseplants" explains how to relate plants to the architecture, to the furniture, to art and accessories. Scale, shape, texture, color, and pattern all come into play in a well-designed room; and although most people recognize the importance of these basic principles, they overlook the fact that the same principles are just as applicable to plant choices as they are to furniture selection. If you feel the solution is to omit any living, growing elements in your decorating scheme, just remove the plants from a well-designed room that you find warm and exciting. Don't the resulting voids prove the importance of well-chosen plants?

Having established the importance of the role that indoor plants play, you next need to decide on your attitude toward them. Are you willing to spend hours nurturing a plant to bring it to its full potential? Or do you consider a plant an attractive accessory you are prepared to sustain but not pamper if it causes problems or gets sick? This will also make a difference in the types of plants you choose. If you belong to the first group, you won't mind caring for a fussy plant. If you belong to the second group, you will be happier and more successful with plants that are not as particular in their horticultural requirements. It is not a matter of the right attitude and the wrong one. It is a matter of recognizing which group you belong to and selecting appropriate plants.

To help with this decision, read the chapter on plant care and look through "A Gallery of Houseplants," which lists the maintenance requirements of individual plants. For the ambitious, there is a chapter on propagation techniques. Others may decide that the time, effort, and patience required to grow a plant from a cutting outweigh the appeal.

On the other hand, flowers appeal to everyone; so there is a special chapter on flowering houseplants. It includes methods for prolonging the blooming period of outdoor annuals and perennials by bringing them inside, as well as methods for forcing bulbs and flowering branches into bloom.

Greenhouses, solariums, and window greenhouses have become such popular architectural features that they also are included in this book. In many houses these additions serve partly as increased living space, partly as solar heat storage components, and partly as a growing environment.

A sick plant is an ugly plant, and the easiest solution is to throw it away. But for some people, that is like suggesting they discard a child. So for them and those not-too-terribly-sick plants, another chapter deals with the recognition and cure of common diseases and infestations.

This book aims to impart the joy of indoor gardening. It contains ideas and practical information, but the primary intent is to encourage you to bring life—houseplants—into your home.

Designing With Houseplants

With every passing year, our world becomes simultaneously more complex and uniform. Highrises, subdivisions, superhighways, shopping malls, and fast-food chains engulf our once-rural landscape. And video games and home computers make astonishingly casual use of a technology that a short time ago was confined to government and business offices. Little wonder so many people feel a need to renew their contact with nature by creating home environments where plants are at least as visible as technology.

Most people recognize that you cannot fill a room with furniture and hope that scale, texture, and color principles will be magically incorporated. By the same token, you cannot merely fill a room with plants and expect it to look like anything other than a greenhouse. The same design principles apply.

Plants are three-dimensional shapes, each one a complete original. Large leaves make bold patterns and cast strong geometric shadows, just as a Calder mobile does. Delicate, lacy leaves evoke images of impressionist paintings. Variegated leaves make as strong a statement as a striped cushion. Feathery fronds drape as romantically as ruffled bedspreads. And flowering houseplants offer as many blooms as chintz upholstery.

Comparing houseplants to furnishings is a useful process. Houseplants can play a dramatic role in the design of a room. This is the reason that you rarely see a photograph in a home magazine without at least one plant in it. This is the reason that lobbies in most offices are furnished with plants. The intent is to make you feel comfortable, to make you feel that this is a space to live in. How to achieve this designed look, rather than merely scattering plants about, is the subject of this chapter.

Flowering and foliage plants add a sense of grace to this elegant sitting area. A moth-orchid (Phalaenopsis), pansy orchid (Miltonia), and lady's slipper orchid (Paphiopedilum) set in an urn lend color and sweep that are echoed by the orchid on the table. The fishtail palm (Caryota mitis) provides a focal point and backdrop for the statue and couch.

Why Plants?

Plants create a dynamic, three-dimensional shape, and within that shape, the parts of the plant (its leaves and stems) form a balanced though not overly precise pattern. In a pattern-on-pattern interior, plants add their own inimitable motif. In a spare interior with primary colors and hard-edge furniture, plants add softness and detail. The "country look" is dependent on plants, and a solarium without a profusion of plants is like an empty greenhouse.

Plants also serve as a contrasting element in an overall design. Much as art deco designers in the 1920s included primitive carvings in sumptuously furnished interiors, adding a green plant to a high-tech environment serves as a contrast or a highlight.

Finally, there is the issue of life itself. Plants add life and warmth to interiors, and the fact that they are living things enhances their contribution to our spaces. If shape alone were the primary consideration, sculpture would suffice. If pattern were the only requirement, plastic plants or dried flowers would do. If contrast were the major design intent, decorative accessories would suffice. Living plants remind us of the wilderness, the beauty, and the diversity of life.

Right and opposite: Without plants, this sunroom seems bare and lifeless, despite a comfortable chair, good light, and pleasant view. The same room with plants is warm and inviting. A kentia palm (Howea forsterana) *and a* kumquat (Fortunella margarita) *frame the chair; oakleaf ivy* (Cissus rhombifolia) *drapes softly across the table and around a geranium* (Pelargonium); *flowering lace-cap hydrangeas, brought in from outside, add color and interest at floor level.*

Decorating With Plants

Decorating with plants is not the same as growing plants. Often, the spot that a houseplant occupies is chosen for pragmatic rather than aesthetic reasons, so by default the plant is displayed where it will grow well with no thought as to where it might have looked the best.

The placement of plants in a room should be a matter of taste and design as well as a question of available light, but are the two compatible? It's possible. Sometimes the place where a plant would look best in a room happens to be near a window. Sometimes the furnishings in a room can be rearranged to accommodate a plant near a window, or special lighting can be installed to keep plants thriving in a dark corner. Nonetheless, decorating with plants does involve some restrictions and pose some problems.

To decorate with plants, you must first establish purpose and intent. Begin by asking yourself where you would put the plant and how you would display it if it were some other decorative object— a large jar or a piece of sculpture. This is the most effective way to make the distinction between growing and decorating.

A delightful example of decorating with houseplants is described in a word picture taken from the biography of Lady Victoria Sackville, the mother of one of England's most famous gardeners, Vita Sackville-West: "Two Bacchanalian little vines, dwarfed but bearing bunches of grapes of natural size, stood in gold winecoolers on either side of the door." Aside from the undeniable charm of the idea, the little potted grapevines were treated like pieces of furniture, like elements of the decorative scheme. Their stations by the doors were fixed, their mode of display constant, and the plants themselves were kept picture perfect by rotation and renewal from a stock of similar fruiting vines in Lady Sackville's greenhouses. This example points out the difference between a view of plants that is strictly horticultural and one that includes the possibility of plants as decoration.

Opposite: This crested euphorbia (Euphorbia lactea 'Cristata') *is no shrinking violet. It proclaims its presence, a vital element in the decorating scheme of this bedroom. The irregular form and complex texture contrast with the clean, smooth surfaces of the walls and floor. The soft color of the plant harmonizes with the muted shades of the walls and carpeting, and the large, strong shape is in keeping with the scale of the other furnishings.*

Perhaps the quickest way to get a feeling for using plants is by observing how others use them. Owners of commercial buildings often employ professional plant designers, who are skilled in putting both foliage and flowering plants into a pleasing arrangement. Home magazines, too, do a fine job of presenting ideas for decorating with plants. Even observing a well-kept garden will show you how different plants can work together.

Keep in mind, however, that some plant arrangements, pleasing though they are to the eye, are not healthy for the plants. Plant care services can replace a plant growing in a poor location when it starts to flag. Magazines can decorate perfectly because they rent or buy plants just for the photography session. The editors and photographers don't have to worry about the future of the plants; they can arrange them how and where they will look best. But can the home decorator or plant grower be equally cavalier with houseplants? Well, yes and no. You can decorate with plants the way magazines do, with design factors uppermost in your mind, but you will still have to provide appropriate plant care. This may mean taking care to choose plants that will thrive in a specific location, or rotating them between two locations: one where the plant looks best and another, possibly in a different part of the house, where it grows best.

Massive size is not the only way of making a statement, as is proved by this air plant (Tillandsia). Its small, round shape resonates with the shapes of the surrounding objects; the soft green of its leaves is reflected in the muted shades of the painting above.

Choosing Plants

Just like furnishings, plants vary in looks, size, and shape. When choosing a plant for a particular spot, you need to consider not only whether the cultural needs of the plant will be satisfied, but also whether the plant will fulfill your decorating needs. For simplicity, plants can be divided into five categories of size and shape: tall, fan shapes; low, bushy shapes; column shapes; soft, feathery shapes; and strong, graphic shapes. Plants with flowers are a separate category; flowering houseplants can make a strong design statement by adding color to an area. The following discussion describes the characteristics of plants in each of these categories. It also suggests some common plants that fall in each category, and how they can be used decoratively in the home.

Tall, Fan Shapes

Tall, fan shapes are the designer's workhorses, often pictured in home magazines. These plants fill the corners, bracket the sofas, back the wing chairs, and hide the radiators. (In real life, of course, hot radiators are anathema to any plant.) Their virtue is that they spread out at the top but take up little floor space. They can be so integral to the design of a room that if they are removed the room looks bare and lifeless.

   Palms are the queens of the tall, fan plants. The fronds rise from a small base and fan out at the top. The best known are the areca palm (*Chrysalidocarpus lutescens*), the date palm (*Phoenix roebelenii*), the kentia palms (*Howea forsterana* and *Howea*

This kentia palm (Howea forsterana) fills and decorates an empty corner, a classic use for tall fan-shaped palms. Be sure to place palms where they will get bright indirect light, and inspect them regularly for spider mites.

belmoreana, which were the original potted palms of Victorian salons), the Chinese fan palm (*Livistona chinensis*), the bamboo palm (*Chamaedorea erumpens*), the reed palm (*Chamaedorea seifrizii*), the fishtail palm (*Caryota mitis*), the lady palms (*Rhapis* species), and the parlor palm (*Chamaedorea elegans*, also called *Neanthe bella*).

The weeping fig (*Ficus benjamina*) is a fashionable replacement for and complement to the palm. It is a tall, delicate, well-shaped tree, suitable for filling high, empty spaces above and between furnishings. Unfortunately, it is particular about where it grows. In most rooms (even ones with several windows), the upper walls and ceiling are too dark. The ideal spot for a tall ficus is an atrium, light well, or solarium. You can achieve some success with overhead spotlights supplementing the natural light, but if you don't have an appropriate spot, choose a different plant for your home and enjoy the weeping fig in the glass atrium at the office.

For a more dramatic effect, the weeping fig can be replaced by its more tolerant cousin, *Ficus maclellandii* 'Alii', whose long, strap-shaped leaves provide the look of the Far East to any interior.

That other office institution, the cornplant (*Dracaena fragrans*), fits well in the home. Three to five individual plants of this trunk-forming species can be placed in a pot to make one full, fan shape. Although palms will not survive behind a sofa, a cornplant usually will as long as there's a window nearby. In dark locations, growth is extremely slow and overwatering becomes a danger.

Another tall, fan shape is the variegated screwpine (*Pandanus veitchii*). A mature specimen is striking and the same size as a large indoor palm. The whorl of long, tapering blades, which spring from the stem in a perfect spiral, are bordered with yellow and striped along their length with pale green bands. It can be killed by prolonged exposure to temperatures below 55° F but will survive nearly every other condition. Give it a sunny location and watch it grow.

In southern California and other warm climates, dwarf banana trees (*Musa* species) in tubs can be brought inside occasionally to provide a tall, fan shape. Patio-grown citrus or loquat (*Eriobotrya japonica*) can also be brought inside. These plants can be grown indoors the year around in an especially sunny location.

Other choices for a tall, fan shape include the spiky, spineless yucca (*Yucca elephantipes*), the spreading umbrella tree (*Brassaia actinophylla*), and the China-doll (*Radermachera sinica*).

Low, Bushy Shapes

Low, bushy plants look handsome sitting alone on the floor next to a low piece of furniture, softening the lines of the furniture by their roundness, or filling any other ground-level design space.

These low, spreading oakleaf ivies (Cissus rhombifolia) fill in space around furniture without distracting the eye from the other design elements in the room. On plant stands, they are at just the desired height and will spread instead of growing too tall for the space.

They are also particularly effective on stands. In fact, if you place one of these plants on a tall stand (at least 4 feet high), it can substitute in design terms for a tall plant. Low, bushy shapes are best used alone rather than in combination with other plants (they are too large to be considered as tabletop plants).

A peace-lily (*Spathiphyllum* 'Mauna Loa') has an excellent low, bushy shape, and like the cornplant (*Dracaena fragrans*), it grows well in low light. When it is thriving, it sends up white flags (the showy spathe cradling the real flowers), signaling contentment, not surrender.

Philodendrons are also highly suitable low, bushy candidates. The lacy-tree philodendron (*Philodendron selloum*) is popular, although its leaves may flop with age and poor light.

A particularly dependable low, bushy shape is the cast-iron plant (*Aspidistra elatior*). The common name carries a genuine recommendation. Unlike most of the tropicals, which grow all through the year, aspidistra has a lengthy dormant period during which it is surprisingly undemanding. During dormancy, it can be used anywhere, window or no, and the cooler the room the better. When growth resumes in late winter, it requires good light, water, and fertilizer. Aspidistra benefits from a summer outdoors, in deep shade, or in a moderately bright, well-ventilated room.

A mature pot of Chinese evergreen (*Aglaonema*), especially of a type such as 'Silver Queen', makes a showy display. This philodendron relative looks like a small dieffenbachia with its gray-green, cream, and emerald leaf patterns, but it is not as coarse as the latter. Chinese evergreen sends up new shoots from the base of mature plants; it soon fills the pot, the many leaves overlapping each other. It, too, is very tolerant of low light.

The Kaffir-lily (*Clivia miniata*), whether in flower or not, is a good decorative choice even though it won't survive in dim light. Design a pot using several individual plants so that there will be several bloom spikes (one per plant). Kaffir-lily spends most of the year in a bloomless state, but its black-green, strap leaves are extremely decorative. When the plant is in bloom, it is resplendent with clusters of yellow-throated, orange trumpets, 10 to 15 on each spike. It requires a cool, bright, dry dormancy in the late fall and early winter; then, in late February or early March, when the flower spikes appear, it needs warmth, light, water, and fertilizer. During the summer, Kaffir-lily can be grown outdoors in deep shade or in bright, indirect light inside.

Orchids (*Cymbidium* species) are also low, bushy plants. In some varieties, both the strap leaves and the flower stalks arch. Orchids do best in a cool greenhouse, but while in bloom they can take a turn in a plant station. The uncut blooms last for six to eight weeks.

Column Shapes

Sometimes space restrictions dictate a column shape—an exclamation point of a plant that stands like a sentinel. A column makes a more formal architectural impression than does the tall, fan shape. Generally speaking, the sparer and more hard-edged the decor (a minimalist or high-tech interior, for example), the more appropriate a columnar plant becomes.

This dramatic pachypodium punctuates the decor like an exclamation point. To be effective, a striking plant needs surroundings that reflect its bold shape. Here, the antlers of the cast-iron statue serve that purpose, and the spreading epiphyllum behind the couch presents a strong counterpoint to the vertical line of the pachypodium.

Giant cacti and succulents, barely distinguishable from contemporary sculpture, are the obvious examples. Many euphorbias are very sculptural in appearance, often looking like branching baseball bats. Peruvian apple (*Cereus peruvianus*) has a similarly sculptural appearance.

Other naturally columnar plants include the coarse-leaved ficus plants, including the familiar rubber plant (*Ficus elastica*). (It should probably be renamed the supermarket ficus, since it's so often sold there.) Although the species is all green, several of its cultivars have greater color interest and will grow in an upright column unless forced to branch by pruning. This is also true of the fiddleleaf fig (*Ficus lyrata*), which deserves more popularity.

Many plants that do not normally grow as columns can be trained into upright forms through the use of cedar slabs, stakes, or osmunda fiber as posts for plants to cling to as they grow. Among them are the large-leaved Red Emerald philodendron, Algerian ivy (*Hedera canariensis* 'Variegata'), kangaroo vine (*Cissus antarctica*), grape-ivy (*Cissus rhombifolia* 'Ellen Danica'), and the arrowhead vine (*Syngonium podophyllum*).

Soft, Feathery Shapes

Airiness can be a desirable characteristic in decorative plants, making them appear soft, refined, and gentle—a green cloud rather than a thunderbolt. Airiness can soften a hard-edged interior or complement a busy, heavily patterned, ultradecorated room.

The weeping fig (*Ficus benjamina*) is the ultimate airy tree, which accounts for much of its popularity in interior decorating. Another popular feathery tree is the ming aralia (*Polyscias fruticosa*). It is also the most fickle of trees, full of leaves one moment, denuded the next, and requiring absolute consistency in care and location.

Podocarpus is also worth investigating. This weeping plant has a long, needlelike leaf and an arching habit. It makes an elegant columnar plant, although it may require permanent staking to keep it upright. A south window and life on the dry side will improve its growth.

*Opposite: Softly draped curtains, a light floral-patterned slipcover, and a spring bouquet are complemented by the feathery plumes of a fern pine (*Podocarpus gracilior*). This plant, like* Podocarpus macrophyllus, *benefits from the bright, filtered light that shines through the filmy fabric. Likewise, the room benefits from the soft play of light through the fern leaves.*

Among the smaller feathery plants, asparagus fern (*Asparagus densiflorus* 'Sprengeri') is a popular choice. This common plant drapes itself over anything in its path, turning hard objects into soft, shapely forms. An upright plant with feathery leaves is the false-aralia (*Dizygotheca elegantissima*). If overwatered, however, it will rapidly lose its leaves.

Strong, Graphic Shapes

Sometimes a background will cry out for a plant with a bold pattern or form that will serve as a focal point, especially against a solid wall of color. Line—not mass—is what's required. In this situation, a good choice is the Madagascar dragontree (*Dracaena marginata*), especially a mature specimen with many trunks. The spiky umbrella of foliage cascades from the ends of the branches, and the interplay of the beige trunks below makes a beautiful display. Many growers deliberately train the trunks into contorted, angular shapes when the plants are young to achieve a striking, graphic effect. The ponytail-palm (*Beaucarnea recurvata*), with its furrowed bark and elephantine base, also has a strong sculptural presence, as do mature, multiple-trunk specimens of *Yucca elephantipes.* In addition, many succulents have strong lines, but they require sunny locations.

*Right: Graphic shapes are generally large, bold ones, like this bird-of-paradise (*Strelitzia*). Though these plants take seven to eight years to mature and bloom, they are worth waiting for. The large flowers, which burst forth in spring and summer, are reminiscent of a bird in flight. A plant this size needs plenty of room and a simple background to show it off to full advantage. Here, a plain clay container, the smooth floor, and the simple lines of the settee fill these design requirements.*
Opposite: Although some people insist that the most striking flowering plants are the ones that fill a room with blossom, there are subtler ways to introduce color. Bromeliads, such as the Aechmea fasciata *shown here, have bright blooms and long-lasting colored bracts. All bromeliads require abundant light and warm temperatures to flower. Overwatering and poor drainage will kill them.*

Flowering Plants

Except for an occasional oleander (*Nerium oleander*) or Chinese hibiscus (*Hibiscus rosa-sinensis*), flowering houseplants seldom achieve sufficient size to make a design statement; in other words, they rarely look most effective standing alone. Flowering plants are best used as tabletop decorations or as centerpieces among foliage plants.

View blooming houseplants as long-lived bouquets. For the price of cut flowers, you can buy a great deal of living color that will last much longer. Instead of a bunch of daisies, for instance, you can buy a pot of cineraria (*Senecio* × *hybridus*). Any quick list of flowering houseplants is rich in variety: kalanchoe, begonia, azalea, guzmania, florist's gloxinia (*Sinningia speciosa*), African violet (*Saintpaulia*), Cape primrose (*Streptocarpus*), primrose (*Primula*), cyclamen, star-of-Bethlehem (*Campanula*), ornamental pepper (*Capsicum*), hydrangea, amaryllis (*Hippeastrum*), heather (*Erica*), pocketbook-flower (*Calceolaria crenatiflora*), sapphire-flower (*Browallia*), flamingo-flower (*Anthurium*). You may have other favorites. Some of these are available only seasonally, but many can be bought the year around.

Although flowering plants are an easy way to add a dash of color, you can't expect them to perform continuously. Cut flowers don't last forever, and neither do flowering plants. You should set them in their plant stations, enjoy them, and then either discard them when their blossoms fade or return them to an out-of-the-way growing station, making space for plants that have just come into bloom.

If you need a more dramatic effect than one or two small plants can give, place several (alike or different) together in a bowl, tray, or basket. You can also add some store-bought plants to your home-grown plants for a more lavish display. (In horticultural circles, adding new plants to a display is known as refreshing your garden.)

Establishing Plant Stations

To design effectively with houseplants, start by deciding where you'd like to locate plants without regard for light or other practical considerations. Would you like to see a plant arching out from behind a favorite table and chair combination, or at the end of the sofa to soften a hard edge? Would you like to flank a doorway with a matched pair of plants to create a sense of formality? Perhaps you've always wanted to put a small plant on a desk or a bookshelf or in the middle of the dining table. The places that seem to call for a plant, places where a plant is a perfect decorative statement, are called plant stations.

A plant doesn't have to be at its station all the time, and the station doesn't have to be occupied by the same plant all the time. The ficus tree by the window can be moved into a dark corner on special occasions and lit from below for drama. Two specimens of the same kind of plant can be alternated weekly between a dark station and a brighter one. For instance, you might rotate two philodendrons between a bright bedroom window where a large plant is needed and a spot in the curve of the grand piano where there is no light at all. If you have a sunny window, a light garden (see page 79), or a greenhouse, you can prepare plants for display and return them when their moment on the stage is over; then the understudies (another set of plants) fill their roles.

How welcoming to walk into a windowless entrance hall and be greeted with a display of bulbs in bloom. Your guests won't know that if they had visited last week the bulbs would have been in hiding and their station taken by aspidistras. Restocking plant stations in this fashion keeps the displays fresh. The coffee table in the living room can be graced by a small plant that's been on a bright windowsill or under fluorescent lights elsewhere in the house. It can be changed from week to week according to what is blooming. Essentially, you can be your own florist.

What would be the plant stations for a corner of a room furnished with a wing chair and a round, pedestal table? An obvious one is on the table, but that may not be the best design solution. The spaces that need filling are around the grouping of furniture, behind and above the table and chair or on each side of them. There are at least three good architectural solutions: a low, fan-shaped plant on the floor beside the table; a tall plant in the corner behind the table and chair; or a combination, with a third plant on the floor on the other side of the chair for balance. There are no rules for plant placement, only ways of thinking about how plants can fill space and relate to other shapes in the room.

An African violet (Saintpaulia ionantha) *will glow like a jewel in an appropriate setting. If you raise many kinds of African violet as a hobby, make a star out of one that is looking its best by displaying it separately. The easiest way to spotlight a plant is to put it in a cachepot that adds to its beauty, set it on a stand, and let the arrangement take center stage on a suitably sized table that does your star justice.*

Another common situation is a long buffet against the dining room wall, with a chair at either end and a large bowl in the middle. Where are the plant stations? The voids are on either side of the bowl. The chairs fill the voids at the ends of the buffet, and the bowl fills the middle. A pair of candlesticks or two vases of flowers could fill the empty areas between, but a pair of plants would lend the same formality to the setting in an unusual manner. A plant could replace the bowl, or the bowl could be moved to one side and balanced with a plant on the other side. If there is space beyond the chairs, plants could be added there at floor level.

Obviously, the more elaborate your facilities for growing and rejuvenating plants, the more display stations you can have and the more frequently you can change the plants. Few people remember that potted plants are not fastened in place; it's easy to move them around. Usually, the plant that starts on the windowsill stays on the windowsill and never graces the dining table. Similarly, the African violet (*Saintpaulia*) that is relegated to the coffee table never gets moved to the windowsill, even if it doesn't bloom.

Solving Design Problems

Striking foliage and flowers make useful, relatively inexpensive design tools. They create divisions within a room, add color, alter scale, fill empty spaces, and obscure architectural defects. A plant can be found to fill almost any need.

Plants as Room Dividers

Many homes feature large, open interiors. Although you may enjoy the sense of spaciousness, undoubtedly there are times when you wish you had the divisions and privacy that walls and partitions afford. With an effective arrangement of plants, you can achieve separation without ruining the open atmosphere.

Even in the sparest of rooms, just the right plant in just the right plant station will complete the decor. This sleek kitchen calls for a bold, out-of-the-ordinary plant choice. Several blooming amaryllis (Hippeastrum) arranged in a basket with sprigs of Scotch broom (Cytisus scoparius) make a striking, colorful accent. Spanish moss (Tillandsia usneoides) obscures the containers.

Fragrant paper-whites (Narcissus) brighten an empty corner and bring the promise of spring during the winter months. They are not particular about light levels once they are blooming, which makes them ideal for dark corners. Narcissus, tulips, hyacinths, and crocus can be forced easily into early bloom indoors.

Mass several medium or large plants, such as croton (*Codiaeum variegatum*), coffee plant (*Coffea arabica*), podocarpus, or schefflera (*Brassaia*). Or perhaps a freestanding weeping fig tree (*Ficus benjamina*) or palm will be enough to block the view and divide the area. Hanging baskets can also divide space—suspend two or three from strong ceiling hooks and fill them with columneas, grape-ivies (*Cissus rhombifolia*), or spiderplants (*Chlorophytum*). A planter box at a right angle to the front door will help create an entrance area in a small house or apartment where the front door opens right into the living room. A two-sided bookcase makes an attractive and functional room divider with plants interspersed with books and other items throughout the shelves.

Plants to Fill Empty and Dark Spaces
How many times have you looked around the house wondering how you could make empty and dull corners, blank walls, and unused areas disappear, or better yet, transform them into attractive

features? Plants are a relatively easy and inexpensive solution. These spots are perfect havens for shade-tolerant plants, such as palms, dracaenas, sansevierias, scheffleras (*Brassaia*), monsteras, or philodendrons. (Supplementary artificial light will noticeably enhance their performance.) Enliven a stairway with trailing plants set in wall brackets or pots lined along the stairs. Use the pools of space often found around furniture arrangements as a station for several plants.

Plants as Camouflage

Plants can disguise architectural obstructions, converting them into striking design features. For instance, when faced with a bothersome pillar or pole in a room, instead of trying to ignore it, use plants to soften its lines and make it blend into the room by encircling the base with a mass of plants or training vines to grow all around it. A warm, sunny corner can be the perfect place to grow plants that prefer dry, warm conditions, such as cacti and succulents, and in turn becomes a focus of interest within the room. An empty fireplace becomes a perfect growing spot for a Boston fern (*Nephrolepis exaltata*) or a cast-iron plant (*Aspidistra elatior*), providing the chimney is closed to prevent drafts. Smaller fireplaces can be decorated with mature jade plants displayed in floor baskets. Protruding angles or recessed areas can be softened and disguised with ferns, piggyback plants (*Tolmiea menziesii*), creeping-charlie (*Pilea nummulariifolia*), and Swedish ivy (*Plectranthus australis*) hung at various levels.

Deciphering a Plant Name

Family, genus, species, variety—the world of plant names can be confusing to the beginning gardener. But once you learn what these words refer to, plant names are no longer a mystery. And since many plants have the same common name, only by using the botanical name can you guarantee that the plant you want is the one you get.

Plants are classified by division, class, order, family, genus, species, subspecies, variety, and cultivar. For the home gardener, however, the important classifications are genus, species, and cultivar.

Genus refers to a group of plants within a broad plant family that are closely related horticulturally.

In a botanical name, the genus is listed first.

Each genus is divided into species. This is the second part of the botanical name. Subspecies and cultivar are often used interchangeably to refer to plants that differ slightly, for example, in flower or foliage color, from the species. A third name listed in italic type is a variety; a name listed in single quotes is a cultivar.

Look through "A Gallery of Houseplants" and you'll quickly spot examples of genera, species, and cultivars. If several species of a plant are described in a reference, just the genus is listed at the beginning of the entry.

Incorporating Plants Into Your Interior Design

Interior designs and decorating styles vary almost as much as the many thousands of different plants we bring indoors. In a room, a handful of basic design elements—wall coverings, furniture, ornamental decorations, and the layout—combine to create the style of the room, whether it's Asian, Early American, Mediterranean, modern, provincial, or Victorian. To help plants advance the theme, consider how they blend with the predominant elements in the settings you have selected.

Matching Plants to Decorating Styles

The right plant just seems to belong in a room. Linear, unpatterned modern interiors become warm and comfortable with healthy green plants in their midst. Graceful palms and weeping fig trees (*Ficus benjamina*), with their striking branches, vibrant greenery, and exotic leaf shapes, inject the atmosphere with a natural vitality and calmness unachievable by the architectural decorating scheme alone.

Traditional interiors, such as many Early American and Victorian homes, look attractive with displays of ferns or palms, which fit in well with ornately carved antiques. A room furnished with provincial pieces takes on an even more antique flavor with the complement of ferns placed on wooden stands.

Southwestern interiors, with their natural colorings, tile flooring, and large windows, are suitable for many plants. Bromeliads, cacti, and succulents—with their striking texture, color, and form—are the most fitting. The more refined Mediterranean interiors will benefit from the stark stems and bursts of pointed foliage of the dracaena, which mixes well with the color and form of patterned upholstery and terrazzo flooring.

Opposite: An unused fireplace is softened and highlighted by the English ivy (Hedera helix) surrounding the logs. When using a fireplace as a plant station, take care to choose plants that will grow well in the available light and check that the chimney is closed to prevent drafts.
Following page: The choice of plants in this living room continues the Asian motif and the subtle browns and beiges of the furniture. Although bonsais are generally outdoor plants, you can bring them inside as temporary decorative accents. The pine (Pinus) on the coffee table is an occasional indoor centerpiece. The same holds true for the Japanese maple (Acer palmatum) temporarily stationed by the window.

Matching Plants to Room Size

Choosing an appropriate size and scale for a plant display is a key factor in making it an attractive focal point within an interior. A plant display of the wrong size or scale can be either visually overbearing or lost.

Small rooms usually look best with a few small plants. You might want to hang a wandering-Jew (*Tradescantia* or *Zebrina* species) in an alcove, grow a mature jade plant (*Crassula argentea*) in a floor basket, and place a podocarpus in a corner. These plants won't cramp the limited space, and their flowing branches may provide a visual relief from the compactness of the room. For a subtle touch of color, try growing a Cape primrose (*Streptocarpus*), florist's gloxinia (*Sinningia speciosa*), or African violet (*Saintpaulia*) on a windowsill, dresser, or coffee table. Some larger plants to grow in small rooms include bamboo palms (*Chamaedorea erumpens*) and false-aralias (*Dizygotheca elegantissima*). These plants are delicate and subtle. They do not branch widely, but rather grow vertically, consuming little of the precious living space while filling the upper reaches of the room.

Large rooms are far more suitable for the big plants, such as weeping figs (*Ficus benjamina*), monsteras, palms, and large orchids, and for group displays of medium and small plants.

Small plants displayed alone tend to be lost in the spaciousness of a large room, unless they form a theme—the same kind of plant in variations of color or form, for example. Small and medium-sized plants will be more noticeable in large rooms when displayed in decorative containers.

Displaying Plants

The presentation of plants can make the difference between decor and mere clutter. Decorating with African violets (*Saintpaulia*), for instance, is no easy job. The plants are small, and avid growers often have dozens of them covering every available surface or crowded into fluorescent light gardens. The crowding detracts

Bird's-nest fern (Asplenium nidus) and living-vaseplants (Aechmea fasciata) turn a tiled tub area into an indoor garden. The staggered heights of the plants and their containers repeat the shape of the stepped surfaces of the bathroom; the sizes of the plants do not overwhelm the proportions of the room. Even the towel has been chosen to repeat the pink of the living-vaseplants. All of these plants appreciate bright, indirect light and the high humidity levels usually found in a bathroom.

from their appeal. Individually, the plants are quite beautiful, but not necessarily noticeable, particularly in an unimaginative green plastic pot. To be decorative, they must be properly presented. One method to show off a single small plant is to place it, pot and all, into a small cachepot (the French term for *hiding pot*) that matches or complements the bloom. Set the cachepot on a round, black stand just slightly larger in diameter than the cachepot. Immediately, the unassuming plant becomes a star.

Two important display principles are illustrated here. First, the mechanics must not show. The green plastic pot with the rolled edge that African violet growers prefer is part of the mechanics. It is serviceable but not attractive. The decorative cachepot makes the presentation work, and since it has no hole in the bottom, it doesn't drip water on the table. Second, whatever you want to display must look important. Isolate a single plant from its fellows, spotlight it, put it in a showy pot, and set it on a stand. Any accessory looks more important when it is placed on a base.

The stand and the cachepot can be placed wherever they look best. The spot becomes a new plant station. The violets can be rotated between the growing area and the display station. Plants that are dressed up and viewed one at a time are often more enjoyable than those customary group arrangements in which some are flowering and some aren't. One special pot will look more attractive than a group of plastic pots set on top of plastic saucers, the complete antithesis of display.

Choosing Containers

Containers can be as fascinating as the plants they contain. There are bonsai pots, antique American redware pots, handmade clay flowerpots from Italy, dimestore-variety clay flowerpots, colorful glazed pots with built-in saucers, and a large assortment of decorative cachepots that serve as covers for utility pots.

In the Japanese philosophy of plant display, the pot must not call attention to itself, unless that's specifically what you have in mind. Among bonsai enthusiasts, commenting on the pot before you say anything about the tree is a polite way of saying that the tree isn't worthy of comment. Although we may enjoy compliments on our unusual pot choices, strong-colored and garishly decorated ones should be avoided so that the beauty of the plant is always shown to its best advantage.

Be aware that there may be a difference between the best pot size for horticultural reasons and the best size for an aesthetic balance. From a horticultural standpoint, it's generally better to use pots that are on the small side. People often repot small plants into large pots, motivated by the generous but anthropomorphic notion that the roots need a big, comfortable pot with room to grow. In fact, what roots need is air, and a giant pot full of wet soil frustrates that need.

If you need a large pot for aesthetic reasons but not for horticultural ones, consider placing the growing container inside a cachepot. When deciding on the size of a cachepot, bear in mind that plants display to advantage when the pot is not overwhelming. The plant itself should always be larger than its pot. Jade plants (*Crassula argentea*), which have notoriously small root systems, are too often potted in immense containers that give the impression they are ingesting the plant.

Perhaps the ideal pot from an aesthetic standpoint is a very deep one. Again, use this pot as a cachepot, elevating the growing container inside the cachepot by placing it on a brick or even another pot turned upside down.

When the aim is to blend a plant into the decor of a room, the container plays just as important a role as the plant itself. On the table, the shallow, oblong clay pot provides a natural base for the sculptural, off-center bonsai birch (Betula). On the mantel, a glazed pot matches the bonsai container and provides a neutral setting for the iris.

Always remember that a special plant should have a special pot. A large, mature, and exquisitely groomed specimen deserves the loveliest pot you can afford. Although the primitive, folksy beauty of redware pots might best set off small ivies, a green antique oriental pot is more suitable for a full-grown sago palm (*Cycas revoluta*). Similarly, although a patterned pot may enhance greenery, it can clash with a flowering plant. The basic principle is to make sure that the container enhances what it contains.

Cornering Plants

Within the home, furniture arrangement is becoming less formal. Seating pieces are being moved away from the walls. The sofa can be set in the middle of the room facing the fireplace or on the diagonal of the room at an angle to the fireplace and either at an angle to or facing other pieces of furniture in the room. Or, if perpendicular to a wall, it can face another sofa or a pair of chairs. The contemporary conversational grouping is a return to the Victorian fashion of having a central table with chairs distributed around it at varying distances. In both the contemporary and the Victorian arrangements, walls are used to display pictures and artwork and are a background for secretaries, breakfronts, armoires, and bookcases. This arrangement leaves the spaces between the walls and the seating areas, especially the corners, open for plants.

Opposite: An empty corner has been turned into an effective plant station in this low-key living room. The lady palm (Rhapis excelsa) and peace-lily (Spathiphyllum), both of which do well in low light, are permanent residents of this corner. The chrysanthemums add seasonal color.

If one of the corner walls includes a sliding glass door or large window, plants will receive enough light to grow well, in addition to contributing to the decor. If, however, the corner is a dark one, what can be done? One solution is to rotate plants from the corner to a growing area in a lighter part of the house. Another solution is to use plant lighting in track lighting.

You can also try the mirror trick. A mirrored, freestanding screen or long mirror panels mounted directly onto the wall can brighten a dim corner. When the mirrors are positioned opposite windows, light is reflected into the foliage of the plant, which may be just the boost that a permanent plant needs (although it will have to be a shade-loving species). The decorative bonus is that the mirror image doubles or triples the plant form, amplifying and magnifying even small plants and making them appear much more important.

Elevating Plants

The indoor gardener who wants to decorate with plants would be wise to accumulate a collection of plant stands and pedestals, as well as plant pots and cachepots. Among the most striking low stands are the oriental footed stands used under Imari bowls or Japanese flower arrangements. These black or brown, wooden stands may have elaborate carving. Using stands like these is instant decorating magic.

Any plant that can be hung can also be set on a stand, often to greater advantage, if there is room for the stand. If height is the goal and there is no skylight, pedestals and tall plant stands are an effective alternative to hanging baskets and free the windows of obstructions.

Opposite: Tall stands and pedestals of different heights add to the visual impact of this indoor garden and act as trunks, elevating the pothos (Epipremnum aureum) to the status of small trees. The mirrored walls double, and sometimes triple, the effect. Pothos thrives in low light, but if the levels are too low, you can add artificial lighting. The translucent pedestals provide supplementary lighting here. The white azalea (Rhododendron) is a temporary visitor to this plant station. It prefers bright, indirect light while blooming, but will tolerate low light for special occasions.

Tall stands and pedestals can also add impact. A photograph of an English Victorian interior reveals plants that seem at first glance to be rubber plant trees (*Ficus elastica*). However, they are not trees at all but short rubber plants on 5-foot stands, each one in a cachepot and the trunk draped or tied with a shawl, hiding the soil and the growing container. The shawls seem a little excessive by modern standards, but the overall idea is ingenious.

Instead of trying to grow a ficus where a ficus can't grow, use a peace-lily (*Spathiphyllum*) or some other low-light plant on a pedestal to give the height and grace of a tree, as well as ease of maintenance. Tall stands can also be topped with seasonal displays of forced blooms. In spring, use tulips (10 bulbs per 10-inch pot); in summer, fill the stands with white geraniums (*Pelargonium*); and at Christmastime, set the stage for the holiday season by displaying pink poinsettias (*Euphorbia pulcherrima*).

Hanging Plants

One of the reasons hanging plants are so popular is that hanging them gets them up high where they can be seen more easily. If light comes from directly overhead, the plants thrive; hanging plants flourish best under a skylight. In fact, some exceptionally beautiful gardens have been created around skylights, using hanging plants in combination with floor plants and planter boxes.

Despite their popularity, hanging plants should be used indoors with discretion. When a plant is hung at a window, light floods in from one side, leaving half the plant in darkness. The top, which needs the most light, receives the least; it's the tips that are bathed in sunlight. Soon the plant turns leggy, stringy, and unattractive, especially when silhouetted against the window. One solution is to use swiveling ceiling hooks and rotate the plant so that it receives light on all sides, allowing for even growth.

In some situations, however, a permanent window obstruction may be just what's required. Many urban gardeners use hanging plants instead of window treatments to obstruct an objectionable view without completely blocking the light. Others hang plants because there is insufficient space for them elsewhere in the room or, in the case of herbs, to have them readily available in the kitchen. In these situations, no matter what the species, the hanging plant must be rigorously groomed and turned to prevent spindly, unbalanced growth.

Hanging plants are magnificent in greenhouses, solariums, and greenhouse rooms. There, hanging plants can be thought of as trees without trunks and placed accordingly, not hanging above other things but tucked behind them. A group of several plants, preferably the same variety, hanging together at different levels is a striking way to fill and soften a corner in a glassed-in space.

This staghorn fern (Platycerium bifurcatum) flourishes under a skylight, benefiting from the even light it receives. The plants lining the tub draw attention to the fact that it's a sunken tub. The peace-lily (Spathiphyllum), oakleaf ivy (Cissus), Boston fern (Nephrolepis exaltata 'Bostoniensis'), maidenhair fern (Adiantum), and weeping fig (Ficus benjamina) benefit not only from the overhead light, but also from the light that reflects off the white walls, which make an effective backdrop for these lush green plants. With sufficient light, many plants will thrive in a humid bathroom, which more closely resembles their native tropical habitat than other rooms in a home. Plants that tolerate low light levels, such as the peace-lily, are ideal for rooms without much light.

Hanging plants are less attractive hung high overhead, when it's mostly the base of the pot that shows, or hung from a rod like a line of clothes put out to dry.

Setting a Stage

Staging, a common practice in flower shows, is another way to elevate plants. Usually it consists of placing a plant on an empty, upturned flowerpot to give it a little extra height and raise it above its companions. A second, smaller plant is then set in front of the staged plant to hide its base. Staging can, of course, be quite elaborate, especially to build lush, tall banks of plants.

At home, proper staging can turn a motley group of undistinguished houseplants into a showy display. At least one common problem can be easily solved with staging. Many houseplants lose their bottom leaves, either as part of their normal growth pattern

The stage for these white-leaved caladiums, bird's-nest ferns (Asplenium nidus), *and ornamental grass is an arched alcove, and the way the plants are grouped reflects this shape. Simple cachepots, made from sections of PVC pipe, raise the individual plants so that they, too, form an arch.*

or because they have dried out once too often. To hide a defoliated stem on a tall plant, stage a companion plant (or two plants at different levels) in front of it, and then disguise the staging with a third plant (or more, if necessary) at windowsill or floor level. This pyramidal grouping will amplify the visual impact and be more attractive than any of the three plants alone.

People who are credited with having an eye for designing with plants often have simply learned to stage well and to fill in the front of a plant display so that there are no visible gaps. If the display is raised, a trailing plant should be added in front. An ivy or any cascading plant whose leaves hang over the edge of the container will break and soften the hard lines of the arrangement, as well as cover up the pots and spaces.

Using Color

The major decorative elements of a flowering houseplant are its color, size, shape, and texture. Plants are often chosen to complement the colors and mood of an entire room or of decorative items such as paintings, floor coverings, pillows, or sculpture. For a constant presence of flower color, it is important to plan for a succession of blooms throughout the year, and it is often desirable to change the types of plants to achieve this effect. To keep a display colorful, you need to become familiar with many types of plants and when they bloom.

The primary objective of decorating with flowering houseplants is to introduce colors into the room. Color is a basic element of design because it is so easily perceived. Furthermore, colors carry familiar connotations of mood and spirit. Some colors are hot and exciting, others are brash and unsettling, and still others are cool and smooth. A brief review of some of the attributes of color will help you select the appropriate indoor flowering plants.

Shades of green will always be a part of the visual effect of even a flowering houseplant. Greens generally promote a soothing, restful mood. Green will unify and pull together yellows and blues, isolate and call attention to reds.

Although white is a neutral decorating color, the whites of blooming houseplants are commonly shades of cream, with accents of yellow, pink, or light blue. White blooms are most striking in large quantities, as in a blooming Easter lily (*Lilium longiflorum*). In groups of flowering houseplants, white improves contrast and creates highlights. It is the most reflective of colors.

Yellow, also a highly reflective color, brightens almost any room. It is full of life and spirit and is especially welcome on indoor plants in spring. Yellow can lighten the heaviness of large blue or purple objects and will accent and complement any blue or green surfaces. Yellows are also useful to warm earth tones.

Orange is a mixture of yellow and red, and carries some of the feelings of both those colors. Orange accents earth tones, and in small amounts will intensify or set apart the coolness of blue.

Red is a strong, hot color, usually used in moderation. Orangereds are commonly used to blend or pick out highlight colors from fabrics or room accessories.

Pink is somewhere between red and blue. Hot pink has the same effect as red; bluish pinks are cool and formal. Pink is a softer color than red and can be used with reds to tone down their effect. Pink flowers convey a warm, friendly mood.

Purple and lavender, like pink, fall between red and blue. Whereas pure reds are rather demanding, shades of purple are cooler and more formal. Lavender is softer than purple. Both colors tend to recede and are sometimes lost in a room, but they can be brought out if combined with white.

Most blue flowers are actually shades of violet or blue-green. Thus some blues appear warm and some cool. Plants with blue blossoms can be blended with greens to create a spacious feeling. Try using houseplants with blue flowers where a stronger-colored flower might overwhelm the setting.

Designing Indoor Gardens

Large, architectural plants and the flowering beauties that temporarily fill plant stations operate as loners for the most part—they
are striking specimens that make a design statement on their own.
Yet most indoor gardeners don't garden with a few striking plants.
If you have more than four potted plants, you probably have a
great many, and if they are bumping against one another and com-
peting for light and attention, they probably look more like a
hodgepodge than a potted garden. Collections of potted plants,
small and large, can, however, make interesting, well-ordered indoor gardens.

The Skylight Garden

Many people who have skylights don't realize that they have an
opportunity for a superb garden. This is the best situation for hanging plants, since all the light is coming from overhead. Many
flowering plants as well as foliage plants are well suited for skylight gardens.

Hang plants around the sides of the skylight, some high and
some low. If there is nothing directly under the skylight, such as a
table or passageway, this striking cascade of plants could reach to
the floor. You might like to build a large pebble tray of the same
size as the skylight and create a floor-level garden to mirror the
one hanging above. Attaching a metal grid below the skylight also
makes a flexible arrangement for hanging plants.

*Opposite: A mix of plant sizes, flowers, and foliages composes an indoor
garden that would bring life to any room. A tall dracaena sets the background, framing a cheery indoor window box filled with bromeliads,
heart-leaf philodendrons* (Philodendron scandens oxycardium), *and asparagus ferns* (Asparagus sprengeri), *which lend color and hide the trunk.*

Designing a hanging garden around a single plant variety can create a spectacular effect. A display of six columneas will draw more praise than a random view of assorted plants. Try using several varieties of the same plant, creating a little variation in color and form. Choose plants that renew themselves from the center. They will maintain their beauty longer and have a more luxurious appearance than vining plants, with their ever-lengthening stems. The spiderplant (originally called the airplane-plant because of its flying offsets) is especially luxurious looking. The all-green variety, *Chlorophytum comosum*, is a stronger grower than the variegated variety. Ferns of all kinds, especially the Boston ferns (*Nephrolepis exaltata* cultivars) and fernlike plants such as the asparagus fern (*Asparagus densiflorus* 'Sprengeri') renew themselves frequently from the center.

Pots of trailing plants can be kept full, high, and bushy in the center by introducing small rooted cuttings of the parent plant into the same pot. The pot, by the way, should be plastic. Hanging plants dry out too quickly to withstand the porosity of clay pots, not to mention their extra weight.

The Windowsill Garden

An unplanned assortment of plants sitting on a windowsill does not make a garden. More often than not, it makes a mess. However, plants can be successfully arranged around a window. In the early 1970s, sills overflowed with plants that cascaded to the floor, and the glass was covered with plants hanging from ingeniously knotted cords. Today, the window garden has become a less overwhelming affair.

An indoor window box can frame and add interest to an otherwise unnoticed window. Tall palms at each end of this arrangement anchor the row of ferns, while daylilies (Hemerocallis) contribute seasonal color. Pots for a window garden should be either uniform or, as here, hidden from view.

The first rule for a genuine sill garden is that all the pots should match. They don't have to be exact clones, but they should, for example, all be clay or all be green. This uniformity focuses attention away from the pots and onto the plants.

Think of the plants as a frame for the window rather than a screen. Tall plants, such as a snakeplant (*Sansevieria trifasciata* 'Laurentii') or an airy false-aralia (*Dizygotheca elegantissima*), go at the edges or on one side. Medium-sized plants come next and then small plants, so that the arrangement slopes down to the center of the sill. Especially suitable are flowering plants and plants with variegated leaves, such as a begonia, cyclamen, kalanchoe, florist's gloxinia (*Sinningia speciosa*), columnar bromeliad (*Vriesea splendens*), or a beautifully marked Moses-in-the-cradle or oyster plant (*Rhoeo spathacea*). Finally, something should cascade below the sill—a creeping fig (*Ficus pumila*) or a wandering-Jew (*Tradescantia* or *Zebrina* species), for example. If you want a hanging plant, don't suspend it in the middle of the window; substitute it for one of the tall side plants. If the window is heavily draped on both sides, or if you want a more formal look, then place one elegant flowering plant on the sill in an attractive pot or cachepot and omit the collection.

Windowsills can be filled from a rotating collection of houseplants that spend most of their time elsewhere. If the plants are permanent residents, however, choose only those that will flourish on the sill. Remember that window plants must be turned regularly to prevent them from bending toward the light.

Deep bay windows can accommodate many plants without appearing overcrowded. To emphasize the feeling of a garden, consider a pebble tray with sides that are high enough to conceal the containers. The overall effect will be further enhanced if the tray matches the shape of the sill. If the bay extends from floor to ceiling, shape the tray to match the floor area defined by the bay. For the healthiest plants, provide artificial lighting on the side facing away from the window.

If the plants are growing too close to the glass, damage and poor health may result from cold drafts or the burning rays of the sun. Filter summer sun with translucent curtains, or choose a window that is shaded by trees in the summer. Also, be aware that in the summer the high angle of the sun and the shade from the trees can drastically reduce light that was strong in the winter and spring. In the autumn, the window will again get more hours of direct sunlight, as the trees lose their leaves and the sun sinks to a lower angle, but autumn sunlight is less intense and often obscured by clouds.

The Tray Garden

A group of plants placed together in a container forms a tray garden. The container can be a tin tray with a layer of pebbles at the bottom or a deep planter that hides the pots.

Bromeliads, sansevierias, and philodendrons form the permanent basis of a tray garden that has been supplemented with cut flowers. Such displays need not be as elaborate as this. Smaller trays placed on a table or in a window can also serve as a decorative accent. Glass vials hidden in the moss are the secret to putting blooms where you want them.

In small trays that hold three to five potted plants, repetition is desirable. Three ferns, three syngoniums, three chrysanthemums, or three Reiger begonias make a much better group than a mixture of three different plants. If you do want a mixture, center a tall plant at the back as the focal point, flank it with shorter plants on both sides (still at the rear of the tray), fill in the front with two matching plants, and complete the ends with a pair of plants that cascade and conceal pots, edges, and foliage. This makes a total of seven plants. If a plant is not tall enough to fill its niche, stage it on an upturned pot or saucer. The final result will be a plant pyramid.

A variegated plant with plenty of white can be a "spotlight" in a tray garden. Use only one, placed low in front so that it draws attention to the tallest plant behind it.

In a large tray garden, such as an indoor raised bed or planter box, many of the same principles apply. There must be tall plants for focus, but you could also add nonliving sculpture or even fountains. An effective arrangement would be a tall, airy umbrella plant (*Cyperus alternifolius*), a weeping fig (*Ficus benjamina*), or a Madagascar dragontree (*Dracaena marginata*) supplemented with shorter, blooming plants, such as kalanchoes, begonias, azaleas, chrysanthemums, hydrangeas, geraniums (*Pelargonium*), or forced bulbs. This is a good place for seasonal or occasional plants, plants that you can buy in bloom and then discard. Alternatively, since variegation can substitute for bloom, in the second tier of plants you might use colorful crotons (*Codiaeum* species), dieffenbachias, peacock-plants (*Calathea*), or peperomias. Fill in the edges with spiderplants (*Chlorophytum*), grape-ivies (*Cissus rhombifolia*), English ivies (*Hedera helix* and its cultivars), or any ferns. When you've finished, no pots should show and there should be no gaps in the foliage.

The ultimate in tray gardens is a raised bed on casters in which the leakproof tray is deep enough to hide the largest pot and the casters are concealed. The exterior finish can be painted or laminated to coordinate with the color scheme of the room.

Opposite: A charming arrangement of ivies, ferns, and star-of-Bethlehems (Campanula) set in a moss basket adds the finishing touch to a breakfast nook. The blooms repeat the color of the cotton lace curtains; the greenery repeats the outdoor landscape.

The Centerpiece

A dining or occasional table can be one of the most important places to make a design statement. You can emphasize a look that your furniture or color scheme already suggests, or you can create a mood for an occasion with an appropriate, individual display. If you think of a centerpiece as a design opportunity rather than as a plant, you will realize that any number of plant arrangements can be placed on a table.

An arrangement of jade plants forms an unusual centerpiece that is hard to equal for beauty and durability. Plant approximately one hundred jade cuttings in a perlite and sand mixture in a shallow bonsai pot. When the cuttings have rooted, set the pot outdoors or in an airy, bright room. The little forest can be brought in and placed on the table at any time. Another striking centerpiece can be made from a beautiful blooming plant, such as the Cape primrose (*Streptocarpus* 'Constant Nymph'), set in a deep bowl. Isolate and elevate the bowl on a pedestal and the centerpiece will look especially rich and elegant for the dining table.

The same bowl, this time containing an assortment of apples, oranges, tangerines, avocados, and bananas, is the basis for yet another centerpiece. Make pockets among the fruit, and tuck in African violets (*Saintpaulia*) or any other small blooming plant. Hide the pots among the fruit and spread the leaves to cover the pockets.

Give your plants as much thought as you would a menu. For a formal dinner, design an arrangement of plants in colors that match the china or linen. For a special party, consider individual plants at each setting. Disguise the containers by wrapping them in napkins that match or set off the ones for your guests. With imagination, your plants will become a complementary part of any table setting.

It is not enough to purchase a plant and set it beside a window. To make a plant feel at home and make a home feel as if the plant belongs, you need to deal with all the design principles that have been described in this chapter. To ensure that plants are happy and healthy at the stations you have chosen (and that you've chosen the right plants), read the following chapters.

Two flourishing lady palms (Rhapis excelsa) *meet the design specifications of this living room. Large palms and fig plants* (Ficus) *are never overpowered by a panoramic vista, and placed carefully, as they are here, they will not obscure it.*

The Basics of Plant Care

Houseplants are domesticated wild plants. Over the years, naturally occurring plants have been cultivated and bred to flourish in an indoor environment. The selected plants have one essential feature in common with their wild cousins—adaptability. They can endure filtered light, widely varying temperatures, and the low humidity found in most offices, stores, and homes.

Today, you can select from a wide choice of houseplants, from familiar favorites to the countless new hybrids specifically adapted to the modern interior. Whatever your tastes, choose plants not only for their shape and appeal but also with an eye to where you will place them and how much care they will require.

To make your choice easier, the following pages describe the basic growing requirements of houseplants. You will find discussions on watering and watering methods, growing media, pots and planting methods, preferred lighting conditions for specific plants, and lots more. All of this will help you choose plants to fit your decorating and horticultural needs, and to ensure that they remain healthy and good looking.

Plants that are healthy and well taken care of, such as this maidenhair fern (Adiantum) and Boston fern (Nephrolepis exaltata 'Bostoniensis') impart a sense of comfort and lushness to their surroundings.

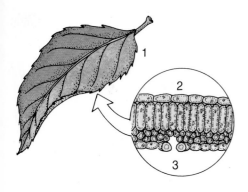

1. Leaves produce food for the plant and release water and oxygen into the atmosphere.

2. Chloroplasts are the chlorophyll bodies within cells in which photosynthesis takes place to manufacture carbohydrates (starches and sugars). They give the leaf its green color.

3. Stomata are specialized breathing pores through which carbon dioxide enters and water and oxygen are released. They close when water is limited.

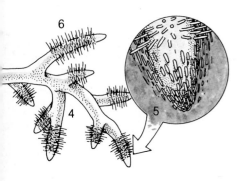

4. Feeder roots grow from the lateral roots and serve to transport water and nutrients absorbed by root hairs.

5. Root caps produce a continuous supply of new cells that are then sloughed off, lubricating the advance of the growing root tip through the soil.

6. Root hairs are microscopic appendages to the feeder roots. They absorb water and nutrients.

Understanding Houseplant Basics

To the beginning indoor gardener, caring for houseplants can be difficult at first. Watering, lighting, fertilizing, grooming, propagating, and seasonal care are initially bewildering; but they become easy and natural once you understand the basic processes of plant growth.

The Parts of a Plant

There are four parts to most plants: roots, stems, leaves, and flowers. All are crucial to plant growth and health.

Roots anchor the plant and absorb the water and minerals that nourish it. Most absorption occurs through the root tips and the tiny hairs on young roots. These tender tissues are easily injured. Transplanting often destroys them, causing the top of the plant to wilt; but under the proper conditions, new root tips will grow within a few days. Roots send water and nutrients to the stem, to start their journey to other parts of the plant. Roots of some plants also store food.

The stem transports water, minerals, and manufactured food to the leaves, buds, and flowers. It also physically supports the plant. Stems can store food during a plant's dormant period, and the stems of some plants also manufacture food. In many houseplants, stems are herbaceous, or soft, rather than woody. Whatever their form, all stems function in a similar manner.

The leaf manufactures food for the plant through photosynthesis, absorbing light over its thin surface area. Its pores absorb and diffuse gases and water vapor during photosynthesis, respiration, and transpiration.

The flower is the sexual reproductive organ of the plant. Most plants flower in their natural environment, but only certain plants will bloom indoors. Flowering houseplants are described in further detail in the fourth chapter.

Photosynthesis: Storing Energy

Like all other living things, plants need food for energy. The basic food element for all living things is sugar or other carbohydrates. Unlike animals, however, plants are able to harness the energy of the sun to manufacture their own sugar, through the process of photosynthesis.

In photosynthesis, light energy, carbon dioxide, and water interact with the green plant pigment chlorophyll to produce plant sugars and oxygen, which is released into the atmosphere. The carbon dioxide is drawn in from the atmosphere by the leaves, and the water is supplied by the roots. Plant photosynthesis supplies most of the oxygen on our planet.

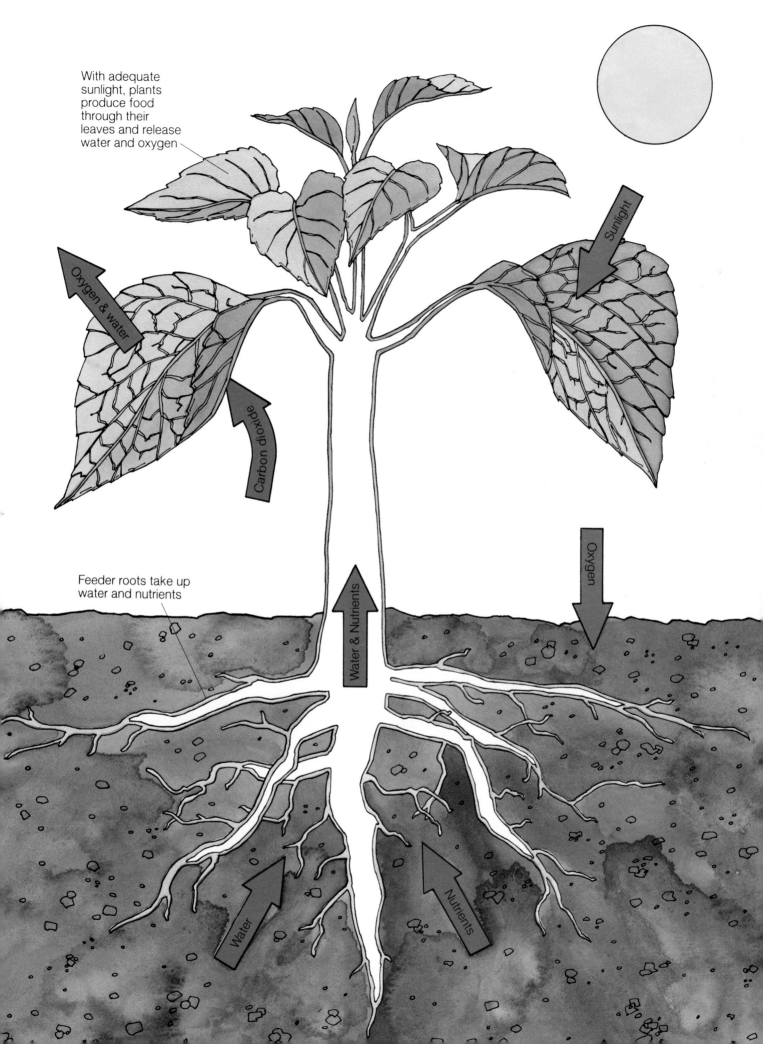

With adequate sunlight, plants produce food through their leaves and release water and oxygen

Oxygen & water

Carbon dioxide

Sunlight

Oxygen

Feeder roots take up water and nutrients

Water & Nutrients

Water

Nutrients

Photosynthesis requires an environment with adequate light, warmth, and humidity. No amount of fertilizer can compensate for an unfavorable environment, since fertilizer provides only nutritional building materials, not the real food—the sugar the plant manufactures by photosynthesis.

Respiration: Supplying Energy

In plant respiration, the sugar created by photosynthesis combines with oxygen to release energy. This energy is used for growth and survival and enables the plant to convert the building materials provided by nutrients in the soil into plant tissues. Respiration produces carbon dioxide, water, and a small amount of heat as by-products, which are released into the atmosphere.

Transpiration

Sunlight falling on a leaf can heat it well above the temperature of the surrounding air. Transpiration, the movement of water vapor from a leaf into the atmosphere, is important in stabilizing leaf temperatures (keeping them cool), in much the same way that human perspiration has a cooling effect.

As water vapor leaves the plant through leaf pores (stomata), the leaf cools. The higher the temperature and the lower the humidity, the faster a plant transpires. If it loses more water than it can absorb through the roots, it wilts; that is why correct watering is so essential to the survival of a houseplant.

Selecting Plants

Florida, California, and (to a lesser degree) Texas are the major foliage plant production areas in the United States. Plants of all types and in all stages of development, from cuttings to 20-foot specimens, are available from multiacre greenhouses and vast growing fields. Depending on the size and type of the foliage and the buyers' specifications, some are shipped directly from the field while others are placed in shade houses to prepare them for the lower light levels they will soon encounter. In either case, they are boxed and carefully loaded into trucks for shipment to florists, nurseries, and garden centers across North America.

Once delivered, the plants will be readied for immediate sale, repotted into larger containers for further growth, or placed under still lower light for more conditioning, or acclimatization.

Shopping for plants from a truck parked at the gas station or at a supermarket is risky business. Plants sold this way have most likely not been acclimatized, and their growing and shipping conditions have probably been far from ideal. They are much less likely to survive than plants purchased from a reputable nursery

or florist. But often, if plants don't survive, the owners feel responsible. Their guilty feelings about not being able to keep the plant alive may cause them to give up plant growing instead of just shopping more carefully for replacements.

Selecting the right plant for a successful indoor garden involves more than simply choosing the first plant that catches your eye.

It is always wise to buy plants from a reputable florist or plant dealer who will be able to offer advice and suggestions.

Starting with the healthiest plants possible is one key to success, but wise beginners will also ask for help in choosing plants that suit their homes and their life-styles. Avoid starting out with such difficult plants as orchids or weeping figs (*Ficus benjamina*). It is far better to begin with something less touchy and to progress, as skills improve, to more demanding species. Wherever you shop, be prepared to answer questions posed by a conscientious florist or plant dealer and to ask your own questions. The following checklists will help you find a suitable plant to fit your needs.

Study Light Levels

The most important variable in plant care is light. Will the plant be living in a garden room with skylights? Or, as is more often the case, will it fill a corner far from any light source? The light level (low, moderate, or high) should dictate the plant choice (see pages 73 to 82 for more information on plant light needs).

Compare Plant Needs and Personal Schedules

Some plants require little care; others require a great deal. Some can withstand erratic treatment, such as overwatering one week and neglect the next; others demand systematic, regularly scheduled care. Decide how much care you will be able to give your plants and choose accordingly.

Consider Room Size and Furniture Scale

Buying a small plant and hoping it will grow to fill a particular location is likely to be a frustrating experience; likewise, having to prune a large specimen continually can be time-consuming and unrewarding. The corner of a room is not a greenhouse, and greenhouse growing conditions can't be simulated in most living spaces. A 2-foot plant is not likely to grow into the 6- or 7-foot tree that the scale of the room demands. And, even if it does, will it grow into a graceful or symmetrical plant that suits its setting? It is better to buy a plant that will fit your needs immediately. Also, mature plants generally adapt more quickly to a new environment.

Closely Examine All the Plants on Display

All plants in the display should be healthy. Pick the healthiest plants you can find, and look them over carefully. Plants should have few brown-edged leaves and few leaves that have been trimmed, particularly on new growth. They should be full and bushy, with small spaces between the leaves. Large gaps between new leaves suggest that the plant has been overfertilized and crowded to induce rapid growth or that it has spent a long period under inadequate light.

Check to be sure that the plant fits comfortably in its container. If the roots are showing through the drainage hole, the plant is pot bound; it is best to choose a different plant. Flowering plants should be properly wrapped or sleeved at the nursery or florist to protect them during transportation from the store to their new home. Be sure to remove the covering once you get home.

Plants received as birthday or anniversary gifts usually arrive decked out in foil, bows, and ribbons. These decorations may be suitable for the occasion but rarely do they look like an integral part of the decorating scheme of a room. Once the celebration is over, and the plant is permanently stationed, remove the bows and ribbons, and replace the foil with a decorative cachepot or a basket that is an appropriate size and shape for both the plant and the room.

Inspect the leaves and junctures of stem and leaves for any sign of insects or disease. Insects or diseases brought into the home on a new plant may infect every other plant in your collection. Avoid plants with algae or slime on the growing medium or the pot. Leaves should be free from dust and grime, but should not look unnaturally shiny.

Flowering plants should have many buds that are just beginning to open. Plants in full bloom may already have exhausted much of their beauty. Buying budded specimens is particularly important with those plants that will never bloom again under less than ideal conditions or plants that will be discarded after the blooms fade. If you wish to get the plant to bloom again, refer to "A Gallery of Houseplants" (pages 199 to 307) for that particular plant's care needs and the fourth chapter, "Flowering Houseplants."

Before buying a plant, inspect it closely. Large gaps on the stems between new leaves suggest that the plant has been overfertilized. Leaves should be free from dust and grime, but not unnaturally shiny.

Consider Plant Costs

Several factors, besides the obvious ones such as rarity and availability, affect the price of a plant. Obviously, if a plant is rare, it will cost more than a plant that is easy to obtain.

The major factor that affects price is the cost that goes into developing the plant before purchase. Species vary enormously in how long it takes or how easy it is to grow them. A kentia palm (*Howea forsterana*), for instance, takes twice as long to reach 5 feet as a parlor palm (*Chamaedorea elegans*); and because it needs twice the labor and energy to grow to 5 feet, the kentia palm costs more.

Some plants are hardier than others and may be grown in open fields rather than under more expensive greenhouse conditions, so they cost less than greenhouse plants. Two seemingly identical plants of the same species may vary in cost because one was shipped directly from the field for immediate sale while the other was shade-grown or held for a period to acclimate it to lower light levels.

Acclimatizing Plants

Plants need to adjust to new surroundings; they may even go through a mild case of shock when first brought home. Over a short period of time, the plant has traveled from the meticulously controlled environment of the commercial greenhouse to a different environment at the retailer's and finally to a home with yet another set of light, humidity, and temperature conditions.

Acclimatization takes several weeks. At first, leaves may yellow and blossoms drop. Pay special attention to plant care during this time. A plant that normally tolerates dim lighting may have been grown under strong light and will need time to adjust to the change. Ease the plant through the transition by placing it in interim locations with decreasing light intensity for periods of several weeks or more before placing it in its final site. Hobbyists, especially, will want to isolate new plants for at least four weeks to prevent unnoticed pests or diseases from affecting their collections.

Keep plants moderately moist during this adjustment period; never allow them to dry out. Water thoroughly each time and discard excess water from the drainage saucer. Once a plant is acclimatized to its permanent surroundings, try not to move it.

Choosing the Right Tools

A few simple tools can make your indoor gardening easier: A long-spouted watering can, good pruning shears, sharp knives, a small trowel, clean cloths, soft sponges, an ostrich feather duster (for small-leaved plants), and soft hairbrushes or paintbrushes are the basic tools the indoor gardener needs. A watering can with a long spout helps you water hard-to-reach plants. Pruning shears and

sharp knives ensure clean cuts, lessening the risks of disease and scarring. A trowel helps when transplanting; cloths, sponges, duster, and brushes help keep leaves free of dust and grime; and you'll find a soft paintbrush useful when you are hand-pollinating plants. Most of these items are available at garden centers, hardware stores, and home supply stores.

Most garden centers also stock inexpensive light meters. Light meters indicate whether the light in a particular spot is low, moderate, or high. The readings are not scientifically exact, but they are accurate enough to enable you to choose a suitable plant for a plant station.

Moisture meters are similarly helpful. They don't measure actual moisture; instead, they measure the presence of electrolytes or fertilizer salts in the soil. Since water carries the electrolytes, a high reading ordinarily indicates the presence of moisture. After a while, however, as salts build up in the soil, the meter will give less accurate readings.

Having the right tools will make plant maintenance simpler. Watering cans and bottles make it easier to attend to those hard-to-reach plants. Trowels are useful when transplanting; scissors, shears, and pruning tools aid in grooming. A mister allows you to increase humidity around plants. A moisture meter indicates the presence of moisture in the soil.

A severely dried-out plant, such as this coleus, should be immersed in a pail of water.

Leave it in water until the soil is well moistened or until the bubbles stop. Let the pot drain and then return it to its growing station.

After a short time, the plant will return to its original healthy state. Try not to let plants dry out often; they will not survive repeated droughts.

Spraying a plant with a mister temporarily increases the humidity around it. More important, misting washes grime from the leaves, and it helps to control pests as well as make plants look healthy and cared for. Other tools that are popular with home gardeners are plastic wrap for layering plants, plastic labels for labeling plants, and a watering wand and a squeeze bottle for watering hanging plants.

You may find you need several sizes of pots, bags of potting soil, plastic flats for rooting cuttings, and powdered rooting hormone. A spray bottle for applying pesticide is also a handy piece of equipment. Be sure to label any pesticide spray bottles and don't store them until they are empty and clean.

Watering Plants

Houseplants are container plants; their roots are confined to the container and cannot reach far for sustenance. Although watering sounds like an easy part of plant care, poor watering is responsible for killing more houseplants than anything else.

Contrary to popular opinion, overwatering is more often the culprit for a plant's water problems than underwatering. Since the roots cannot absorb more water than the plant needs, excess water, unless it drains away, will displace oxygen from the soil. This suffocates the roots and leads to rot. To avoid an overwatering problem, don't assume that a plant needs more water when it doesn't grow as expected; there may be some other reason. Also, never allow a pot to stand in drained water. After watering, pour out any excess in the saucer or remove it with a turkey baster.

Experienced indoor gardeners never water by the calendar. A plant that needs water every day during a hot spell or in a warm room may need it only every other day in cool, cloudy weather or a cooler spot. The amount of water a plant needs varies with the species and its native habitat, the soil in which it is growing, and the light, temperature, and humidity in your home. Plants with a lot of leaf surface or soft, lush foliage will be thirstier than those with less foliage or waxy or leathery leaves.

Water needs are also affected by the growth cycle of the plant. A plant absorbs more water during active growth periods than during rest periods. The size and type of container are other important factors; in a small pot, moisture is absorbed quickly; too large a pot will retain too much water. And water will run through a pot-bound plant without wetting the roots thoroughly. If you can't keep a plant moist, even when you are watering it every day, it needs a larger pot. A plant in a porous clay pot will need water more frequently than one in a plastic or glazed pot. Remember, light, frequent watering is not what most plants need; it is better to water less often and more deeply.

Check soil moisture using the touch test. You will soon learn to tell when a plant needs water.

Evaporation also robs a plant of moisture. Some gardeners solve the evaporation problem by placing one pot inside another and insulating the space between them with peat moss, perlite, charcoal, or gravel. If you do this, be careful not to overwater or the insulation will become soaked. Another way to solve the evaporation problem with small pots is to group them in a wooden box, placing ground bark or peat moss around the pots for insulation and as a temperature-moderating mulch.

To learn exactly when your plant needs water, the simplest method is to test by touch. Poke your finger into the soil to feel the degree of moisture. To double-check, rub a little soil between your thumb and index finger; the soil should feel dry to the touch to an inch below the surface, but not powdery. With a little experience, you'll be able to tell when the plant needs water by how dry the soil feels. You can also use moisture meters, but the final determination should be how the soil feels and how a plant looks.

A plant that is wilting or drooping is thirsty—it needs water at once! Water a plant in this condition thoroughly, and try not to let this happen often—a plant that wilts again and again will not survive long.

Water Temperature

Plants prefer tepid water; cold water can harm roots or foliage, and excessively hot water can kill a plant instantly. Letting water from the cold water tap warm up to room temperature overnight will also allow the dissolved chemicals present in tap water to evaporate.

Water Quality

In parts of the country where the water is particularly hard, it is difficult to grow acid-loving plants, such as camellias and azaleas. However, adding acid soil amendments, such as peat moss, and using acidic fertilizers will help.

Alkaline conditions make it difficult for plants to absorb iron and other trace elements. Regular applications of iron chelate, available at most nurseries, will help to keep the foliage green. When the new foliage on acid-loving plants is yellow, the plant may need extra iron chelate. Water every two weeks with a solution of 1 ounce of iron sulfate in 2 gallons of water until the growth regains its normal color.

Softened water contains sodium that may accumulate in the soil and harm plants. If your home has a water softener, use an outdoor tap for plant water, or install a tap in the water line before it enters the softener so that you'll have a source of unsoftened water for plants. If this is not possible, draw water just before the softener cycle, when the sodium is at the lowest level.

How to Water

Watering plants in the morning allows any moisture on the foliage to evaporate by evening; foliage that remains cool and wet is more prone to disease. Always water thoroughly, until the soil is saturated. If your plant receives only superficial waterings, its roots will grow toward the surface of the soil.

The water should take only a minute or so to drain. If it takes more than 10 or 15 minutes, the drainage hole may be blocked. Unblock it by poking a stick into the hole to loosen compacted soil. Don't let plants sit in water; if the plant is in a saucer, pour off any drained water within an hour. If the plant is too heavy to lift, use a turkey baster to remove the water.

When water drains through the pot rapidly, it may be running down between the rootball and the pot and not soaking in. This may happen after a plant has been allowed to dry out; it can be remedied by submerging the plant in water to its rim.

Many plants benefit from an occasional thorough soaking; it's the frequency that varies. Check the listings in "A Gallery of Houseplants" (pages 199 to 307) to determine the watering needs of your plant.

Special Watering Techniques

There are times when your plants need more than a shower from a watering can. The following techniques are useful for these occasions.

Submerging   For plants that have dried out completely, plants in full bloom, and moisture-loving plants, submerging a pot in water to its rim is excellent. Submerging is also the best way to water hanging plants. Place the plant in a sink or tub and leave it submerged for several minutes, until the air bubbles have stopped. Give plants a good soaking approximately once a month.

Opposite, top left: Plants can be watered either from above or below. It is usually easier and faster to water container plants from above. Use tepid water to avoid harming the roots or foliage.
Opposite, top right: Fuzzy-leaved plants, African violets (Saintpaulia) and other gesneriads, are susceptible to water spots when splashed with cold water. Water these plants from below to avoid the risk of spoiling the leaves.
Opposite, bottom left: If a plant is too heavy to lift, or if you do not want to remove it from its plant station, use a turkey baster to remove any excess water from the drainage saucer.
Opposite, bottom right: Whether watering from above or below, make sure that you water thoroughly and that you pour off any excess drainage water within an hour. If the water takes more than 10 or 15 minutes to drain, the drainage hole may be blocked.

Showering An occasional trip to the shower is an effective way to water plants thoroughly and to rinse dust and dirt from the leaves. Use tepid water, with a gentle flow so that the soil does not wash out of the container.

Leaching Thorough watering will help wash out accumulated salts, which build up from high salt levels in tap water or from overfertilizing and can harm the plant. A whitish deposit on the outside of a clay pot or on the inside of the pot at the soil surface indicates salt buildup. Symptoms of salt damage include brown and brittle leaf tips and margins. To leach out salts, place the plant in a sink, tub, or pail and water it several times, letting the water drain each time. You may need to repeat this process weekly for several weeks. Although salt on the outside of the pot won't harm the plant, cleaning it off will make the pot look better and make it easier to tell if salts are building up again.

Many plants, such as this umbrella tree (Brassaia), *appreciate an occasional trip to the shower to clean the leaves and thoroughly soak the soil. Be sure to use tepid water and a gentle spray so as not to wash the soil out of the container.*

Watering terrariums   Once established, closed terrariums need water only once every month or two. Excess water is difficult to get rid of because there is so little evaporation. The best way to tell when a terrarium needs water is by looking at the container itself. When there is no condensation on the glass, and the plants are beginning to droop, add a little water. If this results in extreme fogging (a sign of overwatering), remove the top until the excess moisture evaporates.

Self-watering systems   If you're going to be away for a few days and can't find someone to take care of your plants, you can easily set up a self-watering system. Simply pad a sink or bathtub with matting or any thick, absorbent material. Set pots with drainage holes directly on the matting and leave a faucet dripping on it. The plants will draw up the moisture.

There's another temporary self-watering method: Make a wick of stocking or nylon clothesline and put it into one of two small holes in the lid of a plastic refrigerator bowl. Run the wick from the hole in the lid to the drainage hole in the plant container. Fill the bowl with water and cover it with the lid. Make sure that the wick is stuffed well inside the drainage hole and is in contact with the soil. Water will soak slowly from bowl to plant. Commercial wick waterers are also available at many garden centers. For information on self-watering containers, see pages 108 to 113.

Lighting Plants

For a plant, light means life. Light regulates three major plant processes: photosynthesis, phototropism, and photoperiodism. *Photosynthesis* is the method by which plants transform light energy into food energy, as discussed earlier.

Phototropism is the natural tendency of plants to grow toward the light source. The process is controlled by auxins (growth hormones) in the stem tips and youngest leaves. Highly reactive to light, these auxins cause the plant to adjust itself to the light source. Indoors, where the natural light source is usually a window, plants will bend toward the window. Rotate plants to avoid excessive growth on the side nearest the light and weak growth on the other side. If you decide to provide supplementary, artificial light, place the fixtures so that the light comes evenly from directly above the plant.

Photoperiodism is the plant's innate programming to its environment. Plants perform best in a rhythmic cycle of light and darkness that closely resembles that of their original habitat. For many plants, the length of the days and nights determines the time they take to reach maturity. Some plants will flower when the days are long (14 hours or more). Other plants, known as short-day

This arrowhead vine (Syngonium) is a victim of phototropism, the natural tendency of plants to grow toward a light source. Note how it is reaching out for more light. Rotate plants that lean toward the light so that their growth will be more even.

Watering Techniques

Peat moss or perlite

Gravel

Charcoal

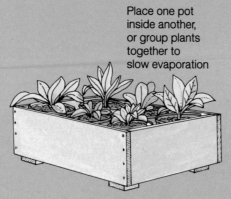

Place one pot inside another, or group plants together to slow evaporation

Watering extension

Drip Irrigation

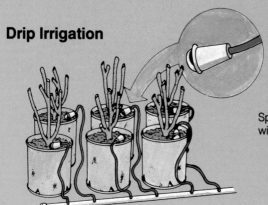

Spaghetti tubes with drip spitters

Wick Watering

Wick tips installed in soil

Wick

Inverted saucer

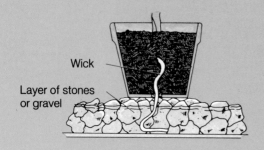

Wick

Layer of stones or gravel

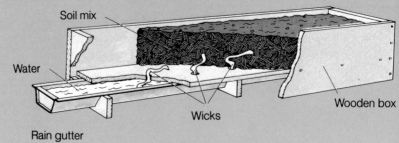

Soil mix

Water

Wicks

Rain gutter

Wooden box

plants, flower when days are short and they receive at least 14 hours of darkness while their flower buds are setting. Most plants, however, bloom without regard to the length of the day, provided there is a cycle of day and night.

Plants depend on light for their survival. Light is as essential to them as food is for humans. For that reason, it is important to study the light available at the plant station before shopping for plants.

Light Categories

Plants are quite adaptable to varying light levels. They can, for example, survive and even grow at light levels well below the optimum range, though they won't flower under such circumstances. At very low light levels, however, plants will gradually die. Given insufficient light, plants will live off their energy reserves for a time; then as these expire, they will be unable to absorb sufficient energy to recuperate from their losses.

There are five commonly used categories for defining plant light conditions. Read the descriptions of the categories and determine which one is closest to the light level in each plant station you've identified in your home, then purchase plants accordingly. It is always easier to use plants adapted to your conditions than to try to adapt your conditions to suit your plants.

Low light   A low light is one in light shade, a position well back from the nearest window. There is enough light to read by without too much strain, but no direct sunlight. Some plants can survive for a while at even lower levels than this, but they will not grow. Few plants thrive in low light: At best they can be said to tolerate it.

Moderate light   Average indoor light, neither sunny nor shady, is defined as moderate light. Most foliage plants will adapt well to this level of light, but few plants will bloom in it. A position directly in front of a north window or slightly back from an east or west one would get moderate light.

Bright indirect light   An all-purpose light level is that of bright indirect light, at which both foliage and flowering plants thrive, although flowering plants will bloom more profusely with some direct sunlight. Bright indirect light is found in a northeast or northwest window that receives a few hours of early morning or late afternoon sun and is well lit the rest of the day. The same effect can be obtained in sunnier windows by moving plants back from the light or drawing sheer curtains during the hottest part of the day.

Some direct sunlight   Direct sunlight for between two and five hours in the morning or afternoon, but not the full strength of midday sun qualifies as some direct sunlight. Usually this is the light found directly in front of an east or west window or a few feet back from a south window. It is the ideal light for many flowering plants, herbs, and vegetables as well as most cacti and succulents, but it's too bright for foliage plants.

Full sun   More than four or five hours of direct sunlight daily is full sun. An unshaded window facing due south during the summer months would receive full sun. Few plants thrive in full sun because of the intense heat, although cacti and succulents tolerate it well. Full sun is easily softened by installing sheer curtains or by moving plants back several feet from the window.

Light Intensity

The farther one travels from the equator, the greater the influence the seasons have on light intensity. In northern climates, for example, there is no equivalent to full sun during the winter months. The brightest winter light is only equal to some direct sunlight or even bright indirect light. At such latitudes, sun-loving plants need the sunniest possible position during the winter months to thrive.

The time of year also affects the light intensities in other ways. Keep in mind that winter sunlight reaches farther into south-facing rooms than summer sunlight because of the low angle of the sun. Plants that receive a few hours of direct sunlight in the middle of a room in the winter may need to be closer to a window in the summer to receive adequate light.

Objects in the light path will also affect light intensity. A south-facing window may receive only bright indirect light or some direct sunlight if it is shaded by nearby buildings or trees or an overhanging roof. Placing objects in the light path is an effective way of gaining shade. Sun-loving plants near a window will moderate the light reaching plants set farther back in the room. Screens on windows, doors, or porches reduce light by at least 30 percent. A white house next door or a light-colored cement driveway will reflect sunlight, increasing the intensity of the light the rooms receive. Snow also reflects a great deal of light and can increase the intensity of light in a room, especially on a sunny day.

How can you tell whether your plant is getting the right amount of light? Just watch its reactions! If new growth is thin and pale and seems to stretch toward the light, the plant is suffering from a lack of light. Move it to a spot where it will receive better illumination. If the plant wilts rapidly, is yellowish in color, and the new growth is unusually compact, the plant is getting too much light. Move it back from the light source. If the plant looks good but doesn't flower as it should, it is probably getting sufficient light for good foliage growth but not enough light for flowering. Moving it just a little closer to the window is probably all that is required.

Types of Artificial Light
Choices in artificial light have changed greatly in the past few years. Once you were limited to standard incandescent lighting, now you can choose among incandescent, fluorescent, high-intensity discharge, and halogen lights.

Incandescent lights Most homes are lit with incandescent light. It is not well balanced in light quality, offering mostly red light and very little blue light. Even specially developed incandescent plant lights, whose light quality has been improved for plant growth, are weak in blue rays. Incandescent light is best used as supplemental light in areas where plants receive some natural light. The advantage of incandescent plant lights over regular incandescent bulbs is that they reflect heat away from the plant, which means that you can place the plant closer to the light source. All incandescent lights are inefficient, however, giving off much of their energy as heat; and they need frequent replacement.

The amount and intensity of sunlight varies according to the window exposure. A south-facing window receives the most intense sun for the longest period while a north-facing exposure receives little direct light. Afternoon sun from the west is warmer than morning sun from the east.

Sunlight at Various Window Exposures

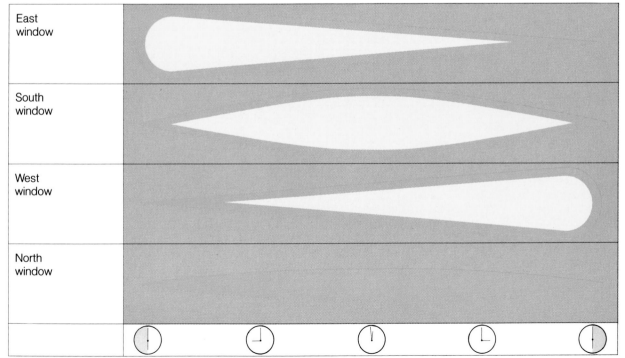

Light Requirements of Various Houseplants

Plants for Low Light
(dim reading-level light)

Botanical Name	Common Name
Aglaonema modestum	Chinese evergreen
Aspidistra elatior	Cast-iron plant
Asplenium nidus	Bird's-nest fern
Dieffenbachia species	Dieffenbachia (dumb-cane)
Dracaena fragrans 'Massangeana'	Cornplant
Spathiphyllum species	Peace-lily, spatheflower

Plants for Moderate Light
(no direct sunlight)

Adiantum species	Maidenhair fern
Araucaria heterophylla	Norfolk Island pine
Asplenium bulbiforum	Mother fern
Cissus antarctica	Kangaroo-ivy
Davallia species	Deer's-foot fern, rabbit's-foot fern
Epipremnum aureum	Pothos, Devil's-ivy
Howea forsterana	Kentia palm
Nephrolepis exaltata 'Bostoniensis'	Boston fern, sword fern
Philodendron bipinnatifidum	Twice-cut philodendron
Philodendron hastatum	Spade-leaf philodendron
Philodendron 'Red Emerald'	Red Emerald philodendron
Philodendron scandens oxycardium	Heart-leaf philodendron
Philodendron selloum	Lacy-tree philodendron
Phoenix roebelenii	Pygmy date palm
Pteris	Table fern, brake fern
Rhapis	Lady palm

Plants for Bright Indirect Light
(away from direct sunlight, or in a north window)

Aloe species	Aloe
Aphelandra squarrosa**	Zebra-plant
Brassaia actinophylla	Schefflera
Ceropegia species	Rosary vine, hearts-entangled
Coleus × hybridus	Coleus
Dizygotheca elegantissima	False-aralia
Episcia species	Episcias, flame-violets
Fatsia japonica	Japanese aralia
Ficus species	Ficus, fig
Hippeastrum species	Amaryllis
Paphiopedilum	Lady's-slipper
Pellaea rotundifolia	Button fern
Phalaenopsis	Moth-orchid
Rhipsalis species	Chain cactus
Saintpaulia species**	African violet
Schlumbergera species	Christmas cactus, Thanksgiving cactus
Vriesea species	Vriesea

Plants for Some Direct Sun
(curtain-filtered sunlight from a south, east, or west window)

Abutilon species	Flowering-maple, Chinese-lantern
Aeschynanthus species	Lipstick-plant, basket vine
Asparagus species	Asparagus fern
Beaucarnea species	Elephantfoot tree, ponytail-palm
Begonia species	Begonia
Caladium species	Caladium
Camellia species	Camellia
Clivia miniata	Kaffir-lily
Columnea species	Columnea
Crassula argentea	Jade plant
Cryptanthus species	Earthstar
Euphorbia pulcherrima	Poinsettia
Ficus species	Ficus, fig
Hydrangea macrophylla	Hydrangea
Platycerium bifurcatum	Staghorn fern
Polypodium aureum	Golden polypody fern, bear's-paw fern, hare's-foot fern
Primula species	Primrose
Rhododendron species*	Azalea, rhododendron
Sedum morganianum	Donkey's-tail, burro's-tail
Senecio rowleyanus	String-of-beads
Streptocarpus species	Cape primrose

Plants for Full Sun
(4 or more hours of direct sunlight)

Aechmea species	Living-vaseplant
Agave species	Century plant
Ananas species	Pineapple
Billbergia species	Vaseplant
Cephalocereus senilis	Oldman cactus
Chrysanthemum × morifolium*	Florist's mum
Codiaeum variegatum	Croton
Echeveria species	Echeveria, hen and chicks
Echinopsis species	Urchin cactus
× Fatshedera lizei**	Tree-ivy, aralia-ivy
Gymnocalycium	Chin cactus, spider cactus
Kalanchoe species*	Kalanchoe
Lithops species	Living-stones
Mammillaria species	Pincushion cactus
Opuntia species	Opuntia, bunny-ears
Cattleya**	Cattleya
Oncidium**	Dancing-lady
Pelargonium species	Geranium
Rosa hybrids*	Miniature roses

Needs full sun to initiate flower buds; bright indirect light will suffice when in flower

**Needs full sun in winter and curtain-filtered sunlight in summer*

Fluorescent lights More efficient than incandescent lights, fluorescent lights convert most of the energy they receive into light rather than heat, so you can place plants within an inch or so of the light source with no danger of burning them. Fluorescents also give off a light more closely balanced in blue and red rays than do incandescent lights. It is quite easy to grow plants under fluorescent lights in areas where there is no natural sunlight at all.

Although most plants will grow perfectly well under ordinary cool white or warm white fluorescent tubes, the full-spectrum fluorescent plant lights give off a more perfectly balanced light quality. Use the full-spectrum on plants that do not bloom well under ordinary fluorescents, such as some orchids, as well as on those that prefer full sun, such as vegetables grown indoors.

To create a light garden with fluorescent lights, set plants so that their upper leaves are 6 to 12 inches from the light source. Place plants requiring full sun closer to the lights than plants preferring moderate light. The basic fixture is a two-tube, 4-foot lamp.

Light is food for a plant. If a plant doesn't get enough natural light, it may be necessary to install supplemental artificial light. In this room, the supplemental light is a dramatic design feature.

This lights a growing space approximately 2 feet wide and 4 feet long: enough for a small indoor garden. For plants preferring full sun, use four-tube lamps; they give off a greater intensity of light. Many people use tiers of plant lights so that they can grow a great many plants in a small space. Fluorescent light gardens are available commercially but are easy to build if you have basic woodworking skills.

The main disadvantage of fluorescent lights is that the intensity of the light diminishes rapidly the farther they are from the plants. Consequently, the top of a tall plant may be well lit while its lower leaves are in deep shade. For that reason, fluorescent lights give better results with low, spreading plants than they do with upright ones.

High-intensity discharge lights   HID lamps are powerful, extremely intense lights. They were originally developed for greenhouses, to supply light as intense as full sun, but they can be adapted to indoor use. HID lamps, such as mercury lamps and high-pressure sodium lights, are so powerful that a single lamp can illuminate an entire indoor garden. However, the extreme intensity of the light they provide, as well as the heat they produce, make them unsuitable for normal home conditions: They are simply too bright and too hot for human comfort. Some people do use HID lamps to grow sun-loving plants like vegetables in a basement, attic, or other dedicated plant room. In such cases, a complete ventilation system is necessary to vent the heat they produce. Be careful not to spray water on HID lamps; they are extremely fragile when hot.

A grow light allows you to create a special display in an area where the natural light is insufficient for normal, healthy plant growth.

Fluorescent Lighting Ideas

Here are three simple light gardens to alter day length or start seedlings. The fluorescent fixture on the adjustable shelf brackets can be moved up or down to give your plants more or less light.

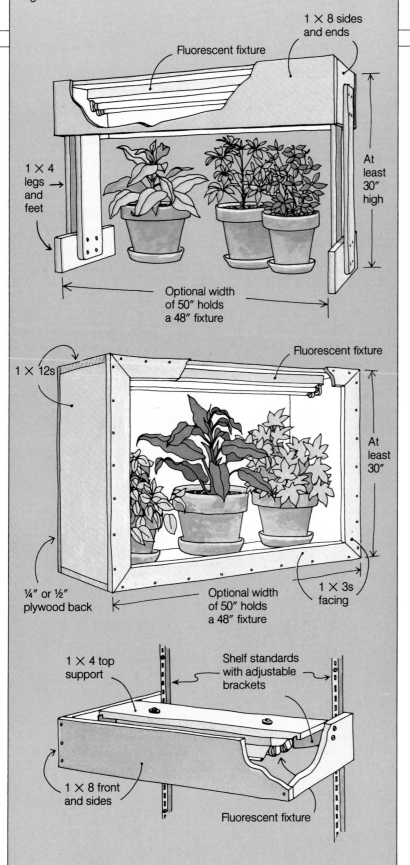

1 × 8 sides and ends

Fluorescent fixture

1 × 4 legs and feet

At least 30" high

Optional width of 50" holds a 48" fixture

1 × 12s

Fluorescent fixture

At least 30"

¼" or ½" plywood back

1 × 3s facing

Optional width of 50" holds a 48" fixture

1 × 4 top support

Shelf standards with adjustable brackets

1 × 8 front and sides

Fluorescent fixture

The bright and focused light of a halogen lamp spotlights the dramatic form of this medicine-plant (Aloe vera) and provides exceptional light quality for its growth. Be careful not to place plants too close to a halogen light source; the intense heat from these lamps can burn plant leaves.

Halogen lights   Miniature versions of HID lamps are known as halogen lights. Currently fashionable in home and office settings, they give off light of exceptional quality, making them good choices for growing indoor plants. They also have the advantage of dramatically drawing attention to the plants they illuminate with such clear intensity. However, they give off a great deal of heat and will burn the leaves of plants that are too close. Because halogen lamps produce beams that are quite narrow, they are most suitable for individual plants or small groups of plants.

Basic potting mixes are available prepackaged from your local nursery or garden center. Shown left to right are mixes for an orchid, a standard houseplant such as a coleus, and a cactus.

Choosing Growing Media

The medium in which a plant grows serves three main purposes. It acts as a support, keeping the plant from falling over; it stores water and nutrients; and it provides sufficient air circulation to keep the roots well oxygenated. Any medium that supplies those three basic needs will give good results.

In the past, garden soils were brought indoors and pasteurized for use in pots, but the results were often poor. That's because growing a plant in a pot indoors involves conditions (limited root space, little action from soil organisms, etc.) that are quite different from the conditions in the ground outdoors. Typical garden soils, as light and airy as they may appear at first, quickly become as compact as cement in a pot indoors. Compaction cuts off oxygen supplies to the plant roots, and without oxygen roots quickly rot. Indoor growers learned with time to amend garden soil with products such as sand, leaf mold, or charcoal to keep it as well aerated as possible.

Today's potting mixes often contain no true soil at all; they go under the name *peat-based mixes* or *soilless mixes*. Typically, they are composed of peat moss or some other partially decomposed plant material, such as fine fir bark, and inorganic elements such as perlite and vermiculite. They offer all the qualities that garden soil offers outdoors: They provide good support for roots and excellent retention of water and minerals; and they are also quite porous, allowing easy circulation of oxygen. Their chief disadvantage is that they are almost totally lacking in natural nutrients, so plants will not thrive unless small amounts of fertilizer are added with each watering. Also, since even the best soilless mix becomes compact with time, it needs to be replaced every year or so.

Measuring Acidity and Alkalinity

An important factor in the composition of any growing medium is its acidity or alkalinity. Acidity and alkalinity are measured in terms of pH. The pH scale ranges from 0 to 14, with 7 being neutral. A pH reading higher than 7 is alkaline, and one lower than 7 is acid. Highly acid mixes cause yellowing and leaf drop. Alkaline soil can cause stunted growth and loss of leaf color.

Most packaged potting mixes are slightly acid; they have a pH of about 6.5 to 6.8, which is ideal for most plants. The mixes suggested here include dolomite lime to raise the pH to a similar level. For acid-loving plants (azaleas, gardenias, citrus, etc.), prepare the mixes without the dolomite lime. Many cacti and succulents prefer a neutral or slightly alkaline soil, easily provided by adding extra lime.

Preparing Your Own Growing Media

Good growing media are usually available ready-made wherever plants are sold. However, the mixes tend to be general-purpose ones and may not be well suited to the type of plants you are growing. If they are not suitable, you can adapt them to your needs by adding one or two ingredients or you can start from scratch and make your own mix.

The ingredients for a homemade houseplant mix are the same as those in commercial mixes. Each plays a specific role in helping houseplants grow and flourish.

Pasteurized garden loam   Many growers like to add some garden soil to soilless mixes. It makes the mix heavier, providing tall plants with more support; and it contains certain nutrients, reducing the need for regular fertilizing. Any soil of garden origin must be pasteurized before use to destroy soil-borne pests and diseases. Do this by thoroughly moistening small quantities and baking them at 200° F for 30 minutes. Alternatively, purchase an already pasteurized mix. The disadvantage of garden soils of any sort is a lack of consistency in their quality: You simply never know what you are getting or how it will react when compacted into a pot.

Peat moss   Made up of various types of partially decomposed bog plants, peat moss is the basic element of most modern potting mixes. Even those indoor gardeners who prefer to grow their plants in soil usually include a fairly large proportion of peat moss in their mixes. It adds lightness to a mix and improves water retention; and since it expands when moist and contracts when dry, it literally pulls air into the soil. The main disadvantages of peat moss are its tendencies to compact with time and become increasingly

An individualized mix for specific planting needs can be created from ingredients such as charcoal, top left; peat moss, top right; fir bark chips, center left; sand, center right; perlite, bottom left; and vermiculite, bottom right.

acid. It contains almost no nutrients. The best-known and most popular type for potting mixes is Canadian sphagnum peat.

Vermiculite Expanded mica is called vermiculite; it looks like little flakes of gold. Because of its excellent soil aeration properties, it has become a basic element of most soilless mixes. It can absorb several times its weight in water and minerals, and releases them slowly. Its main disadvantage is a tendency to become compact with time. The fine and medium grades are most popular. Use only horticultural vermiculite; construction-grade vermiculite sometimes contains harmful impurities.

Perlite   White, expanded volcanic rock, perlite helps to maintain good aeration in a mix. Like vermiculite, it absorbs excess minerals and water and releases them over time. Unlike vermiculite, it does not compact significantly with time, making it a choice ingredient for a mix that will be used to pot mature plants. Coarse to medium grades are preferable. Perlite tends to rise to the surface when watered.

Charcoal   Often absent from commercial mixes, it is worthwhile adding some charcoal even if you don't usually mix your own soil. It acts as a buffer in the potting mix, absorbing potentially harmful excess minerals as well as toxins resulting from decomposition. Use only horticultural- or aquarium-grade charcoal, and sift it first to remove the dust. Never add barbecue charcoal to a potting mix.

Sphagnum moss   A bog moss known as sphagnum moss is used for plants, such as epiphytes, that require a very airy yet humid growing medium. Long-strand sphagnum moss is sometimes sold in living (still green) form; more often it is dried and golden brown. Before use, soak it in warm water, and use it only with some form of lime to counteract its high acidity. Because sphagnum moss has natural fungicidal properties, a milled form is often used in seed mixtures to help prevent damping-off, a fungus that resembles mildew. Milled sphagnum moss is too fine for use in regular potting mixes.

Bark   Fine grades of ground tree bark are sometimes used as a substitute for peat moss. Coarser grades are a common ingredient in epiphytic mixes because they provide excellent aeration.

Styrofoam   Although they are sometimes used as substitutes for perlite, styrofoam beads don't have all its desirable qualities. They do help aerate the mix, but they do not absorb excess water and minerals and release them as needed. Styrofoam is also so light that it floats to the surface when watered. Styrofoam peanuts, a common packaging material, are occasionally used in epiphytic mixes designed for orchids and bromeliads.

Calcined clay   Composed of chunks of kiln-hardened clay, and most widely available in the form of unscented cat litter, calcined clay adds aeration and drainage to a mix and absorbs excess water. It makes a good substitute for vermiculite and perlite when a heavier mix is desired. Always sift it to remove the dust before adding it to a mix.

Coarse sand   Used mainly in succulent mixes, coarse sand adds weight to a medium and improves drainage. Use only horticultural or washed sand.

Dolomite lime   A white powder, dolomite lime is added in small quantities to mixes, especially peat-based ones, to reduce their acidity.

Mix-and-Match Potting Media

Basic Soilless Mix
This is a general-purpose soilless mix well suited to most kinds of indoor plants.

> *1 quart coarse peat moss*
> *1 quart medium-grade vermiculite*
> *1 quart medium-grade perlite*
> *3 tablespoons dolomite lime*
> *1 cup sifted horticultural charcoal*

Soil-Based Mix
This heavier mix is especially useful for plants you don't want to repot annually.

> *1 part pasteurized garden loam*
> *1 part basic soilless mix or commercial soilless mix*

Epiphytic Mix
This mix is suitable for orchids and bromeliads, which derive much of their moisture and nutrients from the air and rain.

> *1 quart long-strand sphagnum moss*
> *1 quart coarse bark*
> *1 quart coarse-grade perlite*
> *1 tablespoon dolomite lime*
> *1 cup sifted horticultural charcoal*

Cactus Mix
This mix is ideal for cacti and succulents, and also for top-heavy plants, which need a weighty soil.

> *2 quarts pasteurized garden loam*
> *1 quart coarse sand*
> *1 quart calcined clay*
> *2 tablespoons dolomite lime*
> *½ cup sifted horticultural charcoal*

Providing the Right Temperature, Humidity, and Air Circulation

The environment also contributes to plant health. Although you may not be able to duplicate the native habitat of a plant in your home, paying attention to the temperature, humidity, and air circulation in your home will help your plants flourish.

Temperature

In concert with light, humidity, and air circulation, temperature affects plant metabolism. Most indoor plants adapt to normal indoor temperatures (55° to 75° F). At night, they almost all benefit from at least a five-degree drop in temperature, which gives them a chance to recover from any rapid water loss that may have taken place during the day. Overnight, the roots continue to take in water, correcting any water deficits in the leaf cells.

Few houses have uniform temperatures in each room. Use a thermometer to check the temperature in different locations of your house, and even at various plant stations within the same room.

Temperatures change with the seasons, even indoors. In the winter, home heating and cold drafts from windows and doors can cause widely fluctuating temperatures. In the summer, the temperature at a south-facing window can soar. Though most plants appreciate changes in temperature, because such changes are natural to their native habitat, some seasonal temperature changes are severe enough to warrant moving plants, especially those growing on windowsills, to a different location.

Humidify the air around a plant by placing the container in a cachepot and adding a layer of moss. The moss will obscure the growing pot and, if kept wet, will add moisture to the air.

A plant set on a pebble tray filled with water to just below the top of the pebbles, never any higher, receives a constant supply of humid air.

Tropical plants native to areas with high temperatures and humidity—episcias, prayer-plants (*Maranta*), and bougainvilleas, for example—may grow best in a room that contains an appliance that vents wet heat, such as a dishwasher, clothes dryer, or humidifier. In a cool room, tropical plants can thrive if the soil is heated by electric heating cables or propagation mats (for more information on these, see page 128). Cold-loving plants (55° to 60° F days, 50° F nights), such as cyclamens, camellias, azaleas, and some orchids, do well in rooms where there is no bright direct sunlight to raise the temperature.

Certain plants require specialized growing conditions, such as a permanent greenhouse environment or an unheated room for a short resting period. Check the individual plant listings in "A Gallery of Houseplants" (pages 199 to 307) and the requirements for flowering plants (pages 137 to 161) for specialized needs.

Humidity

The moisture content of the air defines the term humidity. It is expressed as relative humidity: a percentage of the maximum amount of water vapor the air can hold at a given temperature. Nearly all houseplants grow best in a relative humidity of 50 percent or higher, but this level is difficult to attain in dry climates and indoors in winter. In winter, home heating robs the air of moisture; humidities as low as 4 to 10 percent are common. Some areas of the house are naturally more humid than others. Plants grown in such moisture-rich areas as bathrooms and kitchens benefit from the increased humidity.

A cool-vapor humidifier can increase the humidity considerably on even the coldest days, making the air more comfortable for both people and plants. You can move portable units from room to room or install a humidifier as part of the central heating system. The simplest method for humidifying the air around plants is to use pebble trays: waterproof trays or saucers filled with pebbles, perlite, or vermiculite. Fill these trays with water to just below the surface of the material and place the plants on top. Check that the bottom of the pot is not touching the water; if it is, you are risking root rot. As the water evaporates, it fills the surrounding air with moisture. Add water as necessary. Humidifying trays are strongly recommended for plants growing under artificial lights.

You may also raise humidity by grouping plants together. The combined transpiration from a group of plants raises the humidity around those plants. The leaves will catch and hold the transpired moisture. Leave enough room between the plants to encourage air circulation, which helps prevent disease.

Another popular method of increasing humidity, especially for orchids and ferns, is misting. The spray from a mister should create a fine cloud of moisture. Mist in the morning so that the moisture evaporates during the day. Leaves that are moist for long periods are particularly prone to disease. Fuzzy-leaved plants, such as African violets (*Saintpaulia*), will develop water spots if misted.

Misting, unless done several times a day, raises the humidity only temporarily. In dry rooms, moisture evaporates quickly. Humidifying the air, along with adequate watering, are the only ways to ensure that plants have sufficient moisture.

Air Circulation

Plants enjoy fresh air as much as people do. Soft breezes of warm, humid air supply oxygen and moisture, keeping the plant healthy. Plants that are cramped together or placed in an environment where air does not circulate are more likely to develop fungal diseases. At the same time, drafts also can harm plants. Dry air movement over leaves can cause moisture stress and also leaf burn, especially in direct sunlight. Sudden changes in air movement and temperature can send plants into shock. Be especially careful with plants that are near a window, particularly during winter.

Air pollution affects plants in a number of ways. Fumes from burning propane or butane gas may cause leaves to yellow and leaves and flower buds to drop. Fumes from burning natural gas are not harmful to plants.

Dust and dirt from the air accumulate on plant leaves, clogging the stomata and slowing growth. To keep plants growing well, give smooth-leaved plants a shower or a good rinse once a month (see "Showering Plants," page 72). Between showers and for fuzzy-leaved plants, such as African violets (*Saintpaulia*), you can gently wipe off the dust with a soft rag, brush, or feather duster, taking care not to harm the leaves.

Fertilizing

Photosynthesis provides plants with the sugar and other carbohydrates they need for energy. Fertilizers provide the nutritive minerals they require for healthy growth. Plants that need to be fertilized exhibit slow growth, pale leaves, weak stems, small or nonexistent flowers, or dropped leaves.

Fertilizers come in many different formulations to suit various types of plants. The labels usually list three numbers. These are, in order, the percentages of nitrogen, phosphorus, and potassium that make up the fertilizer. Nitrogen, phosphorus, and potassium are the three major nutrients that plants need. A fertilizer labeled 12-6-6 is 12 percent nitrogen, 6 percent phosphate, and 6 percent potash.

Nitrogen primarily enriches the greenness of the foliage and promotes stem growth. Phosphorus encourages flowering and root growth. Potassium contributes to stem strength and disease resistance. Fertilizers formulated for flowering plants usually contain less nitrogen and more phosphorous and potassium. You can also find specialized fertilizers for some plant groups, such as orchids.

In addition to the three nutrients, plants need three secondary nutrients—sulfur, calcium, and magnesium—and minute quantities of iron, zinc, manganese, copper, chlorine, boron, and molybdenum. These latter are called micronutrients, or trace minerals or elements.

Fertilizer tabs are inserted in the soil, where they release nutrients over time. When applying any fertilizer, always read the label first and follow the directions carefully.

Fertilizers are available in many forms: water-soluble pellets, powders, liquids, dry tablets, time-release pellets, and sticks to insert in the soil. Their value and strength vary widely; if you have questions, consult the houseplant specialist who sold you the plant. When applying fertilizers, always read the label first and follow the directions carefully. Remember that more is not better: Excess fertilizer can burn roots and leaves.

Most fertilizers on the market have been formulated for use once a month, but small biweekly doses are safer than large monthly doses. If monthly doses are recommended, reduce the suggested amount by one half and feed biweekly instead. Most foliage plants need far less fertilizer than flowering plants. Fertilize foliage plants at half strength between March and October. During the winter months you should reduce the applications or stop fertilizing altogether.

Before deciding that a plant needs extra fertilizer, review its other care requirements to determine whether they are being met. If a regularly fertilized plant isn't growing, it's likely that the plant is dormant or sick. The worst time to fertilize is when a plant is ailing. Sickly plants will decline even more rapidly if heavily fertilized, and may even die.

Above: Fertilizer burn is often the cause of brown leaf tips.
Right: Leach out excess salts accumulated from fertilizers and water.

Overfertilization is a common error, particularly with plants on maintenance rather than growth programs. Dormant plants do not require the same amounts of fertilizer as plants growing actively. Too much fertilizer will cause leaf burn, poorly shaped leaves, or a white crust on the pots and the surface of the growing medium; too-frequent fertilization may cause deformed growth.

If you accidentally overfertilize a plant, thorough watering should solve the problem. Thorough watering will also help wash out accumulated fertilizer salts, which can build up and harm the plant. Salt buildup shows as a whitish deposit on the outside of clay pots or as salt burn on the edges of leaves. The condition is a serious one but can be remedied by percolating water through—leaching—the soil. Place the plant in a sink, tub, or pail and water it several times, letting the water drain each time. In mild weather, you can place the plant outdoors and water it with a hose, a technique especially useful for large plants. If salts have become a problem, they will not leach out in one day; you may have to repeat the process weekly for several weeks. As a last resort, you can gently wash the old soil from the roots and repot the plant in fresh soil.

Constant Feeding

Many plants, including African violets (*Saintpaulia*), can be fertilized on a constant-feed program, in other words every time they are watered, the year around. When plants are fertilized this way, growth is more symmetrical and leaf color and size are also more even. However, you must use a fertilizer formulated especially for this purpose. If you do not, you risk overfertilizing and damaging the roots. And remember, plants that require less watering during rest periods also require less fertilizer during those times.

Foliar Feeding

In their native habitats, plants absorb nutrients from rain and bird droppings falling onto their leaves. In a home environment they will absorb specially formulated fertilizers sprayed or misted onto the foliage. Use only fertilizers recommended for foliar application, which are available at garden stores, and follow the label directions. Indoor gardeners often apply trace elements to their plants as foliar sprays.

Foliar feeding acts quickly but lasts a relatively short time. It is best used as a supplement to fertilizers applied directly to the soil.

Grooming

People like plants because they symbolize life and vitality. Yellow leaves and brown tips can quickly destroy that look. Houseplants demand regular grooming, trimming, and pruning to keep them manageable in size and attractive in shape. Good grooming also reduces the possibility of disease and helps flowering plants produce superior blossoms.

Cleaning

Dust and dirt on leaves keep light from reaching the leaf pores, harming the plant as well as making it unsightly. Cleaning the plant allows the leaves to breathe and also helps rid them of insect eggs and mites. Dampen a cloth or soft sponge in mild soapy water to remove grime from smooth-leaved plants. Support the leaf in one hand while gently wiping away from the stem. Avoid cleaning new growth.

Use a dry, soft hairbrush or paintbrush to clean the fuzzy leaves of plants such as African violet (*Saintpaulia*) and velvetplant (*Gynura aurantiaca*). Plants with fuzzy leaves do not react well to having water on their leaves. For large plants with many tiny leaves that are difficult to clean, such as weeping fig (*Ficus benjamina*), a feather duster is ideal.

Exercise caution with all cleaning materials, especially dusters, to avoid transferring pests from an infested plant to a clean one. To

Cacti and Succulents

Cacti and succulents exhibit a wide variety of colors, shapes, textures, and sizes. Succulents are the camels of the plant kingdom; their well-developed water conservation techniques can carry them through periods of drought. Unlike desert cacti, however, not all succulents are native to arid areas. Some come from the tropics, where long dry seasons are followed by a short season of heavy rain. As a group, succulents are easy to grow if their general preferences are followed.

A clay pot just large enough to accommodate the plant without overcrowding its roots is best. If a small plant is placed in too large a pot, its roots may rot in unabsorbed water. Bonsai containers are splendid for displaying succulents, and the drainage holes are the right size for allowing unabsorbed water to drain.

Most succulents need to dry out between waterings. Clay and other porous materials make it easier to control the moisture level, although you can use plastic pots for these plants if you water the plant less frequently. Water quality is especially important for succulents, which are sensitive to mineral salts.

During their growing season, cacti and succulents need watering whenever the soil begins to dry out. During dormancy, however, water sparingly (just enough to keep the roots alive). Don't let them get dehydrated; water before foliage and stems go limp and shrivel. In springtime, when plants show signs of fresh growth, begin thorough watering again. Set the pots in a pan of water and allow them to "drink" until the soil is just moist on top.

Fertilize succulents only during the growing period, and dilute to a quarter of the recommended strength for the fertilizer. Feed in small amounts about every third watering, stopping as soon as plants cease their seasonal growth.

Good air circulation is crucial, since stagnant air encourages mealybugs. Keep the plants cool at night but not cold, and place them where they will get strong light during the day unless, like the tropical cacti, they prefer filtered light.

avoid contamination, clean the cloths, sponges, and dusters in warm, soapy water or a 1:10 solution of household bleach and water and allow them to dry before using them again. You can also spray them with a disinfectant after use. Let them air out for a day or so after disinfecting them, to avoid any plant damage.

The leaves of certain plants look better with a little extra sheen. There are leaf shine products on the market, but they should be used with care and in moderation.

Trimming

Once a leaf has turned entirely yellow, it will never become green again. It should be removed to improve both the look of the plant and its general health. When the tip of a leaf turns yellow or brown, trim away the discolored area for the same reasons. When cutting, use sharp shears and follow the original shape of the leaf, taking as little green, vital material as possible. Small discolored leaves and leaves that have turned completely yellow or brown should be pinched off at the base of their stems.

Yellow and brown leaves are not always signs that the plant is ailing. Some leaf attrition is part of the natural growth cycle of most plants.

Top left: Pinching encourages soft-stemmed plants to branch and become fuller. Pinch out the top of each new shoot as it forms.
Bottom left: Trim off any yellow leaf tips or a leaf that has turned entirely yellow to improve the look of the plant and its general health.
Right: Wiping or brushing off plant leaves removes dust and dirt, which can dull a plant's appearance, and helps stop the spread of pests and diseases.

Pinching

When a young stem tip is pinched off, most plants will branch out below the pinch and become bushier and healthier. For example, a young coleus plant started from a seed or cutting must be pinched during its active growth period or one stem will grow straight up and the plant will become gangly and weak. To avoid this, use thumb and forefinger to nip off the growing tip as soon as the plant has four to six leaves. Dormant buds will spring into active growth, producing additional stems. After two or three weeks, pinch the tips of these new stems and the plant will soon become bushy. Pinching works well for most plants, but is especially recommended for soft-stemmed plants, such as certain begonia species and young geraniums (*Pelargonium*).

Pruning

Removing young, woody stems is known as pruning. When part of a plant is removed, the energy invested in sustaining that part is directed toward the rest of the plant. This explains why a sickly plant may be revived by pruning, and flowering plants encouraged to bloom. Pruning requires care and some basic knowledge, but it is not difficult. With careful shaping, you can create a compact, cared-for, topiary look from shapeless, random growth.

Before you make the first cut, consider the effect you'd like to achieve. Removing a stem at its point of origin will force new growth in the remaining stems or from the base of the plant. Cutting off a stem above a leaf will encourage one or more new growth tips to appear near the cut and make the plant denser. With a sharp pair of small hand-pruners, make cuts on branching plants just above a node or just above a leaf to avoid unsightly bare stems all over the plant. Make the cuts at a slight angle so that the cut surface faces inward, toward the center of the plant.

Vining plants, such as pothos (*Epipremnum aureum*), grape-ivy (*Cissus rhombifolia*), and wandering-Jew (*Tradescantia* or *Zebrina* species), require a different pruning method. To achieve both long stems and fullness at the base, allow just a few vines to grow to full length and pinch all the others well back. Pinching induces branching and will help to keep the plant looking lush. Periodically, vining plants should be cut back severely. Make cuts just above leaf buds or branches, and save the cuttings for rooting. For a particularly full, healthy look, root the cuttings in the same pot as the parent plant.

Sometimes an old, though still healthy plant, loses its lower foliage. To hide the bare stem, place the plant in a large container and add several smaller plants of the same species—or a ground cover, such as pothos (*Epipremnum*)—to fill the empty space.

Pruning young, woody stems gives plants a compact, cared-for look and encourages flowering plants to bloom.

Potting and Transplanting

After months or perhaps a year or more of good care, houseplants grow too large for their original containers and need repotting to stay healthy and continue growing vigorously. Plan to repot your plants periodically as part of a regular maintenance program. The telltale signs of a pot-bound plant will help you decide when it's time to repot.

If a plant seems to need enormous amounts of water, it has probably grown too many roots for its container and needs a larger pot. Long strands of roots coming out of the drainage hole or a rootball that fills the pot completely is a sign of this problem. To see whether the roots are compacted, turn the plant on its side and knock the rim of the pot gently against a solid surface to loosen the rootball. If it doesn't come out, the soil may be too wet. Let it dry a little, then try again. If the roots are massed along the sides of the pot and at the base of the rootball, repot the plant.

Sometimes a newly purchased plant will need repotting. Plants are often shipped to nurseries in a light shipping soil that dries out quickly and needs frequent fertilization. Many small plants are actually rooted cuttings, and these are often underpotted. If, after a week of adjustment to its new home, a new plant still needs constant watering, repot it into a larger pot and a quality growing medium.

Tall plants, such as ficus, avocado (*Persea americana*), and certain dracaenas, need repotting when they start to look overgrown; they may topple if they become top heavy. The final, but no less important, reason for repotting is that plants in handsome new containers can change the look of a room almost as dramatically as new furniture.

As a rule, the new pot should be no more than 2 inches larger than the old one. A repotted plant will not grow well until its roots begin to fill the container. Also, a greatly enlarged mass of soil with few roots retains too much water, leading to root rot.

A second rule of thumb on pot size is that the diameter of the rim should equal one third to one half the height of the plant. Tall, slender plants will grow in small pots, as long as the pots are wide enough to provide a stable base. Vining or trailing plants will also grow in small pots.

Wet the growing medium before using it, preferably a day in advance. If the medium you are using comes in plastic bags, add tepid water and tie the top of the bag tightly to keep the medium moist. If you are using a homemade mix, scoop some into a plastic bag and moisten it in the same way. Or place the mix in a large bowl, knead in water by hand, and leave it overnight covered with plastic wrap or foil.

About an hour before repotting, water the plant thoroughly. If you are potting into a new clay pot, soak the pot thoroughly (until air bubbles no longer rise from it) to ensure that it will not absorb water from the growing medium.

To remove the plant from its existing pot, turn the plant on its side and knock the rim of the pot gently against a solid surface to loosen it. If it doesn't come out, the soil may be too wet. Let it dry a little, then try again. If the pot is large, lay it on its side and run a sharp knife or spatula around the edge of the pot. Pull the plant out—you may need a second pair of hands to steady the pot.

When transferring a pot-bound plant from a round container, you will notice that the roots have circled around the inside of the container. Prune roots that are circling the rootball before transplanting: Make three or four ½-inch-deep cuts from the top of the rootball to the bottom with a sharp knife. The pruning will stimulate new root growth and help the roots penetrate the new mix surrounding the rootball.

To transplant, partly fill the new container with the planting mix. Place the plant at the height it grew in its previous pot. Firm the soil around the rootball, then fill the container with soil. Tamp the planting mix with your fingers, especially near the edges of the container. Water thoroughly, and keep the roots moist until they have spread into the surrounding soil. Repot a plant as quickly as possible so that the roots do not dry out.

Occasionally, a plant will need additional nourishment rather than repotting, especially if it performs better when pot bound. Such plants will benefit from a top dressing. To top-dress a plant, scrape off the top 1 or 2 inches of growing medium with a fork or small rake. Then fill the pot to its original level with fresh potting mixture, tamping it firmly.

Holding the plant securely, tap it out of the container. For large plants, you may need help steadying the pot.

Partially fill the new container with planting mix, then position the plant at the height it grew in its previous pot. Firm the soil around the plant and fill the container with soil.

Once the container is full, firm the soil around the plant and water thoroughly.

Choosing Pots and Containers

Pots directly influence the growth, appearance, and needs of the plants they contain. They can be as casual as a coconut shell or a repainted coffee can or as formal as a glazed bonsai planter. Plastic and cloth bags, old whiskey and wine barrels, stoneware bowls, and pieces of driftwood can all be converted into unusual plant containers. The following containers are the most common.

Plastic Pots

Available in any number of shapes and sizes (generally ranging from 2 to 18 inches in diameter), plastic pots are lighter and less expensive than clay pots. Plants in plastic pots need watering less often than plants in clay pots; since plastic pots are not porous, they retain moisture much longer. However, since air cannot move through the pot walls, plastic pots require growing media with excellent drainage.

Clay Pots

The standard clay pot is both functional and attractive. It is available in the same shapes and sizes as plastic pots and has a drainage hole in the bottom. Clay saucers may be sold with the pots or separately.

The unglazed porous clay allows air and water to move through the pot wall. Clay pots, therefore, should be soaked in a basin of water for several hours before being planted. Otherwise, the dry clay will absorb water from the potting soil, robbing the new plantings of moisture.

Because they are porous, clay saucers will eventually create water stains on surfaces where they're placed. To protect your furniture and floors, cut a round of cork ½ inch thick to fit beneath the saucer, or use a thick cork coaster. A more practical solution is simply not to use clay saucers; instead, choose moisture-proof plastic or glazed ceramic.

Before reusing clay pots scrub them clean with a stiff brush and warm water to eliminate salt buildup on the pot. To sterilize them, run them through a dishwasher or put them into an oven for one hour at 180° F. Or you can soak them in a 1:10 solution of household bleach and water.

Cachepots and Jardinieres

Plants on a growth program eventually require larger pots than the ones they came in. Once, however, a plant has reached the perfect size for the space it fills, maintenance rather than growth becomes the goal. In either case, the grow pot that the plant is potted in may be ideal for the cultural needs of the plant but may not fit in with the decorating scheme of the room. Then it's time to simply

set the pot inside a decorative container, often called a cachepot or jardiniere. Make certain that the container is at least 2 inches higher than the grow pot.

Since the grow pot provides drainage, the outside container need not; it may either be watertight or have a saucer. Put a 1-inch layer of some open material that will not decompose in the bottom of the decorative container; Styrofoam chips and crushed chicken wire are good choices. Set the grow pot in the decorative pot and pack more of the bottom fill material around the sides. To hide the grow pot, spread a mulch of sphagnum moss, Spanish moss, bark chips, or water-polished stones over the surface. Water the grow pot thoroughly at each watering. The water that drains through into the decorative pot should evaporate. If it doesn't, loosen the top mulch to allow more air into the fill material.

Pots directly influence the growth, appearance, and needs of the plant they contain. Clay, ceramic, and plastic containers in a wide variety of shapes and sizes are readily available in plant stores.

As well as being decorative, this brass cachepot prevents water stains on the wood floor.

Squirrel's foot fern or ball fern (Davallia mariesii) looks elegant in a glazed ceramic pot.

Left: Plants and baskets are natural companions. Their textures, shapes, and hues are complementary and, although either can make a statement of its own, the statement they make together is far more dramatic. The natural-color pots and the baskets on the wall and chest harmonize with their shapes and colors; the bright yellow orchid provides an accent. Right: A Chinese steamer conceals the container in which these freesias are growing. The yellow flowers complement the colors of the poster behind them.

Glazed Pottery Pots

Highly decorative, glazed pottery containers lend a distinctive touch to almost any decor. The wide array of sizes and designs includes bonsai pots and trays that are particularly attractive for miniature landscapes or bulbs. Some glazed containers have no drainage holes; these are best used as cachepots for slightly smaller clay or plastic pots.

Woven Baskets

For a less formal or an ethnic-inspired look, woven baskets as plant containers can add just the right touch. Although they look attractive, they can rot quickly from contact with moisture. Some have plastic liners to alleviate the moisture problem, but then they lack drainage. For these reasons, baskets, too, are best used as cachepots, covering a more utilitarian grow pot. Even with an interior saucer or plastic liner to catch moisture, wet baskets can cause extensive moisture damage to surfaces. To avoid this, place baskets on plastic mats or wood-backed cork pads.

Window Boxes and Wood Planters

Planters made of rot-resistant redwood or cypress, though not as popular for houseplants as other types of planters, can fill a decorative niche. Because the construction of wood planters may not be as watertight as that of plastic, clay, or ceramic containers, they are probably best used as cachepots, concealing the grow pots and drainage trays placed inside. Orchids and other epiphytic plants grow extremely well in wood planters; the potting mix dries out rapidly, which suits these plants.

Plastic- and enamel-coated metal window boxes, which are lightweight and available in a variety of colors, are also available. The best of these have drainage holes. On an indoor windowsill, they should also have matching trays to catch the drained water.

Hanging Planters

To add an interesting dimension to a room, try using hanging planters. They will highlight fine architectural details and disguise unattractive ones. They make efficient use of space and avoid monotonous concentration of plants at one level. A trailing plant with its vines cascading over the edges of a planter hung high in the air provides a very graceful effect. However, bear in mind that the vines will cascade only if there is sufficient top light. Hanging plants flourish where they receive light from above, under skylights or in light wells or solariums.

Right: This simple wood planter is handsome enough to use as a centerpiece. Dinner guests can add fresh herbs of their choice to soups or salads.
Opposite: The indoor/outdoor feeling of this sunroom is emphasized by the handsome redwood planter filled with bromeliads that sits below the bank of windows. Using potted plants inside a planter allows you to change them easily to provide year-round color.

Hanging pots   The simplest hanging planter is a clay or plastic pot suspended by a wire hanger that is clamped on or attached through holes in the pot. Most of these simple planters have saucers built into the container or attached underneath; ones without saucers must be watered in the sink and then drained, or they will drip onto the floor. Choose the hangers that have built-in swivels so that you can rotate every side of the planter toward the sun.

Regular pots can be transformed into hanging planters with a simple string or rope macramé cradle, supporting and surrounding both the pot and its saucer. These macramé cradles are available in many plant centers, but they are simple to make using heavy twine or strong, waterproof, nylon cord.

Wood planters   Many hanging planters are made of wood. These are attractive, but dry out quickly. They are popular for growing orchids and other epiphytic plants, however, because these plants prefer a quick-drying soil.

Wire baskets   Since draining water will run unimpeded from a wire basket, use this kind of hanging planter only above a masonry floor. Line the basket with coarse, unmilled sphagnum moss and then fill with soil.

Caring for hanging plants   Whichever type of hanging planter you use, be sure to leave enough watering space at the top. Fill the planter with soil to within ½ inch from the top, not to the rim. In a moss basket, pack sphagnum moss thick and tight around the top inch of the basket to create a watering basin.

Opposite: The beams of an attic bathroom provide the perfect support for hanging planters of variegated ivy (Hedera helix) and columnea. The floor and tub surround also serve as plant stations, for the dwarf anthurium (Anthurium scherzeranum) and maidenhair fern (Adiantum).

A hanging container needs more frequent watering than a pot on the ground or on a windowsill. Exposed to air on all sides, it more quickly loses water to evaporation. Give the soil a thorough soaking whenever you water it, or water it sparingly several times a day. Hanging planters can be watered without too much extra effort by using a squeeze-type plastic watering bottle designed especially for the purpose.

Hanging plants require vigilant grooming. Remove all spent blooms, and cut back straying shoots. To keep the plants looking full and healthy, grow new young shoots in the same pot by pinning tips or vines to the moss with old-fashioned hairpins or paper clips broken apart. Rotate the planter frequently so that all sides get evenly exposed to the sun.

Self-Watering Containers

Do you consider watering plants part of the enjoyment of indoor gardening, or is it a chore? If you prefer to spend your time enjoying your plants rather than remembering to water them, then self-watering containers are for you.

Self-watering containers have a water reservoir that needs attention only when it gets low, usually every couple of weeks. Since fertilizer is usually added to the water at the same time, feeding and watering become tasks to be done every few weeks instead of every few days. Meanwhile, the pot automatically delivers water

Self-watering containers come in a variety of shapes and sizes. This selection shows several types available commercially.

Reservoir Unit

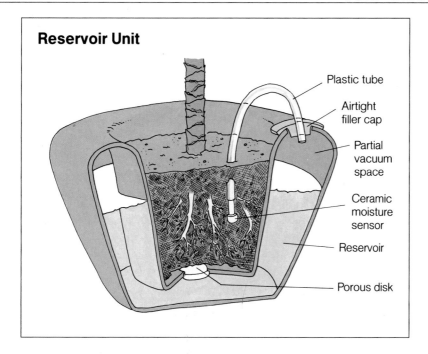

Plastic tube

Airtight filler cap

Partial vacuum space

Ceramic moisture sensor

Reservoir

Porous disk

Wick Watering Unit

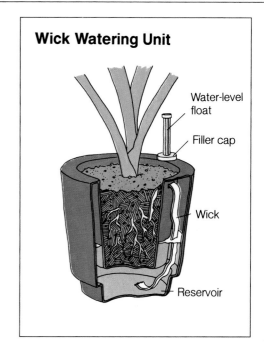

Water-level float

Filler cap

Wick

Reservoir

Hydroponic Unit

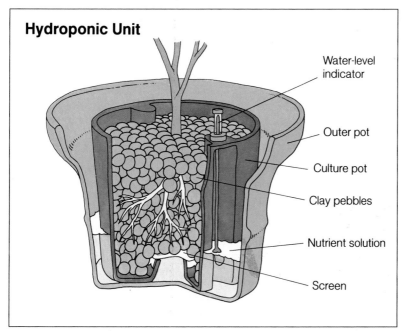

Water-level indicator

Outer pot

Culture pot

Clay pebbles

Nutrient solution

Screen

at the rate the plant uses it, adjusting to changes in light, humidity, or temperature. Plants in self-watering pots are usually more evenly watered than plants in conventional pots.

Self-watering pots operate on the principle of capillary attraction. In the same way that water will move upward to moisten an entire towel when just the tip dips into the sink, water will move from the reservoir into the potting mix above. However, there does need to be a link—a wick of some sort—between the water and the growing medium.

There are many types of self-watering containers. Some have built-in reservoirs. Others are actually two pots: a grow pot and an outer pot or cachepot that fits around the grow pot; the outer pot acts as a reservoir.

Most self-watering containers use a fibrous wick made of a synthetic material (natural fibers rot from constant contact with moisture) to draw water up into the growing medium. In others, the bottom of the grow pot is made of a porous material (often unglazed ceramic), and the water moves through this into the potting medium. The potting medium itself can also act as a wick. In some self-watering containers, the grow pot has deep ridges in its base that descend to the bottom of the reservoir. The ridges are pierced with just a few holes so that water flows in slowly. The narrow column of potting soil filling the ridges is in constant contact with the water in the reservoir and provides moisture to the drier soil above by means of capillary action.

Self-watering pots have different ways of indicating when the reservoir is empty and when it is too full. Some pots show the water level with a float, often colored red for maximum visibility. Others have a clear plastic gauge along one side of the reservoir. In some the entire reservoir is made of a transparent material so that you can see the water level even from a distance. The disadvantage with the latter method is that the water is exposed to light, which encourages the growth of unsightly algae.

There are also different ways of adding water to the reservoir. Containers with built-in reservoirs have an opening in the side or on the top into which you can pour the water. If the grow pot is separate from the outer pot, just lift up the grow pot and pour water directly into the reservoir. Never overfill. If the grow pot is touching the water, the roots may rot.

Making Your Own Self-Watering Pot

It is easy to make a self-watering pot on your own. All you need are a potted plant, an empty refrigerator container, and a strand of fiber that can be used as a wick. Polyester yarn makes an excellent wick, as do thin strips of an old nylon stocking.

Cut the wick to 4 to 6 inches in length. Cut a hole in the center of the lid of the refrigerator container, then cut a second hole close to the edge of the lid. Remove the plant from its pot, and insert the wick through one of the drainage holes in the pot. Wind the wick around the bottom of the pot, letting a few inches hang out. (If you don't want to unpot the plant, you can push the wick up into the potting mix through a drainage hole using a nut pick or

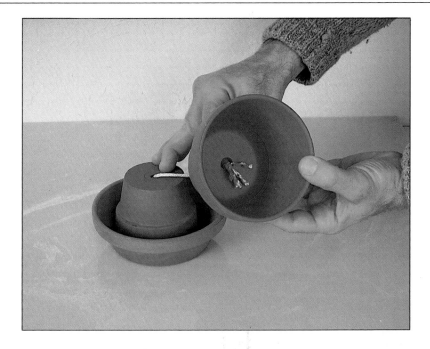

When making a homemade wick watering unit, insert a frayed nylon wick in the bottom of the growing pot to carry the water from the saucer up into the soil.

Place the growing pot on an inverted pot to ensure that it does not sit in water.

knitting needle.) Set the pot on the lid of the container so that the end of the wick hangs down through the hole in the center of the lid. Using the second hole, fill the container with water. Your homemade self-watering pot is complete.

Self-Watering Tips

Although self-watering pots are essentially simple to operate, these few pointers will help you avoid any problems.

• Most wicks need to be primed (premoistened). Soak the wick in water before use. If the grow pot has a porous bottom designed to act as a wick, likewise let it soak in water for two hours before use. After potting up the plant, water it from the top the first time to prime that part of the system too.

• If the potting mix is constantly soggy, install a thinner wick. If it is always too dry, install a thicker wick or a number of wicks.

• Use only soilless mixes in self-watering pots. Garden soil tends to compact quickly when kept constantly moist.

Hydroculture

Hydroculture is one step beyond the self-watering pot. This technique uses no soil or organic material of any kind as a support. The plants grow entirely in stones or, more frequently, clay pebbles. Hydroculture reduces the danger of soil pests and diseases while supplying the plant with exactly the amount of water it needs. It is the ideal technique for people who don't have time to baby their plants, because the plants need watering only every two to three weeks. And those who are allergic to plants (they are generally allergic to soil-borne organisms) may find they can now enjoy houseplants as a hobby. Virtually any houseplant—even cacti and succulents—will adapt to hydroculture.

Hydroculture simply means growing in water. It is a simplified or passive version of another technique, hydroponics. In hydroponic systems, water is recirculated on a regular basis using pumps or other mechanical means. Hydroculture systems consist of an outer pot that serves as a reservoir for a liquid nutrient solution and a grow pot filled with clay pebbles, with a screen between the two pots. In hydroculture systems, water simply moves from one clay pebble to the next by capillary action, much as water moves in a self-watering pot. The texture of the pebbles allows plentiful air circulation, necessary for healthy root growth, while giving the roots all the moisture they require. There are no circulating pumps or bothersome tubes to fuss with.

Before transferring plants to a hydroculture pot, rinse them thoroughly to remove any soil particles, and trim off any dead or dying roots; otherwise rot can result. To make the transition to the new medium easier for the plants, mist them daily for the first 10 days after transplanting. In many cases, rather than transplant soil-grown plants, it is easier to start with new cuttings rooted in the hydroculture pot using special rooting stones, actually small versions of the regular clay pebbles. Transfer the cuttings to their final hydroculture pot once they have rooted. Some merchants stock plants raised in a hydroculture unit.

Using hydroculture pots is simple. You need to add water only when there is none left in the outer pot. In most cases, this means waiting until the indicator reads empty, then delaying two more days. To check that the container is empty, tip it and note whether the indicator moves. Then add enough water to bring the indicator up to the halfway mark. If you fill the pots to the top each time, the roots may rot. Use the maximum capacity of the container only when you will be away for several weeks. Leach the plants every two to three months using room-temperature or tepid water.

Since there is no soil to buffer pH levels and mineral concentrations in the water, it is important to use fertilizers especially formulated for hydroculture. Some liquid and soluble hydroculture fertilizers are designed to be added each time the container is filled with water. Others are slow-release fertilizers, usually in the form of crystals or disks. They should be applied according to instructions, usually once every six months.

• Never put a drainage layer of gravel or pot shards in the bottom of a self-watering pot; it will stall the capillary action.
• Fertilizing a self-watering plant by normal means can be tricky. Instead, each time you top up the reservoir, use a solution of water and soluble fertilizer diluted to one quarter of the recommended strength.
• Leach the potting mix three or four times a year to remove accumulated fertilizer salts. Take the unit to the sink, remove the reservoir, and run tepid water through the soil mix until the drainage water runs perfectly clear.
• Since plants grown in self-watering pots produce fewer roots than plants grown in ordinary pots, they will not need to be repotted as frequently.
• If your system works well for a while, then the soil suddenly remains dry no matter how much water is in the reservoir, it is time to change the wick. Wicks eventually become clogged with mineral salts and no longer work efficiently.

Moving Plants Indoors and Out

After a long, dark winter, many houseplants enjoy a dose of fresh air, filtered sunlight, and rainwater. This treatment rejuvenates them and adds a fresh touch of greenery to porch, patio, or yard. However, it is not highly recommended for plants that you do not want to grow any larger or more vigorously, and it does require care and planning.

Take only the hardiest plants outdoors, those that will stand unexpected wind and cold. Always wait until all threat of frost has passed and temperatures are remaining above 45° F at night. Make the transition gradually, starting the plants out with at least a week in a protected, well-shaded spot. After a few weeks, you can settle most plants in a spot where there's a few hours of filtered sunlight each day and protection from the wind. Never place the plant in full sun. During the first few weeks, keep a close watch for evidence of excessive dryness, pest infestation, or shock.

You can display the plants outdoors in their containers or sink the pots below ground level in the garden, provided the site has good drainage. Dig a bed 3 or 4 inches deeper than the pots and wide enough to accommodate the foliage without it overlapping. Layer the bottom of the bed with 3 inches of gravel and 1 inch of peat moss. Set the pots into the bed and fill with soil up to the rims. The gravel should prevent the roots from spreading out of the drainage holes, but you may want to make sure they don't root into the ground by twisting the pots every few weeks.

As temperatures begin to dip in autumn, prepare to bring the plants back indoors. Set each container on a bench or table where you can examine it carefully, and clip off every yellowed leaf, spent flower, and seedpod. If the plant has grown too large for its indoor location, reshape it with some careful pruning.

Before bringing the plant inside, clean both the plant and the outside of the pot. Examine the foliage carefully for pests and disease, since these might infect your other plants. Treat pest-infested plants with the appropriate control (see pages 185 to 197), following label directions. Once they are back inside, the plants will need to be acclimated (see page 64) just as they did when you first brought them home.

You can also bring outdoor plants inside. If a certain potted plant is in full bloom, why not place it in an indoor spot to enjoy. Before you move it, though, clean the plant and pot thoroughly, checking for insects and disease. Then place the plant at the chosen site, and check to be sure it has sufficient water and light. After the blooms have faded or if the plant is showing signs of stress, return it to its outdoor location. For more information on bringing plants indoors, see "Flowering Houseplants," pages 137 to 161.

Creating Terrarium Gardens

Terrariums are miniature landscapes, created by combining a collection of plants in a glass container. The container can be made from a fish tank, bubble bowl, brandy snifter, or bottle. Depending on the choice of plants, the location, and the type of container, you can create the effect of a woodland dell, a desert, a rocky coastline, or a tiny jungle.

Many hardy houseplants benefit from the fresh air and filtered sunlight of an outdoor location and, in turn, may add a touch of color or pattern to a garden spot that has lost its freshness. Be sure to shield plants from strong light or wind and check them for pests and diseases before bringing them back indoors.

Terrariums are usually thought of as tabletop decorations, but they can also be suspended from ceiling hooks or wall brackets. If there is space in the terrarium, you can even add a shallow container of water to serve as a pond in the midst of the landscape.

Plants do best under clear glass, rather than tinted glass. Bowls, dishes, brandy snifters, and fish tanks are easy to plant and maintain because you can reach inside them with your hands.

Planting Terrariums

You will want to clean and dry the chosen container thoroughly before you start planting. Before you add any plant to a bottle garden or terrarium, inspect it carefully for insects, diseases, and rotted roots. These problems are especially contagious under glass.

Most containers used for terrarium gardening have no drainage holes. To keep the growing medium sweet smelling and healthy, line the bottom of the container with ½ inch of charcoal chips (available where indoor plants are sold). Then add at least 1½ inches of potting mix. The best soils for terrariums are the soilless mixtures or commercially prepared growing media with a little extra vermiculite or perlite added to improve air circulation to the roots.

Small-necked bottles are quite a challenge, requiring delicate, long-handled tools. To place the growing medium in such a bottle, fashion a funnel from a rolled-up piece of newspaper. To move the soil around and shape the terrain, use a slender, wooden stake (a chopstick or bamboo skewer) with a small measuring spoon taped to the end. When you are ready to "bottle" the plants, gently remove most of the potting mix from the roots, drop each plant through the neck of the bottle, coax it into the right position with the "spade," and cover the roots with growing media.

Almost any jar or bottle with a wide mouth can be used as a terrarium. This octagonal container shows off the round form of the maidenhair fern (Adiantum) within.

Resembling a miniature greenhouse, this terrarium would lend a touch of greenery to any setting.

Once the plants are in place, a final mulch or ground carpet of moss will complete the scene. Mist with clear water to settle the roots and to remove soil particles from the leaves as well as from the sides of the bottle.

Maintaining Terrariums

The most common misconception about terrarium plantings is that they require no care and will thrive just about anywhere indoors. In fact, they need occasional watering and regular grooming to remove spent growth and to contain fast-growing plants. A terrarium stuffed with plants will soon be overgrown.

Terrariums do best in bright indirect light—sunlight shining directly through the glass for more than an hour or two is likely to cook the plants. Terrariums will also do well under two fluorescent tubes—one cool white, one warm white, either 20 or 40 watts—for 12 to 14 hours a day.

When the soil appears dry, there are no moisture droplets on the container, or the plants are droopy, add a little water. To remove yellowing leaves, spent flowers, or excess growth from a narrow-necked bottle garden, tape a single-edge razor blade to a thin, wooden stick and use it as a cutting tool. You can remove the clippings with slender pieces of wood, manipulating them like chopsticks (slender, pointed, Japanese-style chopsticks will serve very well). You can also use a mechanic's pickup tool (sold at auto supply stores). Remove dying leaves and flowers before they rot, since a tiny amount of rot can quickly infect healthy leaves and shoots.

Propagating Techniques

Collecting plants is no different from collecting anything else—increased knowledge tends to lead to rarefied tastes and inevitably higher prices. So once you're hooked, indoor gardening can be an expensive hobby. Propagation—the creation of new plants from old—is one of the most rewarding, easy, and economical ways to support your plant-growing habit. It also intimately involves you in the entire cycle of plant growth.

Starting new plants from old ones offers several benefits. You can multiply a few plants into a sizable collection or grow a beautifully symmetrical replacement for an aging favorite specimen. You can reproduce favorites from friends' collections and repay those same friends with gifts reproduced from plants in your collection. All you need is the knowledge of the correct techniques, a minimal investment in propagating materials, a little time and effort, and patience. As long as you allow a young plant some growing time before you expect it to stand in for its parent, you will find that propagation adds an entirely new dimension to the enjoyment of growing plants.

On the following pages, you will find discussions on how to germinate seeds and propagate from stem, leaf, and root cuttings as well as information on how to divide plants, separate and root plantlets, perform layering, and grow ferns from spores. The best propagation method to use depends both on the plant and on your personal preference. If in doubt, check the care guide for each plant in ''A Gallery of Houseplants'' (pages 199 to 307).

Plants propagate in two fundamentally different ways— sexually and asexually. Sexual propagation occurs when pollen from the male parts of the plant fertilizes the female parts to produce seeds. Asexual propagation, or vegetative propagation, occurs when a piece of one plant is cultivated and grown into a new plant. The new plant is simply an extension of the original parent plant.

Creating new houseplants from existing specimens adds to your plant collection and keeps you in touch with the growth cycle of your plants.

Sowing seeds is usually the least expensive way of starting new plants. There is a certain excitement in watching a seedling push through the soil, straighten up, and begin to grow.

Seeds

A seed is a tiny plant waiting for the right conditions to propel it into its life cycle. For germination, it needs a disease-free growing medium, proper warmth and moisture, and adequate light. Propagating from seed allows you to enjoy species not normally available, acquire a number of plants of the same species cheaply, explore genetic variability, and gain a more intimate knowledge of a species.

Most houseplants may be grown from seed, but usually they are easier to propagate vegetatively. A number of excellent houseplants, however, can be propagated only from seed. Single-trunk palms, cyclamen, and many annuals used in hanging baskets fall into this category, as do the herbs parsley, chervil, sweet basil, marjoram, and summer savory. As an experiment, try starting citrus plants from seeds that you've washed and allowed to dry. Lemon, lime, orange, and citron all make lovely houseplants, but you should not expect fruit from these plants. You can delight children by sowing a few dry peas or beans, or unroasted peanuts, all of which are seeds. Under the right conditions, they will burst into growth.

Houseplant seeds are available from garden centers and a few mail-order nurseries. Sow them in the same way you would sow seed for outdoor plants, with bottom heat (70° to 75° F) to expedite germination (see page 128).

For containers, you can use flats, small pots, Styrofoam trays or jugs, cut-off milk cartons, or egg trays with small holes punched in the bottom with a needle. Small plastic or Styrofoam trays with clear plastic covers make excellent seed propagators.

Plastic bags are useful miniature greenhouses. When sealed firmly, drops of moisture form on the inside, creating a humid atmosphere for seeds and cuttings. Prevent the bag from touching a plant by installing stakes or a simple wire frame.

Houseplants to Grow From Seed

Botanical Name	Common Name
Agapanthus	Agapanthus, blue African lily, lily-of-the-Nile
Aglaonema modestum	Chinese evergreen
Asparagus	Asparagus fern
Begonia × *semperflorens-cultorum*	Wax begonia
Bromeliads	
Browallia	Browallia, sapphire-flower
Cacti	
Campanula	Star-of-Bethlehem, bellflower
Carissa macrocarpa	Ornamental pepper
Citrus species	Citrus
Coffea arabica	Coffee plant
Coleus × *hybridus*	Coleus
Crossandra infundibuliformis	Crossandra, firecracker-flower
Cuphea ignea	Cigarplant
Cyclamen persicum	Cyclamen
Exacum affine	Persian violet
Felicia amelloides	Blue marguerite, blue daisy
Gesneriads	
Hypoestes phyllostachya	Hypoestes, pink-polka-dot, freckle-face
Impatiens species	Impatiens
Palms	
Pelargonium	Florist's geraniums
Peperomia species	Peperomia
Persea americana	Avocado
Primula	Primrose
Thunbergia alata	Black-eyed-susan, thunbergia

Large seeds with hard coats should be nicked with a file and soaked in water until the coat softens, and then sown. Slow-germinating seeds (for instance, all species of the carrot family, including parsley and chervil) also benefit from a day or two of soaking.

An easy way to start seeds is to sow them in moistened vermiculite or milled sphagnum moss, both available at garden centers. Sow seeds sparingly so that the seedlings don't get crowded. Scatter tiny seeds on top of moist growing medium and leave them uncovered. Sow medium-sized seeds on the growing medium, then cover them with a thin layer of the medium to hold them in place when they are watered. Cover large seeds to a depth twice their diameter, firming the growing medium around each seed by pressing gently.

Label the seed tray with the seed name, date sown, and any other information you might need. (It may also be useful to keep the seed packets so that you can refer to them for information on

Seed-Starting Accessories

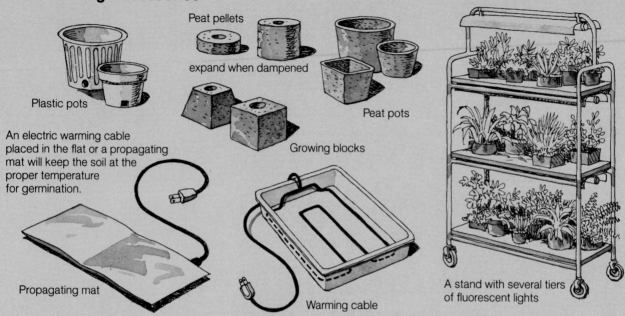

Peat pellets
expand when dampened

Plastic pots

Peat pots

Growing blocks

An electric warming cable placed in the flat or a propagating mat will keep the soil at the proper temperature for germination.

Propagating mat

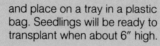

Warming cable

A stand with several tiers of fluorescent lights

One-Step Method

Sow seeds, two at a time, directly into plastic pots, peat pots, or growing blocks. Water thoroughly and place on a tray in a plastic bag. Seedlings will be ready to transplant when about 6″ high.

Two-Step Method

Step 1.

Sow seeds in a tray of damp vermiculite. Set seeds about ¼″ deep; cover; and water lightly. Slip tray into a plastic bag and keep at about 75° F. Withhold water until after germination, then keep soil damp.

Step 2.

Press soil around roots and stem.

When the first true leaves form, transplant to peat pots.

Put the pots on a tray and place the tray in a plastic bag until the plants are well established.

transplanting and suggested growing conditions.) Water lightly, and slip the seed tray into a plastic bag or cover it with paper or glass—the seed packet will indicate whether light or darkness is required for germination. Follow the directions and check seeds daily, watering when necessary. If you are growing tropical houseplants, be prepared to wait—some seeds take several years to germinate!

When seedlings emerge, move them into brighter light. The first two leaves to appear are generally not true leaves but cotyledons, which nourish the stem tip and the true leaves that follow. Wait for true leaves to appear before placing the seedlings in direct sunlight, then give them the same light you would give the mature plant. When the seedlings are three to four weeks old, start to fertilize them every two weeks with a diluted solution of liquid fertilizer (one quarter to one third the regular strength).

Transplant seedlings when they have at least four true leaves. Pry them out carefully, and place them into individual small pots filled with an appropriate potting mix.

If you do decide to try to propagate one of the more challenging plants from seed, learn its needs first. Many specialty seed sources will tell you what they are, as will horticulture reference texts or local plant societies. Be sure you know whether you should cover the seed or sow it on the surface, since some seeds need light to germinate. Learn how long you can expect to wait for germination. Some species can take months to show.

Finally, see if the seeds must be treated before they will germinate. Some require stratification, which is cold treatment in the refrigerator for six weeks or longer at 35° to 40° F. Other seeds have a coat so tough that it must be broken before the seed can germinate. This treatment, called scarification, is achieved by nicking the seed coat with a file or sandpaper.

Cuttings

Inducing a cutting to form roots is the most popular method of vegetative propagation. It is an easy way to duplicate the attractive features of the original plant, since the new plant will be genetically identical. The new plant is in fact called a clone.

Depending on the plant, you can take cuttings from stems, leaves, and roots. Cuttings will root in a number of different media: in a commercial rooting medium, in water, in an artificial soil mix, or in potting mix. Prepare the rooting medium before you take the cutting from the plant.

Although some gardeners routinely dip all cuttings in powdered rooting hormone before rooting them, this step is not usually necessary and may actually inhibit fast-rooting plants, such as coleus and Swedish ivy (*Plectranthus*). Plants with slightly woody stems, such as fuchsia and miniature rose, are more likely to benefit from use of a rooting hormone.

Stem Cuttings

With a very sharp knife or a razor blade, remove a leafy stem that is 1 to 6 inches long. Cut at an angle just below a node—the joint from which the leaf stalk arises—and trim the base with a clean cut about ⅛ of an inch above the lowest leaf node. Make sure the cutting has at least one node.

Strip off all but the top two or three sets of leaves. If the leaves are small and bunched together, you may leave a few more; if the leaves are large, retain only the last two and cut them in half width-wise with scissors. Try to leave about 2 square inches of leaf surface on each cutting—this may be several small leaves or only a part of one large one. Set the stripped end of the cutting in the rooting medium, then pat the soil around it so it is firmly in place.

When taking a stem cutting from a plant with a milky stem, such as poinsettia (*Euphorbia pulcherrima*) or geranium (*Pelargonium*), make the cut, then rub the cut end with alcohol (to prevent disease) and allow it to dry or callus for a few hours out of the sun. When the cut end is dry, proceed with planting.

*Left: Herbaceous plants are easy to propagate from stem cuttings. Take cuttings using a sharp knife, as shown here with a geranium (*Pelargonium*). Right: Remove the lower leaves as well as any excessive top growth.*

Left: With a pencil, make a hole in a moistened soilless medium and insert the trimmed cutting into the hole. Right: Cover the cutting with a plastic cup or a staked plastic bag. Remove the plastic cover after a few days.

Leaf Cuttings

Some plants have the amazing ability to reproduce from a single leaf. The African violet (*Saintpaulia*) is well known for this characteristic, but the same technique works equally well for rex begonias, florist's gloxinias (*Sinningia speciosa*), sedums, kalanchoes, and even some succulents and peperomias.

Certain species will produce new plants from only a section of a leaf, providing the section contains a piece of midrib. Cape primrose (*Streptocarpus*) and a few other plants can be propagated by simply laying leaf sections on top of the rooting medium. Leaf sections of the snakeplant (*Sansevieria trifasciata*) will root and grow if the base of the section is inserted just below the surface of the rooting medium.

To start a plant from a leaf cutting, pull or cut a mature, but not obviously old, leaf away from the parent plant. Cut the leaf stem (petiole) to ½ to 1 inch in length, then set the leaf in the rooting mixture as you would a stem cutting. The leaf should be at a 45-degree angle (it can rest against the pot edge), and the cut end should not be too deep in the medium. Once plantlets form, cut away the parent leaf.

Root Cuttings

Some plants can be propagated from latent buds in their roots. Although relatively few houseplants are propagated this way, they include the edible fig (*Ficus carica*) and the popular Hawaiian ti plant (*Cordyline terminalis*).

To propagate from a root cutting, simply set the root pieces vertically in rooting medium. The ends that were closest to the crown should be at the top. When plantlets form, transplant them as you would other cuttings that have rooted.

Rooting Different Cuttings

Cuttings often fail to root because they dry out before being planted. To avoid disappointment, choose a work area out of direct sunlight and have the container and rooting medium at hand before you take the cutting. After you've severed it from the mother plant, root it quickly. The exception is leaf cuttings from a plant with milky sap, which need to dry and form a callus before rooting.

Various rooting media are suitable for rooting cuttings. Whichever you choose, it should be light and porous, able to hold plenty of water, and coarse enough to allow air to circulate through it. It should also be sterilized. Never use a soil-based mix as a rooting medium; it is too rich for the immature roots of cuttings. One of the best rooting media is a mixture of 1 part sand and 1 part sphagnum peat moss. You can also use straight vermiculite, perlite, or milled sphagnum moss, or a mixture of 10 parts perlite to 1 part

Some plants can be propagated from a single leaf. Use a broken leaf or cut one off the parent plant. Make a diagonal cut at the base of the stem with a sharp knife. Place the cutting in a moistened growing medium, and cover it with plastic for a few days.

peat moss. Once you've made your choice, wet the rooting medium and let it drain.

You can start a plant in almost any container that will hold the rooting medium and stay together. People have successfully propagated plants in egg cartons, cut-off milk cartons, aluminum foil pans, tin cans, and plastic containers. Plastic pots are preferable to clay pots because they retain moisture longer. Commercial flats and pots are also available.

A clear plastic box makes an excellent propagator for multiple cuttings. Use a heated ice pick or awl to punch a few ventilation holes in the lid, lay 2 inches of rooting medium on the bottom, moisten it, then the box is ready for the cuttings. A similar propagating box can be made from a seed flat or fruit box, covered by a sheet of glass or polyethylene film held up by stakes.

Clean any container thoroughly with soap and water before rooting the cuttings. Cuttings rooted in paper containers will need extra nitrogen; those rooted in nonporous containers do better with drainage holes.

Use your index finger or a pencil to make a hole in the rooting medium, insert the cutting, and tamp soil around it until it is firmly in place. Cover the container with glass or plastic (making sure that it doesn't touch the foliage), and set it in a warm, light place with no direct sunlight. Since the cuttings initially have no roots and therefore can't supply the leaves with water, they must not dry out. You may need to water once or twice a day to keep the soil wet if you don't use a plastic or glass cover. However, be careful not to waterlog the growing medium. Since rooting boxes frequently don't have drainage holes, overwatering will lead to root rot. If you are using a plastic bag or glass cover, be sure to open the bag or remove the cover for a few hours every day to allow fresh air to circulate.

Another popular method of rooting cuttings is to place them in a glass of water until roots have formed, then transplant them into a soilless mix. Rooting will occur more quickly if you place each cutting in a separate glass. Don't delay transplanting, since cuttings left too long in water will develop roots that have adapted to growing underwater. These roots may rot when they come into contact with a drier medium. As soon as roots are clearly visible, but no longer than 1 inch, it is time to transplant.

Several plant species that root readily in water can be grown permanently in water if fed frequently with liquid plant food. Wandering-Jew (*Tradescantia* or *Zebrina* species), arrowhead vine (*Syngonium podophyllum*), and philodendrons can easily be grown this way (see the discussion on hydroculture on page 112). Keep in mind that plants growing in water are more susceptible to rot than those in a rooting medium.

Stem Cuttings

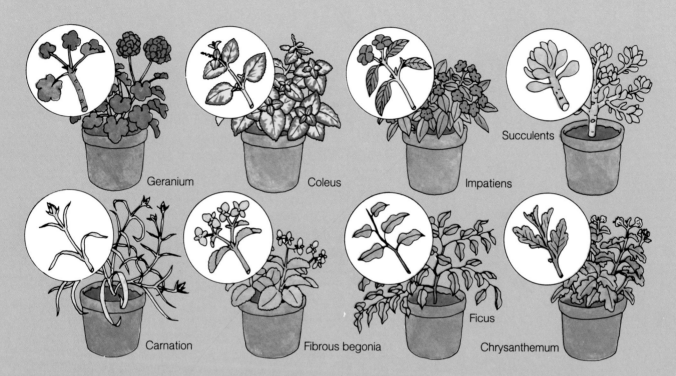

Geranium

Coleus

Impatiens

Succulents

Carnation

Fibrous begonia

Ficus

Chrysanthemum

Herbaceous plants are among the easiest plants to propagate; a selection of them is illustrated above. Cuttings from plants with fibrous or succulent stems should be air dried before planting. This helps prevent rot.

Basic Techniques

Make cuttings 3″ to 5″ long; cut just below a node (where the leaf joins the stem).

Strip off the bottom leaves. The top leaves are necessary for root formation.

Dust the cut end with hormone powder, if desired.

Stick and firm the cutting in the soil mix with leaves just above the soil; firm the soil.

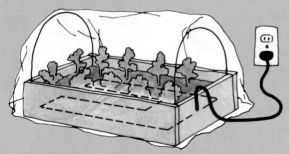

Herbaceous cuttings root readily if given bottom heat and constant high humidity. An electric heating cable (see page 176) in the bottom of a flat, with a plastic cover over the flat, works well.

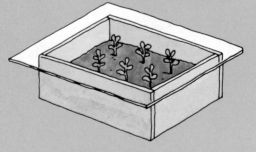

For propagating just a few cuttings, use a pot in a plastic bag or a cutting box with a glass cover to provide the high humidity beneficial to root development. Be sure to open the bag or remove the cover for a few hours every day to allow fresh air to circulate.

Many flowering and foliage plants, such as columneas and begonias, root so easily that you can place the cuttings directly in the final containers. Given reasonable humidity, a porous soil mix, and ample water at the start, the cuttings will root in weeks and produce mature container plants in one season.

Bottom heat   Nearly all cuttings benefit from the addition of bottom heat. They will root particularly quickly if you keep the top of the cutting cool (55° to 65° F) and the bottom warm (70° to 75° F). Experiment with different locations to find the one that works best for cuttings. Many gardeners have had success placing flats on top of the refrigerator or on a gas dryer in the laundry room (the pilot light provides bottom heat).

Inexpensive soil-heating cables are available in various sizes at many garden supply centers. Personnel there can often help you choose the most suitable unit for your needs. If you intend to root cuttings regularly, consider constructing a bottom-heated bench (see page 176). If you install a heating source, adjustable ventilation, and automatic misting, you'll be able to leave cuttings unattended for a few days.

Problems   Rot is the most common problem in rooting cuttings. Try to maintain a healthy environment by renewing the rooting medium in a rooting bench with fresh materials every six months if it's in continual use and by removing any fallen leaves and rotted stems promptly. If the mix is constantly wet, try using pure perlite. If it dries out too quickly, add fine peat moss in the proportion of $1/10$ to $1/5$ of the total mix.

Timing also affects the rooting of cuttings. Many species simply won't root in winter. As you will note from the care guides in "A Gallery of Houseplants" (pages 199 to 307), some cuttings root only when taken from new shoots (softwood cuttings). If a cutting fails to root, or if the new plant dies, try again a few weeks later.

Transplanting Cuttings

Rooting takes from one to six weeks or more, depending on the plant. You can tell that roots have begun to grow when the foliage perks up and the plant puts out new growth. You can test by tugging gently on the cutting; if it doesn't pull out of the soil readily, you will know it has rooted.

Remove the plastic or glass cover once the cutting has rooted, at first for an hour or two daily and then for several hours. Then discard the cover and move the plant to a permanent container.

The best way to determine when the plant is ready to be transplanted is by gently lifting it out of the rooting medium and observing the root length. The roots should not be more than an inch long when you transplant; otherwise, they may tear off.

Move new plants out of the sterile rooting medium and into the permanent growing medium as soon as possible, since rooting media hold no nutrients to feed the plants. Be sure the container is the right size and not too large for the young plant (see page 98).

Indoor Herb Gardens

An indoor herb garden is both practical and decorative. Even an apartment dweller with no outdoor garden space can produce an herb crop. And any cook appreciates the convenience of fresh herbs at the fingertips.

With the right growing conditions, a surprising number of plants can be successfully grown indoors. Most cooking herbs grow well in small- to medium-sized pots. Clay or terra-cotta pots contrast well with herb foliage, but herbs will also grow in glazed pots, a window box, or even, with proper care, a hanging basket.

All herbs require a growing medium with good drainage; herbs with moisture-soaked roots won't flourish. Keep herbs out of the way of gas fumes and areas with abrupt temperature changes, such as by a stove. Finally, be sure the plants receive plenty of light. You may want to rotate the container occasionally to ensure even light and growth. This is especially important if you are growing herbs in a hanging basket.

Your choice of plants should follow your culinary preferences. Perennial favorites include basil, parsley, sage, and mint, but you might also try chives, chervil, dill, French tarragon, lemon thyme, and marjoram. Although rosemary and bay are larger plants that do best in individual pots, they will grow indoors with the proper care.

This kitchen window is the ideal growing spot for an indoor herb garden, providing plenty of light and easy access for the cook. A wire basket lined with moss holds garden sage, thyme, oregano, and chives; the clay pots house silver thyme.

Bromeliads can be propagated by dividing offsets from the parent plant. Slice through the soil with a sharp knife, making sure you take some of the basal growth and roots. Pot the division in its own container, and provide it with the same growing conditions as the parent plant. Water the cup formed by the bromeliad leaves and, very infrequently, moisten the roots.

Divisions

Some houseplants are easiest to propagate by dividing the entire plant, including the root system and foliage, into two or more smaller plants. Plants that form new plant clusters at their base or whose stems emerge from the base of the plant are best propagated by division. Examples are the cast-iron plant (*Aspidistra elatior*), papyrus (*Cyperus papyrus*), ferns, and many begonias, prayer-plants (*Maranta leuconeura*), and cluster-forming succulents, such as certain sedums and jade plants (*Crassula argentea*). Foliage plants should be divided in early spring, when the plants are just beginning to produce new growth. Flowering plants are best divided during their dormant period.

Division is not a delicate technique. Remove the plant from its container, and slice down through the rootball with a sharp knife or sharpened spade. You may need to saw some plants apart, but others you can gently break apart by hand. (Don't worry about damaging the plants or treating the cuts, and once you've taken the divisions, just replant or repot the parent.)

Each division should include some of the main root and stem system. Plant the divisions immediately in permanent containers with potting soil, and water thoroughly. Keep them in bright light but out of direct sun, watering frequently until they root. It may also be helpful to place the divisions inside a clear plastic bag to reduce moisture loss. When they appear upright and healthy, place them in a permanent location and care for them as you would mature plants.

Offsets

Small, new plants that form at the base of the old plant and remain attached to it are known as offsets. They can be broken off and planted to form new plants, just like divisions.

Many succulents and bromeliads produce offsets from dormant buds on the main stem, near ground level. The offsets sometimes completely surround the parent plant and are ready to take over when it dies. Remove them by cutting them off close to the main stem, then place them in an appropriate rooting environment. For most succulents and bromeliads, this means setting the offsets in a slightly smaller pot amid pieces of fir bark.

Detach offsets only when they are mature enough to survive on their own—usually when they have taken on the look of the mature plant. If you provide the temperature and light conditions that the plant prefers, new roots will form quickly. The screwpine (*Pandanus veitchii*), a foolproof houseplant, can be propagated by this method.

Plantlets

Several common houseplants reproduce by sending out miniature new plants on runners or shoots. These include the spiderplant (*Chlorophytum*), flame-violet (*Episcia*), and many varieties of Boston fern (*Nephrolepis exaltata*). When they begin to form aerial roots, the plantlets can be separated from the parent and repotted to form new plants.

Root the plantlets by filling a small pot with moist rooting medium and placing it alongside the parent plant. Without severing the runner, lay the plantlet on top of the soil in the new pot and hold it in place with a piece of wire. Keep the soil moist. New growth will signal that the plantlet has rooted and can be severed from the parent.

Alternatively, clip off the runner and insert the base of the plantlet into a moist propagating medium. Cover with glass or plastic film until the new roots form.

Unlike most plants that propagate by runners, the piggyback plant (*Tolmiea menziesii*) forms plantlets on top of its mature leaves. However, you can root them in the same manner as you would plantlets on runners.

It is not always necessary to remove a plantlet to get it to root. Plantlets formed on the runners or shoots of the spiderplant (Chlorophytum comosum, bottom) or the piggyback plant (Tolmiea menziesii, top) can be pinned into the moist soil in a pot. Leave them growing alongside the parent plant until they root.

Bulbs

Many bulbous plants, such as amaryllis (*Hippeastrum*), can be propagated by dividing their tuberous roots, tubers, or rhizomes or by separating new corms and bulbs from the original plant. In some cases, such as tulips (*Tulipa*) , the old bulb disappears, leaving behind one or more offspring. After flowering, the foliage of most bulbous plants continues to grow, creating food reserves in the bulbs and bulblets for the next season. Then the foliage begins to yellow as the plants enter their dormant period. When this happens, withhold water until all the foliage has died back. Then take the plant out of the container and divide the bulb or separate any small bulblets that have formed beside the parent bulb. It may take several years for a plant started from a bulblet to become large enough to produce a flower.

Bulbs of the scaly type can be increased by peeling off one or two layers of scales and laying them on rooting medium. Easter lilies (*Lilium longiflorum*) reproduce this way. Dust the scales with fungicide and a rooting powder, and seal them in a plastic bag filled with damp vermiculite. Keep the bag at room temperature until bulblets form—about two months—and then cool them in the refrigerator for another two months before planting.

Corms, Rhizomes, and Tubers

Houseplants grown from corms, rhizomes, and tubers have a thickened stem or root, modified for food storage, from which leaves and flowers grow. Timing is important in propagating these plants. If they have a dormant period, propagate when the plant is about to send up green shoots.

Plants that grow from tubers, such as gloxinia, tuberous begonia, and caladium, can be propagated by division. After the eyes have begun to swell in spring, cut the tuber into pieces, making sure each section has a bud. Dust each piece with fungicide and plant just beneath the surface of a moist rooting medium.

To layer a plant, bend a low branch so that it is in contact with the growing medium. Notch the branch at the point of contact and bury it in the growing medium.

Immobilize the rooting branch with a peg or rock. Be prepared to wait several months for it to root.

Tuber division works for large specimens of florist's gloxinia (*Sinningia speciosa*), tuberous begonia (*Begonia × tuberhybrida*), and caladium. After the eyes, or buds, on the tubers have begun to swell in the spring and are clearly visible, simply cut the tuber into pieces, being sure that every section has a bud. Dust the cut surfaces with a fungicide, and plant each piece just below the surface in a moist rooting medium. Provide good air movement to reduce the chance of fungus or bacterial rot; if you see rot beginning, cut off the infected surface and start over.

The lovely glory lily (*Gloriosa rothschildiana*) produces cigar-shaped tubers that can be broken into pieces and replanted. Ferns that form rhizomes can also be cut into pieces and replanted. Theoretically, plants with corms, such as freesias, can be divided, but getting a bud in each division is tricky. It is easiest to replant the many small new corms, called cormels, that form around the parent corm. Separate them and replant them about 2 inches deep.

Layering

Propagation by layering is similar to rooting cuttings, except that the part of the plant (usually a branch) to be rooted remains attached to the parent plant. The great advantage of layering is that the parent plant supplies the cutting with water and nutrients while the roots are forming. Daily maintenance is therefore unnecessary.

To be suitable for layering, a plant needs to have a branch low enough so that you can bend it into contact with the growing medium. If there is such a branch, bend it, notch the point of contact with the mix, then bury that portion of the branch. Securely immobilize it with a peg or a rock. A rock has the additional advantage of keeping the soil beneath it moist.

Layering is best done in the spring. Root formation is likely to take several months. If it does take that long, it may be convenient to leave the layer attached for a full year; spring is also the best time for detaching the rooted branch and growing it on as a separate plant. When you are ready to detach the branch, lift the branch from the potting mix at the point where roots have formed, then cut it from the parent plant and treat it as a rooted cutting.

A number of low-growing species will self-layer. Detach the rooted branch and transplant them in the same way.

To air-layer a plant, cut into, but not through, the stem with a sharp knife and insert a wedge to keep the cut open. Cover the cut with damp moss and wrap it in plastic. When roots appear, cut off the stem and pot the rooted plant.

Air-layering works well for some genera, such as dumbcane (*Dieffenbachia*), flame-violet (*Episcia*), pothos (*Epipremnum aureum*), strawberry-geranium (*Saxifraga stolonifera*), and *Combeya,* that lack branches conveniently close to the ground. It is especially useful for salvaging leggy plants or mature specimens that have lost their lower leaves.

With a sharp knife, make a shallow cut no more than half of the way through a stem at about a foot from the growing tip. Insert a thin piece of wood (such as a matchstick) to hold the cut open. Wrap the stem with a handful of coarse, wet sphagnum moss or a damp sponge, cover with plastic wrap, and secure with tape or rubber bands above and below the cut. When new roots form in the moss, cut off the stem below the rooted section and pot the new plant. If months go by before rooting occurs, you may have to wet the moss by poking a small hole in the wrap and squirting water inside. If the stem fails to produce roots, try again: Open up the wrapping, nick the stem, dust the cut with rooting hormone, and retie.

Fern Spores

Unlike most other plants, ferns produce tiny spores, not seeds, and are challenging to propagate. The spores are tiny, very slow to germinate and grow, and need to be protected continually from dry air. If you want to try propagating ferns, you will need plenty of patience. Look on the undersides of the fronds for ripe spore cases and brush the spores into an envelope. Allow them to dry for a few weeks, before trying to germinate them. The brick-and-box method is perhaps the most effective way of germinating the spores. Place a brick in a transparent plastic box and add 2 inches of water. Cover the top of the brick with ¼ inch of milled peat moss. Wet the brick and moss, and dust the fern spores on top of the moss; cover the box with glass or plastic to retain the moisture. Check the water level every few days while the spores are germinating, adding water when necessary to maintain the water level at 2 inches.

Place the box in a dimly lit spot with moderate temperatures (65° to 75° F), and leave it there for several months. Eventually, the germinated spores will produce a mossy mat on top of the covered brick. This is the sexual stage of the ferns. When the mat looks strong, break off 1-inch pieces and transplant them into a flat filled with an all-purpose potting mix. Keep the flat moist and covered for several more months or until small ferns appear. When the ferns are 2 to 3 inches high, transplant them to individual pots.

Growing ferns from spores takes time and patience, but the results are worthwhile. The young staghorn fern above was recently transplanted into a nest of sphagnum moss.

Flowering Houseplants

If you want to add color and pattern to your indoor garden, there are several foliage plants that fill the bill, but a flowering houseplant will bring a burst of joy to the most cheerless room. Like most good things in life, however, joy doesn't come without some effort. Yet, your efforts will be rewarded when you watch the delicate flowers unfold, adding charm and a touch of spring to your home.

Though definitions of a flowering houseplant vary from person to person, for the purposes of this book, a flowering houseplant is one that can be grown and trained into a size, shape, and form compatible with indoor spaces and the living habits of the occupants of those spaces. Flowering houseplants are further categorized by how they adapt or acclimate to indoor light intensities and temperatures. Some plants, with care, will do fine with indoor light; others will bloom only with special help from you. A few flowering houseplants are outdoor species that have been forced into bloom for indoor use.

The blends of pink and red flowers of this dwarf anthurium, tillandsia, and planter filled with Cape primrose (Streptocarpus), guzmania, and ivy (Hedera) form a pleasing display and draw attention to the garden outside.

Reiger begonias (Begonia ×
hiemalis) *will bloom the year
around in a suitable environment.
Be sure they have at least four
hours of curtain-filtered sunlight
from a south, east, or west window.*

Encouraging Plants to Bloom

Not all flowering plants bloom continuously; a few, in fact, will
not bloom at all indoors unless they receive special care. Flowering
indoor plants are often divided into four categories, according to
the way in which they flower. Two other important considerations that affect how a plant will bloom are the plant's exposure
to light, known as photoperiodism, and the plant's exposure to
temperature, known as vernalization.

Plants That Bloom Continuously

Many African violets (*Saintpaulia*), begonias, and other plants
grown indoors flower continuously, often for many years. These
plants need optimum care in a stable setting. They are truly the
best of the indoor flowering plants.

Plants That Bloom Seasonally or Intermittently

A wider variety of plants, such as peace-lilies (*Spathiphyllum*),
kalanchoe (*Kalanchoe blossfeldiana*), Christmas cactus
(*Schlumbergera*), or geraniums (*Pelargonium*), flower seasonally or
intermittently throughout the year. They are induced to flower
through proper management of temperature, light intensity, light
quality, day length (or night length), and pruning practices. Their
usefulness in indoor gardens rests on their attractiveness as foliage
plants as well as flowering plants. These plants are often moved
about the home, depending on whether they are in flower. However, they shouldn't be neglected once they're out of the limelight;
to encourage bloom, they need proper care.

Plants That Need a Rest Period

Some of the indoor flowering plants that bloom seasonally or intermittently require a rest period (generally after they flower). Florist's gloxinia (*Sinningia speciosa*) is the most widely known plant
in this category. It goes completely dormant, the foliage dies back,
and the tuber is usually removed and stored in moist sphagnum
moss until the next year. Other plants, such as most bromeliads
and clerodendrons, become semidormant; they keep their foliage
but do not produce any new growth during the rest period.

Bulbous plants forced indoors fall into this group of plants. Although some bulbous plants are adapted for years of indoor culture, most wither and go dormant after flowering. Many indoor
gardeners use bulbs as room decorations during their blooming
period and then remove them to an out-of-the-way growing station
when they start to die back. A hidden spot in a well-lit window or
greenhouse will do—but do not neglect them.

Outdoor Plants That Bloom Indoors

Many flowering houseplants are houseplants only while they are in flower. The most popular flowering houseplants are in this category: Tulips, narcissus, chrysanthemums (*Chrysanthemum* × *morifolium*), and Easter lilies (*Lilium longiflorum*) all create a decorative accent indoors while they are in bloom. Afterward, they are either discarded, as is the case with most poinsettias (*Euphorbia pulcherrima*), chrysanthemums, and cinerarias (*Senecio* × *hybridus*), or moved to a greenhouse, a window box, or an outdoor flower bed.

Photoperiodism

Certain plants flower only after exposure to a particular day length. For example, a poinsettia (*Euphorbia pulcherrima*) grown indoors will not ordinarily bloom. The controlling factor is the *photoperiod*, the length of time during each day that the plant is exposed to light. A poinsettia is called a short-day plant because it needs a series of short days and long nights to begin budding. The critical factor is actually the length of the night. Indoors, plants often receive light in the evening from electric bulbs, so a poinsettia will never bloom unless you give it special treatment to mimic the long, dark nights of autumn outdoors.

To initiate flower buds that will mature by Christmastime, in late September or early October place the plant in a closet or other dark area for 12 to 16 hours a night for at least two weeks (preferably six weeks). Be careful not to open the closet door during treatment, and seal any cracks under the door. The dark periods must be total and continuous; even a small amount of light may cause sparse budding or deformed flowers.

The florist's chrysanthemum (*Chrysanthemum* × *morifolium*) industry is organized around the fact that chrysanthemums are also short-day plants. Chrysanthemums flower naturally only in the fall or early winter, but plant producers bring them into bloom throughout the year by using black-cloth shading techniques to simulate long nights.

Few flowers are as sensitive to photoperiodism as poinsettias and chrysanthemums, though researchers have found that photoperiod adjustment encourages flower development in many species, such as begonias and many gesneriads, that do not absolutely require specific photoperiods. Long-day plants, such as tuberous begonias (*Begonia* × *tuberhybrida*), pocketbook-flower (*Calceolaria crenatifolia*), and cineraria (*Senecio* × *hybridus*), can be brought into bloom during fall and winter by providing light at night. Even short bursts of light in the middle of the night may be enough to stimulate flower formation.

Top: Lilies (Lilium) *make colorful flowering houseplants, but once they have bloomed they need a rest period before blooming again. Bottom: Azalea* (Rhododendron) *is best used as an indoor plant only while it is in bloom.*

Poinsettias (Euphorbia pulcherrima), *cheerful winter houseplants traditionally associated with the Christmas season, are short-day plants; they require 10 hours of light or less during the early fall to produce flower buds.*

Vernalization

Some plants, such as the hardy bulbs, need a cold winter to thrive. These plants can be brought into bloom by placing them in cool storage (45° F or below) for several weeks. This process of creating an artificial winter is known as vernalization. Plants that normally lose their leaves in winter, such as hydrangeas and many bulbous plants, can be kept in cool storage for several months. The cooler the area and the longer the storage, the more quickly flowers will develop when the plants are returned to normal growing temperatures. Refrigerators can make appropriate cool storage areas if basements and garages are not cool enough, provided the temperature stays above 35° F to prevent frost damage. Plants in cool storage need to be moist but not wet; some plants need artificial light to prevent excessive leaf drop. Even those species that do not require cooling to produce flowers may be invigorated by vernalization. Often it results in healthier growth and increased flower production.

Prolonging the Flowering Period

Your primary object in caring for your plants while they are flowering is to prolong the flowering period for as long as possible. With proper care, you can double the usual life of blooming plants in a decorative indoor setting. Most plants that have been properly grown before they start to flower will have enough nutrients to carry them through the blooming period. Additional fertilization, especially without thorough watering, may actually damage the roots of plants in bloom.

Never allow the rootball to dry out. The soilless growing media many commercial growers use is especially difficult to wet once it dries out. Excessive drying and root damage causes many plants to suddenly drop their leaves or buds.

Finally, keep blooming plants out of direct sunlight or drafts of hot, dry air. Flower petals cannot replenish lost moisture as easily as can leaves. Petals may burn, fade, or wilt under hot, dry conditions.

Dealing With Reluctant Bloomers

At some point you may find you have a plant that will not bloom. There are many possible causes for this, but the usual one is insufficient light.

Try giving the plant progressively more light. If it is not close to a light source, move it closer to the window or to lights. A drastic change in light intensity may burn the foliage, so make the change gradually. Don't be alarmed if the move bleaches the foliage a little. Unless the leaves turn yellow, the plant will not be damaged. Since placing a plant closer to a light source will cause it to dry out faster, keep a careful eye on it so that you can adjust to its new watering needs.

If a plant will not bloom under good light, it may need a change in day length. If the plant lights are usually on for 12 hours, try a day length of 10 hours for a few weeks, then go back to 12 hours. If this does not work, try a few weeks at 14 hours of light a day (watch carefully to be sure this change does not create too much water stress).

Transplanting disrupts the growing routine and gives the roots more room, which inhibits flowering. Roots need time to grow into new growing medium. Instead of transplanting just before flowering, replace the top third of the soil with new mix until the blooming period is over.

Many plants are simply too young to produce flowers. Often, woody plants must grow for a year or two before they will flower, and bulbous plants started from small bulbs will not flower for two or three years. Most of the newer cultivars of African violets begin flowering when they are quite young, but this is not often the case with other plants.

Pruning and shaping enhance flower production, but only if there is enough foliage left for buds to form. Don't remove flower buds when pruning—pinch back the stems after the plant has finished blooming.

It is important to remove the outer leaves of African violets (*Saintpaulia*) to keep the plants flowering well. Unless they are removed, the inside rows will have no chance to produce flowers. Each row of leaves produces flowers only once. The third row of leaves, counting from the center outward, carries the mature blossoms. The new flower buds are produced in the center of the plant at the first row of leaves. Once a plant has more than five rows of leaves, the blossom number and size will gradually decline until the plant eventually stops flowering altogether.

The acidity of the potting mix is another factor that affects blooming. If the pH level is below 5 or over 8, the plant is unlikely to bloom. Furthermore, plants that are dormant can't be rushed into flowering.

Perhaps your reluctant bloomer just needs a rest. You can try withholding fertilizer and slightly reducing water for a month, then resume regular care. Sometimes flowering plants get into a rut and need a little contrived change of seasons or conditions to force them to develop flower buds. Experiment. You have nothing to lose, and you will learn from your experimentation. If everything you try fails, perhaps it's time to make room for a new plant in your collection.

Once a plant has bloomed, it has different care needs than while it is flowering. Remove spent blossoms and yellowing foliage, and allow it to rest for a time.

Caring for Plants After Flowering

Unless you plan to discard the plant toward the end of its flowering period, you must change the care routine when it stops flowering. If you have distinct display and growing stations, this is most easily accomplished by returning the plant to its growing station. You can then place another flowering plant or a foliage plant in the display station.

Many plants require a rest immediately after flowering. Begin withholding water gradually over a period of a few weeks, and do not fertilize during this time. Withhold water by watering less frequently, not by using less water at each irrigation. There's a temptation to cut back the foliage of bulbous plants once the flowers have faded. However, many bulbous plants need their foliage to produce food reserves for the next flowering cycle. Yellowing foliage naturally signals the onset of their dormancy; remove the foliage then.

Placing African violets (Saintpaulia) near a mirror doubles the amount of color and increases the light they receive. With plenty of bright, indirect light, evenly moist soil, warm temperatures, and high air humidity, African violets will bloom constantly.

To decorate a room successfully with a display of flowering plants, it is important to discard or replace a plant once it is past its prime. Commercial interior landscapers call flowering plants "changeout plants"; they realize that they must keep rotating them to maintain a constantly decorative display.

It is easy to tell when a plant is past its flowering prime: The flowers are fading and no new buds are forming. It will not come back into bloom unless it is pruned and possibly repotted. Move the plant to a growing station and put a new specimen that has just begun to flower into the display station.

Keeping Popular Houseplants Blooming

Choices in flowering houseplants can be as varied as choices in decorating style. Below we list some popular flowering plants for use indoors and tips on keeping these plants in bloom.

African violet (*Saintpaulia*)   Although it will bloom with 10 hours or less of light per day, long days will promote blooming. Leggy stems and the absence of blooms indicate insufficient light. Older varieties may bloom seasonally, with long rest periods between flowerings, but newer hybrids will often bloom nonstop the year around. Perfect for indoor culture because it thrives in night temperatures between 65° and 70° F. Blooms best when roots are crowded.

Begonia (*Begonia* species)   B. × *hiemalis* and other winter-flowering types need a period of lower temperatures and long nights to set buds. Tuberous and fibrous begonias grow best during long days. However, tuberous types require long nights before they go dormant to set flower buds for the next year.

A bougainvillea trained as a topiary wreath and a low, spreading grape-ivy (Cissus) add delicate color, texture, and patterns to this Victorian-inspired dressing table.

Geraniums (Pelargonium) *and orchids team up to add color to a hallway table. These two popular flowering plants fit well into many decorating styles.*

Blue daisy (*Felicia amelloides*)   Pinch flowers off a young plant until it reaches the desired size. Warm temperatures and decreased watering increase blooming, while warm temperatures and bottom heat encourage rapid growth.

Bougainvillea (*Bougainvillea glabra*)   Blooms best in strong light and high temperatures (70° to 80° F). Flowers form when day and night are of equal length. Plants do not like to be moved.

Bromeliad (numerous genera)   Grows well in long days, but many, including the pineapple (*Ananas*), need long nights to set blooms. Keep warm and give plenty of light (60° F minimum at night, 75° F during the day).

Cacti (numerous genera)   Need cool nights (45° to 50° F) to set flower buds. Watering after a long dry period also induces blooming. Cacti need strong light to flower well.

Calceolaria or pocketbook-flower (*Calceolaria crenatiflora*)   Likes cool night temperatures (40° to 45° F) and day temperatures 15° higher. Growing plants to a large size is difficult. Flower buds set in short nights.

Carnation (*Dianthus caryophyllus*)   Blooms best after a period of short nights. Needs strong light to produce its fragrant flowers.

Chrysanthemum (*Chrysanthemum* × *morifolium*)   Needs long, cool nights (45° to 50° F) to set buds, then warm temperatures to help buds develop into blooms; 13- to 14-hour nights also help bud set, providing the temperature remains below 68° F. The combination of warm temperatures and long nights prevents bud formation.

Cineraria (*Senecio* × *hybridus*)   Difficult to force into bloom indoors. Needs cool nights, warm days, and good air circulation.

Citrus (*Citrus* species)   Blooms best in strong light. Cool nights encourage compact growth.

Clerodendrum or glorybower (*Clerodendrum thomsoniae*)   Flowers only on new growth. After flowering, prune and then fertilize to promote new growth for next season.

Columnea (*Columnea* species)   Grows well in long days. Needs cool nights (50° to 60° F) to promote flowering.

Cyclamen (*Cyclamen persicum*)   Flowers like cool temperatures; 40° to 50° F at night is best. Goes dormant in summer and needs this resting period to bloom well.

Cymbidium (*Cymbidium*)   Needs as much light as possible, but watch for burning. Dark green leaves indicate insufficient light. Will not bloom if nights are too warm; night temperatures of 50° to 55° F are best.

Episcia (*Episcia* species)   Similar to African violet, but requires higher light intensities and more humidity to bloom well. Likes long days, crowded roots, and plenty of fertilizer. Keep air around plant humid.

Flamingo-flower (*Anthurium*)   Needs high humidity and high temperatures (80° to 90° F). Long days encourage blooming. Low humidity or low temperatures for even a few days may harm developing flowers.

Florist's azalea (*Rhododendron indica* varieties)   Likes cool temperatures for growth, warmer temperatures for setting flower buds, and then cooler temperatures to mature the buds. Well-pruned, bushy plants will produce more blooms. Move outdoor plants indoors in October to bloom by December.

Fuchsia (*Fuchsia* × *hybrida*)   Needs cool temperatures (50° to 55° F at night, 68° to 72° F during the day). Must have high humidity to perform well. Long days encourage bud set.

Gardenia (*Gardenia jasminoides*)   Needs long, cool nights (below 65° F) to set flower buds. Buds often drop if humidity is low, soil is too wet, or light is too low.

Geranium (*Pelargonium*)   Zonal geraniums (*P.* × *hortorum*), with round leaf edge, bloom in strong light and

Blue is generally a cool color, although blue-lavender is warmer than aqua. Delicate and restrained, Persian violets (Exacum affine) suit this formal setting.

warmth. Martha Washington geraniums (*P. × domesticum*), with jagged leaf edge, need 12- to 13-hour nights to set flower buds and then long days to develop buds into flowers.

Hibiscus (*Hibiscus rosa-sinensis*) Blooms best in long days and high humidity. Does not like to be moved. Prune heavily to keep bushy.

Hoya (*Hoya* species) Fragrant blooms form on stubby twigs. Blooms best in short nights. During winter, needs rest period of less light, water, and fertilizer.

Hydrangea (*Hydrangea macrophylla*) Needs a long, cool storage period during dormancy. Strong light and warmth promote flower development. Fertilize heavily to grow plants to good size. Splitting flower stems indicate too short a cooling period.

Impatiens or busy-lizzy (*Impatiens*) Likes intermediate day length. New Guinea types develop best leaf color with longer days than other impatiens, but bloom best in intermediate days (12 hours light, 12 hours dark).

Kalanchoe (*Kalanchoe blossfeldiana*)   Requires 6 weeks of long nights for flower bud formation. Blooms 3 months after long nights begin.

Lantana (*Lantana*)   Likes high heat (75° to 85° F) and strong light. Will bloom indoors in winter if given short nights after being kept cool and shaded the previous summer.

Marigold (*Tagetes* species)   Grows best in 16-hour days; blooms best in 12- to 15-hour days. Give as much light as possible indoors.

Nasturtium (*Tropaeolum majus*)   Blooms best in long days. Needs cool nights (40° to 55° F) and day temperatures that stay below 70° F.

Orchids (various genera)   Most epiphytic (not grown in soil) orchids grow best in bright light. Need short days and cool nights (65° F or below) to set flower buds. Usually bloom in 4 months if growing conditions are right.

Persian violet (*Exacum affine*)   Needs short nights to bloom well. Growing plants to attain good size indoors is difficult. Give strong light and fertilize heavily.

Petunia (*Petunia* × *hybrida*)   Needs strong light; blooms best with short nights. Needs cool nights (55° to 65° F) to promote flowering indoors in winter.

Poinsettia (*Euphorbia pulcherrima*)   Requires long nights for 6 weeks to form flower buds. Plants given long nights in late September through October will bloom by Christmastime. Bushy plants produce more blooms. Strong light and warmth (75° to 80° F) encourage larger plants and blooms.

Rose (*Rosa*)   Grows best with long days and warm temperatures (60° to 65° F at night, 75° to 80° F during the day). Miniature roses do very well indoors. Increased light improves flower color. Miniatures can be kept in bloom for 8 to 9 months, then they require a rest period of 1 to 2 months. Night temperatures during the rest period should be approximately 40° F, and plants should be shaded.

Snapdragon (*Antirrhinum majus*)   Blooms best with short nights and cool temperatures. Dwarf varieties do well indoors any time of year. Seeds will germinate best if given a cooling treatment before sowing.

Peace-lily (*Spathiphyllum*)   Mature healthy plants bloom best. Likes crowded roots and low-nitrogen soil. Plants kept too wet may grow well but fail to bloom.

Tomato (*Lycopersicon lycopersicum*)   Needs to dry out before flowers will form. Wet plants grow large but will not produce fruit. Long days promote flower formation. Likes bottom heat when grown indoors out of season. Plants given excessive nitrogen may fail to bloom.

Zebra-plant (*Aphelandra squarrosa*)   Blooms best at high temperatures (75° to 80° F) and looks best when cut back to maintain bushiness. Long nights promote flower bud formation.

Zinnia (*Zinnia elegans*)   Needs good air circulation and strong light to grow well indoors. Blooms best during long days. Dwarf varieties are easier to grow indoors.

Forcing Blooms Indoors

Day length, light intensity, and temperature all change naturally in a seasonal cycle, bringing different plants into flower as they change. Gardeners can imitate these changes to force flower development. Forcing is usually defined as an application of extra warmth to induce early flowering, but the full range of techniques

Yellow flowers evoke bright spring sunshine in any season. Here, shrimp-plant (Justicia brandegeana) and miniature primroses sing a harmonious duet.

is far greater. Some plants are photoperiodic, which means that they will bloom only after they have been exposed to the correct ratio of light and dark periods during a day. Other species may require a cool period that imitates winter. Some may not develop flowers, even if the day length is correct, unless the temperature is also correct.

Perhaps the most popular plants to force are bulbs. By duplicating—but shortening—the stages bulbs go through outdoors, you can have tulips, crocuses, daffodils, and hyacinths blooming indoors in the middle of winter. Other plants that can be easily forced include Dutch iris (*Iris xiphium* hybrids), grape hyacinth (*Muscari*), squill (*Scilla peruviana*), and ornithogalum. Several hardy perennials not normally grown as houseplants—hosta, astilbe, bleeding-heart (*Dicentra*), and lily-of-the-valley—can also be forced, along with annual flowers and the branches of flowering shrubs.

The Fragrant Garden

Flowers can add more than just color to a room. Some beautiful bloomers also add a pleasant perfume to the air.

Light is a key ingredient in unleashing the aroma of a bloom. The more light a plant receives, the stronger the perfume. As with all other plants, the proper horticultural care will also help bring out the best in a fragrant houseplant. Check "A Gallery of Houseplants," pages 199 to 307, for further information on the cultural needs of the plants listed here.

Jasmine is the traditional favorite for sweet-smelling flowers. And since the perfume of most jasmines is most powerful at night, many working people can appreciate their fragrance during the hours they are at home. Almost all species of jasmine are fragrant, though not all perform equally well indoors. Two reliable choices are the poet's jasmine (*Jasminum grandiflorum*) and the Confederate-jasmine (*Trachelospermum jasminoides*).

That southern garden favorite the gardenia (*Gardenia jasminoides*) scents the air with a heady aroma reminiscent of a woman's perfume. The African gardenia (*Mitriostigma axillare*) is actually easier to grow indoors than the common gardenia. Keep the air around it humid.

The tender narcissus 'Paper White' is another popular, and heady, aromatic plant. Most often forced for indoor bloom, paper-whites add the look and smell of spring to a winter-encircled home. Be aware, though, that the aroma can be overwhelming in a small room.

Hyacinths (*Hyacinthus orientalis*), an old-fashioned favorite, bloom in late winter, filling a room with the aroma and promise of spring. The fragrant blossoms are red, pink, blue, yellow, or white. Purchase hyacinths in bloom from florists, or force your own from bulbs planted in October.

Citrus blossoms are known for their fresh, clean fragrance. A good choice for indoor gardens is X *Citrofortunella mitis*, a cross between a mandarin orange and a kumquat. With proper care, you can even get fruit for your efforts. It will probably be too bitter to eat fresh from the plant, but you can use it for cooking. Another plant with a similar fragrance is the orange-jasmine (*Murraya paniculata*), with its small, white flowers that combine the aromas of jasmine and orange blossoms.

These bulbs have been cooled and are ready for forcing. A cold frame is not essential; bulbs can be forced in a variety of containers and mediums.

Forcing Hardy Bulbs

Hardy bulbs are perhaps the most rewarding plants to force to bloom. Begin by buying the largest bulbs you can find. Select only those varieties clearly marked "good for forcing" (see chart opposite for a list of bulb varieties for forcing). If you are buying by mail order, place your order as early as possible so that the bulbs will arrive in the early fall. If you can't plant the bulbs immediately after their arrival, store them in opened bags or boxes in a cool place (35° to 55° F) or in the refrigerator, but for no more than a few weeks.

Plant bulbs around the beginning of October for flowers at Christmastime, in the middle of October for February flowers, and in November for March and April flowers. Bulbs can be forced in any number of containers, even ones without drainage holes. However, be sure the container is clean, and use a well-drained growing medium. If you are mixing your own, use equal parts soil, builders sand, and peat moss; to each 5-inch pot of the mix, add a teaspoon of bonemeal (see instructions for mixing your own growing medium on pages 84 to 87). You can also use an all-purpose potting mix.

Pot size depends on the type and quantity of bulbs you are forcing: One large daffodil or tulip bulb or three small crocuses will fill a 4- to 5-inch pot. Six tulips, daffodils, or hyacinths require an 8- to 10-inch pot. When planting several tulips in one pot, place the bulbs with the flat sides facing toward the outside of the pot so that the leaves will emerge facing outward.

Fill each pot loosely with soil mix. Place the bulbs in the pot so that their tops are just below the rim. Cover the tops of tulips, hyacinths, and small bulbs, such as crocus, with an inch of soil, but do not cover the necks and tops of daffodils. Avoid compressing the soil or pressing the bulbs into it; the soil should remain loose so that roots can grow through it easily. After the bulbs are in, water the pots two or three times to moisten the soil, then let excess water drain. Label each pot as you plant it with the name of the flower and the planting date.

Most bulbs need a period of cool temperatures after potting and before forcing so that they can form a vigorous root system to support lush foliage and blooms. Without a potful of roots, bulbs will not bloom prolifically. Some bulbs have been precooled by the producer and can be planted and forced immediately. To prepare bulbs that have not been precooled, place them in a cool, frost-free place, such as an unheated garage or basement, or an old refrigerator, where the temperature is between 35° and 50° F. Keep the soil evenly moist while the bulbs are forming roots; check the pots weekly to see if they need water.

Bulb Varieties for Forcing

Type	Color	Flowering Time
Crocuses		
'Flower Record'	Purple	Late winter, spring
'Joan of Arc'	White	Winter and spring
'Large Yellow'	Yellow	Spring
'Peter Pan'	White	Winter and spring
'Pickwick'	Striped blue and white	Winter and spring
'Purpureus grandiflorus'	Purple	Winter and spring
'Remembrance'	Purple	Winter and spring
Daffodils (*Narcissus*)		
'Barrett Browning'	Orange cup, white perianth	Winter and spring
'Carlton'	Yellow	Winter
'Chinese Sacred Lily'	White	Winter and spring
'Dutch Master'	Yellow	Winter and spring
'Fortune'	Yellow and orange	Winter
'Ice Follies'	Cream cup, white perianth	Winter and spring
'Magnet'	Yellow trumpet, white perianth	Spring
'Mt. Hood'	White	Winter and spring
'Paper White'	White	Winter and spring
'Soleil d'Or'	Yellow	Winter and spring
'Unsurpassable'	Yellow	Winter and spring
Grape hyacinth (*Muscari*)		
'Early Giant'	Blue	Winter and spring
Hyacinths (*Hyacinthus orientalis*)		
'Amethyst'	Violet	Spring
'Amsterdam'	Pink	Winter and spring
'Anne Marie'	Pink	Winter
'Bismarck'	Blue	Winter
'Blue Jacket'	Blue	Spring
'Carnegie'	White	Spring
'Delft Blue'	Blue	Winter
'Jan Bos'	Red	Winter
'Lady Derby'	Pink	Winter
'L'Innocence'	White	Winter
'Marconi'	Pink	Spring
'Ostara'	Blue	Winter and spring
'Pink Pearl'	Pink	Winter and spring
Irises		
'Harmony'	Blue	Winter and spring
'Hercules'	Purple	Winter and spring
Iris danfordiae	Yellow	Winter
Tulips (*Tulipa*)		
'Bellona'	Yellow	Winter
'Bing Crosby'	Red	Winter and spring
'Charles'	Red	Winter
'Christmas Marvel'	Pink	Winter
'Golden Eddy'	Red, with yellow or cream	Spring
'Hibernia'	White	Winter and spring
'Karel Doorman'	Red, with yellow or cream	Winter
'Kees Nelis'	Red, with yellow or cream	Winter
'Olaf'	Red	Winter and spring
'Ornament'	Yellow	Spring
'Paul Richter'	Red	Winter
'Peerless Pink'	Pink	Spring
'Preludium'	Pink	Winter
'Prominence'	Red	Late winter
'Stockholm'	Red	Winter
'Thule'	Yellow with red	Winter

At the forcing stage, bring the pots out of the cool environment into warmth and light, which will trigger the formation of leaves and flowers in three to four weeks. The bulbs are ready for forcing when the tips begin to push up through the soil. For a succession of blooms over a long period, begin forcing only a few pots each week and place them in a sunny, cool (55° to 70° F) spot. The cooler the area, the longer the flowers will last. Keep the soil moist and the bulbs away from radiators and gas heaters; flower buds will fail to open if the soil dries out. Bring all bulbs into a warm and sunny location by late February.

After the flowers fade, keep the foliage in good health by continuing to provide moisture and sunlight. As soon as any danger of hard frosts is past, move the bulbs to an out-of-the-way place outdoors where the foliage can continue to mature and produce food for the next year's blooms. Bulbs will not stand forcing for a second year. Some of them, especially tulips, are best discarded after

Opposite: A container of daffodils (Narcissus) *brings sunshine inside. Daffodils are easy to force and, if kept in a cool room, will last a reasonable time.*
Left: Supplemental light spotlights these paper-white narcissus and allows them to bloom in a shady interior spot.

forcing. Daffodils, however, can be transplanted into the garden in spring and will produce a full bloom again in two or three years.

Problems in forcing bulbs are few:

• Tulips almost always show some aphids, either on the leaves when they emerge from the soil or on the flower buds. See page 186 for information on controls.

• Flower buds of forced bulbs will blast (fail to open) if the soil is allowed to dry out after they've begun to grow.

• Sometimes bulbs succumb to basal rot. If the foliage suddenly turns yellow and stops growing, give it a gentle tug. If the foliage is loose, there's a rootless rotted bulb in the soil. Discard both the bulb and the soil to prevent the disease from spreading.

Forcing Tender Narcissus

Hardy daffodils require a lengthy period of cold temperatures to bloom, but there are also tender narcissus, such as 'Paper White' and 'Grand Soleil d'Or', which are precooled and can be forced relatively quickly even in a somewhat sunny location. Successive plantings made about two weeks apart from mid-October to December will provide indoor blooms from Thanksgiving to St. Patrick's Day. Plant the bulbs among moist pebbles, in a light potting mix, or in a homemade mix with equal parts soil, sand, and peat moss. Place the bases of the bulbs at a depth of 1 to 1½ inches in the growing medium, then water thoroughly. Drain and set away in a cool (50° to 65° F), dark place until the roots form. After the bulbs have grown a good root system—which usually takes two

Hyacinths are easy bulbs to force. The strong purple makes a handsome accent and the aroma is heady. Growing several bulbs in matching containers creates a particularly impressive arrangement.

to four weeks—bring them into a warm room with bright sunlight. They will quickly send up clusters of fragrant white or gold blossoms.

Discard paper-white narcissus after forcing if you live in an area where winter temperatures dip below 20° F. In warmer regions, plant them in the garden outdoors. But don't try to force them again. Buy new stock each year for forcing.

Forcing Hyacinths and Crocuses in Water

Hyacinths and crocuses are often grown in specially designed containers that hold the bulb above a well of water into which the roots grow. These containers are often made of glass, and growing these bulbs in glass containers is especially fun for children, who can watch the roots and flowers develop.

Fill the container so that the base of the bulb is just above the water, and add water as needed to maintain this level. The bulb shouldn't touch the water or it will rot. Change the water every three or four weeks. A small piece of charcoal in the water will deter harmful bacteria. Place the container in a dark, cool area until roots have formed (about 14 weeks), then move it into the light.

Branches of apple, cherry, forsythia, pussy willow, and flowering quince can be forced into early bloom. Arrange them in a vase or plant them in a large container to simulate a blossoming tree.

Forcing Flowering Branches

The delicate beauty of branches of flowering apple, cherry, forsythia, pussy willow, and flowering quince can bring springtime indoors during those cold days of late winter. You can force the blooms on a branch of any of these outdoor plants to use indoors as a flowering accent.

Cut 2- to 3-foot branches during February or March when the flower buds have begun to swell. (If you cut too soon, the flowers will not open.) Smash the cut ends of the branches with a hammer to help the branches absorb water, and then place them in a large container of water in a moderately cool (60° to 70° F), bright room (except pussy willows that have already opened, which should not be placed in water). Change the water every few days. In about two weeks, blossoms will appear.

The blossoms will open quickly in a warm room but will last longer in a cool room. Heat and light promote the development of flowers; cool temperatures and darkness retard flower development and help to make the flowers last longer. To prolong the flowering period once it has begun, some gardeners dip the stem ends into wax to seal the cut surface, and others trim the stem ends every day or so. Placing copper pennies in the vase water, dipping the stems in fruit preservative, and soaking the stems in warm water and then refrigerating them are also popular practices.

Summer comes early when its brightest annual flowers are forced into bloom for indoor color. A centerpiece of marigolds, lobelia, ivy, and sweet alyssum echoes the colors throughout the dining room.

Forcing Annual Flowers

Some of summer's brightest annual flowers force easily in rooms with full sun and a moderately cool (60° to 70° F), humid atmosphere. (Browallia and torenia will make do with less sun—good sunlight from an east window is ample.) In addition to brightening your own indoor garden, they will make cheerful gifts for friends.

A temperature range of 60° to 70° F is ideal for forcing annuals. Pot the flowers in a mixture of equal parts soil, sand, and peat moss, and keep them evenly moist. Fertilize every two weeks with liquid houseplant food. Pinch the growing tips as necessary to encourage compact, bushy plants. Aphids are likely to be troublesome; for control tips, see page 186.

To grow ageratum, sweet alyssum, dwarf balsam, browallia, and dwarf cockscomb indoors for winter and early spring bloom, sow seeds in early August. Follow the same technique for dwarf marigolds, sweet peas, nasturtiums, and morning glories. Once the seedlings are large enough to handle, transplant them to individual pots, and keep moving the plants to larger containers as they increase in size, stopping at 5- to 7-inch containers. Provide a trellis for morning glory and sweet pea vines, and try hanging baskets for the trailing plants.

Lobelia, nicotiana, petunia, snapdragon, torenia, and verbena can be dug from outdoor plantings in autumn, before the first frost, and carefully potted in 5- to 10-inch containers. Disturb roots as little as possible but cut back leaves and stems severely to encourage new growth. Keep plants in a cool, shady place for a few days while they get accustomed to the pots. Then place them in a sunny indoor location, such as on a windowsill, and keep them moist to continue blooming.

Opposite: This pink astilbe, a perennial forced to bloom in time for Easter color, is the perfect complement to the Victorian sitting area. Keep astilbes in a cool, humid room.

Forcing Hardy Perennials

Forcing hardy perennials is a specialized gardening technique that few people ever try. However, if you have an outdoor perennial border that abounds with hosta, bleeding-heart, astilbe, or lily-of-the-valley, you may want to try forcing them in the winter.

Dig vigorous clumps in the early fall, trim them back, and pot them in a moist mixture of soil, sand, and peat moss. Place them in a cold frame, an unheated garage, or cool attic, away from the danger of a severe frost. In the midwinter, bring the pots indoors to a moderately cool (60° to 65° F), sunny windowsill. Keep the soil evenly moist. When new leaves begin to grow, fertilize every two weeks with a houseplant fertilizer. With luck, some of spring's loveliest flowers will appear weeks or months before their outdoor counterparts.

After forcing hardy perennials, replant them outdoors. Do not force the same clumps again for at least two years.

Extending the Flowering Season of Outdoor Plants

Many tender perennial flowers grown outdoors in warm weather as annuals can be brought inside before a frost for an extended flowering season. They will, however, require a sunny indoor location and moist air. On a sunny windowsill, under fluorescent lights, or in a home greenhouse, some plants will bloom indefinitely. Others will merely yield a few more flowers before they finally die.

Plants can be dug out of the garden and potted, although they will suffer more shock than a potted plant that is simply transferred indoors. The best time to dig up and pot a plant is two to three weeks before the first frost date.

Water the plant a day or two before you plan to dig it up. This will make your work easier and will help protect the plant from root damage. Using either a sturdy trowel or a spade, dig up the plant with a sizable chunk of earth surrounding the root system and follow the potting instructions on pages 97 to 99.

Leave the newly potted plant outdoors in a shady, moist spot for several days so that it can acclimatize to the container and the lower light. Scrutinize and groom the plant for pests and diseases as carefully as you would indoor plants that have vacationed outside (see pages 113 to 114).

Annual or tender perennial flowers that send up sturdy new basal growth whenever the tops are cut back are the best to save as houseplants. These include wax begonias (*Begonia* × *semperflorens-cultorum*), geraniums, and impatiens. With careful transplanting and attentive maintenance, you may be able to save heliotrope, French marigold, lantana, and sage.

Once these plants are indoors, keep them moist. After they have adjusted and begun to grow again, feed them monthly with a liquid fertilizer and clip off spent blooms. You can often extend the blooming period for weeks. These plants are ideal for temporarily filling a new greenhouse.

You can bring in frost-sensitive bulbous plants, such as caladium, achimenes, tuberous begonia, and amaryllis. The less hardy herbs, such as borage, lemon verbena, sweet basil, marjoram, young parsley, scented geraniums, and in cold climates, sweet bay and rosemary, can also be potted and brought indoors.

Red caladiums line the window at the end of a hall while a calathea fills in the space next to the chair. Both these plants are tender perennials outdoors but excellent indoor plants.

Greenhouses and Solariums

Entering a greenhouse for the first time is like stepping into another world. It may be snowing outside, but inside a greenhouse you are transported to the steamy, languid tropics or springtime in the desert, surrounded by exotic orchids or lush displays of succulents. Greenhouses and solariums let you create an ideal environment for your plants. They also work well as growing stations, providing you with a year-round supply of houseplants for display stations throughout your home.

Today's greenhouses and solariums are simple, practical, and no longer exclusively the domain of the wealthy. They can be freestanding structures, add-ons to the house, or window extensions over a kitchen sink or in a corner of a living room. A greenhouse fits wherever you have space: in a window, on a balcony, in the background, or on the roof.

This chapter discusses the many types of greenhouses and solariums, their best uses, and some basics on caring for plants in a greenhouse.

The protected environment of a greenhouse is always right for gardening. In a greenhouse, you can grow the plants you love the year around.

Greenhouses

The term *greenhouse* refers to any structure that traps and stores energy by means of transparent panels. In common parlance, however, a greenhouse is a structure specifically designed to have as much transparent surface as possible oriented toward the sun. A sun porch, a sunroom, or even a sunny window can provide some of the benefits of a greenhouse.

Freestanding Greenhouses

Greenhouses are usually either lean-tos or freestanding. Freestanding greenhouses, by far the most common type and what most people mean when they mention greenhouses, are especially popular among serious hobbyists. They use the greenhouse as a general working area, devoting space to aisles, shelves, rows of hanging plants, and a workbench for potting, propagating, and caring for their plants. The layout of the interior space is usually entirely practical, with easy access for a loaded wheelbarrow.

Freestanding greenhouses can be built to any size and covered with glass, acrylic, or fiberglass. The smaller greenhouses that are becoming increasingly available are more appropriate for most gardeners. They allow you to increase the outdoor growing season by intensifying the warmth and humidity of a section of a backyard, or balcony, without going to the trouble of installing a foundation, plumbing, and lights.

Two freestanding greenhouses allow the hobbyist to specialize in plants that require different atmospheric conditions.

A-frame

Gothic

Freestanding

Attached

Top: These sketches indicate some of the more common shapes for greenhouses.
Left: An attached greenhouse is a source of passive solar heating as well as a pleasant setting for conversation or reading.

Solariums and Greenhouse Rooms

Important architectural elements in many modern homes are solariums, or sunrooms. Builders and remodelers install them because of their unique appeal as an indoor-outdoor living space and because of the benefits of adding sun-provided warmth and light to the space. Although these additions are often not primarily designed for indoor gardeners, they are as effective as a greenhouse for plants that enjoy plenty of direct light.

A solarium is an ideal spot for sun lovers—plants and people—yet both can be fried if there are no blinds or screens to control the intensity of the light. Even with screens, a south-facing solarium will be much warmer than other rooms in the home. If you are in doubt as to whether a plant will be happy in a solarium or greenhouse room, check the appropriate listing in "A Gallery of Houseplants" (pages 199 to 307).

Greenhouse Additions

The latest trend in indoor growing space is the greenhouse addition. Unlike the spacious solarium, which is designed primarily for lounging and relaxation and only secondarily for plants, the greenhouse addition is a space devoted to plants. It is usually smaller and more intimate than a solarium and seen not so much as a room of its own but as an extension to the one to which it is attached. A greenhouse addition opens up a room to the outdoors, letting in more light. The kitchen is a perfect room for a greenhouse addition; you can grow herbs and vegetables just where you need them and harvest them without having to deal with the variable conditions of the great outdoors. Greenhouse additions are also just the place for producing attractive flowering plants to decorate less sunny areas of the house while they are in flower.

Greenhouse additions can be custom built to suit the style of the home; more often though they are installed from kits either by the homeowner or by a professional crew. Usually the expense of a new foundation is eliminated by using an existing patio or balcony as a base and the costs for new heating, water, and electric services avoided by simply extending those from the house. In an urban home, a greenhouse addition is a particularly effective design: It takes up little outdoor space yet greatly increases the feeling of space indoors.

Indoors and outdoors appear to meld into one in this enchanting space in a dramatic solarium.

Built on a foundation that also serves as an entry to the house, this greenhouse is accessible from both indoors and outdoors.

Greenhouse Windows

If the idea of a greenhouse interests you, a full-sized one is not the only option and may not be the right one. It can be costly to install and operate and may take up too much space on an urban lot. A greenhouse window, however, is well within most budgets, and just about everyone has at least one window to work with.

Greenhouse windows do not require expensive plumbing, electricity, or heating systems: The systems in the house or apartment will be adequate. Kits are available that can be assembled in as little as one afternoon. And if the greenhouse window becomes too small for your needs, you can always add another greenhouse window or a full-sized greenhouse later.

Start by choosing an appropriate window. Apply the same criterion as you would for choosing a site for a full-size greenhouse: the most light possible with the least obstruction. A spot facing full south is best, although one facing east or west is acceptable. Even a north window is suitable as long as you install fluorescent lights. An overhanging roof is not always a major hindrance and can even be an advantage; it will reduce heat buildup and excessive light in the summer when the sun is directly overhead yet allow the light to flood in, unobstructed, in the winter, when the sun is lower on the horizon. Access to a nearby faucet will make watering easier, which makes kitchen or bathroom windows a good choice, doubly so in the case of a kitchen window as you would be able to grow fresh herbs and vegetables within arm's reach. Try to choose a window that has a view that you won't miss, since a plant-filled greenhouse attached to a window does not allow a clear outlook from the inside of the house. This can be a distinct advantage. Consider using a window greenhouse to divert attention from an uninteresting vista, such as the wall of a neighboring house or apartment building.

Once you've found the right window, choose a kit to fit it. First measure the window carefully. The easiest window greenhouses to install are those that fit directly onto the outside window frame. Kits are available to suit all standard frame sizes. If you can't find a kit that fits your window exactly, buy one slightly larger and install a new frame around the old one. Glass structures are the most popular because they allow a clear view outdoors, but they are

This south-facing greenhouse window at the end of a kitchen corridor houses a prized collection of cacti and succulents.

expensive and also heavy, making installation more difficult. Double-wall acrylic structures are just as durable and are far lighter, making them the next best choice. Choose a structure that suits the style of your house: There is often a choice of frames, including ones made of wood, aluminum, or PVC.

The best window greenhouses come with temperature-controlled vents that open automatically to let out hot air. However, even with these greenhouses, it is wise to install a small circulating fan near the window to blow warm air into the structure in winter and vent hot air in the summer. Due to their small size, window greenhouses tend to heat up quickly during the day and cool off rapidly at night.

There is an extremely simple alternative to even the window greenhouse. You can purchase a miniature indoor greenhouse and place it on a windowsill or on a shelf under lights. Miniature greenhouses have many uses: propagating new plants, curing ailing plants that have been suffering from insufficient humidity, isolating sick plants during treatment, and forcing flowering plants into bloom. They can also make attractive permanent homes for humidity-loving tropical species. Altogether, they are a useful addition to an indoor garden.

Choosing the Site

Deciding where to locate your greenhouse is a critical first step. The primary consideration is sunshine. Look carefully at your property for anything that will block sunlight (houses, walls, and trees). Keep in mind that in winter the sun will be considerably lower than it is in summer. Orientation to the sun is an important factor in determining where to site your greenhouse.

The greenhouse should be placed at a distance from the light-blocking obstacles equivalent to 2½ times their height. For example, if a 10-foot-tall wall casts a shadow on your property, the greenhouse should be 25 feet away from it. However, if a nearby tree is a deciduous one, it can provide shade during hot summer days and allow sunlight in the winter when it loses its leaves. The most important goal is to get maximum value from winter sunlight.

Drainage is the next consideration. Try to avoid building in depressions that will catch rain and snow, or in boggy areas where the soil is constantly wet and unstable. If there is a slope behind the greenhouse, it may be necessary to put in tile or gravel ditches, or some other system to divert runoff.

Select a site that is relatively level, or that can be leveled easily. If you expect to plant directly in the soil, the ground where you build the greenhouse is an important factor. If the soil is full of rocks or clay, you may have to create raised growing beds or plan to do your gardening in containers.

The greenhouse will need water and electricity, so you must plan where to place the hookups. Locating the greenhouse close to these connections will make it easier, and cheaper, to install the utility lines.

Consider the distance you will have to walk to get from the house to the greenhouse. If you have to contend with freezing cold weather or blinding snow, a greenhouse should be close to or, better yet, attached to the house.

Greenhouse Uses

A greenhouse can be put to any number of uses besides growing a range of ornamentals. The most frequent are food production, decoration of the home, plant collections, and solar heating.

Food Production

The environment of a greenhouse is in many ways well suited to food production. Though growing food in a greenhouse is not cost-effective at the outset, using a greenhouse for food production does have benefits: absolute freshness, freedom from contaminants, and the possibility of growing exotic varieties.

Vegetables, fruits, and herbs can all be successfully grown in a greenhouse. Off-season vegetable crops are particularly popular.

Home Decoration

In a greenhouse plants can be grown to a degree of perfection not easy to achieve in the house itself. It is natural to want to show

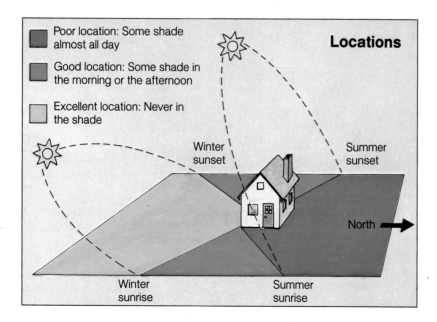

Poor location: Some shade almost all day

Good location: Some shade in the morning or the afternoon

Excellent location: Never in the shade

Locations

Winter sunset

Summer sunset

North

Winter sunrise

Summer sunrise

them off to best advantage by bringing them inside, but keep their stays in the house fairly limited or they will lose their greenhouse luster and perfection.

Plant Collections

A greenhouse is a perfect place to bring similar kinds of plants together in a collection—plants in the same family or genus, plants with the same cultural requirements, or plants that have the same aesthetic impact. The most common such groupings are alpines, begonias, bromeliads, gesneriads, orchids, and succulents.

Top: Many fruits and vegetables grow well in a greenhouse environment. Eating what you've grown is always a thrill, especially in the cold winter months when fresh produce is scarce. Exotic varieties that are not generally sold in the markets are often available as seeds or young plants.

Opposite: Flowering greenhouse plants can be brought into the house to be enjoyed more fully. Their stay, in most cases, should be short. Orchids, such as these phalaenopsis, are especially decorative.

Tuberous begonias (Begonia ✕ tuberhybrida) *show off their colors in the greenhouse. Hobbyists can use greenhouses to increase their plant collections without overrunning their living areas with plants.*

Alpines prefer a cold, bright environment and are particularly suitable for a solar-heated greenhouse. Begonias and gesneriads share a need for both warmth and shade from the summer sun. Epiphytic bromeliads and orchids, the type grown by most fanciers, both require a fibrous, free-draining growing medium. Bromeliad and orchid species run the gamut of temperature tolerance; some will tolerate near freezing temperatures, others need a minimum temperature of 50° F or above. Bromeliads prefer a good deal more summer sunlight than do most orchids. Of all these groups, succulents are best suited to a greenhouse. They accept the extremes of temperature day and night, summer and winter, are unaffected by the sometimes extremely low humidity, and are able to withstand a fair measure of neglect.

Solar Heating

A greenhouse attached to the home is a natural source of passive solar heating. To make the most use of this heating, install a fan or other type of air circulator to force the heated air from the greenhouse into the house. Although there is not likely to be a significant amount of warmth before the first of March or after the middle of October, it can be ample and welcome in March, April, and May.

Growing Plants in a Greenhouse

Since a greenhouse is a controlled environment, there's no trick to growing pineapples or papayas in Montana or Maine. Just choose the exotic fruits you want for Thanksgiving dinner or the flowers for your anniversary centerpiece and follow the care requirements. The real fun is in working with nature. Once you can recognize the natural cycle of a plant, you will learn to care for it according to its needs. In return, it will give you pleasure, personal nourishment, and beauty.

The needs of houseplants in a greenhouse are much the same as of those kept in the home. Most successful commercial plant nurseries use the same growing media for greenhouse container plants as they do for other indoor plants. Watering requirements are also much the same as for houseplants indoors. Remember to water

As long as the sun is out, a greenhouse will trap a significant amount of heat even on the coldest winter days. The occupants (both plants and people) stay warm in this greenhouse/solarium, which was designed to be an integral part of the house.

according to the needs of the plant rather than by the clock or by the calendar.

Whenever any plant is watered, some nutrients leach out of the soil and need to be replaced with a fertilizer. The amount of fertilizer required at any one time is extremely small, but the need is continuous. Mixing a timed-release fertilizer into the soil while you are potting a plant is the easiest way to ensure continuous fertilization.

Bottom Heat

One thing you can do in any sort of greenhouse that you can't do in a home is to heat the growing medium to a controlled temperature. This often produces dramatically healthier and more vigorous plants.

Heating the growing medium has several beneficial effects on the plants. In heated soil, most tropical and subtropical plants can tolerate cooler air temperatures than normal; plants usually grown in hot, humid greenhouses may thrive in a cooler, drier area. Moisture-laden air that escapes from the soil raises the humidity around the plants, a condition favored by tropical and subtropical species. Bottom heat also stimulates root growth and increases a plant's resistance to disease, which in turn stimulates more foliage

Bottom heating by electric coils often produces healthier and more vigorous plants.

growth. In addition, many tropical plants will bloom all year in heated soil.

The merits of providing bottom heat are well known, but the cost of heating the soil has prevented it from becoming a common practice in commercial greenhouses. In small greenhouses or indoor planters, where energy requirements are much lower, it may barely increase the monthly utility bill. In a greenhouse the air can be kept almost 20° F cooler if the soil is heated. This saves on heating costs and brings the temperature and humidity into a range closer to that of indoor living spaces, making the air in the greenhouse more comfortable for you and easing the transition of plants from the greenhouse to the chosen display stations throughout your home.

For optimum growth and flowering, heat the growing medium to around 70° F. Fluctuations below 70° F are acceptable, since these occur in native habitats. However, temperatures over 85° F are undesirable; the soil dries out quickly and small roots will die.

A greenhouse makes it easier to grow orchids, which require a controlled environment.

Check the temperature with a thermometer. To avoid breaking the thermometer, dig a hole and gently place the thermometer in it, then cover the bulb of the thermometer with the growing medium so readings will be accurate.

Many plants respond well to bottom heat. Tropical palms, for instance, generally respond with prodigious root growth. Repot the palm as soon as new roots come through the drainage hole. Many tropical species of the Acanthus family produce more flowers when grown in warm soil. Among these are the lollipop-plant (*Pachystachys lutea*), a medium shrub with bright yellow bracts and unusual, white flowers, and king's-crown (*Justicia carnea*), a shrub with fist-sized clusters of pink flowers.

All the thunbergia vines do well in heated soil. So do the monkey-plants (*Ruellia*), including *R. makoyana*, which has large, rose-red, trumpet-shaped flowers, and *R. graecizans*, which has orange-red bracts and flowers. Many tropical bulbs and tuberous plants also thrive with bottom heat. The spectacular glory lilies (*Gloriosa rothschildiana*), caladiums, achimenes, and florist's gloxinias (*sinningia speciosa*) are in this group. Indoor vegetable gardeners may want to try bottom heat for tomatoes, peppers (both bell and hot varieties), eggplant, chayote, tropical vegetable varieties, and cultivated mushroom species.

There are a number of ways of providing bottom heat to the growing medium. You can do it by applying heat directly. You can also apply heat indirectly to the pot or bench that is in contact with the soil.

Electric cables heat the growing medium directly. Small cables work well in containers, window boxes, and propagation benches. They are simple to install and operate. Use the highest quality cables you can afford, since cheaper ones may crack or deteriorate in damp soil and require frequent replacement. Electric cables are useful for starting seeds, growing plants from cuttings or seedlings, and for establishing large specimen plants during their first year or two after transplanting.

Cables are available in a variety of forms, with and without built-in thermostats. Probably the most convenient is a propagation mat, which resembles an electric heating pad. A propagation mat heats the area it covers.

If you are not buying a mat, the length of cable you need depends on the area you are heating and on the capacity of the particular brand of cable. As a general rule of thumb, use 2 to 4 linear feet of cable, or 10 to 15 watts, per square foot.

Lay the cable on the bottom of the plant container, being careful not to overlap the strands (clothespins are useful to hold the cable in place). Cover the cable with about an inch of sand. Place pieces of screen on top of the sand, to avoid damaging the cable with tools. The growing medium lies on top of the screen.

Another method for heating the growing medium relies on hot water from a gas or electric hot water heater or from a solar collector. In these systems, the hot water circulates through plastic pipes and neoprene tubing. For a hobby greenhouse, ½-inch plastic pipe and ⅛-inch neoprene tubing are adequate. Kits are available, complete with special fittings to attach the tubing to the pipe.

A gardener who grows many different plants in different-sized containers may prefer a simpler system. For small greenhouses, you can easily make a soil-heating system by casting a concrete slab bench. Simply place plastic or copper tubing in the form, pour the concrete, hook up the connections, and place your potted

A greenhouse can shelter a variety of plants or a specialized collection. Here, the owner has created a desert, with plants set directly into the ground.

plants or flats on the heated bench. This kind of bench is easy to clean, and it radiates heat throughout the greenhouse as well as heating the pots directly on top of it.

Many of the supplies needed for a soil-heating system are available at hardware and plumbing stores. Stores selling solar heating supplies are good sources for tubing and valves. Small soil-heating cables are available at many garden stores.

Pots or Not?

There are two general ways to grow plants in a greenhouse, in containers or planted directly in the ground. For greenhouses that form part of the living space, pots will be the first choice. In free-standing greenhouses, the choice depends on the goals of the gardener and the requirements of the plants.

Plants in the ground   Growing plants in the ground allows you to make an integrated garden design. You can grow plants close enough together so that they enhance one another through flower color, foliage pattern, or shape. Growing plants in the ground is also easier. They require much less frequent watering than plants in pots, and they are much less vulnerable to sudden drought stress if watering is delayed. Problems with drainage, feeding, and the buildup of salts are also less likely to occur. In general, plants in the ground are healthier and therefore better looking and more resistant to pests and cold. They grow more vigorously, which is sometimes, but not always, desirable.

Plants in pots   An advantage to plants in pots is that they can be easily moved around the greenhouse or in and out of the greenhouse. They are easier to display indoors at flowering time or to move outdoors for a rest. It is not a good idea to grow plants in pots in a greenhouse where temperatures fall below freezing. The roots are particularly vulnerable to frost damage.

Opposite: Plants in pots are easy to move around a greenhouse and out into the house for display.

Displaying Plants in Greenhouses and Solariums

Plants in attached greenhouses, solariums, and greenhouse windows should contribute to the overall design scheme for the room. Display stations in both areas should be chosen to suit the cultural needs of the plant and the design needs of the room as described in the first chapter.

Display plants in freestanding greenhouses to suit both you and the plant. Ideally, benches and cabinets inside a greenhouse are both functional and attractive. They should fit your own needs, taking your height and reach into consideration so that you can tend your plants comfortably. Many manufactured benches have casters so they will roll back and forth. These benches greatly increase the usable growing area in a greenhouse.

Other popular bench styles include stair-step benches and planter benches. Stair-step benches give you more display room. Shade-loving plants can go under the bench. On any bench you will need to rotate the plants regularly unless they are located against a white wall; otherwise, they will grow unevenly toward the sun.

Planter benches can be filled with soil, but be careful to prevent the plants from becoming waterlogged. Some gardeners fill planter benches with soaked vermiculite and place potted plants on top of them. This way the plants will remain well watered for days.

Whichever benches you choose, they should provide a good display area for the plants and have maximum light exposure. They should allow air to circulate freely through them and among the plants. Use an open material, such as expanded metal or snow fencing, for the bench surface.

*Opposite: Begonias, a maidenhair fern (*Adiantum*), and many different bromeliads are among the plants growing in this greenhouse.*

Solving Specific Plant Problems

Plants, like humans, are susceptible to destructive environmental forces and to individual genetic vulnerabilities. When a plant is weakened—perhaps by loving but inconsistent care—those environmental or genetic elements can cause a variety of problems.

This chapter addresses some of the more serious conditions your plants may develop. For convenience, the chapter is divided into three sections: pests, diseases, and cultural problems. If you notice anything unusual (such as constant wilting) or see a change in your plants (such as spots or bugs on the leaves), consult the individual care guides in "A Gallery of Houseplants." If you've followed those care requirements and still have significant or ongoing problems, check the following pages.

Sometimes the best way to treat a plant is to move it outdoors out of direct sunlight and apply any controls there. This isolates the plant from others in your collection and makes it easier to avoid getting a houseplant insect spray or insecticidal spray on other plants or surrounding surfaces. And if you do use a spray or soap, be sure the plant is listed on the product label and follow label directions carefully.

An ounce of prevention is worth a pound of cure, and the best and simplest way to deal with plant problems is to try to avoid them. Always be careful not to spread a disease or pest from one plant to a whole collection. Don't allow sick plants to come into contact with healthy ones, and don't touch sick plants and then go on to touch or groom healthy ones. When you purchase a new plant, isolate it until you are sure that all it is bringing into your house is joy and beauty. If there is no way to cure a plant, throw it away. Also, throw away the soil it was in. It is wise to discard the pot too, unless you're sure you can sanitize it.

Identifying and curing a problem as soon as it occurs on a plant will help you keep the plant in good health and avoid spreading pests and diseases to your other houseplants.

Pests

Aphids

Aphids

PROBLEM: New leaves are curled, discolored, and smaller than normal. A shiny or sticky substance may coat the leaves. Tiny (⅛-inch), wingless, green, soft-bodied insects cluster on buds, young stems, and leaves. Aphids in small numbers do little damage, but they are extremely prolific and populations can rapidly build up to damaging numbers on houseplants. Damage results when the aphids suck sap from the leaves and stems. Aphids are unable to digest all the sugar in the plant sap and excrete the excess in a fluid called honeydew, which often drops onto leaves or surfaces below.

SOLUTION: Wipe off small infestations with cotton swabs dipped in rubbing alcohol. Spray larger infestations with a houseplant insect spray containing acephate (Orthene®), resmethrin, malathion, or pyrethrins. Make sure your plant is listed on the product label and follow label directions carefully.

Cyclamen Mites

Cyclamen mite damage

PROBLEM: The stem tips or the newest growth in the plant center becomes severely stunted. Leaves become stunted, brittle, stay very small, and may be cupped or curved. Color may change to bronze, gray, or tan. Flower buds fail to develop properly and open. Cyclamen mite (*Steneotarsonemus pallidus*) is an extremely small mite related to spiders. These mites attack a number of houseplants and can be particularly damaging to cyclamens. They infest the new growth most heavily, but will crawl to other parts of the plant or to other plants. Cyclamen mites reproduce rapidly.

SOLUTION: Spray infested plants several times with a household insect spray containing dicofol, resmethrin, diazinon, or insecticidal soap. Make sure your plant is listed on the product label and follow label directions carefully. Isolate mildly infested plants. Discard severely infested plants. Scour the pots and wash the area where the pots were sitting with a solution of 1 part household bleach to 9 parts water. Observe nearby plants closely so that you can spray if symptoms appear. Avoid touching leaves of infested plants and then touching leaves of other plants.

Fungus Gnats

PROBLEM: Small (up to ⅛ inch), slender, dark insects fly around when plants are disturbed. They frequently run across the foliage and soil and may also be found on windows. Roots may be damaged and seedlings may die. Fungus gnats are small flies that do little damage, but they are unpleasant when present in large numbers. They lay their eggs in soil that contains organic material. After a week the eggs hatch and the larvae crawl through the upper layer of the soil. The larvae are white, ¼ inch long, and have black heads. They feed on fungi that grow on organic matter. The larvae usually do not damage plants, but when present in large numbers they may feed on the roots of some plants, killing very young seedlings. The larvae feed for about 2 weeks before maturing into adults. There can be many generations in a year.

SOLUTION: Spray with a houseplant insect spray containing diazinon. Make sure your plant is listed on the product label and follow label directions carefully. It may be necessary to repeat applications.

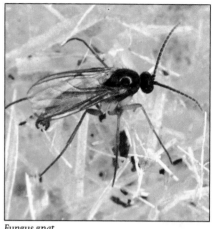

Fungus gnat

Leaf Miners

PROBLEM: Irregular, winding, white tunnels or patches appear on upper leaf surfaces. Small, dark-headed, white grubs can sometimes be seen in the tunnels. Leaf miners live inside the leaves of susceptible species, such as chrysanthemums and cinerarias (*Senecio × hybridus*). They spread through contact with other plants and may also come indoors through open windows.

SOLUTION: Remove infested leaves. Take plants outside and spray with acephate (Orthene®). Make sure your plant is listed on the product label and follow label directions carefully. For long-term control, apply disulfoton systemic insecticide granules around the base of the plant.

Leaf miners

Mealybugs

PROBLEM: White cottony or waxy insects up to ¼ inch long cluster on the undersides of leaves, on stems, and in the crotches where leaves are attached. Egg masses may also be present. A sticky substance called honeydew may cover the leaves or drop onto surfaces below the plant. Leaves may be spotted or deformed. Infested plants are unsightly, do not grow well, and may die if severely infested.

SOLUTION: Control is difficult. If only a few mealybugs are present, wipe them off with a damp cloth or use cotton swabs dipped in rubbing alcohol. Wipe off any egg sacs under the rims or on the bottom of pots. For larger infestations, thoroughly spray stems and both sides of leaves with a houseplant insect spray containing acephate (Orthene®), or with a resmethrin and oil spray; general-purpose sprays containing malathion are also effective if carefully applied. Make sure your plant is listed on the product label and follow label directions carefully. Continue spraying for a while after it appears the mealybugs have been controlled. Discard severely infested plants, and do not take cuttings from them. Clean the growing area with soapy water before starting new plants.

Citrus mealybugs

Scales

Begonia scale

PROBLEM: Nodes, stems, and leaves or fronds are covered with white, cottony, cushionlike masses, brown crusty bumps, or clusters of flattened, reddish gray or brown scaly bumps that can be scraped off easily. Leaves or fronds turn yellow and may drop. A shiny or sticky material called honeydew may cover the stems and leaves or fronds and drip on surfaces below. Scale insects of several different types attack houseplants. The young, called crawlers, are small (about ¹/₁₀ inch), soft-bodied, and move about on the plant and onto other plants. After a short time they insert their mouth parts into the plant so that they can feed on the sap. The legs disappear, and the scales remain in the same place for the rest of their lives. Some develop a soft covering, and others are hard.

SOLUTION: Pick off by hand or spray with a houseplant insect spray containing acephate (Orthene®) or resmethrin and oil. Make sure your plant is listed on the product label and follow label directions carefully. Repeated applications may be necessary. Spraying is most effective against the crawlers rather than the stationary adults.

Spider Mites

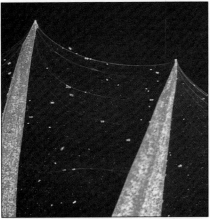

Spider mites

PROBLEM: Leaves are stippled, yellow, and dirty; they may dry out and drop. There may be webbing over flower buds, between leaves, or on the lower surfaces of the leaves. To determine whether a plant is infested with mites, hold a sheet of white paper beneath an affected area and tap the leaf or stem sharply. Minute green, red, or yellow specks the size of pepper grains will drop to the paper and begin to crawl around. The pests are easily seen against the white background. Spider mites, related to spiders, are major pests of many houseplants. They cause damage by sucking sap from the undersides of the leaves. Under warm, dry conditions, these insects multiply rapidly.

SOLUTION: Spray infested plants with a houseplant insect spray containing hexakis (Vendex®) or a spray containing acephate (Orthene®) and resmethrin or an insecticidal soap. Make sure your plant is listed on the product label and follow label directions carefully. Plants need several weekly sprayings to kill the mites as they hatch. Inspect new plants thoroughly before bringing them into the home.

Springtails

Springtail

PROBLEM: Plants have small, white to black insects up to ¹/₅ inch long that jump when plants are watered. Lower leaves and young seedlings may occasionally be nibbled. Springtails are common insects in indoor conditions and seem to prefer potting mixtures rich in peat moss. They do little damage to mature plants but can be harmful to seedlings.

SOLUTION: Allow the potting mixture to dry out slightly between waterings, as springtails thrive only in damp conditions. Use pasteurized mixtures when sowing seed, and cover seed containers with plastic film to prevent the pests from reaching young seedlings. In severe cases, apply diazinon to the soil around the base of the plant.

PROBLEM: Flowers and leaves are abnormally mottled or streaked with silver. Young leaves and flowers may be distorted. Pollen sacs on African violets (*Saintpaulia*) spill open, leaving yellow powder on flowers. Dusty black droppings collect on leaves or flowers. Tiny (1/16-inch-long) insects scuttle away when the plant is breathed on. Thrips damage plant surfaces with their rasping mouth apparatus. Larvae are pale in color and wingless; adults are dark and, although they bear feathery wings, tend to hop rather than fly. Eggs are laid inside plant tissues or in the potting mix and are therefore relatively immune to pesticide treatments.

SOLUTION: Remove heavily damaged leaves and flowers to reduce infestation. Spray weekly with a pesticide containing acephate (Orthene®) or resmethrin until no further symptoms are apparent. Make sure your plant is listed on the product label and follow label directions carefully.

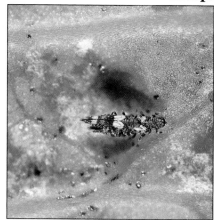

Greenhouse thrips

Whiteflies

PROBLEM: When you touch the plant, tiny, winged insects flutter around it. Leaves may be mottled and yellow. Whiteflies feed mainly on the undersides of the leaves. They cannot digest all the sugar in the sap and excrete the excess in a sugary material called honeydew, which coats the leaves and may drop from the plant.

SOLUTION: If only a few leaves are infested, wipe off larvae with a damp cloth or cotton swab soaked in alcohol, or shake the plant and vacuum up the cloud of flies. Spray severe infestations with a houseplant insect spray containing acephate (Orthene®), a resmethrin-petroleum oil spray, malathion, pyrethrins, or insecticidal soaps. Check labels to determine which material can be used on your particular plant. Spray weekly as long as the problem persists. Remove heavily infested plants as soon as you spot the problem.

Greenhouse whiteflies

Diseases

Bacterial Stem Blight

Bacterial stem blight

PROBLEM: Soft, sunken areas with water-soaked margins appear on the stems. Cracks sometimes appear in the affected areas. Lower leaves may turn yellow and become severely wilted. They tend to hang on the stem even when collapsed. If the condition is severe, the stem may rot through so that the top of the plant breaks off. Inner stem tissue is discolored brown. Cuttings from infected stems may produce infected plants, or they simply may not root. Bacterial stem blight is caused by the bacterium *Erwinia chrysanthemi*.

SOLUTION: There is no cure for this disease. Discard severely infected plants. If some stems are still healthy, cut them off above the diseased area and reroot them. Do not use any stems that have brown streaks.

Botrytis

Botrytis

PROBLEM: Light brown patches appear on leaves, stems, or flowers, gradually darkening and turning soft and moist. A grayish mold covers the affected surfaces. Infected plant parts curl up and fall off. Botrytis, or gray mold, is a common air-borne fungal disease that affects a wide range of plants. It spreads quickly to other nearby plant parts. When the plant stem is affected, the entire plant may rot away. It is especially common during periods of intense humidity and inside closed containers, such as terrariums.

SOLUTION: Remove infected plant parts. Treat the rest of the plant with a fungicide, such as chlorothalonil. Make sure your plant is listed on the product label and follow label directions carefully. To prevent this disease, avoid overly humid air and improve air circulation around the plants. To avoid spreading the disease, do not mist susceptible plants.

Crown, Stem, and Root Rot

PROBLEM: Plants fail to grow. Leaves appear dull and then turn black. Lower ones may turn yellow and drop. Leaves in the center of the plant turn dark green and then black. Roots are dead and rotted. When the condition is severe, all the roots are rotted and the plant may wilt and die. Rot is caused by soil-dwelling fungi (*Pythium* species), also known as water molds, that attack the roots and usually indicates that the plant has been watered too frequently or that the soil mix does not drain well. The fungi are common in garden soils and can be introduced on a plant or dirty pot, or transferred on dirty fingers or tools. Rot spreads quickly through a root system if the soil remains wet. Plants weakened by other factors are more susceptible to fungi.

SOLUTION: If the plant is only mildly affected, let the soil dry out between waterings. If the soil mix is heavy or the container does not drain well, transplant into fast-draining soil mix in a container that drains freely. Discard severely infected plants and soil. Soak pots in a mixture of 1 part household bleach to 9 parts water for 30 minutes. Rinse with plain water, and dry thoroughly before reuse. You can also sterilize the pots. After handling infected plants, wash your hands thoroughly before touching healthy plants.

Crown, stem, and root rot

Leaf Spot

PROBLEM: Circular, reddish brown spots appear on the leaves. The spots are surrounded by a yellow margin. Several spots may join to form blotches. Badly spotted leaves may turn yellow and die. Fusarium leaf spot is caused by a fungus (*Fusarium moniliforme*). In most cases spotting is unsightly but not harmful; but if spotting is severe, the leaf may weaken and die.

SOLUTION: Clip off badly spotted leaves. Water carefully to avoid leaf splash, and keep the foliage dry to prevent the spread of the fungus. If spotting continues, spray the plant with a fungicide containing chlorothalonil. Make sure your plant is listed on the product label and follow label directions carefully.

Fusarium leaf spot

Powdery Mildew

PROBLEM: White or gray, powdery patches appear on the leaves, stems, and flowers. Leaves and flowers may be covered with the powdery growth. The mildew usually appears first on older leaves and on the upper surfaces of the leaves. Tissue under the powdery growth may turn yellow or brown. Affected leaves may drop. Powdery mildew is caused by several genera of fungi. The powdery patches are fungus strands and spores. The wind-borne spores are capable of infecting leaves, stems, and flowers on the same plant or on nearby plants. The disease is favored by dim light and warm days with cool nights. Older leaves are more susceptible than new leaves. Plants in dry soil are more susceptible than plants kept evenly moist.

SOLUTION: Remove infected leaves and spray with a fungicide, such as triforene, or chlorothalonil until the disease is gone. Make sure your plant is listed on the product label and follow label directions carefully. Move plants to locations with more light. Keep plants out of cool drafts and in rooms with temperatures as even as possible, and provide better air circulation.

Powdery mildew

Sooty Mold

Sooty mold

PROBLEM: Patches of thin, black powder appear on both surfaces of the leaf. Leaves yellow and die from lack of light. Sooty mold is not a plant disease in itself but rather a side effect from an infestation of sucking insects, such as mealybugs, scale insects, or whiteflies. These insects give off honeydew, which spreads over the leaf surface and on which sooty mold develops.

SOLUTION: Remove yellowed leaves and rinse off healthy ones with soap and water. Treat plant for whatever insect is excreting the honeydew.

Virus

Virus-infected lily

PROBLEM: Plants grow slowly and without energy. Leaves are often lightly mottled or streaked with yellow; they may also show ringed yellow spots. Leaves can be distorted. Virus diseases are often subtle, with the main symptoms being stunted growth and a generally lackluster performance. They are carried from plant to plant by insects or on infected tools.

SOLUTION: There is no cure for infected plants. Destroy them. To prevent viruses, keep insects at bay through preventative treatment. When pruning always dip tools into a disinfectant (bleach, rubbing alcohol, etc.) between each cut.

Cultural Problems

Bud Blast

PROBLEM: Flower buds form but fail to open. They may turn brown shortly after forming or attain nearly full size before brown patches appear. Sometimes they simply drop off with no other symptom. Dry air is the most common cause. Air pollution is another common cause, and there are a number of other causes: excessive heat or cold, too much fertilizer, too little or too much water, fungal disease, etc. Bud blast is normal in certain circumstances, such as when a plant has produced more buds than it has energy to feed. Young plants, for example, will often lose many of their flower buds at their first flowering.

SOLUTION: Increase air humidity as flowering approaches by placing plants on a humidifying tray or in a room with a humidifier. You might also move plants out of direct sunlight, as air loses humidity as it heats up. Beware also of the drying effects of air conditioning. Look for any other symptoms that may explain the cause of the buds blasting (wilting from too much or too little water, sudden temperature change, etc.) and treat accordingly.

Bud blast

Edema

PROBLEM: Brown, corky patches form on stems or leaves. When scratched away, the underlying cells are found to be healthy. Too much water, especially during dull weather, is the usual cause. Cells swell up with moisture and burst, then scab tissues form as the plant heals, leading to a corky appearance. Edema on some plants, notably succulents, may also be caused by sucking insects, such as spider mites. Many plants tend to develop edema on their lower stems as they age.

SOLUTION: Once edema appears, it can only be cured by cutting away the affected tissues. It can, however, be prevented by less frequent watering, especially when the air is humid and light levels are low. Also check for symptoms of spider mites and treat accordingly.

Edema

Guttation

Guttation

PROBLEM: Drops of water or sap form at leaf tips or on the underside of the leaf. They may blacken or form translucent crystals as they dry. Too much soil moisture is the most common cause. The plant absorbs more water than it can use, causing it to secrete the excess through its leaves. In some plants, like *Cissus* species, West Indian holly (*Leea*), and chestnut vine (*Tetrastigma voinieranum*), a certain amount of guttation is normal.

SOLUTION: Reduce watering so that the plant does not absorb excessive amounts of liquid. Improved light will help the plant to use the water rather than secrete it through its leaves. Increase air circulation and lower air humidity so that any liquids that are exuded evaporate rapidly rather than accumulate.

High Temperature

High-temperature damage

PROBLEM: Outer leaves turn yellow. Leaves may die and turn brown. Stems become soft. Plants stop flowering. High temperatures cause problems for cool-weather plants. They will tolerate warm days as long as they have cool nights (below 55° F). Cool temperatures initiate flower buds. Constant high temperatures inhibit flower buds, and plants stop flowering. High temperatures also keep plants from growing well, causing leaves to lose their green color and die.

SOLUTION: Grow cool-weather plants in a cool room with as much light as possible. If a cool room is not available, put them near a window at night. If temperatures are not below freezing, put the plants outside at night. Under alternating temperatures, they will flower for long periods. Keep plants adequately watered and fertilized.

Insufficient Water

Dry poinsettia

PROBLEM: Leaves are small; plant fails to grow well and may be stunted. Plant parts or whole plants wilt. Margins of broad leaves or tips of narrow leaves may dry and become brittle but still retain a dull green color. Bleached areas may occur between the veins. Leaf tissues may die and remain bleached or turn tan or brown. Plants may die.

SOLUTION: Water plants immediately and thoroughly. If the soil is completely dry, soak the entire pot in water for a couple of hours.

Iron Deficiency

PROBLEM: The newest leaves turn yellow at the margins. The yellowing progresses inward, so that in the advanced stages the last tissues to lose their green color are the veins. In severe cases, the entire leaf is yellow and small. The plant may be stunted. Iron deficiency is a common problem for acid-loving plants, which grow best in soil with a pH between 5.5 and 6.5. Although soil is seldom deficient in iron, when the pH is 7.0 or higher the iron is chemically unavailable to some plants.

SOLUTION: To correct iron deficiency, make a solution containing chelated iron, and spray the foliage with it and apply it to the soil in the pot. Use acid-based fertilizers for feeding the plant. When planting or transplanting acid-loving plants, use an acidic growing medium that contains at least 50 percent peat moss. Use a minimal amount of lime or dolomite in the soil mix.

Iron deficiency

Lack of Light

PROBLEM: Plants fail to grow well. Leaves may be lighter green and smaller than normal. Lobes and splits normal in mature leaves may not develop. Lower leaves may yellow and drop. Stems and leaf stalks may elongate and be spindly and weak. Plants grow toward a light source. Flowering plants fail to produce flowers, and plants with colorful foliage become pale. Variegated plants may lose their variegation and become green. Although foliage plants generally need less light than plants grown for their flowers or fruit, plants with colorful foliage have a relatively high need for light.

SOLUTION: Gradually move the plant to a brighter location. To avoid sunburn on sensitive plants, close lightweight curtains when the sun shines directly on the plant. If the available light is not bright enough, provide supplemental lighting, as described on pages 77 to 82.

Spindly growth from lack of light

Low Humidity

PROBLEM: Growth is slow and leaves tend to curl downward. Plants wilt rapidly and need frequent watering. Flower buds and new leaves wither or fail to develop properly. Leaf edges and tips may turn brown and dry up. Low air humidity causes plants to lose water to the air more quickly than they can replace it. It is a major problem, especially during the heating season when air indoors is naturally drier.

SOLUTION: Place plants on a humidifying tray or keep them in a room with a humidifier. Group plants together so that the transpiration given off by each increases the air humidity around the plants. Regular misting can also help, as can moving the plant to a cooler, less sunny spot. Grow plants that require very high air humidity in terrariums.

Dieback caused by low humidity

Nitrogen Deficiency

Nitrogen deficiency

PROBLEM: The oldest leaves, usually the lower ones, turn yellow and may drop. Yellowing starts at the leaf margins and progresses inward without producing a distinct pattern. The yellowing may progress upward until only the newest leaves remain green. Growth is slow, new leaves are small, and the whole plant may be stunted. Nitrogen is easily leached from soil during regular watering. Of all the plant nutrients, it is the one most likely to be lacking in the soil.

SOLUTION: For a quick response, spray leaves with a foliar fertilizer. Fertilize plants with a soluable plant food, such as a 23-19-17 fertilizer. Add the fertilizer at regular intervals, as recommended on the label.

Salt Damage

Salt damage

PROBLEM: The leaf margins of plants with broad leaves or the leaf tips of plants with long, narrow leaves turn brown and brittle. This browning occurs on the older leaves first; but when the condition is severe, new leaves may also be affected. On some plants the older leaves may yellow and die. Salt damage is a common problem on container-grown plants. Salts can accumulate from water or from the use of fertilizers, or they may be present in the potting soil. Salts also accumulate faster if plants are not watered thoroughly.

SOLUTION: Leach excess salts from the soil by flushing with water as described on page 72. Never let a plant stand in the drainage water. If the plant is too large to lift, empty the saucer with a turkey baster. Do not overfertilize. Trim off dead stem tips with scissors.

Sunburn or Leaf Scorch

Sunburn

PROBLEM: Tan or brown dead patches develop on leaves exposed to direct sunlight. Leaf tissues may lighten or turn gray. In some cases the plant remains green but growth is stunted. Damage is most severe when the plant is allowed to dry out. Sunburn or leaf scorch occurs when a plant is exposed to more intense sunlight than it can tolerate. Plants that are grown in low light burn easily if they are suddenly moved to a sunny location.

SOLUTION: Move plants to a shaded spot or close curtains when the plant is exposed to direct sunlight. Prune off badly damaged leaves, or trim away damaged leaf areas to improve the appearance of the plant. Keep plants properly watered.

Too Much Water or Poor Drainage

Overwatering damage

PROBLEM: Plants fail to grow and may wilt. Leaves lose their glossiness and may become light green or yellow. An examination of the rootball reveals brown, mushy roots without white tips. The soil in the bottom of the pot may be soggy and have a foul odor. Plants may die.

SOLUTION: Discard severely wilted plants and those without white root tips. For plants that are less severely affected, do not water again until the soil is almost dry (barely moist). Prevent the problem by using a light soil with good drainage.

Water Spots

Water spots

PROBLEM: White to light yellow blotches in various patterns, including circles, occur on the older leaves. Small islands of green may be left between the discolored areas. Brown spots sometimes appear in the colored areas. Water spots are a common problem for African violets (*Saintpaulia*) and other fuzzy-leaved plants. They occur most commonly when cold water is splashed on the leaves while the plant is being watered.

SOLUTION: Avoid getting cold water on leaves when watering. Or use tepid water, which will not cause spotting if it touches the leaves. Spotted leaves will not recover. Pick them off if they are unsightly.

A Gallery of Houseplants

As a result of scientific research and dedication by both amateur gardeners and botanists, there is a dazzling array of houseplants available to you. "A Gallery of Houseplants" is a catalog of possibilities to help you choose and care for plants that suit both your horticultural fancy and your design ideas.

The listings are divided into three categories—flowering plants, foliage plants, and cacti and succulents. Since many favorite houseplants are not exclusively one or the other, you'll find them placed according to their most interesting feature. A few of the plants are listed in both the flowering and foliage plants sections.

Entries are in alphabetical order, by botanical name. Some plants are grouped by family and alphabetized under the family name. Bromeliads, citrus, gesneriads, and orchids are grouped in this way in the Flowering Houseplants section. Jasmines, cestrum, gelsemium, and trachelospermum are grouped together under Jasmines. In the Foliage Houseplants section, cissus, dracaenas, ferns, figs, palms, philodendrons, and spiderworts are grouped together.

Beneath the botanical name for each entry are the most familiar common names. These are followed by a description of and general information about the plant and its growth pattern. For family groups and some of the larger and more varied genera—dracaenas and begonias, for example—the introductory paragraphs cover the entire group. If you don't know a botanical name, use the index on pages 308 to 311 at the end of this chapter, which lists plants by common names first.

Each listing describes plant care requirements in the following categories: light, water, humidity, temperatures, fertilization, propagation, grooming, repotting, and problems. Use these care guides as a horticultural reference to help you select plants that fit your life-style and home.

Available in a variety of sizes, shapes, and even colors, houseplants fit into any decorating scheme.

Flowering Houseplants

Plants that produce beautiful flowers are extremely popular for indoor gardens. Care requirements for these plants may vary according to whether they are grown primarily for their flowers or for their foliage. The cultural information provided in this section promotes flowering.

Quite a few flowering houseplants are purchased as mature specimens already in bloom. Many of them are not well suited to being kept indoors after flowering, except in a greenhouse or solarium setting with a great deal of light, space, and humidity. These might be classified as plants used indoors while flowering. Some of the most common indoor plants, such as poinsettias, Easter lilies, and chrysanthemums, are in this category. In these cases, the care guides will help you to prolong the indoor life of a plant. The care guides generally describe the conditions necessary to keep the plants growing and bring them into bloom year after year.

Many bulbous plants that can be brought into flower indoors are included in this section of the gallery. Many bulbs can be placed almost anywhere indoors as decorative items when in bloom and then planted outdoors after flowering. Others need tending after flowering to initiate a dormancy period before they bloom again. Bulbous plants for flowering indoors are listed separately in the gallery. The individual care guides explain the requirements after flowering.

Abutilon hybridum

Abutilon
Abutilon, flowering-maple, Chinese-lantern

A tropical, viny shrub of the Hollyhock family, abutilon is extremely vigorous, growing several feet each year. Its bell-shaped flowers are striking, and its leaves, sometimes dappled with yellow or white, are shaped like a maple's. Its stems can be espaliered or trained onto a trellis.

The popularity of abutilon has spurred the development of hybrids with large blossoms in a wide range of colors. *A. hybridum* (Chinese-lantern) produces white, yellow, salmon, or purple blooms. *A. megapotamicum* 'Variegata' (trailing abutilon) features red and yellow blossoms with large, dark brown, pollen-bearing anthers. *A. pictum* 'Thompsonii' (formerly *A. striatum* 'Thompsonii') has an orange-salmon flower. Both *A. megapotamicum* 'Variegata' and *A. pictum* 'Thompsonii' have decorative yellow mottling on their leaves.

With bright, curtain-filtered light and moist soil, abutilon should grow rapidly and blossom most of the year. Fertilize monthly.

Light: Provide at least 4 hours of curtain-filtered sunlight from a bright south, east, or west window.

Water: Keep very moist, but do not allow to stand in water.

Humidity: Average indoor humidity levels.

Temperatures: 50° to 55° F at night, 65° to 70° F during the day.

Fertilization: Fertilize all year, more heavily in summer.

Propagation: Take cuttings from stems or shoots before they have hardened or matured.

Grooming: Because the plant grows so rapidly, pruning is a must for retaining its shape and size. Prune during the slow growth period in winter. Keep to desired height and shape with light pruning or clipping at any time.

Repotting: Repot in winter or early spring, as needed.

Problems: Dry soil or a high level of soluble salts may damage roots, causing plant to die back. If light is too low, plant will become spindly and weak.

Acalypha
Acalypha, copperleaf, beefsteak-plant, chenille-plant

Acalypha hispida is called the chenille-plant because its long plumes (more than 20 inches) of tiny, red flowers resemble chenille fringe. This plant blooms most heavily summer through fall, but will bloom the year around under good conditions. It needs light and warmth during blossoming. *A. wilkesiana* is usually grown for its distinctive leaves, which have red, copper, and pink tones that look like beefsteak. Winter flowers are tiny and not noteworthy. *A. repens*, a newer variety, is also becoming popular. Acalyphas are bushy plants that will get too big for indoor culture unless they are pruned several times a year.
Light: In winter, keep in direct sunlight for about 4 hours. In summer, provide curtain-filtered sunlight from a south or west window.
Water: Keep evenly moist. Water thoroughly and discard drainage.
Humidity: Average indoor humidity levels.
Temperatures: 55° to 60° F at night, 70° to 75° F during the day.
Fertilization: Fertilize only during late spring and summer months.
Propagation: Take cuttings from stems or shoots that have recently matured.
Grooming: Prune in early spring. Keep to desired height (2 or 3 feet is best) and shape with light pruning or clipping at any time. Give plant plenty of room.
Repotting: Repot infrequently. Plants need a large container for blooming and attaining proper form.
Problems: Leaves will drop if soil is too wet or too dry. If plant is in a draft or dry air, leaves will scorch.

Agapanthus
Agapanthus, blue African lily, lily-of-the-Nile

Agapanthuses are large plants, bearing clusters of lilylike blue or white flowers in summer. They bloom better when allowed to mature and get slightly pot bound. They need room and should not get too dry between waterings. The dwarf agapanthus (*A.* 'Peter Pan' and others) reaches a height of 8 to 12

inches and is well adapted to indoor growing. Most of the other species are approximately 2 feet tall.
Light: In winter, keep in direct sunlight for about 4 hours. In summer, provide curtain-filtered sunlight from a south or west window.
Water: Keep evenly moist. Water thoroughly and discard drainage.
Humidity: Average indoor humidity levels.
Temperatures: 50° to 55° F at night, 65° to 70° F during the day.
Fertilization: Fertilize only when plant is growing actively or flowering.
Propagation: Start new plants by dividing an old specimen. Seeds are available but can be more difficult than division.
Grooming: Pick off yellowed leaves.
Repotting: Repot infrequently.
Problems: Low light or soil that is too wet or too dry will cause leaves to yellow.

Allamanda
Allamanda, golden trumpet vine

Allamanda is a woody vine with large, fragrant, yellow blossoms in spring and summer. The plant needs warmth and lots of light. It will probably also need staking or training onto a trellis. *A. cathartica* is a vigorous climber that bears golden yellow flowers. It does well in a pot if vigorously pruned. Allamanda is occasionally available from specialist growers.
Light: Provide 4 hours or more of direct sunlight from a south window. Does best in a greenhouse setting.
Water: Keep evenly moist. Water thoroughly and discard drainage. In winter, keep plant a little drier, watering less frequently.
Humidity: Requires moist air. Use a humidifier for best results.
Temperatures: 55° to 60° F at night, 70° to 75° F during the day.
Fertilization: Fertilize only during late spring and summer months.
Propagation: Take cuttings from stems or shoots before they have hardened or matured.
Grooming: Pinch back new stem tips, being careful not to pinch off flower buds.
Repotting: New plants have to grow in a medium to large pot until almost root bound before they will bloom.

Acalypha hispida

Allamanda neriifolia
Agapanthus 'Peter Pan White'

Anthurium scherzeranum
Aphelandra squarrosa

Transplant into larger pots as needed.
Problems: Plant will not bloom if light is too low. In a draft or dry air, leaves will scorch. Susceptible to mealybugs.

Anthurium
Anthurium, flamingo-flower, tailflower

Anthuriums are among the best-known tropical flowers. Blossoms on *A. andraeanum* are long lasting and often used in weddings on Hawaii and other Pacific islands. They are popular in cut-flower arrangements around the world. The red or orange portion of the bloom is actually a bract (modified leaf); the tiny flowers appear on the spike, or spadix. New, everblooming varieties, such as 'Lady Jane' and 'Southern Blush', are now widely available.

Most anthuriums are large. *A. scherzeranum* is a small species, more suited for indoor or greenhouse culture. Keep anthuriums in humid air and fertilize them well when they are growing actively.
Light: Provide at least 4 hours of curtain-filtered sunlight from a bright south, east, or west window.
Water: Keep evenly moist. Water thoroughly and discard drainage.
Humidity: Requires moist air. Use a humidifier for best results.
Temperatures: 55° to 60° F at night, 70° to 75° F during the day.
Fertilization: Fertilize lightly throughout the growing season.
Propagation: Remove plantlets or rooted side shoots as they form.
Grooming: Mound up soil as high crowns form. Remove aerial roots.
Repotting: Leave room at the top to mound up soil as crown develops. Repot infrequently.
Problems: In a draft or dry air, leaves will scorch. Will not bloom if light is too low.

Aphelandra squarrosa
Aphelandra, zebra-plant

For 6 weeks in the fall, aphelandra provides an impressive, orderly display of color: large, conical, deep yellow flowers emerge from golden bracts. This small, evergreen shrub, a favorite of Victorian conservatories, also has unusual foliage—dark, elliptical leaves striped with ivory veins that create a zebra effect. The variety 'Louisae', the most

readily available cultivar, is compact with relatively small leaves. 'Apollo White' and 'Dania' are even more compact and produce leaves with striking vein patterns.

Aphelandra tends to become gangly. To combat this, cut it back after flowering, letting 1 or 2 pairs of leaves remain. Feed when the plant is growing actively or flowering, never allow the rootball to dry out, and keep the plant warm in winter.
Light: Place in a bright south, east, or west window with indirect sunlight.
Water: Keep very moist during growth and flowering; at other times keep evenly moist. Water thoroughly and discard drainage.
Humidity: Requires moist air. Use a humidifier for best results.
Temperatures: 55° to 60° F at night, 70° to 75° F during the day.
Fertilization: Fertilize only when plant is growing actively or flowering.
Propagation: Take cuttings from stems or shoots that have recently matured.
Grooming: Prune in early spring.
Repotting: Repot in winter or early spring, as needed.
Problems: If plant is in a draft or dry air, leaves will scorch. Leaves will drop if soil is too wet or too dry.

Ardisia
Ardisia, coralberry

Ardisias are woody ornamental shrubs that grow outdoors in warm climates. Their red berries at Christmastime make them particularly popular. The foliage is shiny and waxy, with small, fragrant, white or pink flowers. As indoor plants, they must have good light in winter. Cut them back severely in late winter, keeping them dry until they begin to grow. Keep only the strongest shoots, and train them to grow upward. Many gardeners place ardisias in shaded patio gardens during summer, to ensure better fruiting for the holidays.
Light: In winter, keep in direct sunlight for about 4 hours. In summer, provide curtain-filtered sunlight from a south or west window.
Water: Keep evenly moist. Water thoroughly and discard drainage.
Humidity: Requires moist air. Use a humidifier for best results.

Temperatures: 50° to 55° F at night, 60° to 65° F during the day.
Fertilization: Fertilize only during late spring and summer months.
Propagation: Take cuttings from stems or shoots before they have hardened or matured. Seeds are available, but can be more difficult than cuttings.
Grooming: Prune just before the heavy blossoming period, being careful not to cut off flower buds.
Repotting: Repot infrequently.
Problems: Susceptible to spider mites, especially if plant is dry, and to scale. If plant is in a draft or dry air, leaves will scorch. Dry soil or a high level of soluble salts may damage roots, causing plant to die back. Will not bloom if light is too low.

Azalea

See **_Rhododendron_**.

Begonia

The begonia family contains more than 1,500 known species, offering a vast array of beautiful flowers, foliage shapes, and colors. Moreover, begonias are adaptable to almost any indoor environment. Many begonias are grown primarily for their foliage. This section describes some flowering varieties. Florists and garden centers offer many of these plants already in bloom for home decoration.

With a minimum of trouble, you should be able to keep your begonias healthy and blooming all year. In general, plenty of bright light, an average indoor temperature that drops slightly at night, and light applications of fertilizer will ensure constant blooms. Begonias are sensitive to overwatering, so take care to use soil that is rich in organic matter and drains well.

Begonia × cheimantha
Christmas begonia, Lorraine begonia

Begonia × cheimantha hybrids are popular because they bloom profusely in winter. They are bushy, dwarf plants, most frequently used in hanging baskets because the stems tend to arch outward attractively. Given enough light, Christmas begonias become covered with pink or white single flowers on long stems, or racemes. Since they bloom in winter, be sure to provide enough light and warmth and keep them evenly moist. After flowering, the plants become semidormant until late spring. Keep them drier during this period.
Light: Provide at least 4 hours of curtain-filtered sunlight from a bright south, east, or west window.
Water: Keep very moist during growth and flowering; at other times, allow to dry between waterings.
Humidity: Average indoor humidity levels.
Temperatures: 65° to 70° at night, 75° to 80° F during the day.
Fertilization: Fertilize only when plant is growing actively or flowering.
Propagation: Take stem cuttings at any time.
Grooming: Prune after flowering has ended, being careful not to remove flower buds.
Repotting: Cut back and repot when flowering stops.
Problems: Subject to crown rot in overly moist conditions. Leaves will drop if soil is too wet or too dry. Some varieties may get powdery mildew.

Begonia × hiemalis
Rieger begonia, hiemalis begonia, elatior begonia

Hiemalis begonias originated through hybridization of a winter-flowering begonia with hardy and vigorous tuberous begonias. Many varieties are available in florist shops. Hiemalis begonias are low growing and exceptionally bushy. Many are pendulous and are used in hanging baskets. Some of the newer cultivars have bronze or red foliage. The flowers are usually large and double; they come in yellow, red, white, and orange. Hiemalis begonias prefer cooler locations than most begonias, but do not like drafts. Give them plenty of light during their winter flowering period. These plants are hard to maintain through the summer and are often best treated as temporary flowering plants, to be discarded when blooming ceases.
Light: Provide at least 4 hours of curtain-filtered sunlight from a bright south, east, or west window.
Water: Keep evenly moist. Water thoroughly and discard drainage.
Humidity: Average indoor humidity levels.
Temperatures: 50° to 55° F at night, 65° to 70° F during the day.
Fertilization: Fertilize all year, more heavily in summer.

Begonia × hiemalis

Ardisia crispa

Begonia × semperflorens-cultorum

Bougainvillea 'Raspberry Ice'

Begonia × tuberhybrida 'Nonstop Orange'

Propagation: Take stem cuttings at any time.
Grooming: Pinch back new stem tips to improve form. Keep to desired height and shape with light pruning or clipping at any time. Be careful not to remove flower buds when pruning.
Repotting: Cut back and repot when flowering stops.
Problems: Subject to crown rot in overly moist conditions. Some cultivars are susceptible to powdery mildew.

Begonia × *semperflorens-cultorum*

Wax begonia, fibrous-rooted begonia

Wax begonias are the most popular of the fibrous-rooted begonia species. Many cultivars and hybrids exist. They are bushy plants with shiny, waxy, heart-shaped leaves. Given ample light, they bloom profusely in a variety of colors. Wax begonias are most commonly used as outdoor bedding annuals or in hanging baskets for patio gardens. However, they will flourish indoors with light fertilization, good light, and sufficient warmth.
Light: Provide at least 4 hours of curtain-filtered sunlight from a bright south, east, or west window.
Water: Keep evenly moist. Water thoroughly and discard drainage.
Humidity: Requires moist air. Use a humidifier for best results.
Temperatures: 65° to 70° F at night, 75° to 80° F during the day.
Fertilization: Fertilize lightly throughout the growing season.
Propagation: Take stem cuttings at any time. Seeds are available, but can be more difficult than cuttings.
Grooming: Pinch back new stem tips to improve form. Keep plant to desired height and shape with light pruning or clipping at any time. Be careful not to remove flower buds when pruning.
Repotting: Cut back and repot when flowering stops.
Problems: Subject to crown rot in overly moist conditions. If plant is in a draft or dry air, leaves will scorch. If light is too low, plant will get spindly and weak. Watch for mealybugs and powdery mildew.

Begonia × *tuberhybrida*

Tuberous begonia

Cultivars of tuberous begonias produce the largest flowers of all begonias grown indoors. Most are large plants that need good light, cool temperatures, and moist soil and air. It is best to buy a mature tuber, plant it, enjoy a flowering period, and then discard it or place it in the garden. Older plants tend to get spindly and weak indoors.
Light: Provide at least 4 hours of direct sunlight in winter. Provide curtain-filtered sunlight in summer, from a south or west window.
Water: Keep very moist at all times, but do not allow to stand in water.
Humidity: Use a humidifier for best results.
Temperatures: 50° to 55° F at night, 60° to 65° F during the day.
Fertilization: Fertilize lightly. Do not fertilize when in flower.
Propagation: Start new plants from the bulblets that develop beside the parent.
Grooming: Discard after flowering.
Repotting: Not usually done.
Problems: Subject to crown rot in overly moist conditions. Leaves will scorch if plant is in a draft or dry air.

Bougainvillea glabra

Bougainvillea

Bougainvilleas are among the most popular and most beautiful flowering shrubs in warm climates. Indoors, they must be pruned and trained to be manageable. They will probably not bloom in winter unless they are in a warm greenhouse. These plants can sometimes be purchased from a florist.
Light: Does best in a greenhouse setting.
Water: Let plant approach dryness before watering, then water thoroughly and discard drainage.
Humidity: Requires moist air. Use a humidifier for best results.
Temperatures: 55° to 60° F at night, 70° to 75° F during the day.
Fertilization: Fertilize only during late spring and summer months.
Propagation: Take cuttings from stems or shoots before they have hardened or matured. Seeds are available, but can be more difficult than cuttings. Root cuttings are another option.

Grooming: Prune after flowering.
Repotting: Repot in winter or early spring, as needed.
Problems: Will not bloom if light is too low. Poor drainage, too-frequent watering, or standing in water will cause root rot. Susceptible to mealybugs.

Bromeliads

Many gardeners have discovered that although bromeliads have exotic tropical foliage and flowers, they are not difficult to grow indoors. The most distinctive feature of bromeliads is the cup-shaped rosette of leaves, which holds the water that nourishes the plant. In some varieties, flowers and large, colorful bracts emerge from the center, creating a spectacular display. The bracts are modified leaves that grow from the same axils as the flowers. Originating in the tropics, most bromeliads are epiphytes (air plants). They grow suspended in trees and on rocks in their native habitat, gathering moisture and nutrients from rainfall and particles in the air.

Bromeliads are available in flower in many florist shops and garden centers. Display them in pots or hanging baskets, or attach them to boards. If you decide to keep them in pots, use a light soil that drains easily and pots that look a little small. Too-large containers and overwatering can be fatal to their small root system. When growing these plants in a pot, water mainly by filling the rosette, but don't forget to moisten the potting mix occasionally as well. Bromeliads need lots of sun and high temperatures to bloom. If you're having trouble inducing a bromeliad to flower, place it in a plastic bag with a ripe apple for a few days. The ethylene gas from the apple will initiate flower buds. When the plant stops flowering, the rosette starts to die, a slow process that can last as long as 3 years. Planting the offsets that form at the base of the plant will give you a collection that blooms year after year.

There are more than 2,000 bromeliad species. Some are grown for their flowers, others for their foliage. The following are particularly suitable for an indoor garden.

Aechmea
Living-vaseplant, urnplant, coralberry

The most common aechmea is *Aechmea fasciata* (living-vaseplant, urnplant). Its broad, thick leaves are mottled with gray and sea-green stripes and its conical rosette of pink bracts and large, dark blue flowers creates a splendid effect. An upright rosette of thick, silver-banded leaves distinguishes the striking *A. chantinii.* Its flowers last for several months.

A. fulgens discolor, commonly known as the coralberry, has broad leaves that are green on top and purple underneath. The contrast in the foliage is heightened by the purple flower. Red berries form after the flower dies.

Ananas comosus
Pineapple, ivory pineapple

If you know what a pineapple is, then you know an ananas. Pineapples are the fruit of *A. comosus.* You can grow one by cutting off a piece of the fruit along with the tuft (the crown of leaves at the top of the plant), planting it in a pot of soil, and placing it in full sun. Narrow, gray-green leaves with prickly ribbing on the side will form a striking rosette. The pineapple fruit will spring from the center for an unusual display, but this will happen only after several years. *A. comosus* 'Variegatus' (ivory pineapple) has the more attractive foliage.

Billbergia
Vaseplant, queen's-tears

Vaseplants are among the easiest bromeliads to grow, but they flower for only a short time. *B. nutans* (queen's-tears) has grassy, gray-green leaves and an arching spray of pink and green flowers. *B. pyramidalis* and *B. pyramidalis striata* sport long, green, strap leaves, bright red bracts tipped with violet, and upright, scarlet flowers with yellow stamens.

Cryptanthus
Earthstar, starfish-plant, rainbow-star

Called earthstars because of the shape of their rosettes, these plants are small and show great variation in leaf color, making them attractive plants for small spaces or dish gardens. *C. acaulis* (starfish-plant) has small, wavy-edged leaves in varying shades of yellow and green.

Bromeliad: *Aechmea fasciata*

Bromeliad: *Ananas comosus*

Bromeliad: *Billbergia vittata*

Bromeliad: *Dyckia fosterana*

Bromeliad: *Guzmania lingulata*

Bromeliad: *Neoregelia*
Bromeliad: *Cryptanthus*

Bromeliad: *Nidularium procerum*

C. bromelioides tricolor (rainbow-star) displays a colorful array of stripes down the length of its wavy leaves. *C. zonatus* (zebra-plant) resembles zebra skin, banded in ivory and shades of brown. *C. bivittatus* has green leaves with creamy white stripes. Some of the common hybrids of *C. bivittatus* include 'Starlite', 'It', and 'Pink Starlite'.

Dyckia species
Dyckia

Dyckias are slow-growing, medium-sized bromeliads with dark green, spiny foliage. In bright light during summer, the plants will produce orange flowers on spikes. One popular species is *D. brevifolia.*

Guzmania
Guzmania

The vase-shaped rosettes of guzmanias can grow to 20 inches wide. They bloom from late winter to summer, depending on the species. The true flowers are small but are surrounded by large, showy bracts in reds, yellows, or oranges. *G. lingulata,* a popular species, has brightly colored bracts ranging from red to yellow, and white flowers.

Neoregelia
Blushing bromeliad,
painted-fingernail-plant

Neoregelias produce large rosettes of thick, shiny leaves. When mature, *N. carolinae* 'Tricolor' (blushing bromeliad) reaches a diameter of 30 inches. Lightly toothed leaves, variegated in cream and green, jut out in an orderly pattern. Just before flowering, the young leaves in the center turn bright red. *N. spectabilis* features green leaves with pink-tipped ends, inspiring the name *painted-fingernail-plant.*

Nidularium
Bird's-nest bromeliad

The center of the leaf rosette of nidulariums changes color many weeks before the flowers appear. Various species are available with foliage of different shades and patterns. Among the most popular is *N. innocentii,* with its small, red leaves that cradle white flowers at the center. The plants will tolerate moderate light, but may bloom only in bright light.

Tillandsia
Tillandsia, air plant, Spanish moss

Many species of tillandsias are available to indoor gardeners. Even the *T. usneoides* (Spanish moss) commonly seen as an epiphyte in the South is occasionally grown indoors. Most tillandsias have narrow, arching foliage, either like grass leaves or palm leaves. Some of the smaller species are popular as hanging plants or dish-garden plants. Sword-shaped flower spikes appear in summer. *T. cyanea* has a rosette of bright green leaves, deep pink or red bracts, and violet blue flowers. *T. ionantha* has miniature silver gray leaves and violet flowers.

Vriesea
Vriesea, flaming-sword

The genus *Vriesea* features many plants attractive for both their foliage and flowers. *V. splendens,* a popular variety, forms a rosette of wide, purple-banded leaves. The common name, flaming-sword, refers to the flower, a long spike of red bracts and yellow flowers. The bloom will last for several weeks.

Care of Bromeliads

Light: Abundant light. An east or west window is best. Ananas and Dyckia require full sun.
Water: Always keep the cup of rosette-type bromeliads filled with water (preferably rainwater), changing it occasionally. Allow plants growing in pots to dry out, then water lightly so that they are barely moist. Overwatering and poor drainage will kill bromeliads. Spray epiphytic bromeliads not growing in pots with warm water regularly.
Humidity: Dry air is generally not harmful.
Temperatures: Average constant temperatures of 65° to 70° F are fine for foliage types and plants in flower. Warmer temperatures (75° to 80° F) are needed to initiate flower buds.
Fertilization: Fertilize lightly once a year, in early spring.
Propagation: Remove mature offsets and a sizable section of roots from large plants and pot shallowly in light soil. Keep warm.
Grooming: Wash leaves occasionally.

Repotting: Rarely necessary.
Problems: Brown areas on leaves usually indicate sunburn; move plant out of direct sunlight. Brown tips on leaves result from dry air. Watch for scale and mealybugs on foliage and flowers.

Browallia
Browallia, sapphire-flower

Browallia is a woody plant usually grown in a hanging basket, since its shoots tend to spread and trail. In a regular pot, it will need pruning and staking. Given enough light, the plant will bear blue or white, medium-sized flowers all year. In winter, keep it watered with room-temperature water and continue to fertilize it lightly until it has finished flowering.
Light: In winter, keep in about 4 hours of direct sunlight. In summer, provide curtain-filtered sunlight from a south or west window.
Water: Keep very moist at all times, but do not allow to stand in water.
Humidity: Requires moist air. Use a humidifier for best results.
Temperatures: 55° to 60° F at night, 70° to 75° F during the day.
Fertilization: Fertilize all year, more heavily in summer.
Propagation: Start from seeds. Sow in a small pot and transplant seedlings as needed. Or take cuttings from stems or shoots that have recently matured.
Grooming: Prune after flowering.
Repotting: Repot each year, in early summer, for best growth.
Problems: If plant is in a draft or dry air, leaves will scorch. Will not bloom if light is too low. Susceptible to whiteflies.

Brunfelsia
Yesterday-today-and-tomorrow

The common name for brunfelsia comes from the fact that as it ages, its flowers change from dark purple to almost white. The mildly fragrant, medium-sized flowers grow in clusters almost all year long if they have plenty of light. They need a moderate rest period in late spring.
Light: In winter, keep in direct sunlight for about 4 hours. In summer, provide curtain-filtered sunlight from a south or west window.

Bromeliad: *Tillandsia cyanea*

Bromeliad: *Vriesea splendens*

Browallia speciosa 'Major'

Brunfelsia pauciflora var. *calycina*

Calliandra haematocephala
Calceolaria crenatiflora

Water: Keep very moist during growth and flowering; at other times, allow to dry between waterings.
Humidity: Average indoor humidity levels.
Temperatures: 50° to 55° F at night, 65° to 70° F during the day.
Fertilization: Fertilize only when plant is growing actively or flowering.
Propagation: Take cuttings from stems or shoots before they have hardened or matured.
Grooming: Prune well in early spring. Pinch back new stem tips to improve form. Be careful not to destroy flower buds when pruning.
Repotting: Cut back and repot when flowering stops.
Problems: Will get spindly and weak if light is too low. Dry soil or high level of soluble salts may damage roots, causing plant to die back.

Calceolaria crenatiflora
Calceolaria, pocketbook-flower, slipper-flower

The intricate flowers of calceolaria (often sold as *Calceolaria herbeohybrida*) are shaped like a sac. Cultivars come in many colors, including red, pink, maroon, and yellow. Most have purple or brown markings on the petals. The plants are difficult to grow from seeds because they are sensitive to improper watering and fertilizing. They like cool nights and are suited to a small greenhouse or window box. Before they flower, pinch back stems to train them into bushy plants.
Light: Blooming plants can be placed anywhere. Growing plants need curtain-filtered sunlight in summer and direct sunlight in winter.
Water: Keep evenly moist. Water thoroughly and discard drainage.
Humidity: Requires moist air. Use a humidifier for best results.
Temperatures: 40° to 45° F at night, 60° to 65° F during the day.
Fertilization: Fertilize lightly throughout the growing season. Do not fertilize blooming plants.
Propagation: Start from seeds. Sow in a small pot and transplant seedlings as needed.
Grooming: Pinch back new stem tips to improve form, stopping when the flowering period approaches. Discard after flowering.

Repotting: Transplant seedlings several times, as they grow.
Problems: Subject to crown rot if planted deeply, watered over the crown, or watered late in the day. If plant is in a draft or dry air, leaves will scorch. Susceptible to whiteflies.

Calliandra
Calliandra, powder-puff, flame bush

Given lots of sunlight, calliandras will produce large, red, or pink flower heads with many stamens, resembling powder puffs. They are winter-flowering, bushy shrubs. Their compound leaves are like the honeylocust's. Calliandras will get quite large and should be pruned to a height of 3 feet. Because they need warmth and light, they are best suited for greenhouses or solariums. Usually available only from specialist nurseries.
Light: Provide 4 hours or more of direct sunlight from a south window. Does best in a greenhouse setting.
Water: Let plant approach dryness before watering, then water thoroughly and discard drainage.
Humidity: Requires moist air. Use a humidifier for best results.
Temperatures: 65° to 70° F at night, 75° to 80° F during the day.
Fertilization: Fertilize only during late spring and summer.
Propagation: Take cuttings from stems or shoots that have recently matured.
Grooming: Prune in early spring. Keep to desired height and shape with light pruning or clipping at any time.
Repotting: Repot in winter or early spring, as needed.
Problems: Will get spindly and weak if light is too low.

Camellia
Camellia

Camellias are evergreen shrubs with dark green, glossy leaves. In spring they produce large, fragrant flowers in shades of white, pink, or red. *C. japonica*, a species commonly grown indoors, has more than 2,000 cultivars in a variety of colors, sizes, and shapes.

This is basically a plant for cool greenhouses or outdoor use in moderate climates; it requires a set of exacting conditions to succeed indoors. A cool room with good air circulation is a must. When buds appear in winter or spring, do not move the plant, and guard against fluctuations in temperature and soil moisture or the buds will drop.

Light: Keep in about 4 hours of direct sunlight in winter. Provide curtain-filtered sunlight in summer, from a south or west window.

Water: Keep evenly moist. Water thoroughly and discard drainage.

Humidity: Average indoor humidity levels.

Temperatures: 40° to 45° F at night, 60° to 65° F during the day.

Fertilization: Use an acid-based fertilizer during late spring and summer, and add trace elements once in spring.

Propagation: Take cuttings from stems or shoots that have recently matured.

Grooming: Prune after flowering. Pinch back new stem tips to improve form. Be careful not to remove flower buds when pruning.

Repotting: Repot infrequently.

Problems: If plant is in a draft or dry air, leaves will scorch. Leaves will drop if soil is too wet or too dry. Somewhat susceptible to mealybugs and, to a lesser degree, to scale.

Campanula
Campanula, star-of-Bethlehem, bellflower

Campanulas are small, bushy plants that bear an abundance of flowers from August through November. The flowers are purple, blue, or white, and many species have bell-like flowers, giving the plant one of its common names. *C. isophylla* and *C. isophylla* 'Alba' have heart-shaped leaves and hanging stems up to 2 feet long. Many indoor gardeners prefer to plant campanula in a small hanging basket.

Light: Keep in about 4 hours of direct sunlight in winter. Provide curtain-filtered sunlight in summer, from a south or west window.

Water: Keep very moist during growth and flowering; at other times, allow to dry between waterings.

Humidity: Average indoor humidity levels.

Temperatures: 50° to 55° F at night, 65° to 70° F during the day.

Fertilization: Fertilize only during late spring and summer.

Propagation: Take cuttings from stems or shoots before they have hardened or matured.

Grooming: Cut back in late fall or early winter, as needed. Pinch back new stem tips for 6 to 8 weeks to improve form, being careful not to remove flower buds.

Repotting: Repot in winter or early spring, as needed.

Problems: If plant is in a draft or dry air, leaves will scorch. Poor drainage, too-frequent watering, or standing in water will cause root rot. Subject to crown rot in overly moist conditions.

Capsicum
Ornamental pepper

Ornamental peppers are not particularly noteworthy until they become loaded with fruit in late summer and fall. Since it takes very good light to accomplish heavy blossoming and fruit set, ornamental peppers are best suited for greenhouse culture. The fruit changes from green to yellow to its final coloration—usually bright red—as it matures. Even small plants set fruit. They make attractive tabletop or windowsill decorations. The fruit is edible, but being a chili pepper, it is extremely hot. Keep away from small children.

Light: Provide 4 hours or more of direct sunlight from a south window. Does best in a greenhouse setting.

Water: Keep evenly moist. Water thoroughly and discard drainage.

Humidity: Average indoor humidity levels.

Temperatures: 55° to 60° F at night, 70° to 75° F during the day.

Fertilization: Fertilize only when plant is growing actively or flowering.

Propagation: Start from seeds. Sow in a small pot and transplant seedlings as needed.

Grooming: Prune in spring. Pinch out new stem tips to improve form. Be careful not to remove flower buds when pruning. Discard after fruiting.

Repotting: Repot in winter or early spring, as needed.

Problems: Will not bloom if light is too low. Leaves will drop if soil is too wet or too dry. Susceptible to aphids and spider mites.

Camellia japonica 'Debutant'

Campanula isophylla

Capsicum annuum

Carissa macrocarpa

Chrysanthemum frutescens

Chrysanthemum × morifolium

Carissa macrocarpa
Natal plum

Dwarf cultivars of Natal plum (sometimes sold as *Carissa grandiflora*) do well in greenhouses or solariums and are popular indoor bonsai subjects. They produce abundant foliage on woody stems. Their large, white flowers are fragrant and are followed by red, plumlike fruits. These are edible, but have a bitter, cranberry taste. Fruit and blossoms appear together on the plant at certain times of the year. Keep Natal plums pruned to between 2 and 3 feet to prevent legginess. Though you may find the plant in outdoor nurseries in the South, it is usually available only from specialty growers elsewhere.

Light: Provide 4 hours or more of direct sunlight from a south window. Does best in a greenhouse setting.

Water: Keep evenly moist. Water thoroughly and discard drainage.

Humidity: Average indoor humidity levels.

Temperatures: 55° to 60° F at night, 70° to 75° F during the day.

Fertilization: Fertilize lightly throughout the growing season.

Propagation: Take stem cuttings at any time.

Grooming: Keep to desired height and shape with light pruning or clipping at any time.

Repotting: Repot in winter or early spring, as needed.

Problems: Will get spindly and weak if light is too low.

Chrysanthemum frutescens
Marguerite, Boston daisy, Paris daisy

Marguerites are vigorous growers that produce yellow or white flowers intermittently throughout the year. Their lacy foliage has a distinctive aroma. The plants need lots of light to grow indoors. They tend to look rangy if not clipped. Keep them well branched and approximately 12 inches tall. Replace them when they get weak and spindly.

Light: Provide 4 hours or more of direct sunlight from a south window. Does best in a greenhouse setting.

Water: Keep evenly moist. Water thoroughly and discard drainage.

Humidity: Average indoor humidity levels.

Temperatures: 40° to 45° F at night, 60° to 65° F during the day.

Fertilization: Fertilize all year, more heavily in summer.

Propagation: Take stem cuttings at any time.

Grooming: Pinch back new stem tips to improve form, being careful not to remove flower buds. Start new plants to replace old specimens when they get weak.

Repotting: Repot at any time.

Problems: Spider mites can be a problem, especially if plant is too dry. Will not bloom, and will get spindly and weak, if light is too low.

Chrysanthemum × morifolium
Florist's chrysanthemum, florist's mum

Greenhouse hybrid chrysanthemums, or florist's chrysanthemums, are often given as gifts. They are considered houseplants because they are usually purchased while blooming, for display indoors. They can be transplanted into the garden, but are difficult to grow outdoors. Think of florist's mums as cut flowers that last a long time.

Commercial growers apply dwarfing chemicals to the plants and ensure year-round production by placing them in the dark to induce flowering during the long days of spring and summer. The large flowers come in every color of bloom except blue.

Look for plants with a few open blossoms and plenty of buds. Place the plant in a cool room on a windowsill where it will receive about 4 hours of direct sun daily. Morning or evening sun is best. It should bloom for 6 to 8 weeks.

Florist's mums are usually discarded after flowering, but if you want to save the plant, prune it back and reduce watering; then plant it in the garden. Without growth retardants, it will probably become quite leggy. Pinch it back often to maintain a full, bushy plant. Florist's mums are not hardy in cold climates and need to be indoors in a cold but frost-free room for winter.

Light: Place in a bright south, east, or west window.

Water: Keep evenly moist. Water thoroughly and discard drainage.

Humidity: Average indoor humidity levels.

Temperatures: 50° to 55° F at night, 60° to 65° F during the day.

Fertilization: Do not fertilize when in flower. Fertilize lightly at other times.

Propagation: Take cuttings from stems or shoots before they have hardened or matured.

Grooming: Discard after flowering.

Repotting: Not usually done.

Problems: Spider mites can be a problem, especially if plant is too dry.

Citrus
Citrus

Plants in the citrus family have something for all seasons: shiny, dark green foliage; attractively scented, white flowers that appear intermittently throughout the year; and colorful, long-lasting fruits. The latter range in color from green to yellow or orange, depending on the species and the maturity of the fruit. Often fruits at various stages of development and color are found on the plant at the same time. All citrus are shrubby plants that normally become large with time, but they can be kept in check with regular pruning. Avoid trimming off branches with flowers or buds if you want a crop of fruit. Some citrus bear numerous thorns; others are mostly or entirely thornless.

Citrus fruits produced indoors tend to be sour or bitter and cannot be eaten fresh. They can, however, be used in any recipe that calls for citrus: marmalades, candies, and so on. To ensure fruit production indoors, pass from flower to flower, dusting each with a small paintbrush.

Growing citrus from store-bought fruit is a popular pastime. Sow the seeds in small pots in a moist growing medium, and cover with plastic wrap. Place the pot in a warm, brightly lit spot. The seedlings will appear in 2 or 3 weeks and become attractive, long-lived foliage plants. It is unlikely that plants raised from store-bought fruit will ever flower or produce fruit indoors, as the parent plants were selected for outdoor conditions. For good fruit production, start new plants from stem cuttings of selections that do bloom well indoors or buy plants that are already in bloom. The latter can be expensive, but they give quick results; young plants can be years away from flowering.

The best choice for indoor growing is × *Citrofortunella mitis,* actually a cross between *Citrus reticulata* (mandarin orange) and the closely related genus *Fortunella* (calamondin or miniature orange) so commonly seen in garden centers and florist shops. It blooms and produces fruit the year around. It also remains nicely compact with only minimal pruning. *Citrus limon* 'Meyer' (meyer lemon) is also productive indoors, bearing yellow fruits identical to store-bought lemons. *C. limon* 'Ponderosa' (ponderosa lemon), another good choice, produces enormous fruits with a thick, rough skin, usually only one or two at a time. Occasionally, *C. sinensis* cultivars (sweet oranges) are also offered. They require ideal conditions to produce fruit indoors. Another citrus worth noting is *Fortunella margarita* (kumquat), which produces small, orange-yellow, oblong fruits.

Light: Provide 4 hours or more of direct sunlight from a south window. Does best in a greenhouse setting.

Water: Let plant approach dryness before watering; then water thoroughly and discard drainage each time.

Humidity: Average indoor humidity levels.

Temperatures: 50° to 55° F at night, 65° to 70° F during the day.

Fertilization: Use an acid-based fertilizer. Add trace elements once a year, in spring.

Propagation: Take stem cuttings at any time.

Grooming: Keep to desired height and shape with light pruning or clipping at any time.

Repotting: Repot infrequently.

Problems: Will not bloom if light is too low. Leaves will drop if soil is too wet or too dry. Subject to infestations of mealybugs, scale, and spider mites. Lack of trace elements (particularly iron) may cause leaf yellowing.

Clerodendrum
Clerodendrum, glorybower, bleeding-heart

Clerodendrums are actually woody shrubs that get quite large when growing outdoors. The most popular cultivar is *C. thomsoniae,* which inspired the name "bleeding-heart" because of its beautiful and intricate white and red flowers. It is often found in florist shops. The flowers cluster on trailing stems, so the plant is commonly used in

Citrus limon 'Lisbon'

Fortunella margarita 'Nagami'
Citrus × *limonia* 'Rangpoor'

Clerodendrum thomsoniae

Clivia miniata

Crinum 'Cape Dawn'

hanging baskets. Keep clerodendrums warm and give them plenty of room.

Light: Provide at least 4 hours of curtain-filtered sunlight from a bright south, east, or west window.

Water: Keep very moist during growth and flowering; at other times, allow to dry between waterings.

Humidity: Average indoor humidity levels.

Temperatures: 55° to 60° F at night, 70° to 75° F during the day.

Fertilization: Fertilize only during late spring and summer.

Propagation: Take cuttings from stems or shoots before they have hardened or matured.

Grooming: Prune after flowering. Pinch back new stem tips to improve form. Be careful not to remove flower buds when pruning.

Repotting: Repot infrequently.

Problems: Spider mites can be a problem, especially if plant gets too dry. Also susceptible to mealybugs. Poor drainage, too-frequent watering, or standing in water will cause root rot.

Clivia miniata
Kaffir-lily

A herbaceous plant, *Clivia miniata* is a member of the amaryllis family and is named after Charlotte Clive, Duchess of Northumberland, who developed it in 1866 as an indoor plant. Thick stems 12 to 15 inches long emerge from a crown of leathery, strap leaves and support large clusters of orange, trumpet-shaped flowers with yellow throats. French and Belgian hybrids bloom in yellow to deep red-orange. After flowers fade in late spring, ornamental red berries form and add a touch of lasting color.

This winter bloomer does well in a room that receives plenty of indirect sunlight and cools down during the night. Houses in cold climates are most suitable. Crowded roots that are left undisturbed for years produce the best blooms; repotting is rarely necessary.

Light: Provide at least 4 hours of curtain-filtered sunlight from a bright south, east, or west window.

Water: Keep very moist during growth and flowering; at other times, allow to dry between waterings.

Humidity: Average indoor humidity levels.

Temperatures: 50° to 55° F at night, 60° to 65° F during the day in fall and winter. Normal room temperatures are fine during spring and summer.

Fertilization: Fertilize only when plant is growing actively or flowering. During fall the plant rests; apply no fertilizer and reduce water. From January to August, fertilize monthly.

Propagation: Start new plants from the plantlets that develop beside the parent bulb.

Grooming: Pick off yellowed leaves. Cut flower stalks if you wish.

Repotting: Repot infrequently.

Problems: Subject to crown rot if planted deeply, watered over the crown, or watered late in the day.

Crinum
Crinum, Bengal lily, milk-and-wine-lily

Crinums are one of the largest bulb plants grown indoors. The pink, red, or white flowers are fragrant and sometimes 6 inches across. They are borne in clusters on top of a 3-foot stalk. The leaves are narrow and 4 feet long. Crinum is a magnificent plant, and needs a lot of room. It flowers indoors in spring and summer, although it can also bloom in autumn. Keep it well lit, moist, and fertilized from spring until October, and give it a moderately dry resting period during winter.

Light: Provide curtain-filtered sunlight in summer, from a south or a west window.

Water: Keep very moist during growth and flowering; at other times, allow to dry between waterings.

Humidity: Average indoor humidity levels.

Temperatures: 50° to 55° F at night, 65° to 70° F during the day.

Fertilization: Fertilize only when plant is growing actively or flowering.

Propagation: Start new plants from the bulblets that develop beside the parent bulb.

Grooming: Remove old leaves as plant goes dormant. Cut flower stalks after blooming if you wish. Give plant plenty of room.

Repotting: Repot infrequently.

Problems: No significant problems.

Crocus
Crocus

Crocuses, because of their small size, make an excellent midwinter-flowering pot plant. Florists often sell them in bloom in winter. Since the plants usually grow only a few inches tall, they look best in a broad, shallow pot, planted in clumps. Crocuses are available in many colors and shades. The corms must be given a cold (35° F) treatment in the pot before forcing. Many indoor gardeners pot newly purchased mature corms in October, place them in a cool (not freezing) place until January, and then bring them inside for flowering. After the foliage has died back, place the plants in the garden or discard.

Light: Place in a bright, indirectly lit south, east, or west window.

Water: Keep evenly moist. Water thoroughly and discard drainage.

Humidity: Average indoor humidity levels.

Temperatures: 40° to 45° F at night, 60° to 65° F during the day.

Fertilization: Do not fertilize when plant is in flower. Fertilize lightly at other times.

Propagation: Start new plants from the bulblets that develop beside the parent bulb. It will take several years to get a new corm to blooming size.

Grooming: Remove flowers as they fade. Discard after flowering.

Repotting: None needed.

Problems: No significant problems.

Crossandra infundibuliformis
Crossandra, firecracker-flower

Given ample light and fertilizer, crossandras will bloom almost continuously. The flowers appear on short stalks at the ends of growing shoots, overlapping one another. They are bright salmon red. Cut them back as needed to maintain shape. Discard them when they get leggy or pot bound.

Light: Provide 4 hours of direct sunlight in winter. Provide curtain-filtered sunlight in summer, from a south or west window.

Water: Keep evenly moist. Water thoroughly and discard drainage.

Humidity: Requires moist air. Use a humidifier for best results.

Temperatures: 55° to 60° F at night, 70° to 75° F during the day.

Crocus vernus

Crossandra infundibuliformis

Cuphea hyssopifolia

Cuphea ignea
Cyclamen persicum

Fertilization: Fertilize all year, more heavily in summer.

Propagation: Start from seeds. Sow in a small pot and transplant seedlings as needed. Or, take stem cuttings at any time.

Grooming: Keep to desired height and shape with light pruning or clipping at any time. Start new plants to replace old specimens when they get weak or old.

Repotting: Transplant seedlings several times, as they grow.

Problems: Poor drainage, too-frequent watering, or standing in water will cause root rot.

Cuphea
Cigarplant, elfin-herb,
Hawaiian heather

Two quite different cupheas are grown as houseplants. The elfin-herb, also known as Hawaiian heather (*Cuphea hyssopifolia*), bears bell-shaped, six-petaled flowers, usually pink but also purple or white, and has needlelike leaves. It is commonly grown as an indoor bonsai. The cigarplant (*C. ignea,* sometimes labeled *C. platycentra*) bears red, tubular flowers with a white tip that resemble a burning cigar, giving it its common name. Its leaves are small and broad. Both are bushy plants that require some pruning to maintain their shape. Given good light, they will grow well and flower at any season.

Light: Provide 4 hours or more of direct sunlight in winter; provide bright, indirect light the rest of the year. Attractive plant for light gardens.

Water: Keep evenly moist. Water thoroughly and discard drainage.

Humidity: Cigarplant requires moist air; use a humidifier for best results. Elfin-herb or Hawaiian heather tolerates average indoor humidity levels.

Temperatures: 55° to 65° F at night, 70° to 75° F during the day.

Fertilization: Fertilize when plant is growing actively.

Propagation: Take stem cuttings at any time. Cigarplant is also readily grown from seed. Start in February for summer flowering, and again in July for winter blossoms.

Grooming: Prune and pinch as needed. Cigarplant is usually discarded after blooming.

Repotting: Can be repotted at any time. Grow in small pots for plentiful flowers. Transplant seedlings several times, as they grow.

Problems: Will not bloom in low light.

Cyclamen persicum
Cyclamen

The heart-shaped, dark green leaves of cyclamen surround upright stems that are topped with butterfly blossoms from midautumn until midspring. Of the 15 species in the genus, *C. persicum* is most commonly grown indoors and is readily available from florists. Purchase plants in early fall when the blooming season begins for indoor color.

Cyclamen does best in a cool room with good air circulation but no drafts. When blooming, it needs as much sun as possible. Fertilize every 2 weeks.

Many people discard cyclamen after blooming, but the plants can be kept if they are given special care. When blooming ceases and the foliage dies back, put the plant in a cool spot and let the soil dry. In midsummer repot the corm with new soil in a small pot, and place it in a warm area to encourage root growth. As the plant grows, gradually return it to a cool location (55° F) to induce blooming.

Light: Place in a bright, indirectly lit south, east, or west window.

Water: Keep evenly moist. Water thoroughly from the bottom and discard drainage.

Humidity: Average indoor humidity levels.

Temperatures: 50° to 55° F at night, 60° to 65° F during the day.

Fertilization: Fertilize only when plant is growing actively or flowering.

Propagation: Start from seeds. Sow in a small pot and transplant seedlings as needed. It may take 2 years to get a blooming plant.

Grooming: Pick off yellowed leaves.

Repotting: Repot each year, in midsummer.

Problems: Subject to rot if water accumulates in the top of the corm. Somewhat susceptible to both mealybugs and scale.

Erica
Heath, heather

The heaths are a large group of plants grown outdoors in cool northern landscapes. A few cultivars are commercially grown for cut flowers. Many of the smaller types, such as *E. gracilis* and *E. hyemalis,* make fine indoor plants if given enough light and cool temperatures the year around. The blooms are of varying colors and are usually quite fragrant. The plants are bushy and produce dense branches and tiny, narrow leaves that can be easily pruned or clipped. Heaths are very sensitive to soluble salts from excessive fertilizer or improper watering.

Light: Provide at least 4 hours of curtain-filtered sunlight from a bright south, east, or west window.
Water: Let plant approach dryness before watering, then water thoroughly and discard drainage.
Humidity: Requires moist air. Use a humidifier for best results.
Temperatures: 50° to 55° F at night, 60° to 65° F during the day.
Fertilization: Fertilize lightly once a year, in early spring.
Propagation: Take cuttings from stems or shoots that have recently matured.
Grooming: Keep to the desired height and shape with light pruning or clipping at any time.
Repotting: Repot in winter or early spring, as needed. A peat-based mix is essential.
Problems: Will not bloom if light is too low. Dry soil or a high level of soluble salts may damage roots, causing plant to die back.

Eucharis grandiflora
Amazon lily

Amazon lilies are easy-to-grow bulbs that will flower even in indirect light indoors. They are large plants with a wonderful fragrance. The flowers are white and borne in groups of 3 to 6 on a 2-foot stalk. The bulb may bloom as many as three times a year. Keep the plant very moist and well fertilized while it is growing. Only a short resting period is needed. Never let it get excessively dry, and keep the plant warm, especially at night.

Light: Place in a bright, indirectly lit south, east, or west window.

Water: Keep very moist during growth and flowering; at other times, allow to dry between waterings.
Humidity: Requires moist air. Use a humidifier for best results.
Temperatures: 65° to 70° F at night, 75° to 80° F during the day.
Fertilization: Fertilize only when plant is growing actively or flowering.
Propagation: Start new plants from the bulblets that develop beside the parent bulb.
Grooming: Give plant plenty of room to grow.
Repotting: Repot infrequently.
Problems: If plant is in a draft or dry air, leaves will scorch. Poor drainage, too-frequent watering, or standing in water will cause root rot.

Euphorbia pulcherrima
Poinsettia

The poinsettia was first found in Mexico in the 1800s, growing as a wildflower. It has since become the most popular living Christmas gift in the United States. The large, white, pink, red, yellow, lime green, or bicolor flowers are actually groups of bracts that surround a small, inconspicuous true flower. Ranging in height from 1 to 3 feet, the plants produce blossoms that are 6 to 12 inches wide.

With proper care these plants will continue to bloom for several months, and some can be made to blossom the following season. While blooming, the plants simply need plenty of sunlight and protection from drafts and sudden changes in temperature. Reduce water during the rest period from spring to midsummer, then increase waterings and apply fertilizer every 2 weeks. These plants normally flower in the fall, when the nights are long. Beginning about October 1, they need 2 weeks of long (14-hour) nights, uninterrupted by any light, before flowers are initiated. If your plant is indoors, be sure that household lights do not interrupt this darkness. You may have to place the plant in a dark closet at night or put it outdoors in a protected spot.

Light: Place in a bright, indirectly lit south, east, or west window.
Water: Keep evenly moist. Water thoroughly and discard drainage.
Humidity: Average indoor humidity levels.

Erica

Eucharis grandiflora

Euphorbia pulcherrima

Exacum affine

Felicia amelloides 'San Luis'

Freesia × *hybrida*

Temperatures: 50° to 55° F at night, 65° to 70° F during the day.
Fertilization: Fertilize when actively growing.
Propagation: Take cuttings from stems or shoots before they have hardened or matured.
Grooming: Prune after flowering. Pinch back stem tips of young or regrowing plants to improve form. Be careful not to remove flower buds when pruning.
Repotting: Repot infrequently in winter or early spring when needed.
Problems: If soil is too wet or too dry, or if plant is suddenly moved to a spot where light is low, leaves will drop. Poor drainage, overwatering, or standing in water will cause root rot.

Exacum affine
Persian violet

Persian violets are popular because they will bloom in small pots. Plants are commonly covered with tiny, blue or white flowers with yellow centers. Many florist shops carry them throughout the fall and winter in a variety of sizes from seedlings to blooming plants. The seedlings must be handled carefully, because slight injuries may lead to stem rot and cankering. Keep the seedlings in moist air and out of direct sun. As the plants get bigger, provide some direct sun in fall to encourage blooming. Never place the plants in cool drafts or water them with cold water.
Light: Keep in about 4 hours of direct sunlight in winter. Provide curtain-filtered sunlight in summer, from a south or west window.
Water: Keep evenly moist. Water thoroughly and discard drainage.
Humidity: Requires moist air. Use a humidifier for best results.
Temperatures: 55° to 60° F at night, 70° to 75° F during the day.
Fertilization: Fertilize only during late spring and summer.
Propagation: Start from seeds in spring. Sow in a small pot and transplant seedlings as needed. Or take stem cuttings, but cuttings do not produce as fine a plant as one grown from seed.
Grooming: Discard after flowering.
Repotting: Transplant seedlings several times, as they grow.

Problems: Dry soil or a high level of soluble salts may damage roots, causing plant to die back. Subject to crown rot in overly moist conditions. Susceptible to whiteflies.

Felicia amelloides
Felicia, blue marguerite, blue daisy

If they get an abundance of light, felicias produce their blue, yellow-centered blooms almost continuously. The plant is normally a little leggy and will need frequent clipping, but be careful not to clip off the stalks with flower buds. The leaves are ½-inch long, with a rough texture. Do not overfertilize this plant in winter.
Light: Provide 4 hours or more of direct sunlight from a south window.
Water: Let plant approach dryness before watering, then water thoroughly and discard drainage.
Humidity: Average indoor humidity levels.
Temperatures: 50° to 55° F at night, 65° to 70° F during the day.
Fertilization: Fertilize all year, more heavily in summer. Do not overfertilize in winter.
Propagation: Start from seeds in midsummer. Sow in a small pot and transplant seedlings as needed. Or take cuttings in spring.
Grooming: Keep to desired height and shape with light pruning or clipping at any time, being careful not to clip off the stalks with flower buds.
Repotting: Repot in winter or early spring, as needed.
Problems: Dry soil or a high level of soluble salts may damage roots, causing plant to die back. Will get spindly and weak if light is too low.

Freesia
Freesia

Freesias are bulbs grown widely in Europe and the United States for cut-flower arrangements. The flowers are extremely fragrant and come in many colors and patterns. You can force them into bloom as you would tulips or daffodils. Purchase mature bulbs in fall, pot them, and place the pot in a cool (not freezing) location until January. Then move the pot to a warm, brightly lit spot for forcing. Freesias can grow quite tall and may need staking. Unless you live in a mild-winter area, it is best to discard this plant after flowering. Freesias will not survive outdoors where it freezes in winter.

Light: Keep in about 4 hours of direct sunlight in winter while in bloom.
Water: Keep evenly moist. Water thoroughly and discard drainage.
Humidity: Average indoor humidity levels.
Temperatures: 50° to 55° F at night, 60° to 65° F during the day.
Fertilization: Do not fertilize.
Propagation: Buy mature bulbs or start new plants from the bulblets that develop beside the parent bulb.
Grooming: Generally discarded after blooming. In mild climates, bulbs may be planted outdoors.
Repotting: Not needed.
Problems: No significant problems.

Fuchsia × hybrida
Fuchsia, lady's-eardrops

The showy flowers and thin, green or variegated leaves of fuchsia make it a striking shrub. The sepals, which enclose the flower buds, are green on most plants; however, fuchsias have colored sepals that flare open to reveal pendant petals. The petals can be the same color as the sepals or a different hue. Colors range from white through pink, red, lavender, violet, and purple, in countless combinations. There are thousands of fuchsia strains, in a great number of shapes and sizes. Many make excellent hanging plants.

During summer, fuchsias can be moved outdoors to a cool-shaded spot. Feed frequently and always keep the soil moist. Plants in hanging baskets dry out quickly, so check them frequently.
Light: Keep in about 4 hours of direct sunlight in winter. Provide curtain-filtered sunlight in summer, from a south or west window.
Water: Keep very moist at all times, but do not allow to stand in water.
Humidity: Average indoor humidity levels.
Temperatures: 50° to 55° F at night, 60° to 65° F during the day.
Fertilization: Fertilize only during late spring and summer.
Propagation: Take cuttings from stems or shoots before they have hardened or matured.
Grooming: Prune in early spring. Pinch back stem tips of young or regrowing plants to improve form. Be

careful not to remove flower buds when pruning.
Repotting: Repot each year.
Problems: Summer heat may cause plant to die back. If soil is too wet or too dry, leaves will drop. Susceptible to whiteflies. Check carefully for insects before bringing back indoors at the end of the summer.

Gardenia jasminoides
Gardenia, cape jasmine

Discovered in China in the 1700s, gardenia species now number about 200. The heady aroma of the creamy, spiraling blossoms is sure to please everyone. *G. jasminoides* has large, glossy, dark green leaves and produces an abundance of flowers. It is the type most often grown indoors. Some varieties bloom only in summer; others bloom throughout the year. Oil extracted from the flower is used in perfumes and tea. Gardenias also make excellent cut flowers.

These plants are popular additions to the greenhouse, and rightly so. Gardenias kept indoors need high humidity and cool nights as well as plenty of sunlight. The plant will not set flower buds if night temperatures exceed 65° F.
Light: Keep in about 4 hours of direct sunlight in winter. In summer, provide curtain-filtered sunlight from a south or west window.
Water: Keep very moist at all times, but do not allow to stand in water.
Humidity: Requires moist air. Use a humidifier for best results.
Temperatures: 50° to 55° F at night, 65° to 70° F during the day.
Fertilization: Use an acid-based fertilizer, and add trace elements once in spring.
Propagation: Take cuttings from stems or shoots that have recently matured.
Grooming: Prune in early spring. Pinch back stem tips of young or regrowing plants to improve form. Be careful not to remove flower buds when pruning.
Repotting: Repot infrequently.
Problems: Bud drop results from plant stress, caused by overly dry air, high temperatures, or a sudden change in environment. Plants purchased in bud, for example, will often lose all their flowers due to stress. If soil is too wet or too dry, leaves will drop. Will not bloom if light is too low.

Fuchsia × hybrida

Gardenia jasminoides

Gesneriad: *Aeschynanthus* 'Flash'

Gesneriad: *Achimenes* 'Menuette'

Gesneriads

African violets are the gesneriads most familiar to indoor gardeners. Once considered rather temperamental, they have been much improved in recent years. Many other, lesser-known gesneriads, such as nematanthus, gloxinias, and streptocarpus, are also available in florist shops, garden centers, and supermarkets.

The variety of forms and colorings of the more than 120 genera and 2,000 species in this family is truly outstanding. Gesneriads are classified according to rooting type and growth habit. African violets and episcias are two of the best known of the fibrous-rooted type. Tuberous-rooted gesneriads include florist's gloxinias (*Sinningia speciosa*). Achimenes is an example of the gesneriads that form scaly rhizomes underground. Most genera hybridize and cross easily within species, which leads to the development of many varied cultivars. Dwarf cultivars are now being developed, furthering both the usefulness of gesneriads and their popularity. Most gesneriads are easy to propagate, when plant patents permit. They serve well as children's plant projects or as gifts for plant-collecting friends.

Gesneriads are usually grown for their blossoms. Many, such as the episcias and columneas, have equally attractive foliage. Some get quite large and are useful as specimen plants to dominate arrangements in hanging baskets, or as pedestal plants. Many indoor gardeners grow gesneriads in a place with ideal conditions, then move them temporarily to display areas. Maintaining symmetry in the rosettes of foliage is the key to a specimen-quality gesneriad. Grow them on an evenly lit light bench for best results.

Since gesneriads have such variety, the following plant descriptions each include a care guide. In general, gesneriads adapt well to indoor culture. Most bloom for long periods, given good light. Many will adapt to lighted indoor gardens, plant shelves, or terrariums. They need warmth, even moisture, light fertilization, and no direct sunlight. The tuberous-rooted gesneriads and some of the rhizomatous kinds require a rest period after flowering, during which water and fertilizer should be reduced or completely withheld for a few weeks.

Achimenes
Achimenes, rainbow-flower, magic-flower, widow's-tear

Achimenes cultivars offer a variety of flower colors, including light blue, deep red, and yellow. They are often found in florist shops. Like their African violet relatives, they need warmth to grow well and ample light to blossom. Achimenes are bushy plants that are often used in hanging baskets. The foliage of many cultivars is attractive by itself, especially if the branches are properly pinched and trained when the plants are young. Achimenes are usually started from dormant rhizomes in spring. They will flower throughout the summer.

Light: Provide at least 4 hours of curtain-filtered sunlight from a bright south, east, or west window.

Water: Keep evenly moist. Water thoroughly and discard drainage. Do not water during dormant period.

Humidity: Requires moist air. Use a humidifier for best results.

Temperatures: 65° to 70° F at night, 75° to 80° F during the day.

Fertilization: Fertilize lightly each month while plant is growing actively.

Propagation: Start new plants by dividing and potting up rhizomes at the end of the dormant season. Or sow seeds in spring.

Grooming: Pinch back stem tips of young or regrowing plants to improve form, being careful not to remove flower buds.

Repotting: When plant has died back after flowering, remove rhizomes and repot. Store the rhizomes at 60° F, packing them in dry peat moss or vermiculite. Repot in spring. Keep recently potted plants warm and only moderately moist.

Problems: Will not bloom if light is too low. If soil is too wet or too dry, leaves will drop. Dry soil or a high level of soluble salts may damage roots, causing plant to die back.

Aeschynanthus
Basket vine, lipstick-plant

Basket vine is a hanging basket gesneriad that generally bears thick, waxy leaves on trailing or bushy stems. Depending on the variety, the tubular flowers are born either at the leaf axils or in clusters at the ends of the stems.

They are usually brightly colored in shades of red, orange, pink, or yellow. The common name, lipstick-plant, comes from the fact that the base of the flower is encased in a tubular calyx, like lipstick extended from its tube.

Some varieties bloom strictly according to season, often in fall; others bloom intermittently throughout the year. The best-known species is *A. radicans* (sometimes found under the name *A. lobbianus*), a trailer with red blooms extending from a purplish calyx. *A. longicaulis* (formerly *A. marmoratus*) bears green and brown flowers that are not altogether attractive, but its purplish green, yellow-veined leaves have made it popular as a foliage plant. *A. hildebrandii* is a small, shrubby plant with numerous, bright orange flowers. Under good conditions, it may be ever-blooming.

These plants require night warmth and good winter light. They can be purchased from florists. Small plants will take some time before they will fill a large basket.

Light: Provide at least 4 hours of curtain-filtered sunlight from a south, east, or west window.

Water: Let dry slightly between waterings, then water thoroughly and discard drainage.

Humidity: Average indoor humidity levels.

Temperatures: 65° to 70° F at night, 75° to 80° F during the day.

Fertilization: Fertilize lightly each month from January through September.

Propagation: Take cuttings from stems or shoots before they have hardened or matured.

Grooming: Prune after flowering. Start new plants to replace old specimens when they get weak.

Repotting: Repot infrequently.

Problems: Will not bloom if light is too low. Dry soil or a high level of soluble salts may damage roots, causing plant to die back. Watch for mealybugs.

Alsobia
Alsobia, laceflower vine

Alsobias (formerly included in the genus *Episcia*) bear lightly hairy, dark green leaves, often with a reddish tinge in bright light, and form dense rosettes. From the rosettes, numerous creeping stems, or stolons, emerge, producing plantlets that root wherever they touch the potting mix. As the stolons arch downward, they form an attractive, thick covering of greenery, making alsobia an ideal hanging-basket plant. Heavily fringed, white flowers with various degrees of purple spotting appear intermittently throughout the year. Removing some of the stolons will increase flower production.

Light: Provide at least 4 hours of curtain-filtered sunlight from a bright south, east, or west window.

Water: Keep evenly moist when growing actively. Water thoroughly and discard drainage.

Humidity: Average indoor humidity levels.

Temperatures: 65° to 70° F at night, 75° to 80° F during the day.

Fertilization: Fertilize when the plant is growing actively or flowering.

Propagation: Remove and root plantlets, or propagate by layering.

Grooming: Remove yellowed leaves and faded flowers.

Repotting: Repot in late winter or spring as necessary.

Problems: Will not bloom if light is too low.

Chirita
Chirita

Chirita sinensis, the most popular chirita species, is known for its silver, marbled leaves and slow-growing, lavender flowers. It has a rosette growth pattern and is well suited to light benches or window boxes. It likes cool temperatures and is quite tolerant of dryness, being a near-succulent.

Light: Keep in about 4 hours of direct sunlight in winter. Provide curtain-filtered sunlight in summer, from a south or west window.

Water: Water thoroughly. Allow to dry out slightly between waterings.

Humidity: Average indoor humidity levels.

Temperatures: 55° to 60° F at night, 65° to 70° F during the day.

Fertilization: Fertilize regularly during the growing season.

Propagation: Take leaf cuttings at any time or propagate by division or from seed.

Gesneriad: *Alsobia dianthaflora*

Gesneriad: *Columnea sinensis*

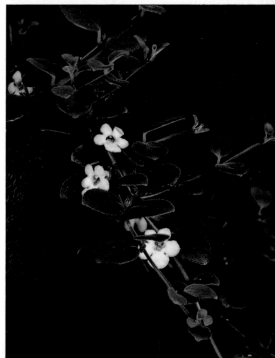

Gesneriad: *Codonanthe digna*

Gesneriad: *Columnea* 'California Gold'

Gesneriad: *Episcia cupreata*

Grooming: Remove faded flowers and leaves promptly.
Repotting: Repot in spring, as needed.
Problems: Will not bloom in low light.

Codonanthe
Codonanthe

This gesneriad bears small, elliptic or rounded leaves on trailing stems, making it a good subject for hanging baskets. Flowers are small and white and, though not long lasting, are produced regularly throughout the year. If flowers are pollinated, colorful berries, often orange, white, or pink, will follow.
Light: Place in a bright, indirectly lit south, east, or west window.
Water: Keep thin-leaved varieties evenly moist at all times. Allow thicker-leaved varieties to dry slightly between waterings.
Humidity: Average indoor humidity levels.
Temperatures: 65° to 70° F at night, 75° to 80° F during the day.
Fertilization: Fertilize when plant is growing actively or flowering.
Propagation: Take stem cuttings anytime.
Grooming: Remove yellowed leaves and faded flowers. Prune excessively long stems.
Repotting: Repot infrequently.
Problems: Will not bloom if light is too low.

Columnea
Columnea

There are 150 different species of columnea. They come from Central America, South America, and the West Indies; their natural habitat is the damp tropical forest. Because they are semi-upright or trailing plants, they look especially fine in hanging baskets. The brightly colored, tubular flowers are orange, scarlet, or yellow, and many hybrids bloom continuously throughout the year. Flowers range in size from ½ to 4 inches, depending on the variety. Leaves vary from button size to 3 inches in length. *C.* × *banksii,* which has waxy leaves, is one of the easiest to grow. *C. gloriosa* has hairy leaves and red flowers. Two of the better-known hybrids are 'Early Bird' and 'Mary Ann'.

Columneas aren't the easiest plants to grow, but keeping the air moist will help them stay healthy and blooming. Water carefully during winter, and keep them away from heat sources.
Light: Provide at least 4 hours of curtain-filtered sunlight from a bright south, east, or west window.
Water: Keep moist during growth and flowering; at other times, allow to dry between waterings.
Humidity: Requires moist air. Use a humidifier for best results.
Temperatures: 55° to 60° F at night, 70° to 75° F during the day. Some species require much cooler night temperatures in winter to bloom well.
Fertilization: Fertilize only when plant is actively growing or flowering.
Propagation: Take cuttings from stems or shoots that have recently matured.
Grooming: Prune after flowering or fruiting. Pinch back new stem tips to improve form. Be careful not to remove flower buds when pruning.
Repotting: Repot infrequently.
Problems: Subject to crown rot in overly moist conditions. Will not bloom if light is too low.

Episcia
Episcia, flame-violet

Episcias are available in many cultivars, each with distinctive foliage texture and variegated coloring. Many gardeners value them for their foliage alone. In the summer, they produce small flowers that are red, yellow, orange, pink, lavender, or white. The plants produce short-stemmed rosettes of large leaves and trailing stolons on which smaller leaves appear. Episcias are generally used in hanging baskets or as ground covers in well-lit terrariums and dish gardens.
Light: Place in a bright, indirectly lit south, east, or west window or, even better, under fluorescent lights.
Water: Keep evenly moist during growth and flowering; at other times, allow to dry between waterings.
Humidity: Requires moist air. Use a humidifier for best results.
Temperatures: 65° to 70° F at night, 75° to 80° F during the day.
Fertilization: Fertilize when plant is growing actively or flowering.
Propagation: Pot plantlets or rooted side shoots as they form. Alternatively, layer the stolons or take leaf cuttings.

Grooming: For large leaves and plentiful flowers, thin stolons occasionally. Remove faded flowers and leaves.
Repotting: Repot in winter or early spring, as needed.
Problems: If plant is in a draft or dry air, leaves will scorch. Poor drainage, too-frequent watering, or standing in water will cause root rot.

Gesneria
Gesneria

Small plants with shiny, dark green, spoon-shaped leaves, gesneria are popular as terrarium plants. Within the moist confines of a terrarium, they are everblooming, with yellow, orange, or red tubular flowers. They require a high humidity to do well in the open. Gesnerias produce seed prolifically, often reseeding themselves throughout their terrarium homes. They get off to a fast start, often blooming only 4 months after seed is sown, but thereafter are extremely slow growing.
Light: Place in a bright, indirectly lit south, east, or west window or, even better, under lights.
Water: Keep evenly moist at all times.
Humidity: Requires very moist air. Use a humidifying tray or grow in a terrarium.
Temperatures: 65° to 70° F at night, 75° to 80° F during the day.
Fertilization: Fertilize when plant is growing actively or flowering.
Propagation: Start from seed or take stem cuttings from mature plants.
Grooming: Remove yellowed leaves and faded flowers.
Repotting: Repot infrequently.
Problems: Will not bloom if light or humidity is too low. May wilt or die if allowed to dry out.

Kohleria
Kohleria

Kohlerias are one of the gesneriads with herbaceous stems and soft, hairy foliage, typical of many members of this large family. Their tubular flowers are usually purple, red, pink, or yellow with strikingly marbled throats. They produce rhizomes and are easy to grow, but tend to get leggy when subjected to poor light. They are most often used in hanging baskets. Winter-flowering cultivars are common, but they need plenty of light. Kohlerias go dormant after flowering. They can be cut back during this period.
Light: Provide at least 4 hours of curtain-filtered sunlight from a bright south, east, or west window.
Water: Keep very moist during growth and flowering. Spray occasionally when dormant.
Humidity: Requires moist air. Use a humidifier for best results.
Temperatures: 50° to 55° F at night, 60° to 65° F during the day.
Fertilization: Fertilize only when plant is growing actively or flowering.
Propagation: Take stem cuttings at any season, or divide rhizomes.
Grooming: Prune after flowering.
Repotting: Repot after flowering.
Problems: Will get spindly if exposed to low light and too much warmth.

Miniature Sinningia

Miniature sinningias, sometimes still referred to by their old name, gloxineras, are currently particularly popular, especially with gardeners who appreciate their ability to flower throughout the year with little care. They originated from crosses between large sinningias and the microminiature sinningias *S. pusilla* and *S. concinna*. Miniature sinningias bear tubular flowers with flared tips on short-stemmed rosettes rarely over 8 inches in diameter and often less than 2 inches in diameter. They come in a wide variety of flower colors.

Older varieties tend to go into dormancy after blooming, but modern hybrids produce new shoots even before the previous ones have faded, thus providing blooms throughout the year. The small hybrids are ideal for well-lit terrariums.
Light: Provide at least 4 hours of curtain-filtered sunlight from a bright south, east, or west window; or, even better, place under fluorescent lights.
Water: Water thoroughly and discard drainage. If tubers enter dormancy, stop watering until new growth appears.
Humidity: Requires moist air. Use a humidifier for best results.
Temperatures: 65° to 70° F at night, 75° to 80° F during the day.
Propagation: Remove and root extra rosettes. Or sow seed; many bloom in less than 5 months from seed.

Gesneriad: *Kohleria* 'Flirt'

Gesneriad: Miniature sinningias (left to right): 'Coral Baby', 'Ruffled Wood Nymph', 'Lyndon Lyon'

Gesneriad: *Nematanthus* 'Black Gold'

Gesneriad: *Saintpaulia ionantha*

Grooming: Remove faded rosettes.
Repotting: Repot annually in early spring or as plant comes out of dormancy.
Problems: Will not bloom if light is too low. Leaves will scorch if plant is in a draft or dry air.

Nematanthus
Goldfish-plant

Goldfish-plant produces flowers along its trailing stems, primarily in late summer and fall. The flowers resemble goldfish, complete with tiny "mouths." The foliage is small and grows close to the stems, which can reach 2 feet long or longer. Keep the plant in a hanging basket, out of drafts and dry air.
Light: Provide at least 4 hours of curtain-filtered sunlight from a bright south, east, or west window.
Water: Keep evenly moist. Water thoroughly and discard drainage.
Humidity: Average indoor humidity levels.
Temperatures: 55° to 60° F at night, 70° to 75° F during the day.
Fertilization: Fertilize only when plant is growing actively or flowering.
Propagation: Take stem cuttings at any time.
Grooming: Prune in early spring. Pinch back stem tips of young or re-growing plants to improve form. Be careful not to remove flower buds when pruning.
Repotting: Repot infrequently, in winter or early spring when needed.
Problems: Will not bloom if light is too low. Dry soil or a high level of soluble salts may damage roots, causing plant to die back. Susceptible to spider mites, especially if plant is too dry.

Saintpaulia
African violet

Originally collected in Africa in the late nineteenth century, African violets are first in any list of favorite flowering plants. No other plant can match their ability to thrive and bloom indoors for months on end.

Rosettes of velvety leaves on short stems surround clusters of flowers in white or shades of pink, red, violet, purple, or blue. The compact size of an African violet makes it perfect for windowsills, small tabletop arrangements, and hanging displays.

There are thousands of named African violets from which to choose. Some favorite standards include 'Swifty Thriller', 'Half Moon Bay', 'Nob Hill', 'Something Special', and 'Granger's Wonderland'. Consult local experts or plant catalogs to find your favorite.

Despite their reputation for being temperamental, African violets generally are not difficult to grow. The fact that millions of indoor gardeners grow and collect them attests to their ease of flowering. Plenty of bright, indirect light is the key to constant bloom. Supplement with artificial light if the plant stops blooming, especially in winter when it receives less than 12 hours of bright light a day. Evenly moist soil, warm temperatures, high humidity, and monthly feedings are the other important factors for growth. The plants will flower best with only one crown.

Miniature African violet varieties have recently gained popularity. Potted in 2½-inch pots, they grow only 6 inches wide, making them useful additions to terrariums or miniature greenhouses. Semi-miniatures have somewhat smaller leaves and crowns than the standards, but their flowers are almost as large. One of the most reliable miniatures is 'Mickey Mouse'. Outstanding semi-miniatures include 'Precious Pink', 'Snuggles', and 'Magic Blue'. Popular micro-miniatures include 'Optimara Rose Quartz' and 'Optimara Blue Sapphire'. Many trailing miniatures and semi-miniatures are available; among the most popular are 'Falling Snow', 'Snowy Trail', and 'Pixie Blue'. These do well in hanging baskets no larger than 4 inches in diameter. Group two or three in one basket.

In addition to the care techniques for standard African violets, there is an especially valuable tip for the miniatures and semi-miniatures: Keep the soil always moist. This can be difficult, because there isn't much soil in the small pots and it dries out quickly. For this reason, many growers like to keep these plants in self-watering containers.
Light: Bright light. Direct sunlight in winter is fine, but summer sun may be too strong. During winter, supplement with artificial light so that the plant receives at least 14 hours of light a day.

Water: Keep evenly moist. Use only room-temperature water. Avoid wetting foliage; cold water will spot the leaves. Leach soil occasionally.

Humidity: Provide moist air by surrounding base of plant with moist peat moss or by placing plant on humidifying tray.

Temperatures: 60° to 65° F at night, 72° to 75° F during the day. Keep plants away from cold windows. Sudden changes in temperature are harmful.

Fertilization: Fertilize all year, more heavily in summer.

Propagation: In spring, take leaf cuttings or sow seeds.

Grooming: Remove all dead leaves and flowers promptly (stems included). Shape by removing side shoots.

Repotting: Plant does best when slightly pot bound. Use pot about half the width of the plant. Plant rooted leaf cuttings in 2½-inch pots.

Problems: Mushy, brown blooms and buds indicate botrytis blight. Pick off diseased parts, provide good air circulation, avoid high humidity, and use fertilizer with less nitrogen.

Yellow rings on leaf surface are caused by cold water touching foliage. Streaked, misshapen leaves with irregular yellow spots are infected by a virus. There is no cure, so discard plant. If a healthy plant suddenly wilts, it has crown rot, which results from an erratic watering routine and is fatal. Do not allow the soil to dry out between waterings. Maintain a constant level of soil moisture. Severe temperature changes may also cause crown rot.

Lack of flowers is most often caused by inadequate light. Supplement daylight with artificial light. Extremely dry or cold air may also inhibit flowering. And repotting or moving the plant to a new location can inhibit flowering for a long time.

Yellowing leaves result from dry air, too much sun, incorrect watering, or improper fertilization. Follow fertilizer directions closely. Brown, brittle leaves develop if soil is deficient in nutrients. Repot if soil is old; otherwise, fertilize regularly.

Slow growth and leaves curled downward indicate that the temperature is too low. Soft foliage and few flowers indicate that the temperature is too high. Brown-edged leaves and small flowers result from low humidity. Place plants in humidifying trays.

Gesneriad: *Saintpaulia* 'Wine Country'

Gesneriad: *Saintpaulia* 'Snowy Trail'

Gesneriad: *Saintpaulia* 'Snuggles'

Gesneriad: *Saintpaulia* 'Little Rose Quartz'

Gesneriad: *Sinningia cardinalis*

Gesneriad: *Sinningia speciosa*

Gesneriad: *Smithiantha* 'Carmel'

Sinningia cardinalis, S. canescens
Cardinal flower, Brazilian edelweiss

These plants—cousins of the popular florist's gloxinia—were classified as *Rechsteineria* until recently. They are taller than florist's gloxinias and have tubular, red flowers about 2 inches long. Given enough light, they will bloom during the winter holidays and on into spring and summer. Like most gesneriads, they should be kept warm and only lightly fertilized. They may go completely dormant for long periods.

Light: Keep in about 4 hours of direct sunlight in winter. Provide curtain-filtered sunlight in summer, from a south or west window.
Water: Let plant approach dryness before watering, then water thoroughly and discard drainage.
Humidity: Requires moist air. Use a humidifier for best results.
Temperatures: 65° to 70° F at night, 75° to 80° F during the day.
Fertilization: Fertilize only during late spring and summer.
Propagation: Sow seeds in a small pot and transplant seedlings as needed. Or take cuttings in spring.
Grooming: Remove faded growth when plant goes dormant.
Repotting: Transplant seedlings several times, as they grow.
Problems: Subject to crown rot in overly moist conditions. Will not bloom if light is too low. Dry soil or a high level of soluble salts may damage roots, causing plant to die back.

Sinningia speciosa
Florist's gloxinia

Florist's gloxinias, originally from Brazil, have large, velvety leaves encircling bell-shaped flowers with ruffled edges. The flowers are borne well above the foliage.

To grow well and last for many years, florist's gloxinias need humidity, full sun in winter, and shade in summer. Keep the soil moist but not too wet, and be sure to use tepid water. After blooming, the plant needs a dormant period. While they are growing, gloxinias need fertilizing every 2 weeks.

Light: Place in a bright, indirectly lit south, east, or west window.

Water: Keep evenly moist. Water thoroughly and discard drainage. After flowering, gradually withhold water until the stems and leaves die back, then put the plant in a cool, dark place for 2 to 4 months while the tuber rests. Water sparingly until new growth appears, then repot into fresh soil, move into light, and provide moisture.
Humidity: Average indoor humidity levels.
Temperatures: 55° to 60° F at night, 70° to 75° F during the day.
Fertilization: Fertilize only when plant is growing actively or flowering.
Propagation: Sow seeds in a small pot and transplant seedlings as needed. Or take leaf or stem cuttings.
Grooming: Pick off yellowed leaves.
Repotting: Repot after dormancy, when growth resumes.
Problems: Subject to crown rot in overly moist conditions. Will not bloom if light is too low. Flower buds blast (buds form, but fail to open) when air is too dry.

Smithiantha
Temple-bells

This gesneriad produces an attractive spike of bell-shaped flowers from fall through winter, depending on the cultivar. The flowers are about 2 inches long and red, orange, yellow, or white. The semiwoody stems bear large, velvety leaves. Temple-bells need warmth and constant moisture to bloom well. They require less light than many other gesneriads, however. Some cultivars are large plants and will need plenty of room. After the plants bloom, allow them to go dormant, remove the rhizomes, and divide and store them until it is time for repotting in late summer.

Light: Place in a bright, indirectly lit south, east, or west window.
Water: Keep very moist during growth and flowering; at other times, allow to dry between waterings.
Humidity: Requires moist air. Use a humidifier for best results.
Temperatures: 65° to 70° F at night, 75° to 80° F during the day.
Fertilization: Fertilize only when plant is growing actively or flowering.
Propagation: Divide rhizomes. Seeds are also available, but can be more difficult than division.

Grooming: Remove old leaves as plant goes dormant. Cut flower stalks if you wish. Give plenty of room.
Repotting: Repot each year in late summer.
Problems: Leaves will scorch if plant is in a draft or dry air. Subject to crown rot in overly moist conditions.

Streptocarpus
Cape primrose

These plants are relatives of the African violet and the florist's gloxinia and can be grown under similar conditions. There are two quite distinct groups of streptocarpus: the stemless *Streptocarpus streptocarpus,* and the stem-bearing *Streptocarpus streptocarpella.* In common terms, the plants of the first group are streptocarpuses and those of the second are streptocarpellas.

Streptocarpus

These are commonly known as the Cape primrose because they are native to the southern tip of Africa and because their straplike leaves resemble those of the English primrose. Arching flower stalks, each bearing from two to over a dozen blooms, are borne directly from the stemless, narrow leaves. The latter can be up to 12 inches long. Many colorful varieties in white, pink, red, violet, or blue are available, often with contrasting veins and a yellow throat. Certain varieties, such as the seed-grown Weismoor hybrids, bear flowers over 3 inches in diameter on large plants, but bloom for only a few months, usually during summer. Smaller-flowered varieties, such as the Nymph hybrids (1- to 2-inch flowers) or the Mount Olympus hybrids (1-inch flowers), are more prolific, blooming the year around on smaller, more compact plants.

Cape primroses prefer cooler winter temperatures than their cousin the African violet. If the leaves go limp yet the potting medium still seems moist, the plant is suffering from overwatering or excess heat. Keep the plant drier than usual and place it in a shady spot until it has recovered.
Light: Place in a bright, indirectly lit south, east, or west window. Full winter sunlight will stimulate off-season bloom in these plants.

Water: Keep moist during growth and flowering; at other times, allow to dry between waterings.
Humidity: Requires moist air. Use a humidifier for best results.
Temperatures: 55° to 60° F at night, 70° to 85° F during the day.
Fertilization: Fertilize when plant is growing actively or flowering.
Propagation: Easily reproduced by division, seeds, or leaf cuttings. Leaves cut into sections and laid on the surface of rooting medium will each produce several plants.
Grooming: Pick off yellowed leaves and trim back those with brown tips. Cut flower stalks back after last bloom has faded.
Repotting: Repot in late winter or spring as necessary.
Problems: Wilting may occur if kept too moist or too hot. Will not bloom at high temperatures or in low light.

Streptocarpella

The stems of the streptocarpella bear small, thick leaves and arch gracefully over the edges of the pot, making it perfect for hanging baskets. Flowers are small but extremely numerous, especially during the summer months. Colors range from pale lavender to blue to deep purple, often with a lighter throat. Thick-leaved, pale-flowered *Streptocarpus saxorum* is the best known of the streptocarpellas; it needs full sun and blooms only during summer. The more modern hybrid streptocarpellas, such as deep blue 'Good Hope', bloom throughout the year with only moderate light.
Light: Provide at least 4 hours of curtain-filtered sunlight from a bright south, east, or west window. Full winter sunlight will stimulate off-season growth. *Streptocarpus saxorum* needs full sun to bloom.
Water: Keep moist during growth and flowering; at other times, allow to dry between waterings.
Humidity: Requires moist air. Use a humidifier for best results.
Temperatures: 65° to 70° F at night, 75° to 80° F during the day.
Fertilization: Fertilize when plant is growing actively or flowering.
Propagation: Take stem cuttings, although can be propagated also by division, seeds, or leaf cuttings.

Gesneriad: *Streptocarpus*

Gesneriad: *Streptocarpella* 'Good Hope'

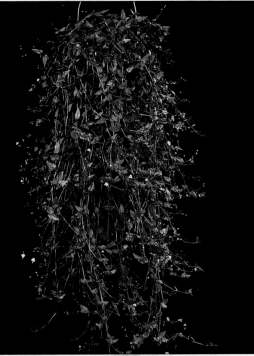

Gibasis geniculata

Gloriosa rothschildiana
Haemanthus katharinae

Grooming: Pick off yellowed leaves and trim back those with brown tips. Cut flower stalks back after last bloom has faded.
Repotting: Repot in late winter or spring as necessary.
Problems: Wilting may occur if kept too moist or too hot. Will not bloom at high temperatures or in low light.

Gibasis
Tahitian bridal-veil

This hanging-basket plant has small, pointed leaves—green above, purple below—borne oppositely along trailing stems. Given enough light, the plant will bear a profusion of tiny, delicate, white flowers on thin stalks above the foliage. This is where the name "bridal-veil" comes from. The plant is particularly sensitive to dry air and dry soil.
Light: Place in curtain-filtered sunlight to promote blooming, but no direct sunlight.
Water: Keep very moist at all times, but do not allow to stand in water.
Humidity: Requires moist air. Use a humidifier for best results.
Temperatures: 55° to 60° F at night, 70° to 75° F during the day.
Fertilization: Fertilize all year, more heavily in summer.
Propagation: Take stem cuttings.
Grooming: Pinch back stem tips of young or regrowing plants frequently to improve form, being careful not to remove flower buds. Start new plants to replace old specimens when they get leggy or weak.
Repotting: Repot in winter or early spring, as needed.
Problems: Will not bloom if light is too low. Dry soil or a high level of soluble salts may damage roots, causing plant to die back.

Gloriosa
Glory lily, climbing lily

Glory lily is a vining plant that has an extremely intricate, lily flower that grows to 4 inches across. The plant climbs vigorously and must be trained on a trellis. It will cling to the trellis with tendrils or "hooks" at the ends of its leaves. Glory lilies must be allowed moderate dormancy periods between growth cycles. The normal blooming period is midsummer through fall;

however, it is possible, by varying the watering of the plant, to alter the resting-growing cycle and promote winter flowering. For winter flowering, the plant needs a well-lit location with good night warmth. *G. rothschildiana* has large, wavy-edged flowers that are brilliant red banded with yellow. *G. simplex* has orange-yellow flowers with slightly wavy edges. *G. superba* flowers are crimped along the edges, yellow aging to red.
Light: Keep in about 4 hours of direct sunlight in winter. Provide curtain-filtered sunlight in summer, from a south or a west window.
Water: Keep very moist during growth and flowering; at other times, allow to dry between waterings.
Humidity: Average indoor humidity levels.
Temperatures: 55° to 60° F at night, 70° to 75° F during the day.
Fertilization: Fertilize only when plant is growing actively or flowering.
Propagation: Start new plants from the bulblets that develop beside the parent bulb.
Grooming: Prune after flowering.
Repotting: Repot in winter or early spring, as needed.
Problems: Will not bloom if light is too low.

Haemanthus
Blood-lily

This bulbous plant is fairly easy to grow and will provide a splendid bloom to reward your efforts. The best-known species is *H. katharinae,* sometimes sold as *Scadoxus multiflorus subspecies katharinae,* whose feathery salmon flowers are borne in a globe-shaped flower head up to 9 inches across. *H. multiflorus* has a marbled flower stalk and bright red flowers in a cluster up to 6 inches across. Both bloom in early summer before or just after the foliage appears. The strap leaves, borne on a short stalk, remain on the plant throughout the summer, then fade as the plant enters winter dormancy. *H. albiflos* differs from the others not only in the flower—creamy white stems surrounded by a greenish white bract—but in that its stemless strap leaves do not die back in the winter.
Light: Provide at least 4 hours of curtain-filtered sunlight from a bright south, east, or west window.

Water: Keep evenly moist during growth and flowering; at other times, allow to dry between waterings.
Humidity: Requires moist air. Use a humidifier for best results.
Temperatures: 50° to 55° F at night, 65° to 70° F during the day.
Fertilization: Fertilize when plant is growing actively or flowering.
Propagation: *H. albiflos* produces bulblets, which can be removed and rooted. Others must be multiplied by seed, a long process beyond the skills of most home gardeners.
Grooming: Remove old leaves as plant goes dormant. Give plant plenty of room.
Repotting: Repot infrequently, since pot-bound plants bloom more profusely. Plant with the tip of the bulb protruding out of the soil.
Problems: Dry soil or a high level of soluble salts may damage roots, causing plant to die back.

Heliconia
Lobster-claw

Lobster-claw is a tropical New World plant grown for its exotic appearance. It bears smooth, often colorfully-veined leaves, like banana leaves, and striking and long-lasting inflorescences, either upright or arching downward, in combinations of yellow, orange, red, and green. The inflorescence is composed of triangular bracts in two ranks, which give the plant its common name. Most varieties available are dwarf selections, but even so they require large pots and plenty of space. They are often available as rhizome sections, which root easily.
Light: Place in a bright, indirectly lit south, east, or west window.
Water: Keep plant evenly moist at all times.
Humidity: Requires high humidity; grow on a humidity tray.
Temperatures: 65° to 70° F at night, 75° to 80° F during the day.
Fertilization: Fertilize when plant is growing actively or flowering.
Propagation: Divide rhizomes at any time.
Grooming: Remove yellowed leaves and faded flower bracts.
Repotting: Repot in spring as necessary.
Problems: Leaves scorch in low air humidity. Will not bloom in low light. Spider mites are a problem in dry air.

Heliotropium
Heliotrope

Heliotropes are semiwoody shrubs that can be grown as bushy plants (12 inches tall) or as single stems (3 to 4 feet tall). They are popular because of their extremely fragrant flowers, but they bloom only if given plenty of light. There are many hybrids available with purple, blue, or white flowers. The flowers are small and are borne in clusters 3 to 4 inches wide.
Light: Provide 4 hours or more of direct sunlight from a south window. Does best in a greenhouse setting.
Water: Keep evenly moist. Water thoroughly and discard drainage.
Humidity: Requires moist air. Use a humidifier for best results.
Temperatures: 50° to 55° F at night, 60° to 65° F during the day.
Fertilization: Fertilize all year, more heavily in summer.
Propagation: Take stem cuttings at any time. Or sow seeds, but seeds can be more difficult than cuttings.
Grooming: Prune after flowering.
Repotting: Transplant seedlings several times, as they grow. Repot in winter or early spring, as needed.
Problems: Will not bloom if light is too low. If soil is too wet or too dry, leaves will drop.

Helxine soleirolia

See *Soleirolia soleirolii*

Hibiscus rosa-sinensis
Hibiscus

A woody shrub, hibiscus is popular in outdoor landscapes in warm regions. Given plenty of light and kept pruned to about 3 feet, it is attractive and easy to grow indoors. The plants have large blooms, available in pink, red, yellow, orange, or white. Single and double flower forms are available. Individual hibiscus flowers are short-lived, but the plant blooms throughout the year. The plant is usually treated before purchase with a growth retardant to keep it dense and compact without any pruning. When the effect wears off, the plant will become more open and require pruning.

Heliconia latifolia

Heliotropium

Hibiscus rosa-sinensis 'Hula Girl'

Hippeastrum

Hoya carnosa 'Krinkle'

Light: Provide 4 hours or more of direct sunlight from a south window.
Water: Keep evenly moist. Water thoroughly and discard drainage.
Humidity: Requires moist air. Use a humidifier for best results.
Temperatures: 55° to 60° F at night, 70° to 75° F during the day.
Fertilization: Fertilize all year, more heavily in summer.
Propagation: Take cuttings from stems or shoots before they have hardened or matured.
Grooming: Keep to desired height and shape with light pruning or clipping at any time. Give plant plenty of room to grow.
Repotting: Repot in winter or early spring, as needed.
Problems: Susceptible to spider mites, especially if air is too dry. If plant is in a draft or dry air, leaves will scorch. Will not bloom in low light.

Hippeastrum
Amaryllis, Barbados lily

The strap leaves of the lilylike amaryllis emerge after it blooms. Its 1- to 2-foot stems have flower clusters that are 8 to 10 inches wide. They come in a wide array of colors: 'Apple Blossom' is pink, 'Beautiful Lady' is salmon-orange, 'Fire Dance' is bright red, and 'Scarlet Admiral' is deep scarlet. Seed-grown bulbs are sold by color in stores. Strains available through mail-order firms tend to produce more robust flowers.

The plant blooms in late winter and is moderately easy to grow; with proper care it lasts for many years. Pot bulbs in October. When a flower spike appears, place in a well-lit, cool (60° F) location. As buds grow and eventually flower, keep moist and fertilize monthly. After flowering, the foliage will grow for several months, then die back; allow the plant to dry out and become dormant.
Light: Place in a bright, indirectly lit south, east, or west window.
Water: Keep moist during growth and flowering; at other times, allow to dry between waterings.
Humidity: Average indoor humidity levels.
Temperatures: 50° to 55° F at night, 65° to 70° F during the day.
Fertilization: Fertilize only when plant is growing actively or flowering.

Propagation: Start any new plants from bulblets that develop beside the parent bulb.
Grooming: Pick off yellowed leaves.
Repotting: Repot every three to four years when bulb outgrows its pot.
Problems: Subject to crown rot in overly moist conditions.

Hoya
Hoya, waxplant

Hoyas are vining plants with thickened leaves produced on self-branching stems. Given enough light, they will produce clusters of extremely fragrant, waxy flowers in summer or fall, depending on the cultivar. The flowers form on the same spurs year after year, so be careful not to prune off these leafless vine extensions. Train the plants on a trellis or use them in a hanging basket. The vines will get quite long, but you can double them back to give the plant a denser appearance. Many forms have variegated or variously colored leaves. The most common plants are varieties of *H. carnosa*. *H. bella* is a small-leaved species that is also popular.
Light: Place in a bright, indirectly lit south, east, or west window.
Water: Keep very moist during growth and flowering; at other times, allow to dry between waterings.
Humidity: Average indoor humidity levels.
Temperatures: 50° to 55° F at night, 60° to 65° F during the day.
Fertilization: Fertilize only when plant is growing actively or flowering.
Propagation: Take stem cuttings at any time.
Grooming: Keep to desired height and shape with light pruning or clipping at any time, being careful not to cut off the flower spurs.
Repotting: Repot infrequently. New plants need to grow in a medium-to-large pot until almost root bound before they will bloom.
Problems: Will not bloom if light is too low.

Hyacinthus orientalis
Hyacinth

Hyacinths are usually purchased from florists for indoor blooms in late winter. Their fragrant blossoms are red, pink, blue, yellow, or white. During flowering they can be placed almost anywhere indoors, but need bright light to flourish. To force your own flowers, buy mature bulbs in October, pot them, and allow them to root in a cool, dark spot for 8 weeks. They should bloom 2 or 3 weeks after being brought into a warmer and brighter spot. Tend the plant until it dies back, then plant it in the garden.

Light: Provide at least 4 hours of curtain-filtered sunlight from a bright south, east, or west window after flowering has ceased.

Water: Keep very moist during growth and flowering; at other times, allow to dry between waterings.

Humidity: Average indoor humidity levels.

Temperatures: 50° to 55° F at night, 60° to 65° F during the day.

Fertilization: Do not fertilize when plant is blooming. Fertilize lightly at other times.

Propagation: Start new plants from the bulblets that develop beside the parent bulb.

Grooming: Remove old leaves as plant goes dormant. Cut flower stalks if you wish.

Repotting: Plant bulb in the garden after it goes dormant.

Problems: Poor drainage, too-frequent watering, or standing in water will cause root rot.

Hydrangea macrophylla
Hydrangea

Hydrangea flowers are 8 to 10 inches in diameter, immense clusters of ½- to 1-inch flowers. Shiny, oval leaves 2 to 6 inches long set off the flowers. The blooms are pink, red, white, blue, or mauve. Blue flowers will turn pink in neutral or alkaline soil. Adding aluminum sulfate or iron sulfate to the soil will produce blue flowers; applying lime or wood ashes will neutralize the soil pH and produce pink or red flowers.

The plant can be purchased in bloom during the spring or summer. It is easy to care for while flowering but will not usually bloom in the home the following season. For blooms to last 6 weeks, two conditions must be met: The plant must be in a cool location and the soil must never be allowed to dry. Daily watering may be necessary during flowering. If your tap water is especially hard, be sure to leach the soil frequently; use rainwater whenever possible. In mild

climates you can plant hydrangea outdoors for summer blooms.

Light: Provide at least 4 hours of curtain-filtered sunlight from a bright south, east, or west window.

Water: Keep very moist, but do not allow to stand in water.

Humidity: Average indoor humidity levels.

Temperatures: 50° to 55° F at night, 65° to 70° F during the day.

Fertilization: Fertilize when plant is growing actively or flowering.

Propagation: Take cuttings from stems or shoots that have recently matured.

Grooming: Discard after flowering, or prune and plant outdoors.

Repotting: Not usually done.

Problems: Dry soil or a high level of soluble salts may damage roots, causing plant to die back. If plant is in a draft or dry air, leaves will scorch.

Impatiens
Impatiens, balsam, patient-lucy, busy-lizzy

Growing impatiens is an easy way to bring natural color indoors all year. They're excellent decorations for a sunny table, window box, or windowsill. Regular care of impatiens will reward you with a constantly blossoming plant to brighten your home.

I. balsamina (common balsam) is an annual; it will bloom profusely for months in summer and winter, then die. Taller varieties of this species are usually grown in the garden. Although you may be tempted to bring outdoor plants indoors, their large size and lanky shape become more apparent and distracting once they are indoors. Dwarf varieties are far more attractive. Another species, *I. wallerana* (busy-lizzy), an everblooming perennial, is also easy to raise indoors. It is also known as *I. holstii* and *I. sultanii*. It grows up to 15 inches high, and has flowers 1 to 2 inches across in a wide array of colors—pink, red, orange, purple, white, and variegated. 'Tangerine' features a richly colored flower and handsome leaves.

The New Guinea hybrids (*I. × hawkeri*) were developed from a number of species native to New Guinea. These plants are perennials grown as annuals and are well suited to container culture. The flowers are large, and pink, red, orange, lavender, or purple. New Guinea

Hydrangea macrophylla

Impatiens wallerana 'Blitz'

Impatiens × hawkeri (New Guinea hybrid)

Ixora duffii

Jasmine: *Jasminum polyanthum*

hybrids need plenty of water and fertilizer and more light than other impatiens.

Light: Provide at least 4 hours of curtain-filtered sunlight from a bright south, east, or west window.

Water: Keep evenly moist. Water thoroughly and discard drainage.

Humidity: Average indoor humidity levels.

Temperatures: 50° to 55° F at night, 60° to 65° F during the day.

Fertilization: Fertilize all year, more heavily in summer.

Propagation: Start from seeds. Sow in a small pot and transplant seedlings as needed. Or grow from cuttings.

Grooming: Pinch back leggy branches to control shape and encourage blossoms.

Repotting: Transplant seedlings several times, as they grow. Plants that are slightly pot-bound will bloom more profusely.

Problems: Susceptible to spider mites, especially if air is too dry. If soil is too wet or too dry, leaves will drop. Will not bloom if light is too low. If you bring an impatiens in from the garden in fall, be sure it is free of pests, particularly whiteflies and spider mites.

Ixora
Ixora, flame-of-the-woods, jungle-geranium

Ixoras are compact, shrubby plants that bloom over an extended period beginning in summer. The stems bear large clusters of medium-sized flowers in red, yellow, orange, or white. The flower clusters tend to bend the stems, so you may wish to stake them during flowering. These plants need plenty of light and warmth to do well year after year.

Light: Provide 4 hours or more of direct sunlight from a south window. Does best in a greenhouse setting.

Water: Keep evenly moist. Water thoroughly and discard drainage.

Humidity: Requires moist air. Use a humidifier for best results.

Temperatures: 55° to 60° F at night, 70° to 75° F during the day.

Fertilization: Fertilize all year, more heavily in summer.

Propagation: Take cuttings from stems or shoots before they have hardened or matured.

Grooming: Prune after flowering.

Repotting: Repot in winter or early spring, as needed.

Problems: If light is too low, will get spindly and weak, and will not bloom.

Jasmines

Many types of plants are known under the name jasmine or jessamine. Those grown indoors generally have in common attractively perfumed flowers that are white to yellow in color and most highly scented at night. Most are twining and viny, requiring staking and regular pinching. The foliage is often shiny, making the plant attractive even when it is not in bloom. Their family background is varied: true jasmines (*Jasminum*) are in the Olive family; the others are in the Dogbane family, the Logania family, or the Nightshade family. Their flowering season also varies, but the most popular ones are winter or early spring bloomers.

Among the true jasmines, *J. polyanthum* is probably the most commonly grown. A winter bloomer, it bears dozens of scented, white, star-shaped flowers at a time, even as a small plant. Also popular is *J. grandiflorum* (poet's jasmine), bearing scented, white flowers in the summer. *J. sambac* 'Maid of Orleans' and *J. sambac* 'Grand Duke of Tuscany', known as Arabian jasmines, produce rose-shaped semidouble or double flowers that open a creamy white and fade to purple. Pungently scented, they bloom intermittently throughout the year. Arabian jasmines are more shrubby than most other jasmines.

Among the false jasmines, *Cestrum nocturnum* (night-blooming jasmine) bears greenish cream flowers from summer to fall. As the common name suggests, they are scented only at night. Both *Gelsemium sempervirens* (Carolina jessamine), which bears scented, yellow, trumpet-shaped blossoms, and *Trachelospermum jasminoides* (confederate-jasmine), with highly perfumed, white, star-shaped flowers, are hardier than the mostly subtropical true jasmines and can be grown outdoors in areas where temperatures do not drop far below zero. Indoors, both bloom in late winter or early spring.

Light: Provide 4 hours or more of direct sunlight from a south window. Does best in a greenhouse setting.

Water: Keep evenly moist during growth and flowering; at other times, allow to dry slightly between waterings.

Humidity: Average indoor humidity levels.

Temperatures: During summer, 65° to 70° F at night, 75° to 80° F during the day. During winter, lowering temperatures to 40° to 50° F at night will help stimulate flowering. Arabian jasmines prefer warmer winter night temperatures (60° to 65° F).

Fertilization: Fertilize all year, but more heavily during the growing season.

Propagation: Take stem cuttings at any time. *Gelsemium sempervirens* can be air-layered.

Grooming: Prune after flowering, removing overly long branches. Pinch back to improve form. Be careful not to pinch off flower buds. Can be trained up a trellis or other support.

Repotting: Repot at any time.

Problems: Will not bloom if light is too low. If soil is either too wet or too dry, leaves will drop. Spider mites are a problem when air is dry.

Justicia brandegeana
Shrimp-plant

The floral parts of the shrimp-plant, formerly classified as *Beloperone guttata,* are 3 to 4 inches long and hang downward. The tiny flowers are borne between scale-shaped bracts; together they resemble a shrimp. Cultivars are available in yellow, salmon, or red. The plants are woody shrubs that can grow quite large. Indoors, keep them pruned to about 2 feet.

Light: Keep in about 4 hours of direct sunlight in winter. Provide curtain-filtered sunlight in summer, from a south or west window.

Water: Let plant approach dryness before watering, then water thoroughly and discard drainage.

Humidity: Average indoor humidity levels.

Temperatures: 50° to 55° F at night, 65° to 70° F during the day.

Fertilization: Fertilize all year, more heavily in summer.

Propagation: Take stem cuttings at any time.

Grooming: Prune in early spring. Pinch back stem tips of young or regrowing plants to improve form. Be

Jasmine: *Gelsemium sempervirens*

Jasmine: *Trachelospermum jasminoides*

Justicia brandegeana

Justicia carnea

Lachenalia aloides

Lantana camara

careful not to remove flower buds when pruning.

Repotting: Repot at any time.

Problems: Will get spindly and weak if light is too low.

Justicia carnea
King's-crown, Brazilian-plume

King's-crown is a large plant that bears groups of rose-colored flowers on spikes that grow above the foliage. It blooms in late summer. The leaves are 4 to 8 inches long, oval, and borne all along 2- to 3-foot stems. Keep the plant warm at all times; reduce fertilization after flowering.

Light: Keep in about 4 hours of direct sunlight in winter. Provide curtain-filtered sunlight in summer, from a south or west window.

Water: Keep evenly moist. Water thoroughly and discard drainage.

Humidity: Requires moist air. Use a humidifier for best results.

Temperatures: 55° to 60° F at night, 70° to 75° F during the day.

Fertilization: Fertilize all year, more heavily in summer.

Propagation: Take cuttings from stems or shoots before they have hardened or matured.

Grooming: Prune after flowering.

Repotting: Repot in winter or early spring, as needed.

Problems: If light is too low, will get spindly and weak, and will not bloom.

Lachenalia
Cape cowslip, leopard lily

Cape cowslips are becoming increasingly popular. They are bulbs and easy to force into bloom. Their striking multicolored yellow and red flowers add color and cheer to any household in winter. The leaves are large and sometimes have purple spots, adding interest to the plant. Most cultivars that bloom in late winter are planted in fall. As with any other bulb, the plant needs a dormancy period after the foliage has died back.

Light: Four hours or more of direct sunlight from a south window.

Water: Keep very moist during growth and flowering; at other times, allow to dry between waterings.

Humidity: Average indoor humidity levels.

Temperatures: 40°F to 45° F at night, 60° to 65° F during the day.

Fertilization: Fertilize only when plant is growing actively or flowering.

Propagation: Start new plants from the bulblets that develop beside the parent bulb.

Grooming: Remove old leaves as plant goes dormant.

Repotting: Repot infrequently.

Problems: Will not bloom if light is too low. Poor drainage, too-frequent watering, or standing in water will cause root rot.

Lantana
Lantana

Lantanas are small, woody shrubs that bear clusters of fragrant blossoms in red, yellow, white, and various bicolors. The flowers change color as they age, so a cluster usually will have a pleasing combination of light and dark flowers. The foliage has a distinctive aroma when crushed or bruised. The stems are prickly.

Indoors, lantanas bloom most profusely in early summer, but will bloom a little throughout the year if given plenty of light. The plants tend to get leggy if not clipped frequently. Lantanas are often used in hanging baskets; some cultivars are quite trailing in habit. If you are a devoted and patient gardener, you can train and prune lantanas into the shape of a tree. It would be best to do this in a greenhouse. Lantana, which can look and smell like lemon verbena, is quite poisonous.

Light: Provide 4 hours or more of direct sunlight from a south window. Does best in a greenhouse setting.

Water: Keep soil slightly moist at all times during the growing season, drier when the plant is resting.

Humidity: Requires moist air. Use a humidifier for best results.

Temperatures: 50° to 55° F at night, 65° to 70° F during the day.

Fertilization: Fertilize all year, more heavily in summer.

Propagation: Take stem cuttings at any time.

Grooming: Prune just before the heavy blossoming period. Keep to desired height and shape with light pruning or clipping at any time. Be careful not to cut off flower buds when pruning.

Repotting: Repot in winter or early spring, as needed.

Problems: If light is too low, will not bloom, and will get spindly and weak. If plant is in a draft or dry air, leaves will scorch. Whiteflies can be quite a nuisance; watch also for spider mites, aphids, and mealybugs.

Lilium longiflorum
Easter lily

Easter lilies are one of the most popular flowering potted plants sold in the United States. They are occasionally used as cut flowers. Blooming plants will last longer if they are kept cool, out of drafts, and constantly moist. To prolong the life of the flowers, remove the pollen-bearing, yellow anthers just as the flowers open. After flowering, care for the plant until the foliage yellows, placing it in a bright window and fertilizing it lightly. Most gardeners then plant the bulb outdoors in the garden, where it will flower every summer. You might get another Easter flowering if you leave the plant in its pot and move it outdoors, protect it from early freezes, and bring it indoors in late November. Force it to flower with high light and warmth.

Light: Will survive in low (reading-level) light. After flowering, place plant in a bright, indirectly lit south, east, or west window.

Water: Keep evenly moist. Water thoroughly and discard drainage.

Humidity: Average indoor humidity levels.

Temperatures: 50° to 55° F at night, 60° to 65° F during the day.

Fertilization: Do not fertilize when plant is in flower. Fertilize lightly at other times.

Propagation: Start new plants from the bulblets that develop beside the parent bulb.

Grooming: Remove faded flowers.

Repotting: Plant outdoors after foliage dies back.

Problems: Poor drainage, too-frequent watering, or standing in water will cause root rot.

Malpighia coccigera
Holly malpighia, miniature-holly

Malpighias are suitable for indoor gardens because they bloom as small plants, grow slowly, and seldom get more than a foot tall. Their leaves are similar to those of outdoor holly; though on the same plant some leaves are spiny and others not. The summer flowers are small and pink and are followed by red berries. Keep malpighias pruned into a shrub form.

Light: Provide at least 4 hours of curtain-filtered sunlight from a bright south, east, or west window.

Water: Let plant approach dryness before watering, then water thoroughly and discard drainage.

Humidity: Average indoor humidity levels.

Temperatures: 50° to 55° F at night, 65° to 70° F during the day.

Fertilization: Fertilize lightly throughout the growing season.

Propagation: Take cuttings from stems or shoots that have recently matured. Seeds are available, but can be more difficult than cuttings.

Grooming: Prune after flowering or fruiting.

Repotting: Repot infrequently.

Problems: Will not bloom if light is too low. Dry soil or a high level of soluble salts may damage roots, causing plant to die back.

Mandevilla sanderi
Dipladenia

Dipladenia is a woody-stemmed climber grown for its trumpet-shaped, five-petaled flowers. Up to 3 inches across, the flowers are light pink to deep rose with an orange to yellow throat. They appear from spring through autumn. The stems will twine around a support, or you can trim back the rampant growth to give the plant a shrubby appearance. Flowers appear on new growth, so heavy pruning will help stimulate new blooms.

Light: Place in a bright, indirectly lit south, east, or west window.

Water: Keep evenly moist during the growing season. During the winter rest period, allow to dry out between waterings.

Humidity: Average indoor humidity levels.

Lilium longiflorum var. *eximium*

Malpighia coccigera

Mandevilla 'Alice du Pont'

Mandevilla splendens

Mitriostigma axillare

Temperatures: 65° to 70° F at night, 75° to 80° F during the day. During the winter rest period, cooler temperatures (down to 50° F) are appreciated.
Fertilization: Fertilize when plant is growing actively or flowering.
Propagation: Not easy to propagate. Try taking stem cuttings, at any time, and rooting at warm temperatures using a rooting hormone.
Grooming: Remove yellowed leaves and faded flowers. Prune in fall to encourage plentiful new growth.
Repotting: Repot annually in spring.
Problems: Will not bloom if light is too low. Subject to spider mites and leaf drop in dry air.

Manettia cordifolia var. glabra
Firecracker vine

This plant is usually trained onto a small trellis. It is a little leggy for use in a hanging basket. Given good light, it will blossom throughout the year. The flowers are tubular, red, and tipped with yellow. They resemble a lighted firecracker.
Light: Provide at least 4 hours of curtain-filtered sunlight from a bright south, east, or west window.
Water: Keep evenly moist. Water thoroughly and discard drainage.
Humidity: Average indoor humidity levels.
Temperatures: 50° to 55° F at night, 65° to 70° F during the day.
Fertilization: Fertilize all year, more heavily in summer.
Propagation: Take stem cuttings at any time.
Grooming: Keep to desired height and shape with light pruning or clipping at any time.
Repotting: Repot in winter or early spring, as needed.
Problems: Will get spindly and weak if light is too low.

Medinilla magnifica
Medinilla

Medinilla magnifica is a well-chosen name for this plant, for it is indeed magnificent when in bloom. The drooping flower stalks, measuring up to 16 inches in length, are composed of pink bracts

and clusters of bell-shaped, carmine flowers. The plant itself is quite striking, with woody, four-sided stems and large, leathery leaves with prominent veins. Prune it back harshly after each flowering to keep it at a reasonable size.
Light: Place in a bright, indirectly lit south, east, or west window.
Water: Keep evenly moist during the growing season. During the winter rest period, allow to dry out between waterings.
Humidity: Requires very high humidity. Place on a humidifying tray for best results.
Temperatures: 65° to 70° F at night, 75° to 80° F during the day.
Fertilization: Fertilize when plant is growing actively or flowering.
Propagation: Not easy to propagate. Try taking stem cuttings, at any time, and rooting at warm temperatures using a rooting hormone.
Grooming: Remove yellowed leaves and faded flowers. Prune after flowering.
Repotting: Repot annually in spring.
Problems: Will not bloom if light is too low. Subject to spider mites and leaf drop in dry air.

Mitriostigma axillare
African gardenia

This is a shrubby plant with deep green, ruffled, shiny leaves and small, trumpet-shaped, white flowers borne at the leaf axils. Its relationship to the gardenia is shown by the heady perfume the flowers give off. But it is far easier to grow indoors than a gardenia, adapting well to most indoor conditions.
Light: Place in a bright, indirectly lit south, east, or west window.
Water: Keep plant evenly moist at all times.
Humidity: Average indoor humidity levels.
Temperatures: 60° to 65° F at night, 70° to 75° F during the day.
Fertilization: Fertilize when the plant is growing actively or flowering.
Propagation: Take stem cuttings in spring.
Grooming: Prune to encourage plentiful new growth.
Repotting: Repot annually in spring for best growth.
Problems: Leaves may yellow if soil dries out or temperature is too low.

Murraya paniculata
Orange-jasmine

This tropical shrub, once restricted mainly to greenhouse use, is now finding a new life as a subject for indoor bonsai and topiary. It also makes an attractive indoor tree or shrub. It bears pale brown branches and glossy green, compound leaves. Its most attractive feature, however, is the small, perfumed, white flowers that combine the odors of jasmine and orange blossoms. It will bloom several times a year under good conditions. Well pruned, it can be kept to 3 feet high or less, but allowed to grow to its full height, it will reach an impressive 10 feet.

Light: Place in a bright, indirectly lit south, east, or west window.

Water: Keep evenly moist.

Humidity: Average indoor humidity levels.

Temperatures: 65° to 70° F at night, 75° to 80° F during the day. During the winter rest period, cooler temperatures (down to 50° F) are appreciated.

Fertilization: Fertilize when plant is growing actively or flowering.

Propagation: Take stem cuttings at any time.

Grooming: Remove yellowed leaves. Prune after flowering.

Repotting: Repot annually in spring for best growth.

Problems: Will not bloom if light is too low.

Muscari
Grape hyacinth

Small bulb plants, grape hyacinth are popular because they are easy to force into bloom. Their size makes them ideal windowsill or desk plants. The tiny, blue or white flowers are borne on 6-inch stalks in midwinter or early spring. They are fragrant and last for quite a while. The leaves are narrow and grassy, and arch outward from the bulb tip. Force them as you would other common bulbs: Purchase mature bulbs in October, pot and keep cool until January, then bring them into a warm room for flowering. Tend the plants until the foliage dies back, and then plant them in the garden.

Light: Place in a bright, indirectly lit south, east, or west window.

Water: Keep evenly moist. Water thoroughly and discard drainage.

Humidity: Average indoor humidity levels.

Temperatures: 40° to 45° F at night, 60° to 65° F during the day.

Fertilization: Do not fertilize when in flower. Fertilize lightly at other times of the year.

Propagation: Start new plants from the bulblets that develop beside the parent bulb.

Grooming: Pick off yellowed leaves.

Repotting: Transplant to outdoor location in spring.

Problems: No significant problems.

Narcissus
Daffodils, narcissus

There are two types of narcissus bulbs used indoors for forcing. The plants that produce a single, trumpet-shaped flower on a 12-inch stalk are called daffodils and are hardy bulbs. Those that produce a group of small flowers on a single stem are called Tazetta narcissus and are hardy only in the South. Many cultivars in either group are suitable for indoor gardens. Buy mature bulbs in the fall and put them in potting soil, pebbles, or sand so that half of the bulb sits above the water or planting medium. Keep them at 35° to 40° F for several weeks until they sprout about 4 inches of growth. Then bring them into a well-lit room for flowering. Keep them cool during this time and do not fertilize. Discard the plant after flowering, or if it is hardy, place it outdoors in a flower bed. Allow the leaves to die back naturally.

Light: Will survive in low (reading-level) light. After flowering, place in a bright window until foliage dies back.

Water: Keep very moist while flowering.

Humidity: Average indoor humidity levels.

Temperatures: 40° to 45° F at night, 60° to 65° F during the day.

Fertilization: Do not fertilize when plant is in flower. Fertilize lightly at other times.

Propagation: Buy mature bulbs or take a large division from the bulb of a garden plant.

Grooming: Discard or plant outdoors after flowering.

Repotting: Not necessary.

Problems: No special problems.

Muscari armeniacum

Narcissus poeticus

Nerium oleander

Neomarica gracilis
Apostle-plant, walking-iris

The flattened, elongated leaves and general shape of the flower give the apostle-plant a resemblance to the iris. The plants are large, with blue and white flowers borne on tall stalks. Each stalk usually has one flower open at a time. It will last only for a day or two, but then another opens. It is a winter bloomer, so usually needs some direct winter sunlight. Plantlets will form at the tops of the flower stems. You can root them to start other blooming specimens.
Light: Keep in about 4 hours of direct sunlight in winter. Provide curtain-filtered sunlight in summer, from a south or west window.
Water: Keep evenly moist. Water thoroughly and discard drainage.
Humidity: Average indoor humidity levels.
Temperatures: 50° to 55° F at night, 65° to 70° F during the day.
Fertilization: Fertilize all year, more heavily in summer.
Propagation: Remove plantlets or rooted side shoots as they form.
Grooming: Cut flower stalks for better appearance if you wish.
Repotting: Repot infrequently. Pot-bound plants will bloom more abundantly.
Problems: Will not bloom if light is too low.

Nerium oleander
Oleander

Oleander is a popular indoor shrub, reaching over 6 feet tall under average home conditions. It bears narrow, glossy, willowlike leaves on upward-growing branches. Clusters of often highly scented, white, yellow, pink, or red flowers bloom in summer. Both single and double forms are available, and some varieties have the added attraction of variegated leaves. Oleander is often grown in tubs and placed outdoors for the summer. This stimulates heavier flowering. All parts of this plant are extremely poisonous, and it should not be grown where small children or pets have access to it. Always wash your hands after pruning and taking cuttings, to be sure you don't accidently ingest the sap.

Light: Keep in direct sunlight in winter. In summer provide 4 hours of bright, indirect sunlight from a south, east, or west window.
Water: Let the plant approach dryness before watering, then water thoroughly and discard drainage.
Humidity: Average indoor humidity levels.
Temperatures: 60° to 65° F at night, 70° to 75° F during the day. During the winter rest period, cooler temperatures (down to 50° F) are appreciated.
Fertilization: Fertilize when plant is growing actively.
Propagation: Take stem cuttings in early summer from branches not bearing flower buds.
Grooming: Prune severely after flowering. Pick up and destroy fallen leaves and faded flowers.
Repotting: Repot annually in spring for best growth.
Problems: Needs some direct sunlight to bloom. Watch for scale and spider mites.

Orchids

Growing exquisite orchids is regarded by most people as the supreme gardening achievement. But in fact, some species of orchids grow quite well indoors and require less routine care than other houseplants. In addition, improved breeding techniques have significantly increased the availability and lowered the cost of many cultivars. Placed on a windowsill in the living room, an orchid is sure to be the center of attention.

Orchids may have striking flowers, but their foliage is generally unattractive. They often have wrinkled, lumpy pseudobulbs at the base of the leaves and bear thick, aerial roots that many people find objectionable. Some indoor gardeners grow orchids among other houseplants, where their 'ugly duckling' appearance is not so noticeable, then move them to a more visible spot when they bloom.

It is wise to purchase mature, blooming orchids, as young plants can take years to flower. Described here are some of the orchids that grow well under average indoor conditions.

Orchid: *Brassavola perrinii*

Aerides
Foxtail orchid

Aerides is a summer-flowering epiphyte of moderate size. Given full sun, this orchid blooms profusely, with fragrant flowers in red, pink, or white on long stalks that arch outward from the plant. *A. odorata* is particularly fragrant and popular with indoor orchid growers.

Angraecum
Comet orchid

Many angraecums are small plants well suited to indoor gardens. *A. superbum* 'Eburneum', which is larger than most, bears waxy, greenish white flowers and strap-shaped leaves. It, as do most angraecums, flowers in winter. The plants need brightness and even moisture, but are tolerant of cool night temperatures and normal household humidity.

Brassavola
Lady-of-the-night

Brassavolas are popular plants for beginners, since they bloom readily even under adverse conditions. The flowers are usually quite large for the size of the plant and greenish in color. Their most notable characteristic is that they are intensely fragrant, but only at night, which gives the group its common name. Best known are *B. nodosa* and *B. digbyana* (the latter is more properly classified as *Rhyncholaelia digbyana*). Brassavolas require abundant watering and full sun when in active growth.

Brassia
Spider orchid

Brassias bear flowers with long, narrow sepals that give rise to their common name. The plants are fairly large, with 15-inch flower spikes and leaves that grow to 10 inches long. They generally bloom in fall or winter if given sufficient sunlight.

Bulbophyllum

Bulbophyllums are the largest and most varied genus in the orchid family. Some are especially large plants with equally large flowers, but the most popular are dwarf or even miniature plants, which

fit easily on even a narrow windowsill. Cultural requirements vary widely according to their native habitats, but most prefer warm temperatures, some shade from direct sun, and regular waterings while they are growing actively.

Cattleya

The genus *Cattleya* is not nearly as popular as the numerous hybrid genera derived from crosses between it and related orchids, such as *Rhyncholaelia, Laelia,* and *Sophronitis.* These breeder-made genera—among them × *Brassolaeliocattleya,* × *Laeliocattleya,* × *Sophrolaeliocattleya,* and × *Potinara*—are generally referred to by orchid fanciers as cattleyas or "catts." Cattleyas in the large sense include both the old-fashioned corsage orchids and an increasingly popular range of miniature hybrids with smaller blooms. The vigorous plants produce gorgeous blooms when they receive plenty of sun.

Cymbidium

The miniature cymbidiums are especially well suited for many indoor gardens. Yet even with miniatures, the narrow, arching foliage needs room. Give the plants cool nights to promote flowering, which usually occurs in late summer or fall. There are many hybrids available in a wide variety of colors. The flowers are long lasting, even in arrangements.

Dendrobium

Dendrobiums are mostly epiphytic orchids; both evergreen and deciduous types are available. Large flowers bloom in clusters or in a row along the stem. They last between a week and several months, depending on the species, and need plenty of sun, as do most orchids.

Epidendrum
Buttonhole orchid, clamshell orchid

Epidendrums are a large family of orchids, some growing as canes and others as pseudobulbs. Many species are small and suitable for warm, indoor window boxes in winter sun. Some species may bloom continuously under suitable conditions.

Orchid: *Cattleya*

Orchid: *Miltoniopsis*

Orchid: *Dendrobium*

Orchid: *Oncidium*

Orchid: *Cattleya*
Orchid: *Brassia*

Orchid: *Masdevallia veitchiana* 'Williams'

Orchid: *Miltonia*

Orchid: *Odontoglossum*

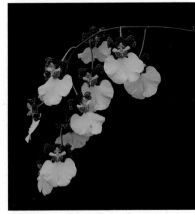

Orchid: *Oncidium*

Orchid: *Haemaria*

Haemaria discolor var. dawsoniana
Jewel orchid

The jewel orchid is one of several orchids grown as much for its exceptional foliage as for its bloom. This plant will grow in regular potting soil. It may reach a height of 8 inches or so on somewhat trailing stems. Its leaves are a velvety, purplish green, with a prominent network of red and white veins. Small, white or pinkish flowers grow on long spikes. When given good, indirect light, jewel orchids will bloom in winter.

Masdevallia
Tailed orchid

Masdevallias are cool-loving orchids that have curiously unorchidlike flowers: broad sepals partially joined at the base and pointed at the tips. They like bright light with little direct sun, and high humidity.

Miltonia
Pansy orchid

The flat-faced, heavily marbled flowers of pansy orchids give them their common name. The original genus has been subdivided into two closely related ones: *Miltonia* and *Miltoniopsis*. The former, which has two-leaved pseudobulbs, prefers warm temperatures the year around. *Miltoniopsis*, which has one-leaved pseudobulbs, prefers cooler temperatures. Both require filtered light and high air humidity.

Odontoglossum

Odontoglossums need moist air and stable growing conditions. They are best suited for greenhouses where they can get direct sunlight in winter and filtered light in summer. There are many species and hybrids available, most bearing large flowers that are fragrant and long lasting. Many bloom twice a year.

Oncidium
Dancing-lady

Oncidiums are a large group of epiphytic orchids. They generally produce stalks of yellow flowers speckled with brown. Flower size depends on the species, but is usually quite small. For the most part, they require bright light with protection from direct summer sunlight.

Paphiopedilum
Lady's-slipper

The long-lasting flowers of the paphiopedilum bear a distinctive pouch. Mostly terrestrial, paphiopedilums prefer a more humid, less airy growing medium than other orchids, which can be provided by adding extra sphagnum moss to their mix. There are two main groups: those with green leaves, which prefer cool growing conditions, and those with variegated leaves, which adapt well to regular indoor temperatures. All prefer filtered light.

Phalaenopsis
Moth-orchid

Moth-orchids are probably the best orchids for beginners. They adapt well to regular indoor temperatures (75° F during the day and 65° F at night), do not require excessively high air humidity, and are generally well suited to the average home. Unlike the many orchids that are grown solely for their flowers, moth-orchids often have attractively marbled foliage. They produce sprays of 2- to 3-inch flowers in a wide range of colors. Modern hybrids may bloom throughout much of the year. Close relatives requiring similar care include *Doritis* and the hybrid genus × *Doritaenopsis.*

Rodriguezia

Most of the orchids in the *Rodriguezia* genus are miniatures, less than a foot tall. The plants bloom abundantly, producing large clusters of small, fragrant flowers, usually white or pinkish. Keep these plants moist and in damp air.

Vanda

Standard vandas are too large for most homes, but miniature hybrids are now available that are more suited to home culture. These plants prefer sunlight from a south window. They do well in greenhouses because of their need for strong light.

Care of Orchids

Orchids are an extremely varied group of plants, and their cultural requirements vary considerably, not only from one genus to another but from one species to another. This diversity makes it hard to give a general summary of orchid care, but it also means that there is an orchid that will adapt to just about every indoor situation. Always check on the cultural needs of an orchid before purchasing it; it is far easier to find an orchid that suits your conditions than to change your conditions to suit a particular species.

Light: Most orchids fall into one of two categories: those requiring direct sunlight and those preferring filtered light. The first group should be given full sun throughout the winter months, preferably in a south-facing window, and bright light with some shading from direct midday sun in summer. If they take on a yellowish tinge, all is well; if their foliage is bright green, they need more light. This group may need supplemental artificial light during the winter. The orchids that prefer filtered light are suited to either east or west windows or curtain-filtered summer windows the year around. They also do well under fluorescent lights.

Water: Varieties with thick leaves and large pseudobulbs prefer to be watered thoroughly, then allowed to dry out before the next watering. Those with thin roots and no pseudobulbs generally prefer being watered as soon as the potting mix starts to dry. Most orchids appreciate a short period of dry conditions in autumn to stimulate flowering.

Temperatures: Daytime temperatures of 70° to 75° F are generally acceptable throughout much of the year. A night temperature up to 15° F lower is appreciated. An annual period of cool temperatures (down to 50° F) combined with reduced watering will induce flowering in many orchids.

Fertilization: Fertilize lightly throughout the year, more heavily in summer.

Propagation: Most orchids can be divided every few years; at least three pseudobulbs should be left in each pot. Some also produce *keikis*, or plantlets, at the bases or on the flower stalks. These can be removed and potted up once they have produced roots.

Orchid: *Paphiopedilum*

Orchid: *Phalaenopsis*
Orchid: *Vanda*

Oxalis regnellii

Pachystachys lutea

Grooming: Pick off yellowed leaves and cut back flower stalks to the nearest green joint after blooming.

Repotting: Allow roots to extend beyond pot as long as plant continues to grow well. When growth is inhibited, repot into a larger container using an appropriate orchid potting mix. Very few orchids grow well in regular potting mixes, since they don't allow sufficient air circulation to the roots. Use a special orchid mix (generally a mixture of bark, perlite, sphagnum moss, and other bulky products). Many orchids will also grow on bark or on pieces of osmunda fiber. Tie them solidly to the support until they are well rooted.

Problems: Limp leaves or flowers are caused mainly by insufficient light, but can also be due to improper watering (usually overwatering). Yellowing leaves can be expected if leaves are old or plant is deciduous; otherwise, yellowing results from overwatering or sunburn. Brown spots are due to too much sun or to leaf spot disease.

Oxalis
Oxalis, peppermint stripe

Most oxalis are bulbous plants that rarely grow above 6 or 8 inches, although some with fibrous roots and upright stems do grow taller. Since they produce relatively large flowers (1 to 2 inches) all winter long, they make popular windowsill plants. Various cultivars are available in pink, white, or red. The foliage resembles clover, sometimes with a reddish hue. Cut off the flower stalks to prevent the messy petals and seed pods from dropping. Most bulbous types require a rest in the summer; they will die back as summer approaches. *O. braziliensis* produces wine red flowers in early spring over dense clumps of shiny, three-lobed leaves. *O. lobata* has yellow flowers held well above the foliage. *O. purpurea* (or *O. variabilis*) grows easily, with large, pink to rose red flowers. *O. regnellii* is one of the most distinctive and easiest to grow, with strong stalks of white flowers and precisely triangular leaf segments. *O. versicolor* (peppermint stripe) has an abundance of white flowers that are etched in red.

Light: Provide 4 hours or more of curtain-filtered light from a south window.

Water: Keep moist during growth and flowering; at other times, allow to dry between waterings.

Humidity: Average indoor humidity levels.

Temperatures: 50° to 55° F at night, 65° to 70° F during the day.

Fertilization: Fertilize only when plant is growing actively or flowering.

Propagation: Start new plants from the bulblets that develop beside the parent bulb. Grow fibrous-rooted oxalis from stem cuttings.

Grooming: Keep stemmed types to desired height and shape with light pruning or clipping at any time. Remove dead leaves and flowers from both types.

Repotting: Repot each year.

Problems: Susceptible to spider mites, especially if air is too dry. If plant is in a draft or dry air, leaves will scorch. Will get spindly and weak if light is too low.

Pachystachys lutea
Lollipop-plant

Lollipop-plant is a fast-growing shrub with decorative and long-lasting yellow bracts and short-lived but abundant white flowers. The leaves are large and puckered, slightly wavy along the edges. The bracts appear in conical clusters 4 to 6 inches long at the ends of the branches during the summer, or intermittently throughout the year under artificial light.

Light: Place in a bright, indirectly lit south, east, or west window. Grows well under artificial light.

Water: Keep evenly moist.

Humidity: Prefers high humidity. Keep plant on a humidifying tray during winter.

Temperatures: 65° to 70° F at night, 75° to 80° F during the day.

Fertilization: Fertilize when plant is growing actively or flowering.

Propagation: Take stem cuttings at any time; they root easily.

Grooming: Prune heavily after flowering to encourage plant to branch from the base. Most attractive when kept under 3 feet in height.

Repotting: Repot annually in spring for best growth.

Problems: Will not bloom if light is too low. Bottom leaf loss is normal, but can be reduced by heavy pruning.

Passiflora
Passionflower

Passionflowers are large, rapidly growing vines that cling with long tendrils to supports. The large flowers (4 to 6 inches wide) are complex and quite striking. *P. caerulea* has purple, white, and blue flowers in summer and autumn, followed by yellow, nonedible fruits. *P. coccinea* has showy, crimson flowers with protruding, bright yellow stamens. Its edible fruits are orange or yellow, striped with green. *P.* 'Incense' has fragrant, wavy, royal purple flowers in summer. *P. quadrangularis* is a standard fruiting passionflower with fragrant, white, pink, or violet flowers in summer. Because of its size, growth habit, and light requirements, this plant does best in a greenhouse or solarium. It should not require much care, except light pruning to keep it under control. However, it does need a dormancy period in late fall or early winter.

Light: Provide 4 hours or more of direct sunlight from a south window. Does best in a greenhouse setting.

Water: Keep moist during growth and flowering; at other times, allow to dry between waterings.

Humidity: Requires moist air. Use a humidifier for best results.

Temperatures: 55° to 60° F at night, 70° to 75° F during the day.

Fertilization: Fertilize only when plant is growing actively or flowering.

Propagation: Take stem cuttings at any time. Seeds are available, but can be more difficult than cuttings.

Grooming: Prune just before the heavy blossoming period, being careful not to remove flower buds.

Repotting: Repot infrequently.

Problems: Will not bloom if kept in low light.

Pelargonium
Florist's geranium, ivy geranium, Martha Washington geranium

Natives of South Africa, geraniums are versatile and appealing, available in thousands of species and named varieties. Some are grown outdoors; others can be easily moved indoors from outside. Common geraniums are hybrids of *P. ✕ hortorum* and often have a dark green or blackish ring in each leaf. Varieties are available in red, salmon, apricot, tangerine, pink, and white.

Geraniums can add distinction to an indoor decor all year. They bloom in every season, but are most appreciated in January and February when little else is in flower. Many get quite large and need plenty of room, but there are also miniature and dwarf varieties of *P. ✕ hortorum.* Fancy-leaf geraniums have varicolored leaves, often in bronzes, scarlets, and yellows.

P. ✕ domesticum (Martha Washington or regal geranium) grows to about 2½ feet. It is most noteworthy for its flowers, which are large and come in a wide range of striking colors, some brilliantly blotched. Leaves are dark green, solid looking, with crinkled margins.

Scented-leaf varieties are grown primarily for the sharp, evocative fragrances of their leaves. *P. crispum* smells like lemon; *P. graveolens* and others, like rose; *P. ✕ nervosum,* like lime; *P. odoratissimum,* like apple. They bear flowers that would be considered satisfactory in another genus but seem pale beside their larger cousins. In general the scented-leaf plants are smaller and less easygoing than the other geraniums. For example, they are more sensitive to over- or underwatering.

Ivy geraniums, varieties of *P. peltatum,* bear leathery leaves with a shape similar to English ivy and sport many clusters of showy flowers, often veined with a darker shade of the overall color. These are excellent in hanging baskets near windows.

Geraniums are easy to care for in the proper environment. A sunny windowsill where it is cool (never above 75° F) and dry is ideal. Fertilize once a week, and water when the soil is dry.

Light: Provide 4 hours or more of direct sunlight from a south window.

Water: Let plant approach dryness before watering, then water thoroughly and discard drainage.

Humidity: Average indoor humidity levels.

Temperatures: 55° to 60° F at night, 70° to 75° F during the day.

Fertilization: Fertilize all year, more heavily in summer.

Propagation: Take stem cuttings at any time. Seeds are also available for many cultivars.

Grooming: Pinch back stem tips of young or regrowing plants in autumn to improve form, being careful not to remove flower buds. Remove faded blossoms.

Passiflora caerulea

Pelargonium peltatum 'Galilee'

Plumbago auriculata

Pentas lanceolata
Primula malacoides

Repotting: Repot in winter or early spring, as needed. Transplant seedlings several times, as they grow.

Problems: If light is too low, plant will get spindly and weak, and will not bloom. Sometimes troubled by white-flies and by rots.

Pentas lanceolata
Pentas, Egyptian star-cluster

Pentas will bloom all year if given plenty of light. The small flowers, which are red, purple, pink, or white, are borne in clusters at the ends of the branches. Pinch and train the plant into a bushy form approximately 12 to 16 inches tall, but be careful not to cut off developing flower clusters. Stake the plant if flowers pull the shoots over.

Light: Provide 4 hours or more of direct sunlight from a south window.

Water: Keep evenly moist. Water thoroughly and discard drainage.

Humidity: Average indoor humidity levels.

Temperatures: 50° to 55° F at night, 65° to 70° F during the day.

Fertilization: Fertilize all year, more heavily in summer.

Propagation: Take stem cuttings at any time.

Grooming: Keep to desired height and shape with light pruning or clipping at any time.

Repotting: Repot in winter or early spring, as needed.

Problems: If plant is in a draft or dry air, leaves will scorch.

Plumbago indica
Plumbago, leadwort

Plumbago, a large-leaved semiwoody plant, tends to trail and is usually grown in a hanging basket or staked in a pot. It produces clusters of pale blue or white flowers. Plumbago grows slowly indoors and must be given ample light and warmth. For these reasons, it is best suited for greenhouses or solariums.

Light: Provide 4 hours or more of direct sunlight from a south window. Does best in a greenhouse setting.

Water: Keep evenly moist. Water thoroughly and discard drainage.

Humidity: Requires moist air. Use a humidifier for best results.

Temperatures: 65° to 70° F at night, 75° to 80° F during the day.

Fertilization: Fertilize all year, more heavily in summer.

Propagation: Take stem cuttings at any time. Seeds are available, but can be more difficult than cuttings.

Grooming: Keep to desired height and shape with light pruning or clipping at any time.

Repotting: Repot in winter or early spring, as needed.

Problems: If light is too low, will get spindly and weak, and will not bloom.

Primula
Primrose, Chinese primrose, fairy primrose, German primrose

Primroses produce magnificent clusters of flowers on stalks above a rosette of light green leaves in winter. Cultivars are available in red, yellow, blue, white, and bicolors. It takes plenty of light, moist air, and very cool nights to get these plants to flower properly. They are usually purchased already in bloom, although they can be started and grown in a home greenhouse, provided they are kept moist. Any stress will make them susceptible to spider mite infestation.

The three species especially suited to growing indoors are *P. malacoides, P. obconica,* and *P. sinensis.* The largest is *P. malacoides,* commonly called the fairy primrose. Star-shaped, scented flowers are borne in tiers on tall stalks. *P. obconica* (German primrose) reaches a foot in height and blooms in white, lilac, crimson, or salmon. *P. sinensis* (Chinese primrose) is the primula usually carried by florists. This small plant features delicate, ruffled flowers in a wide range of colors, pink being the most common. All these primroses need similar care.

A well-lit, cool area, such as a sun porch, is ideal. If the plant is near a warm, sunny window, pack coarse sphagnum moss up to the rim of the pot to help keep both the soil and the roots cool.

Light: Place in a bright, indirectly lit south, east, or west window while in flower. Before flowering, does best in a greenhouse setting.

Water: Keep evenly moist. Water thoroughly and discard drainage.

Humidity: Requires moist air. Use a humidifier for best results.

Temperatures: 40° to 45° F at night, 60° to 65° F during the day.

Fertilization: Do not fertilize when in flower. Fertilize lightly during the rest of the year.

Propagation: Start from seeds. Sow in a small pot and transplant seedlings as needed.

Grooming: Pick off yellowed leaves, and blossoms as they fade.

Repotting: Repot in winter or early spring, as needed.

Problems: Susceptible to spider mites, especially if air is too dry. If in a draft or dry air, leaves will scorch. Dry soil or a high level of soluble salts will damage roots, causing plant to die back.

Punica granatum 'Nana'
Dwarf pomegranate

Dwarf pomegranate, a form of the well-known tropical fruit tree, will do well in a greenhouse or solarium. The plant has small leaves similar to myrtle leaves. It produces showy red flowers, mainly in early summer. The 2-inch fruits are edible and will mature on the plant if kept warm and moist. Since the fruits tend to pull the branches over, the plant may require staking. Prune frequently to produce a woody shrub.

Light: Provide 4 hours or more of direct sunlight from a south window. Does best in a greenhouse setting.

Water: Keep evenly moist. Water thoroughly and discard drainage.

Humidity: Requires moist air. Use a humidifier for best results.

Temperatures: 55° to 60° F at night, 70° to 75° F during the day.

Fertilization: Fertilize only when plant is growing actively or flowering.

Propagation: Take cuttings from stems or shoots before they have hardened or matured.

Grooming: Keep to desired height and shape with light pruning or clipping at any time.

Repotting: Repot infrequently, in winter or early spring when needed.

Problems: Will not bloom if light is too low.

Rhododendron
Azalea, rhododendron

Many cultivars of azaleas and a few rhododendrons are available in bloom as houseplants. After flowering, many are simply used as indoor foliage plants. Some may survive if planted outdoors,

although most azaleas sold as houseplants are not hardy enough for northern gardens. To encourage an azalea to bloom again inside the home, put the plant outside in early summer. Bring it back inside in early winter, after the cool days of fall, and put it in a cool place until it blooms again.

Light: May be placed anywhere when in bloom. After flowering, provide at least 4 hours of curtain-filtered sunlight from a bright south, east, or west window.

Water: Keep evenly moist. Water thoroughly and discard drainage.

Humidity: Requires moist air. Use a humidifier for best results.

Temperatures: 55° to 60° F at night, 70° to 75° F during the day.

Fertilization: Fertilize only when plant is growing actively or flowering. Use an acid-balanced fertilizer, and add trace elements once in spring.

Propagation: Take cuttings from stems or shoots before they have hardened or matured.

Grooming: Prune after flowering.

Repotting: Repot infrequently.

Problems: If plant is in a draft or dry air, leaves will scorch. Susceptible to spider mites, especially if air is too dry.

Rosa
Miniature rose

Although usually thought of as exquisite additions to outdoor gardens, miniature roses will also lend grace to your home. Delicate 1- to 1½-inch blooms are available in a wide range of colors. Grown as small bushes, climbers, or standards, they make an appealing indoor display. Their limited popularity stems from the difficulty gardeners have had in making them flourish indoors. However, new hybrids have eliminated many problems. 'Starina', 'Rainbow's End', 'Cupcake', 'Snow Bride', and 'Rise 'n' Shine' are a few reliable choices.

To grow miniatures successfully, give them the same care you would give them outdoors. Place them in a spot with abundant light and cool, well-circulated air. High humidity is a must, so place a humidifying tray beneath the pots. Allow the soil to dry slightly between thorough waterings. Apply a high-nitrogen fertilizer every 2 weeks. Rinse the leaves regularly with water, remove yellowing leaves, and clip off

Punica granatum 'Nana'

Rhododendron (Azalea)

Rosa 'Red Minimo' (Miniature)

Ruellia

Russelia equisetiformis

Scilla peruviana

the blossoms as soon as they fade. When pests, such as aphids or mites, invade, treat them immediately. After the last blossoms of summer have faded, prune back the plant severely.

Light: Keep in about 4 hours of direct sunlight in winter. Provide curtain-filtered sunlight in summer, from a south or west window.

Water: Keep evenly moist. Water thoroughly and discard drainage.

Humidity: Requires moist air. Use a humidifier for best results.

Temperatures: 50° to 55° F at night, 60° to 65° F during the day.

Fertilization: Fertilize all year, more heavily in summer.

Propagation: Take stem cuttings at any time.

Grooming: Keep to desired height and shape with light pruning or clipping at any time.

Repotting: Repot at any time.

Problems: Will not bloom if light is too low. If soil is too wet or too dry, leaves will drop. Susceptible to spider mites, especially if plant is too dry. Rinsing plant twice weekly sometimes prevents spider mites.

Ruellia
Monkey-plant, trailing velvetplant

The most commonly grown ruellia is *R. makoyana,* the monkey-plant. It blooms most heavily during fall and winter, producing rose red, trumpet-shaped flowers up to 2 inches in diameter. This plant remains attractive throughout the year because of its colorful leaves, which are silver-veined and velvety, olive green above and purple underneath. Another species, usually listed as *R. graecizans,* bears bright red, tubular flowers throughout the year over plain green foliage.

Light: Place in a bright, indirectly lit south, east, or west window.

Water: Keep evenly moist.

Humidity: Requires moist air. Use a humidifier for best results.

Temperatures: 65° to 70° F at night, 75° to 80° F during the day.

Fertilization: Fertilize when plant is growing actively or flowering.

Propagation: Take stem cuttings in spring or summer. *R. graecizans* can also be grown from seed.

Grooming: Pinch back regularly for full growth. Prune after flowering.

Repotting: Repot annually in spring for best growth.

Problems: Will not bloom if winter light is too low. Aphids can be a problem.

Russelia equisetiformis
Coralplant, fountain-plant

Russelias are hanging-basket plants that have arching branches of tiny leaves shaped like either needles or scales. The red flowers are borne on the ends of the branches, giving a cascading appearance. The plants are large, sometimes growing to 3 feet or more across. They must have plenty of light to continue blooming and to maintain a thick, vigorous branching habit.

Light: Provide 4 hours or more of direct sunlight from a south window. Does best in a greenhouse setting.

Water: Let plant approach dryness before watering, then water thoroughly and discard drainage.

Humidity: Requires moist air. Use a humidifier for best results.

Temperatures: 50° to 55° F at night, 65° to 70° F during the day.

Fertilization: Fertilize all year, more heavily in summer.

Propagation: Take cuttings from stems or shoots before they have hardened or matured.

Grooming: Start new plants to replace old specimens when they get weak. Give plant plenty of room.

Repotting: Transplant eventually to an 8-inch basket.

Problems: Poor drainage, too-frequent watering, or standing in water will cause root rot. Will not bloom if light is too low.

Scilla
Squill

Squill bulbs are commonly grown outdoors for their early spring flowers. The bell-shaped, blue flowers are produced on stalks 12 inches high. The moderate size of most squills makes them especially suited for winter flowering on a windowsill in the home. Plant several mature bulbs together in a pot in October and place in a cool, not freezing, spot until January. After they have flowered and the foliage has declined, you can plant them in the garden.

Light: Provide at least 4 hours of curtain-filtered sunlight from a bright south, east, or west window.
Water: Keep very moist during growth and flowering; at other times, allow to dry between waterings.
Humidity: Average indoor humidity levels.
Temperatures: 40° to 45° F at night, 60° to 65° F during the day.
Fertilization: Do not fertilize indoors.
Propagation: Start new plants from the bulblets that develop beside the parent bulb.
Grooming: Cut flower stalks if you wish. Remove old leaves as plant goes dormant. Plant outdoors when dormant.
Repotting: Not necessary.
Problems: No serious problems.

Senecio × *hybridus*
Cineraria

Cinerarias (also known by the name *Senecio cruentus*) are popular winter-blooming plants. Many florists stock them regularly. They can be grown easily from seed under cool conditions to produce a large cluster of flowers in colors from pink to dark blue. Some of the hybrid seedlings have dark foliage with a purplish cast when viewed from below. It is interesting to start with a seed mixture and see what different forms and flower colors you get. Give the plants plenty of light before flowering so that they will not become leggy. Keep them cool when blossoming.
Light: Provide at least 4 hours of curtain-filtered sunlight from a bright south, east, or west window.
Water: Keep evenly moist. Water thoroughly and discard drainage.
Humidity: Average indoor humidity levels.
Temperatures: 40° to 45° F at night, 60° to 65° F during the day, or cooler during flowering.
Fertilization: Do not fertilize when in flower. At other times, fertilize lightly.
Propagation: Start from seeds. Sow in a small pot and transplant seedlings as needed.
Grooming: Discard after flowering.
Repotting: Transplant seedlings several times, as they grow.
Problems: Subject to infestations of whiteflies, aphids, and spider mites. Powdery mildew is sometimes present.

Serissa foetida
Serissa, snow-rose

Bonsai enthusiasts can be credited with having introduced this attractive plant to indoor growers. Dwarf in all respects, serissa makes an attractive miniature tree or shrub, rarely reaching over 1 foot in height. It supports pruning well, allowing it to be trained into topiary or bonsai forms. The tiny leaves are elliptical and may be variegated in yellow. The flowers, borne most heavily in spring and summer, are barely ¼ inch in diameter and can be pink or white, single or double, depending on the clone. Although the epithet *"foetida"* means "foul smelling," the flowers themselves have no scent. The plant's disagreeable odor is noticeable only during root pruning. Plants with plain green leaves tend to flower more heavily than those with variegated leaves.
Light: Place in a bright, indirectly lit south, east, or west window.
Water: Keep evenly moist.
Humidity: Average indoor humidity levels.
Temperatures: 65° to 70° F at night, 70° to 75° F during the day.
Fertilization: Fertilize when plant is growing actively or flowering.
Propagation: Take stem cuttings in spring.
Grooming: Prune as needed.
Repotting: Repot annually in spring for best growth.
Problems: Will not bloom if light is too low. Spider mites a problem when air is too dry.

Solanum pseudocapsicum
Jerusalem cherry, Christmas-cherry

Jerusalem cherries are related to tomatoes, though the fruit is not edible. They need an abundance of light to bloom and set fruit properly. Many gardeners grow them outdoors and bring them in from September through the holidays. Given enough light, they will bear blossoms, green (immature) fruit, and orange or red (mature) fruit all at the same time. If you bring them in from outdoors, be sure they are free of pests, such as spider mites, whiteflies, and aphids. Pinch back the shoots on younger plants to keep their size to approximately 1 foot. If grown indoors the

Senecio × hybridus

Solanum pseudocapsicum

Spathiphyllum 'Mauna Loa'

Sprekelia formosissima

year around, the flowers should be hand-pollinated. Jerusalem cherries are usually treated as annuals and discarded after blooming, but they can be kept from year to year if trimmed back harshly.

Light: Provide 4 hours or more of direct sunlight from a south window. Does best in a greenhouse setting.
Water: Keep evenly moist. Water thoroughly and discard drainage.
Humidity: Requires moist air. Use a humidifier for best results.
Temperatures: 50° to 55° F at night, 60° to 65° F during the day.
Fertilization: Fertilize only when plant is growing actively or flowering.
Propagation: Start from seeds. Sow in a small pot and transplant as needed.
Grooming: Discard after flowering or fruiting. If treated as a perennial, prune harshly after flowering or fruiting. Pinch back stem tips of young or regrowing plants to improve form. Be careful not to remove flower buds when pruning. Discard when plant becomes too leggy.
Repotting: Repot in winter or early spring, as needed.
Problems: Foliage has an odor that some find objectionable. Susceptible to spider mites, whiteflies, and aphids.

Spathiphyllum
Peace-lily, spatheflower, snow flower, white anthurium

The distinctive flower of this plant gives it its common name, the peace-lily. The spathe is a pure white bract that encloses the true flowers. Sometimes more than 4 inches wide and 6 inches long, it unfurls to form a softly curved backdrop for the central column of tiny, closely set flowers. The blossom clearly resembles its relative anthurium. Spoon-shaped leaves on long stalks surround the flower and mirror its shape.

When not in flower, the peace-lily makes a particularly attractive foliage plant. Choose the plants by size: *S. 'Clevelandii'* (white anthurium) grows to a height of 2 feet. *S. floribundum* (snowflower) has leaves less than a foot tall. The most common, *S. 'Mauna Loa'*, reaches 3 feet. Other popular varieties include 'Sensation'®, the largest peace-lily, and 'Petite'. They bloom in spring and sometimes in autumn. A few days after it unfurls, the white spathe turns pale green.

Of the large flowering plants, this is one of the easiest to grow, especially under limited light conditions. A few hours of bright indirect light daily, normal to warm house temperatures, and regular watering and feeding are all that is needed to bring this plant to bloom.
Light: Will survive in low (reading-level) light.
Water: Keep very moist during growth and flowering; at other times, allow to dry between waterings.
Humidity: Average indoor humidity levels.
Temperatures: 55° to 60° F at night, 70° to 75° F during the day.
Fertilization: Fertilize only when plant is growing actively or flowering.
Propagation: Start new plants by dividing an old specimen.
Grooming: Pick off yellowed leaves.
Repotting: Repot infrequently.
Problems: Poor drainage, too-frequent watering, or standing in water will cause root rot. Will bloom poorly if light is too low. Cold drafts will harm plant. Wash leaves occasionally to protect plant from scales and mites.

Sprekelia formosissima
Aztec-lily, jacobean-lily, St. James lily

Aztec-lilies will last for several years in a pot if given ample light after blooming and allowed to rest in fall. The leaves of this medium-sized, bulbous plant are about 18 inches long and not particularly attractive, but they must be maintained to build the bulb for its next flowering. Keep the plant warm and well fertilized while growing.
Light: Provide 4 hours or more of direct sunlight from a south window.
Water: Keep moist when growing. When dormant, keep mostly dry, watering very occasionally.
Humidity: Average indoor humidity levels.
Temperatures: 60° to 65° F at night and 70° to 75° F during the day in the growing season (February through September); much cooler during fall and early winter.
Fertilization: Fertilize only when plant is growing actively or flowering.
Propagation: Start new plants from the bulblets that develop beside the parent bulb.
Grooming: Cut flower stalks if you wish. Remove old leaves as plant goes dormant.

Repotting: Repot every 3 or 4 years. Plant so that top of bulb is out of soil.
Problems: No serious problems.

Stephanotis floribunda
Stephanotis

Stephanotis is a vining plant that can grow quite large. It has thick, leathery leaves similar to those of waxplants. The flowers, which usually appear in June, are traditionally used in wedding bouquets. They are white and extremely fragrant. Given enough light, stephanotis will bloom most of the year. Allow the plant to rest during winter.
Light: Provide 4 hours or more of direct sunlight from a south window. Does best in a greenhouse setting.
Water: Keep very moist during growth and flowering; at other times, allow to dry between waterings.
Humidity: Average indoor humidity levels.
Temperatures: 55° to 60° F at night, 70° to 75° F during the day.
Fertilization: Fertilize only when plant is growing actively or flowering.
Propagation: Take stem cuttings at any time.
Grooming: Pinch back stem tips of young or regrowing plants to improve form. Prune after flowering. Be careful not to remove flower buds.
Repotting: Repot infrequently. New plants need to grow in a medium to large pot until almost root bound before they will bloom.
Problems: Susceptible to scale and mealybugs. Will not bloom if light is too low.

Strelitzia
Bird-of-paradise

Bird-of-paradise flowers are famous throughout the world for their beauty and form. They are large and are borne on a long stalk; many say they resemble the head of a tropical bird. The plant is also large, and will bloom only when mature. Bird-of-paradise is best suited for a greenhouse.
Light: Provide 4 hours or more of direct sunlight from a south window. Does best in a greenhouse setting.
Water: Water thoroughly, but allow to dry between waterings.
Humidity: Average indoor humidity levels.

Temperatures: 50° to 55° F at night, 65° to 70° F during the day.
Fertilization: Fertilize three times a year: spring, midsummer, and early fall.
Propagation: Start new plants by dividing an old specimen.
Grooming: Give plant plenty of room.
Repotting: New plants need to grow in a medium to large pot until almost root bound before they will bloom.
Problems: No serious problems.

Streptosolen jamesonii
Streptosolen

This is a winter-flowering, woody shrub; it produces clusters of bright orange flowers about 1 inch across. It tends to get leggy, so train it onto a small trellis or plant it in a hanging basket. Many gardeners prune it into a tree shape, with weeping or semitrailing growth at the top. Even in this form, it will need a trellis. Pruning regrowing stems will help maintain form but may limit blossoming. Though not common, it is occasionally available from specialty growers.
Light: Keep in about 4 hours of direct sunlight in winter. Provide curtain-filtered sunlight in summer, from a south or west window.
Water: Keep evenly moist. Water thoroughly and discard drainage.
Humidity: Average indoor humidity levels.
Temperatures: 50° to 55° F at night, 60° to 65° F during the day.
Fertilization: Fertilize all year, more heavily in summer.
Propagation: Take stem cuttings at any time.
Grooming: Prune in early spring. Pinch back stem tips of young or regrowing plants to improve form. Be careful not to destroy flower buds when pruning.
Repotting: Repot infrequently. New plants need to grow in a medium to large pot until almost root bound before they will bloom.
Problems: Will get spindly and weak if light is too low. If soil is too wet or too dry, leaves will drop.

Stephanotis floribunda

Strelitzia reginae

Streptosolen jamesonii

Tabernaemontana divaricata

Thunbergia alata

Tulbaghia fragrans

Tabernaemontana divaricata
Butterfly-gardenia, crape-jasmine, Adam's-apple, Nero's-crown

Butterfly-gardenia (sometimes classified as *Ervatamia coronaria*) is a large shrub. It produces clusters of fragrant flowers that are about 2 inches across. Most of the flowers appear in summer, but good light will prolong the blooming period. *T. divaricata plena* is a species with double-petaled flowers. The plants will grow to about 2 feet and should be pruned into a neat shape. Although a slow grower, several years of good care should produce a specimen plant. Always water thoroughly to prevent a buildup of soluble salts, which will cause the plant to decline.

Light: Provide 4 hours or more of direct sunlight from a south window. Does best in a greenhouse setting.
Water: Keep very moist at all times, but do not allow to stand in water.
Humidity: Average indoor humidity levels.
Temperatures: 65° to 70° F at night, 75° to 80° F during the day.
Fertilization: Fertilize all year, more heavily in summer.
Propagation: Take cuttings from stems or shoots before they have hardened or matured.
Grooming: Prune in early spring.
Repotting: Repot infrequently.
Problems: Will not bloom if light is too low. Dry soil or a high level of soluble salts may damage roots, causing plant to die back.

Tetranema roseum
Mexican foxglove

Mexican foxglove bears groups of tiny, pink blossoms on 8-inch stalks, all year long. The dark green leaves of this small plant are formed in a rosette on a short stem. To keep it blooming, give it warmth, even moisture, and plenty of winter light. Keep Mexican foxglove out of cold drafts. Works well as a terrarium plant.

Light: Keep in about 4 hours of direct sunlight in winter. Provide curtain-filtered sunlight in summer, from a south or west window.
Water: Keep evenly moist. Water thoroughly and discard drainage.
Humidity: Average indoor humidity levels.

Temperatures: 55° to 60° F at night, 70° to 75° F during the day.
Fertilization: Fertilize all year, more heavily in summer.
Propagation: Grow from seed, which is generally available and easy to germinate, or start new plants by dividing an old specimen.
Grooming: Pick off yellowed leaves. Cut flower stalks if you wish.
Repotting: Repot at any time.
Problems: If plant is in a draft or dry air, leaves will scorch.

Thunbergia alata
Thunbergia, black-eyed-susan, clock vine

A spring-flowering plant popular with florists, thunbergia is generally used in a hanging basket for a patio garden. It can also be trained onto a small trellis. Its yellow flowers with black centers resemble the pastureweed common in northern states. In the South, thunbergia grows as a perennial vine. Indoor gardeners can keep it from year to year, but it needs plenty of light to flower well. The plants may get weak and spindly after a few years, even with the best care.

Light: Provide 4 hours or more of direct sunlight from a south window. Does best in a greenhouse setting.
Water: Keep evenly moist. Water thoroughly and discard drainage.
Humidity: Average indoor humidity levels.
Temperatures: 55° to 60° F at night, 70° to 75° F during the day.
Fertilization: Fertilize only when plant is growing actively or flowering.
Propagation: Start from seeds. Sow in a small pot and transplant seedlings as needed. Sow in early to midsummer for fall and winter flowers.
Grooming: Cut back straggly vines at the base. Trim the others lightly. Pinch off faded flowers to prolong flowering.
Repotting: Cut back and repot when flowering stops.
Problems: Will not bloom if light is too low.

Tulbaghia fragrans
Fragrant tulbaghia, society-garlic, violet tulbaghia

Although tulbaghias are bulbs, they bloom repeatedly throughout the year if given plenty of light, water, and fertilizer.

The flowers are borne in clusters on 15-inch stalks. They are usually lavender and mildly fragrant. Do not bruise or break the leaves unless you like the smell of garlic in your indoor garden. The bulbs multiply rapidly and require frequent division.

Light: Give 4 hours or more of direct sunlight from a south window.

Water: Keep evenly moist. Water thoroughly and discard drainage.

Humidity: Average indoor humidity levels.

Temperatures: 40° to 45° F at night, 60° to 65° F during the day.

Fertilization: Fertilize all year, more heavily in summer.

Propagation: Start new plants by dividing an old specimen.

Grooming: Pick off yellowed leaves.

Repotting: Repot each year.

Problems: Will not bloom if light is too low.

Tulipa
Tulip

There are hundreds of tulip varieties. Most are suitable for indoor forcing, though the smaller varieties may be the easiest to force successfully. Tulips can be purchased already in bud from many florists. To force your own, purchase several mature bulbs in October, put them together in a pot with the flat side outward to get better foliage orientation, and place them in a cool spot until January or February. Many devoted indoor gardeners use an old refrigerator to keep the bulbs cool. After the bulbs have flowered and the foliage has died back, most varieties can be placed in the garden. The bulbs of some varieties will divide readily; others are more difficult to propagate.

Light: Place anywhere during flowering. Before and after flowering, provide at least 4 hours of curtain-filtered sunlight from a bright south, east, or west window.

Water: Keep very moist during growth and flowering; at other times, allow to dry between waterings.

Humidity: Average indoor humidity levels.

Temperatures: 50° to 55° F at night, 60° to 65° F during the day.

Fertilization: Lightly fertilize after flowering.

Propagation: Start new plants from the bulblets that develop beside the parent bulb.

Grooming: Cut flower stalks if you wish. Remove old leaves.

Repotting: Repot each year.

Problems: Subject to crown rot in overly moist conditions.

Vallota
Scarborough-lily

This bulb produces up to 10 bright red-orange flowers in a cluster on a 2-foot stalk. It usually flowers in summer or early fall. The leaves are narrow and about a foot long. After they have died back, give the bulb a rest until summer. Repot it gently each summer, disturbing the roots in the center of the rootball as little as possible.

Light: Provide 4 hours or more of direct sunlight from a south window.

Water: Keep very moist during growth and flowering; at other times, allow to dry between waterings.

Humidity: Average indoor humidity levels.

Temperatures: 50° to 55° F at night, 60° to 65° F during the day.

Fertilization: Do not fertilize when flowering. Fertilize lightly at other times.

Propagation: Start new plants from the bulblets that develop beside the parent bulb.

Grooming: Cut flower stalks if you wish. Remove old leaves as plant goes dormant.

Repotting: Repot each year.

Problems: Subject to crown rot in overly moist conditions.

Veltheimia
Veltheimia, forest lily

Veltheimias are large bulbs. The tubular pink, rose, or white flowers are borne in winter and early spring on a stalk 12 to 15 inches high. The glossy green leaves are 12 inches long and arch outward from the base of the flower stalk. Give bulbs a rest in summer.

Light: Provide at least 4 hours of curtain-filtered sunlight from a bright south, east, or west window.

Water: Keep very moist during growth and flowering. Allow to dry out during the summer.

Humidity: Average indoor humidity levels.

Temperatures: 50° to 55° F at night, 60° to 65° F during the day.

Tulipa

Vallota

Veltheimia

Zantedeschia aethiopica

Zephyranthes candida

Fertilization: Fertilize only when plant is growing actively or flowering.
Propagation: Start new plants from the bulblets that develop beside the parent bulb.
Grooming: Pick off yellowed leaves. Cut flower stalks if you wish.
Repotting: Repot when growth starts in fall.
Problems: No serious problems.

Zantedeschia
Calla lily, golden calla, pink calla

The elegant flower of the calla lily, actually a colored leaf, called a spathe, which curls around a fragrant, yellow column of flowers, needs no introduction. Most people recognize it on sight. Besides being a popular cut flower, calla lilies also make good houseplants.

The best-known calla lily is the largest: *Zantedeschia aethiopica*. It bears creamy white spathes, 5 to 10 inches in length, atop wide, glossy, arrow- or heart-shaped leaves. It can reach 4 feet or more in height when in flower, but some cultivars are much smaller. Other species include *Z. elliottiana* (golden calla), which has white-spotted, arrow-shaped leaves, and *Z. rehmannii* (pink calla) with strap-shaped leaves often covered with white dots. Hybrid callas in shades of white, pink, yellow, orange, and red, often dwarf plants no more than 18 inches in height, are becoming increasingly popular.

Callas are native to bogs that dry up completely during the dry season, which gives a clue as to their culture. Since their flowers are most appreciated during the winter months, begin watering lightly in fall, increasing the amount until the plant is in full growth. Alternatively, start them in spring for summer bloom. Keep the potting mix evenly moist during growth and flowering. *Z. aethiopica* especially likes moist soil; it will grow even with its pot sitting permanently in water. When blooms fade, reduce watering, removing the leaves as they yellow. If the plant goes entirely dormant, keep the rhizome nearly dry, watering it only enough to keep it from shriveling, until the following growing and flowering season. Some cultivars will maintain their foliage throughout the year, and these should be kept slightly moist at all times.

Light: Keep in 4 hours of direct sunlight in winter. Provide curtain-filtered sunlight in summer from a south or west window.
Water: Keep thoroughly moist during growth and flowering; at other times, allow to dry between waterings.
Humidity: Requires moist air. Use a humidifier for best results.
Temperatures: 50° to 55° F at night, 65° to 70° F during the day. During dormancy, temperature is not a major factor.
Fertilization: Fertilize only when plant is growing actively or flowering.
Propagation: Start new plants by dividing an old specimen.
Grooming: Pick off yellowed leaves. Cut faded flower stalks.
Repotting: Repot the rhizome at the end of dormancy.
Problems: If plant is in a draft or dry air, leaves will scorch. Spider mites can be a problem if air is too dry.

Zephyranthes
Zephyr-lily

Many species and hybrids of zephyr-lilies are available. Most are of moderate size and are easy to grow. They bloom at various times, sometimes more than once a year. Flowers are pink, yellow, orange, or white and are borne singly on a stalk, like a daffodil. The foliage is grassy and about a foot long. Give the plants a rest period of 2 months after the foliage has died back. Keep in a sunny, cool spot for flowering.

Light: Provide 4 hours or more of direct sunlight from a south window.
Water: Keep very moist during growth and flowering; at other times, allow to dry between waterings.
Humidity: Average indoor humidity levels.
Temperatures: 40° to 45° F at night, 60° to 65° F during the day.
Fertilization: Fertilize only when plant is growing actively or flowering.
Propagation: Start new plants from the bulblets that develop beside the parent bulb.
Grooming: Cut flower stalks if you wish. Remove old leaves as plant goes dormant.
Repotting: Repot each year.
Problems: Poor drainage, too-frequent watering, or standing in water will cause root rot.

Foliage Houseplants

A brief look at this section reveals the wide range of plants considered noteworthy for their foliage. Foliage attributes include color, variegation, and texture and also the size and arrangement of the leaves on the stems and branches. Even though striking and colorful foliage is important, the size, shape, and form of a plant are the major criteria for its selection as a decorative accent or part of an indoor garden. It is the combination of these characteristics—size, shape, form, and foliage—that gives an indoor garden its special charm. The ability to determine the relative importance of these characteristics enables interior plant designers to create striking indoor settings.

Many foliage plants produce flowers from time to time, but in general their flowers are less significant for design purposes than are their other characteristics. In some cases a plant may produce flowers only under precise cultural conditions, limiting its usefulness as a flowering specimen.

When selecting foliage plants, use the cultural information given here to find a plant that will fit both your design purposes and setting.

Acorus gramineus 'Variegatus'

Acorus gramineus
Miniature flagplant, Japanese sweet flag

Flagplants are often grown outdoors in southern climates, but two cultivars are suited for indoor gardening: a dwarf variety that has green leaves and a taller, variegated form. Their leaves look like stiff, thick blades of grass. The plants are easy to grow in a variety of indoor settings. They do best in bright light, moist soil, and high humidity. In locations with only moderate light, keep them drier and fertilize less. Flagplants do well in cool spots if not overwatered.
Light: Provide at least moderate light but no direct sunlight.
Water: Keep evenly moist. Water thoroughly and discard drainage.
Humidity: Provide moist air. Use a humidifier for best results.
Temperatures: 40° to 45° F at night, 60° to 65° F during the day.
Fertilization: Fertilize lightly throughout the growing season.
Propagation: Start new plants by dividing an old specimen.
Grooming: Pick off yellowed leaves.
Repotting: Repot at any time.
Problems: Leaves will scorch if plant is in a draft or dry air. Dry soil or a high level of soluble salts may damage roots, causing plant to die back.

Aglaonema
Chinese evergreen

Chinese evergreen, which can grow to 2 feet, is a favorite indoors because it tolerates a wide range of conditions, including poor light and dry air. Any number of common species and cultivars are available, including *A. modestum*, *A.* 'Silver Queen', *A. crispum*, and *A. commutatum*. Its oblong, lance-shaped leaves are 6 to 9 inches long and 2 to 3 inches wide. The leaves can be anything from entirely green to heavily marbled with silver and white. Creamy, waxy flowers like calla lilies bloom in late summer and early fall. Tight clusters of 1-inch-long, yellowish red berries follow the flowers. Growth slows during winter.
Light: Will survive in low (reading-level) light. Never place plant in direct sunlight.
Water: Keep evenly moist (somewhat drier in winter). Water thoroughly and discard drainage.
Humidity: Average indoor humidity levels.
Temperatures: 55° to 60° F at night, 70° to 75° F during the day.
Fertilization: Fertilize all year, more heavily in summer.

Aglaonema 'Silver Queen'

Alocasia 'African Mask'

Alpinia sanderae

Propagation: Take root divisions or stem cuttings in spring and summer. Seeds are available, but can be more difficult than divisions and cuttings.
Grooming: Remove yellowed leaves.
Repotting: Repot at any time. Blossoms best when pot bound.
Problems: Leaf edges will turn brown if level of soluble salts is too high or if plant is in a draft or dry air.

Alocasia
Alocasia

The striking foliage of the alocasia is arrow-shaped, often with lobed or wavy edges. Most varieties have shiny leaves, and some have a silvery overlay on much or part of the leaf. They grow from tubers, each producing a half dozen or so large leaves. Juvenile forms of alocasia are often quite small, but adult plants can reach 4 feet in height. The best known and most widely available is *Alocasia* × *amazonica,* which has dark green, almost black leaves and ivory veins. Several cultivars of this plant are available .
Light: Place in a bright, indirectly lit south, east, or west window.
Water: Water thoroughly, but allow to dry between waterings.
Humidity: Requires moist air. Use a humidifier for best results.
Temperatures: 65° to 70° F at night, 75° to 80° F during the day.
Fertilization: Fertilize lightly throughout the growing season.
Propagation: Divide in spring.
Grooming: Pick off yellowed leaves.
Repotting: Repot infrequently.
Problems: Subject to crown rot in overly moist conditions.

Alpinia sanderae
Variegated ginger

Its yellow to cream, feathered variegation and its modest stature in a genus of otherwise extremely tall plants has made the variegated ginger a popular houseplant in recent years. The thin canes with lance-shaped leaves arch away from the pot. For an attractive display, always plant 3 divisions to a pot, each stem facing in a different direction. The flowers are attractive but are rarely seen indoors.
Light: Provide at least 4 hours of curtain-filtered sunlight from a bright south, east, or west window.

Water: Water thoroughly, but allow to dry between waterings.
Humidity: Requires moist air. Use a humidifier for best results.
Temperatures: 65° to 70° F at night, 75° to 80° F during the day.
Fertilization: Fertilize lightly throughout the growing season.
Propagation: Divide in spring.
Grooming: Pick off yellowed leaves and cut out faded canes.
Repotting: Repot as necessary.
Problems: Subject to crown rot in overly moist conditions.

Anthurium
Anthurium

Although many attractive anthuriums are grown especially for their flowers, some are becoming increasingly popular as foliage plants. And with over 600 species in the wild in a bewildering variety of forms, there is an abundance to choose from. *A. crystallinum* is one that is often available. It has heart-shaped, emerald green leaves up to 12 inches across and 20 inches long, overlaid with attractive silver veins. *A. hookeri* 'Alicia' has thick, leathery dark green leaves with wavy edges and extremely short petioles that form a bird's nest rosette. *A. pedioradiatum* 'Fingers' bears shiny, broad leaves with finger-like, pointed projections. The latter two are especially tough and are well adapted to home care.
Light: Place in a bright, indirectly lit south, east, or west window.
Water: Water thoroughly, but allow to dry between waterings.
Humidity: Requires moist air. Use a humidifier for best results.
Temperatures: 65° to 70° F at night, 75° to 80° F during the day.
Fertilization: Fertilize lightly throughout the growing season.
Propagation: Remove and root offsets, or take cuttings from varieties with visible stems.
Grooming: Pick off yellowed leaves.
Repotting: Repot infrequently.
Problems: Subject to crown rot in overly moist conditions.

Araucaria heterophylla
Norfolk Island pine, bunya-bunya

Norfolk Island pine is popular for indoor use because of its formal, treelike appearance. It grows slowly indoors, so you may prefer to purchase a mature specimen. A related plant, *A. bidwillii* (bunya-bunya), has a less formal shape, with sharp needles in two rows along its stem, and also grows indoors. Norfolk Island pine resembles a fir tree and can be decorated at Christmastime.

Light: Provide at least moderate light but no direct sunlight.

Water: Keep evenly moist. Water thoroughly and discard drainage.

Humidity: Average indoor humidity levels.

Temperatures: 50° to 55° F at night, 65° to 70° F during the day.

Fertilization: Fertilize lightly throughout the growing season.

Propagation: Home propagation is not practical.

Grooming: Pick off yellowed leaves.

Repotting: Repot infrequently.

Problems: Leaves will scorch if plant is in a draft or dry air. Poor drainage, too-frequent watering, or standing in water will cause root rot. Leaves will drop if soil is too wet or too dry.

Asparagus
Asparagus fern

Two of the most popular asparagus ferns are *A. densiflorus* 'Sprengeri', which has arching 18- to 24-inch stems covered with thousands of 1-inch, flat needles, and *A. setaceus,* a trailing vine with 12- to 18-inch stems covered with dark green, ⅛-inch needles. Both look best in hanging baskets. A third variety, also popular, is *A. densiflorus* 'Myers', which has stiff, upright stems to 2 feet and dark green, needle leaves, which give it an airy, feathery look.

These plants have been favorites for generations because they are so easy to care for. Unlike true ferns, they tolerate a wide range of temperatures and light, do not require a humid atmosphere, and can be propagated easily. To keep the plants bushy, pinch back their long stems periodically.

Light: Provide bright indirect or curtain-filtered sunlight.

Water: Water thoroughly, but allow to dry between waterings.

Humidity: Average indoor humidity levels.

Temperatures: 60° to 65° F at night, 68° to 72° F during the day.

Fertilization: Fertilize lightly throughout the growing season.

Anthurium crystallinum

Anthurium hookeri

Araucaria heterophylla

Asparagus densiflorus 'Sprengeri'

Aspidistra elatior 'Variegata'

Aucuba japonica 'Picturata'

Bamboo: *Arundinaria pygmaea*

Propagation: Divide thick roots of old plants in any season.
Grooming: Pinch back stems to keep bushy; if plant gets leggy, cut stems to soil level. Fresh new stems will soon begin to grow.
Repotting: Repot any time plant becomes overcrowded.
Problems: Leaves will turn yellow and drop if plant is suddenly moved to a location with low light.

Aspidistra elatior
Cast-iron plant

This tough plant was one of the most popular houseplants of the Victorian era. It's a tough plant; it can survive extreme heat and low light that would be deadly to most other plants. Its leaves are oblong, shiny, dark green, and leathery, growing 15 to 30 inches long and 3 to 4 inches wide. They intermingle above a clump of 6-inch stems. In spring, dark purple, bell-shaped flowers are borne singly at the soil surface.

This slow-growing, long-lasting plant responds well to proper attention, but it can survive poor treatment for a long time. Place out of direct sun, in average warmth and a moderately bright and well-ventilated room, and water regularly from spring to fall. Reduce water and keep the plant cool during winter, when it rests. Although it can withstand most types of abuse, this plant cannot endure soggy soil or frequent repotting.
Light: Will survive in low (reading-level) light.
Water: Water thoroughly, but allow to dry between waterings. In winter, keep plant dry and water infrequently.
Humidity: Dry air is generally not harmful, but keep plant out of drafts.
Temperatures: 50° to 55° F at night, 60° to 65° F during the day.
Fertilization: Fertilize lightly throughout the growing season.
Propagation: Start new plants by dividing an old specimen.
Grooming: Pick off yellowed leaves.
Repotting: Can be repotted at any time, but infrequent repotting is best.
Problems: Poor drainage, too-frequent watering, or standing in water will cause root rot. Susceptible to spider mites. Will not withstand frequent repotting.

Aucuba japonica
Japanese aucuba, golddust-tree

Aucubas are woody shrubs grown outdoors in many climates. The various cultivars have yellow variegation patterns or speckles on shiny, green leaves when grown in bright light. Keep the plants cool at night and out of direct sunlight during the day. Be careful not to overfertilize. Prune in early spring to train into a bushy plant.
Light: Provide at least 4 hours of curtain-filtered sunlight from a bright south, east, or west window.
Water: Let soil get almost dry before watering, then water thoroughly and discard drainage.
Humidity: Average indoor humidity levels.
Temperatures: 40° to 45° F at night, 60° to 65° F during the day.
Fertilization: Fertilize lightly throughout the growing season.
Propagation: Take root cuttings at any time.
Grooming: Prune in early spring.
Repotting: Repot in winter or early spring, as needed.
Problems: Poor drainage, too-frequent watering, or standing in water will cause root rot. Dry soil or a high level of soluble salts may damage roots, causing plant to die back.

Bamboo

Several genera of plants are known as bamboo, including *Bambusa, Phyllostachys,* and *Arundinaria. A. pygmaea* (formerly known as *Sasa pygmaea*) is tolerant of most indoor conditions. It is a dwarf, growing only to about 1 foot, but many other bamboos are large plants that grow rapidly, given enough warmth and moisture. Bamboo can work well in an interior design because of its columnar shape; for example, at a window, it can frame or partially obscure a view.
Light: Provide 4 hours or more of direct sunlight from a south window.
Water: Keep very moist at all times, but do not allow to stand in water.
Humidity: Provide moist air. Use a humidifier for best results.
Temperatures: 55° to 60° F at night, 70° to 75° F during the day.
Fertilization: Fertilize all year, more heavily in summer.

Propagation: Take cuttings from rhizomes or underground stems at any time.
Grooming: Cut back and thin out old shoots at any time.
Repotting: Repot infrequently.
Problems: No serious problems.

Begonia

There are thousands of begonia species, hybrids, and cultivars. Most of the ones mentioned in this book are popular as flowering plants, but some are more useful and attractive as foliage plants. Even these will produce small flowers on long, graceful stalks if given enough light. These plants often do well outdoors on a shaded patio during summer.

Cultivars of foliage begonias are usually selected for the color, shape, and variegation of the foliage. Because many have shades of red or maroon in the foliage, a plant light (bluish purple) will greatly enhance the brightness of the leaf colors. In fact, foliage begonias altogether thrive under lights. For best results, keep these begonias warm and avoid crown rot by never overwatering.

Cane begonias
Angel-wing begonia

The leaves of cane begonias are borne vertically on erect, smooth stems with swollen nodes somewhat like those of bamboo. They are asymmetrical and quite diverse in color, size, and variegation. The plants are not normally self-branching, but instead send up new stems from the base. Many cultivars grow quite large and need plenty of room. Although grown primarily for their foliage, they will bloom intermittently throughout the year if given enough light.

Best known are the angel-wing begonias, which have large leaves, silver-spotted on top and red underneath. The old-fashioned hybrid B. corallina 'Lucerna' (or 'Corallina de Lucerna') is the most common angel-wing. It bears coral flowers and can reach over 4 feet at maturity. B. coccinea is similar but of intermediate height. Some, such as B. 'Orange Rubra', are pendulous in habit, making them good choices for hanging baskets. Others, such as B. 'Sophie Cecile', are upright in growth and have deeply cut leaves.

Light: Provide bright but indirect light from a south, east, or west window.
Water: Let plant approach dryness before watering, then water thoroughly and discard drainage.
Humidity: Average indoor humidity levels.
Temperatures: 65° to 70° F at night, 75°F to 80° F during the day.
Fertilization: Fertilize lightly throughout the growing season.
Propagation: Take stem cuttings at any time.
Grooming: Cut back long stems to promote new growth.
Repotting: Repot annually in spring for best growth.
Problems: Subject to crown rot in overly moist conditions.

Rhizomatous begonias
Iron-cross begonia, beefsteak begonia, lettuceleaf begonia, eyelash begonia, star begonia

The rhizomatous begonias are the largest group of begonias. Their jointed rhizomes grow along or under the soil surface and hang over the edge of the pot. The rhizomes are not attractive, but generally they are hidden from view by the plant foliage, which is often attractively mottled and textured. In ample light, many rhizomatous begonias bear tall stalks of white or greenish white flowers held well above the leaves. B. masoniana (iron-cross begonia) is one of the best known of this group; it produces large, bumpy, heart-shaped leaves in yellow-green with a dark burgundy, Maltese-cross pattern in the center. Some old-fashioned hybrids with thick rhizomes and extralarge leaves are still popular, such as B. × erythrophylla (beefsteak begonia), with round, shiny bronze leaves, and B. erythrophylla 'Bunchii' (lettuceleaf begonia), with highly crested leaf edges. More popular these days, though, are the smaller varieties, such as the tiny B. boweri (eyelash begonia), the larger B. heracleifolia (star begonia), and the numerous intermediate hybrids, such as B. 'Maphil', B. 'Chantilly Lace', and B. 'Bow-Nigra'. Some of the small rhizomatous begonias need high humidity and are best grown in terrariums. One of these is B. prismatocarpa, which bears bright buttercup yellow flowers throughout the year.

Begonia 'Mandarin Orange' (Cane begonia)

Begonia masoniana (Rhizomatous begonia)

Begonia luxurians (Shrub begonia)

Begonia × *rex-cultorum* 'Cleopatra'

Brassaia actinophylla

Light: Provide bright but indirect light from a south, east, or west window.
Water: Let plant approach dryness before watering, then water thoroughly and discard drainage.
Humidity: Provide moist air. Use a humidifier for best results.
Temperatures: 65° to 70° F at night, 75° to 80° F during the day.
Fertilization: Fertilize lightly throughout the growing season.
Propagation: Take leaf or rhizome cuttings at any time.
Grooming: Shape with pruning or clipping at any time. Excessively long rhizomes can be cut back.
Repotting: Repot infrequently.
Problems: Subject to crown rot in overly moist conditions. Will not bloom if light is too low.

Shrub begonias
Trout-leaf begonia

Shrub begonias branch abundantly, hiding their stems from view. Unlike many cane begonias, however, they tend to flower only seasonally and so are grown almost exclusively for their foliage. The bare-leaf types have smooth, metallic-looking leaves; the old-fashioned bare-leaf hybrid *B.* × *thurstonii* has bronze-green leaves with a red underside that are remarkably reflective. The trout-leaf begonia, *B.* × *argenteo-guttata*, is also in the bare-leaf category, although its silver-spotted leaves make it resemble a miniature angel-wing begonia. Bare-leaf begonias generally require more sunlight than other begonias. Another type of shrub begonia has leaves covered in thick hair or felt. *B. scharffiana*, for example, has bronze-green leaves dusted with white hair. Hairy-leaf begonias prefer diffuse light. The fern-leaf begonias are best known for their unusual foliage: *B. foliosa* has tiny, ovate leaves that liberally coat its arching stems, and *B. luxurians* has giant leaves that are divided into narrow leaflets attached together at the base like spokes on a wheel.
Light: For hairy-leaf begonias, provide bright but indirect light from a south, east, or west window. Give bare-leaf begonias some direct sunlight.
Water: Let plant approach dryness before watering, then water thoroughly and discard drainage.
Humidity: Average indoor humidity levels.

Temperatures: 65° to 70° F at night, 75° to 80° F during the day.
Fertilization: Fertilize lightly throughout the growing season.
Propagation: Take stem cuttings at any time.
Grooming: Cut back long stems to promote branching.
Repotting: Repot annually in spring for best growth.
Problems: Subject to crown rot in overly moist conditions.

Begonia × rex-cultorum
Rex begonia

Rex begonias are a sizable group of plants grown primarily for their foliage. They will bloom if given good light, producing tiny flowers on long stems. The leaves of most cultivars are large and have asymmetrical blades with diverse, brilliant coloration and textures. The rex begonias are rhizomatous in habit; their stems may grow horizontally across the soil surface. Keep them warm and take care not to overwater. Fertilize lightly.
Light: Provide bright but indirect light from a south, east, or west window.
Water: Let plant approach dryness before watering, then water thoroughly and discard drainage.
Humidity: Average indoor humidity levels.
Temperatures: 65° to 70° F at night, 75° to 80° F during the day.
Fertilization: Fertilize lightly throughout the growing season.
Propagation: Take rhizome or leaf cuttings at any time. Seeds are available, but can be more difficult than cuttings.
Grooming: Keep to desired height and shape with light pruning or clipping at any time. Give plant plenty of room.
Repotting: Repot infrequently.
Problems: Subject to crown rot in overly moist conditions.

Brassaia
Schefflera, umbrella tree

Scheffleras are often used in commercial settings because they grow fast and are relatively easy to care for. *B. actinophylla*, although sold as a small seedling, can become huge. Its leaves are palmately compound and may be a foot or more across, spreading out like the sections of an umbrella. *B. actinophylla* 'Amate' has become a popular choice within the past few years. For information on the miniature schefflera, sometimes listed as *B. arboricola,* see *Heptapleurum arboricola.*

Light: Provide bright but indirect light from a south, east, or west window.
Water: Let plant approach dryness before watering, then water thoroughly and discard drainage.
Humidity: Average indoor humidity levels.
Temperatures: 50° to 55° F at night, 60° to 65° F during the day.
Fertilization: Fertilize lightly throughout the growing season.
Propagation: Take stem cuttings at any time. Seeds are available, but can be more difficult than cuttings.
Grooming: Give plant plenty of room. Pick off yellowed leaves.
Repotting: Repot infrequently.
Problems: Will get spindly and weak if light is too low. Leaves will drop if soil is too wet or too dry. Spider mites can be a problem, especially if air is too dry.

Buxus
Boxwood

Boxwood is a woody shrub found in many outdoor gardens. It can easily be made into a formal hedge. Many boxwoods are becoming popular as indoor plants, especially for bonsai. They have a dense branching habit, resulting in thick masses of tiny, green leaves. They can be cut and pruned to almost any shape. Keep boxwoods cool at night and do not overwater or overfertilize.

Light: Provide at least 4 hours of curtain-filtered sunlight from a bright south, east, or west window.
Water: Let plant approach dryness before watering, then water thoroughly and discard drainage.
Humidity: Average indoor humidity levels.
Temperatures: 50° to 55° F at night, 60° to 65° F during the day.
Fertilization: Fertilize lightly throughout the growing season.
Propagation: Take cuttings from stems or shoots that have recently matured.
Grooming: Keep to desired height and shape with light pruning or clipping at any time.

Repotting: Repot infrequently.
Problems: Dry soil or a high level of soluble salts may damage roots, causing plant to die back. Spider mites can be a problem, especially if air is too dry.

Caladium
Caladium

Caladiums, with their dozens of different leaf patterns and colors, can create a display of color to rival that of any flowering plant. Masses of exquisite paper-thin, heart-shaped leaves, 12 to 24 inches long, are borne on long stalks. The plant is perennial yet dies back for a 4-month period during winter. *C. bicolor* features wide, red leaves bordered with green that are 14 inches long and 6½ inches wide. *C. humboldtii* is a miniature plant; its light green leaves are splotched with white.

Light: Provide at least 4 hours of curtain-filtered sunlight from a bright south, east, or west window.
Water: Keep evenly moist, although plant can tolerate some dryness between waterings. Allow to dry out and become dormant in fall.
Humidity: Provide moist air. Use a humidifier for best results.
Temperatures: 55° to 60° F at night, 70° to 75° F during the day.
Fertilization: Fertilize lightly throughout the growing season.
Propagation: Start new plants from the bulblets that develop beside the parent bulb. Pot these bulblets in late winter, when plant is dormant.
Grooming: Remove old leaves as plant goes dormant.
Repotting: Repot each year.
Problems: Leaves will scorch if plant is in a draft or dry air. Plant will get spindly and weak if light is too low.

Calathea
Calathea, peacock-plant

Calatheas have what many consider to be the most beautifully variegated foliage of any indoor plant. The stems are often red, and the large, blade leaves have various patterns of greens on top. Some cultivars have purples and reds on the undersides of the leaves. Calatheas will not tolerate dry air or drafts; they are often grown in lit terrariums. Give the plants plenty of room, since they can grow 2 feet high, with individual leaves 8 inches across.

Buxus sempervirens 'Suffruticosa'

Caladium 'Red Flash'

Calathea louisae

Chlorophytum comosum 'Vittatum'

Cissus antarctica

Light: Will survive in low (reading-level) light.
Water: Keep very moist at all times, but do not allow to stand in water.
Humidity: Provide moist air. Use a humidifier for best results.
Temperatures: 65° to 70° F at night, 75° to 80° F during the day.
Fertilization: Fertilize lightly once a year in early spring if plant is in a dimly lit spot. Otherwise, fertilize lightly throughout the growing season.
Propagation: Start plants by dividing an old specimen.
Grooming: Pick off yellowed leaves.
Repotting: Repot at any time.
Problems: Leaves will scorch if plant is in a draft or dry air. Dry soil or a high level of soluble salts may damage roots, causing plant to die back.

Chlorophytum comosum
Spiderplant

The familiar spiderplant has been grown indoors for nearly 200 years, when Goethe, the German writer and philosopher, brought the plant inside because he was fascinated by its habit of producing miniature plants on shoots. The spiderplant can grow to be 3 feet tall. Wiry stems up to 5 feet long, bearing plantlets, spring forth among grassy, green, arching leaves striped with yellow or white. This plant is perfect for a hanging basket.

The spiderplant will grow in almost any location—sunny or shady, dry or damp. Water freely from spring to autumn, and keep in a moderate to cool location. Feed every other week. The plantlets can be left on the stems of the parent plant for a full look, or they can be removed for propagation. The plant will produce the most plantlets when slightly pot bound.
Light: Provide at least moderate light but no direct sunlight.
Water: Keep very moist during growth and flowering; at other times, allow to dry between waterings.
Humidity: Average indoor humidity levels.
Temperatures: 50° to 55° F at night, 60° to 65° F during the day.
Fertilization: Fertilize all year, more heavily in summer.
Propagation: Remove plantlets or rooted side shoots as they form.
Grooming: Give plant plenty of room to grow.

Repotting: Repot in winter or early spring as needed.
Problems: Brown leaf tips can be caused by a high level of soluble salts. Dry soil or soluble salts may damage roots, causing plant to die back.

Cissus

Cissus is a member of the grape family, a trailing or vining plant that becomes woodier with age. It is attractive in hanging baskets or trained onto a trellis. Of all the genera in the grape family, *Cissus* is the one most suitable for indoor culture, given moderate light and dry air. Several species are mentioned here. Although their culture is similar, enough differences exist to warrant individual care guides.

Cissus is popular in commercial settings. The plants also grow rapidly in the home and acclimate easily to poor light and infrequent watering. With care, plants can be maintained for many months in adverse conditions, but they will not flourish unless they are given bright indirect or even full sunlight and kept moderately moist and well fertilized. Prune stem tips and train the vines frequently to encourage plant to grow in an attractive shape.

Cissus antarctica
Kangaroo-ivy, kangaroo vine

Kangaroo-ivy is a vigorous indoor climber, an obvious member of the grape family. It is usually trained onto a trellis, string, or post, but can be used also in hanging baskets. The foliage is large and shiny, but may be sparse along the stem if the plant is not in good light. To counter a spindly appearance, many indoor gardeners train or wrap several vines together to make the foliage look denser.
Light: Provide at least moderate light but no direct sunlight.
Water: Let plant approach dryness before watering, then water thoroughly and discard drainage.
Humidity: Average indoor humidity levels.
Temperatures: 50° to 55° F at night, 65° to 70° F during the day.
Fertilization: Fertilize lightly throughout the growing season.
Propagation: Take stem cuttings at any time.

Grooming: Keep to desired height and shape with light pruning or clipping at any time.
Repotting: Repot at any time.
Problems: Will get spindly and weak if light is too low.

Cissus discolor
Begonia-treebine

Begonia-treebine is a vigorous vine that will grow to 6 feet or more unless pruned. It needs more light than its cousins kangaroo-ivy and grape-ivy. The leaves resemble those of a rex begonia, velvety with toothed edges and red veins. In ample light, pink and white colorations will appear.
Light: Provide 4 hours or more of direct sunlight from a south window.
Water: Keep evenly moist. Water thoroughly and discard drainage.
Humidity: Requires moist air. Use a humidifier for best results.
Temperatures: 55° to 60° F at night, 70° to 75° F during the day.
Fertilization: Fertilize all year, more heavily in summer.
Propagation: Take stem cuttings at any time.
Grooming: Keep to desired height and shape with light pruning or clipping at any time.
Repotting: Repot in winter or early spring as needed.
Problems: Will get spindly and weak if light is too low.

Cissus rhombifolia
Grape-ivy, oakleaf ivy

Grape-ivy grows wild in the West Indies and South America. It is a grape family vining plant best grown in a hanging basket. Its stems and buds are brown and have reddish hairs, and its shiny, 3-leaflet leaves are similar to those of poison ivy. Its two cultivars, 'Mandaiana' and 'Ellen Danica', are grown most often. Grape-ivy is popular with indoor gardeners because it tolerates a wide range of growing conditions and grows rapidly, even in moderate light.
Light: Will survive in low (reading-level) light.
Water: Let plant approach dryness before watering, then water thoroughly and discard drainage.
Humidity: Dry air is generally not harmful, but keep plant out of drafts.

Temperatures: 50° to 55° F at night, 60° to 65° F during the day.
Fertilization: Fertilize lightly throughout the growing season.
Propagation: Take stem cuttings at any time.
Grooming: Keep to desired height and shape with light pruning or clipping at any time.
Repotting: Repot at any time.
Problems: Leaves will drop if soil is too wet or too dry. Dry soil or a high level of soluble salts may damage roots, causing plant to die back. Powdery mildew occurs occasionally.

Clusia rosea
Balsam-apple

Balsam-apple is an attractive indoor tree with extremely thick, spoon-shaped leaves measuring up to 8 inches long and 4 inches wide. It takes up a great deal of space if allowed to grow to its natural height and spread, but regular pruning will keep it under control. The pink to white flowers are rarely borne indoors.
Light: Place in a bright, indirectly lit south, east, or west window.
Water: Water thoroughly, but allow to dry between waterings.
Humidity: Average indoor humidity levels.
Temperatures: 65° to 70° F at night, 75° to 80° F during the day.
Fertilization: Fertilize lightly throughout the growing season.
Propagation: Take stem cuttings in spring.
Grooming: Pick off yellowed leaves. Prune as needed.
Repotting: Repot infrequently.
Problems: Lower leaves drop as plant ages.

Codiaeum variegatum
Croton, Joseph's coat

The varied leaf shapes and exotic leaf colors of the croton make it an especially attractive indoor plant. Growing to 3 feet high, it produces lance-shaped, leathery leaves that reach up to 18 inches long. Foliage colors of the many varieties include red, pink, orange, brown, and white. Color markings vary considerably among leaves on the same plant. In addition, the plant may change color as it matures.

Cissus discolor

Cissus rhombifolia

Codiaeum variegatum var. *pictum*

Coffea arabica

Coleus × *hybridus*

Cordyline terminalis 'Kiwi'

C. variegatum var. *pictum* (Joseph's-coat) is a popular croton. Its oval, lobed leaves somewhat resemble oak leaves, and it grows as a narrow shrub that usually attains a height of 2 to 4 feet.

Crotons are not easy to grow unless you can satisfy all their environmental needs. Plenty of sunshine and a warm, draft-free location are essential. The key to success is keeping the air humid enough so that the plant can cope with the sun and warm temperatures. Place it on a humidifying tray to ensure adequate moisture. Dry air or dry soil will cause the leaves to wither rapidly and die.

Light: Provide 4 hours or more of direct sunlight from a south window.
Water: Keep evenly moist. Water thoroughly and discard drainage.
Humidity: Requires moist air. Use a humidifying tray for best results.
Temperatures: 65° to 70° F at night, 75° to 80° F during the day.
Fertilization: Fertilize lightly throughout the growing season.
Propagation: Take cuttings from stems or shoots before they have hardened or matured. Or propagate by air layering.
Grooming: Clean leaves and inspect for pests regularly. Pinching or pruning occasionally will cause plant to branch and become fuller.
Repotting: Repot in winter or early spring as needed.
Problems: Leaves will scorch if plant is in a draft or dry air. They will drop if soil is too wet or too dry. Susceptible to spider mites.

Coffea arabica
Coffee plant

Is it possible to grow your own coffee in the living room? Actually, coffee plants tend not to flower indoors, but they do make attractive, bushy shrubs up to 3 or more feet in height. The dark green, elliptic leaves have wavy margins. Keep pruned for a bushy look.

Light: Place in a bright, indirectly lit south, east, or west window.
Water: Water thoroughly, but allow to dry between waterings.
Humidity: Requires moist air. Use a humidifier for best results.
Temperatures: 55° to 60° F at night, 65° to 70° F during the day.
Fertilization: Fertilize lightly throughout the growing season.

Propagation: Start new plants from unroasted coffee beans or from cuttings.
Grooming: Pick off yellowed leaves. Prune and pinch as needed.
Repotting: Repot annually in spring for best growth.
Problems: May lose inner and lower leaves if soil is too moist or too dry. Maintain high air humidity to prevent spider mites.

Coleus × hybridus
Coleus

Coleus is a fast-growing, tropical shrub. So richly colored are its leaves that many people choose it as a colorful, inexpensive substitute for croton. The velvety, oval, scalloped leaves taper to a point and come in a multitude of colors with toothed or fringed margins, depending on the variety. Dark blue or white flowers form in fall.

Light: Place in a bright, indirectly lit south, east, or west window.
Water: Keep evenly moist. Water thoroughly and discard drainage.
Humidity: Average indoor humidity levels.
Temperatures: 55° to 60° F at night, 70° to 75° F during the day.
Fertilization: Fertilize only when plant is growing actively.
Propagation: Take stem cuttings at any time.
Grooming: Prune in early spring. Pinch back stem tips of young or regrowing plants to improve form.
Repotting: Repot each year.
Problems: Some leaf drop will occur in winter. Will get spindly and weak if light is too low.

Cordyline terminalis
Cordyline, Hawaiian ti

Cordylines are large outdoor plants in their native South Sea Islands. The narrow leaves, which can be 18 inches long, are often used for hula skirts. Popular indoor cultivars will grow to about 3 feet and have foliage with pink variegations and stripes along the leaf edges. Although cordylines will tolerate low light, foliage color will not develop well under such conditions. For a more interesting look, use several plants to a pot. Cordyline is difficult to grow to perfection indoors because of its need for extremely humid air.

Light: Will survive in low (reading-level) light.
Water: Let plant approach dryness before watering, then water thoroughly and discard drainage.
Humidity: Requires moist air. Use a humidifier for best results.
Temperatures: 65° to 70° F at night, 75° to 80° F during the day.
Fertilization: Fertilize lightly throughout the growing season.
Propagation: Take stem cuttings at any time. Or start new plants by air layering.
Grooming: Pick off yellowed leaves.
Repotting: Repot at any time.
Problems: Leaves will scorch if plant is in a draft or dry air. Spider mites can be a problem, especially if air is too dry.

Cycas revoluta
Fern-palm, sago palm

Although fern-palm resembles a palm tree, it is more closely related to modern conifers. The leaves are shiny and extremely stiff. Although they appear tough, they are actually quite easily damaged, and since the plant produces only one new set of leaves each year, any damage remains visible for a long time. The plant forms a trunk like a palm trunk, but only after many years' growth. Fern-palm is very slow growing; if you want a plant with a trunk, buy one that has already reached that stage. Other types of cycads occasionally grown indoors include *Ceratozamia, Dioon, Encephalartos,* and *Zamia.*
Light: Provide at least 4 hours of curtain-filtered sunlight from a south, east, or west window.
Water: Water thoroughly, but allow to dry between waterings.
Humidity: Requires moist air. Use a humidifier for best results.
Temperatures: 55° to 60° F at night, 70° to 75° F during the day.
Fertilization: Fertilize lightly in spring and summer.
Propagation: Growing from seed is a slow process best left to professionals. Offsets are unlikely under home conditions.
Grooming: Pick off yellowed leaves.
Repotting: Repot infrequently.
Problems: Spider mites can be a problem if air is dry.

Cyperus
Umbrella plant, pygmy papyrus

Cyperus papyrus, which is common in the Middle East, was used historically to make the writing material known as papyrus. The long, green stems bear whorls of leaves, resembling the spokes of an umbrella. These "leaves" are actually bracts, among which small green to brown flowers appear. Dwarf cultivars are available as small plants, but most soon grow to 2 to 4 feet. The most popular species used indoors is *C. alternifolius.* Cyperus is a member of the sedge family. Like all the sedges, it is semiaquatic and likes wet conditions, preferring to stand in water at all times. The leaves may scorch or burn in dry indoor air. Tall plants may require staking.
Light: In winter, keep in about 4 hours of direct sunlight. In summer, provide curtain-filtered sunlight from a south or west window.
Water: Keep very moist at all times. Can stand in water.
Humidity: Requires moist air. Use a humidifier for best results.
Temperatures: 40° to 45° F at night, 60° to 65° F during the day.
Fertilization: Fertilize lightly throughout the growing season.
Propagation: Start new plants by dividing an old specimen. Or start from seed, but seeds are more difficult than division. *C. alternifolius* is most easily propagated from cuttings of leaf clusters.
Grooming: Pick off yellowed leaves.
Repotting: Repot in winter or early spring as needed.
Problems: Spider mites can be a problem, especially if air is too dry. Leaves will scorch if plant is in a draft or dry air.

Dieffenbachia
Dieffenbachia, dumb-cane

When touched by the tongue, sap from the cane stems of dieffenbachia can cause temporary speechlessness and much pain, hence the name "dumb-cane." This handsome evergreen features a single, thick trunk when young; as it matures it can be potted with multiple trunks together to form a palmlike appearance. Mature plants reach ceiling height. They have few equals for

Cycas revoluta

Cyperus alternifolis

Dieffenbachia 'Tropic Snow'

Dionaea muscipula

planter and large container decorations. Arching, oblong, pointed leaves, 10 to 12 inches long, spiral around the trunk. *D. maculata* 'Rudolph Roehrs' has chartreuse leaves marbled with ivory and divided by a dark green central rib. The newer hybrids, 'Tropic Snow' and 'Camile', are clumping and stay compact longer than the older varieties.

Light: Will survive in low (reading-level) light, but prefers a moderately bright spot such as a north or east window.

Water: Water thoroughly, but allow to dry between waterings.

Humidity: Average indoor humidity levels.

Temperatures: 50° to 55° F at night, 65° to 70° F during the day.

Fertilization: Fertilize all year, more heavily in summer.

Propagation: Take stem cuttings or air-layer at any time.

Grooming: Pick off yellowed leaves and wash leaves occasionally.

Repotting: Repot at any time.

Problems: Poor drainage, too-frequent watering, or standing in water will cause root rot.

Dionaea muscipula
Venus's-flytrap

Venus's-flytrap is a carnivorous plant grown as a curiosity; it's especially popular with young children. The leaf tips are divided into traps that close on flies and other small insects or when touched with a finger. It really does not need to be fed indoors, but occasional insects can be supplied. Never give it red meat of any kind. It is also unwise to stimulate the traps too often, as they die after responding only a few times.

Venus's-flytrap is relatively easy to grow for short periods indoors, but hard to keep from one year to the next because its cultural needs are difficult to meet indoors. It is best grown in a terrarium. It goes into dormancy in winter and requires cool conditions at that time. Remove flower stems as they weaken the plant needlessly.

Other carnivorous plants that will grow indoors under similar conditions include *Drosera* (sundew), *Darlingtonia californica* (cobraplant), and tropical *Nepenthes* (pitcher plant).

Light: Provide at least 4 hours of curtain-filtered sunlight from a south, east, or west window.

Water: Keep evenly moist except during winter dormancy. Use only rain or distilled water.

Humidity: Requires very moist air. Does best in a terrarium.

Temperatures: 45° to 50° F at night, 55° to 60° F during the day. During dormancy, near-freezing temperatures (under 40° F) are preferred.

Fertilization: Do not fertilize. Feed occasionally with insects.

Propagation: Propagate by division or leaf cuttings in spring.

Grooming: Pick off blackened leaves.

Repotting: Repot each spring into pure sphagnum moss.

Problems: Subject to crown rot if conditions are too warm.

Dizygotheca elegantissima
False-aralia

False-aralia is one of the most graceful plants you can grow indoors. Thin, dark green leaves with lighter veins spread into nine fingers with saw-toothed edges. You can buy small seedlings for a terrarium or a mature plant large enough to sit under. The leaves of mature plants have a decidedly different look from the juvenile leaves.

With proper care, this slow grower should cause few problems. It is, however, extremely sensitive to soil moisture and won't tolerate either soggy soil or a dry rootball. Don't move it around often; it does best when kept in the same location. Moist air is another important factor in keeping it healthy.

Light: Place in a bright, indirectly lit south, east, or west window. Older plants can endure less light.

Water: Keep evenly moist. Water thoroughly and discard drainage. In winter, keep plant almost dry, watering infrequently.

Humidity: Average indoor humidity levels.

Temperatures: 55° to 60° F at night, 70° to 75° F during the day.

Fertilization: Fertilize lightly throughout the growing season.

Propagation: Difficult to propagate. Try sowing seeds in a small pot and transplant seedlings as necessary.

Grooming: Keep to desired height and shape with light pruning or clipping at any time.

Repotting: Repot infrequently, in winter or early spring when needed.

Dizygotheca elegantissima

Problems: Leaves will drop if soil is too wet or too dry. Spider mites can be a problem, especially if air is too dry.

Dracaena

Dracaenas usually have tall stems like palm trees, with tufts of narrow, sword-like leaves near the top. Most grow into large plants, often 10 feet or more in height. To offset its natural tendency for tall, leggy growth, stems of different heights are often planted together in the same pot or the stems are contorted to achieve different heights. Many indoor gardeners air-layer the plants to reduce their height. The canes that are left after the air layers are removed will usually sprout new leafy growth.

Many dracaena varieties are available. Most are selected for their foliage and form, used for large-scale architectural plantings indoors. Some have narrow, spiky foliage; others have wider, more arching leaves. Most of the popular cultivars are variegated. *D. fragrans* 'Massangeana' occasionally produces sprays of extremely fragrant, white flowers among its large leaves. In many commercial interiors these flowers are removed because their aroma is overpowering.

If conditioned properly, dracaenas will tolerate low light and infrequent watering; but they will grow little, if at all, under such conditions. Because their care depends somewhat on the cultivar chosen, an individual care guide is given for each species.

Dracaena deremensis
Warneckii dracaena,
Janet Craig dracaena

Warneckii and Janet Craig dracaenas grow as single-stemmed plants with long, narrow leaves arching outward all along the stem. It is common to cluster several plants of differing heights in one pot to give more visual interest. 'Janet Craig', the larger of the two, has dark green, shiny leaves and will grow to 5 or 6 feet if given ample light. A dwarf cultivar, 'Janet Craig Compacta', is also available. 'Warneckii' has narrower leaves with thin, white stripes along the leaf edges. These dracaenas are quite tolerant of stressful indoor environments, but avoid overwatering or overfertilizing plants that are growing in low light to keep them at their best.

Light: 'Warneckii' will survive in low (reading-level) light. 'Janet Craig' needs moderate or bright light. Neither will tolerate direct sunlight.
Water: Let plant approach dryness before watering, then water thoroughly and discard drainage.
Humidity: Average indoor humidity levels.
Temperatures: 55° to 60° F at night, 70° to 75° F during the day.
Fertilization: Fertilize all year, more heavily in summer.
Propagation: Take stem cuttings at any time, or start new plants by air layering.
Grooming: Pick off yellowed leaves. Trim brown leaf tips.
Repotting: Repot at any time.
Problems: Leaves will drop if soil is too wet or too dry. Leaf tips will turn brown from excessively dry potting mix or a high level of soluble salts.

Dracaena fragrans 'Massangeana'
Cornplant

The leaves of the cornplant are long and narrow, although broader than those of *D. deremensis*, with a yellow stripe down the center, resembling corn leaves. The plant is grown in two ways: as a single stem with leaves reaching outward all along the trunk, or as a series of bare stems that have been topped to produce clusters of foliage on stalks that sprout from the cuts. In ample light, the cornplant may occasionally produce an extremely fragrant flower. It can tolerate many abuses, but be careful not to overwater or overfertilize a plant growing in low light.
Light: Will survive in low (reading-level) light.
Water: Let plant approach dryness before watering, then water thoroughly and discard drainage.
Humidity: Average indoor humidity levels.
Temperatures: 55° to 60° F at night, 70° to 75° F during the day.
Fertilization: Fertilize all year, more heavily in summer.
Propagation: Take stem cuttings at any time, or start new plants by air layering.
Grooming: Pick off yellowed leaves. Trim brown leaf tips.
Repotting: Repot at any time.

Dracaena deremensis 'Janet Craig'

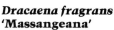
Dracaena deremensis 'Warneckii'

Dracaena fragrans 'Massangeana'

Dracaena marginata 'Colorama'

Dracaena reflexa 'Song of Jamaica'

Dracaena sanderana

Problems: Leaves will drop if soil is too wet or too dry. Leaf tips will turn brown from excessively dry potting mix or a high level of soluble salts.

Dracaena marginata
Madagascar dragontree, red-margined dracaena

Dracaena marginata has the narrowest leaves of all the commonly grown dracaenas. All cultivars have red striping on the edges of the leaves; 'Tricolor' and 'Colorama' are striped lengthwise in pink or cream but need more light and humidity than the species to do well indoors. The plants are normally grown as a series of stems with the foliage at the top. As the plants grow, the older leaves will yellow and die back, but the older stems may branch at the top. Avoid leaf tip burn by keeping the plant evenly moist and out of drafts.

Light: Provide at least moderate light but no direct sunlight.
Water: Keep evenly moist. Water thoroughly and discard drainage.
Humidity: Average indoor humidity levels.
Temperatures: 55° to 60° F at night, 70° to 75° F during the day.
Fertilization: Fertilize lightly throughout the growing season.
Propagation: Take stem cuttings at any time, or start new plants by air layering.
Grooming: Pick off yellowed leaves. Trim leaves with brown tips.
Repotting: Repot at any time.
Problems: Leaves will scorch if plant is in a draft or dry air. Watch for spider mites, especially if air is dry.

Dracaena reflexa
Pleomele

Pleomele, until recently classified as *Pleomele reflexa*, grows into a large plant with reflexed, or downward-pointing, leaves closely set along cane-like stems. There are several variegated cultivars, of which the best known is *D. reflexa* 'Song of India', with white- or cream-edged leaves. Because pleomele is tolerant of many indoor environments, it is often seen in commercial interiors. Keep it away from drafts and cold air.

Light: Provide at least moderate light but no direct sunlight.

Water: Let plant approach dryness before watering, then water thoroughly and discard drainage.
Humidity: Average indoor humidity levels.
Temperatures: 65° to 70° F at night, 75° to 80° F during the day.
Fertilization: Fertilize lightly throughout the growing season.
Propagation: Take stem cuttings at any time, or start new plants by air layering.
Grooming: Pick off yellowed leaves. Trim brown leaf tips.
Repotting: Repot infrequently.
Problems: Leaves will drop if soil is too wet or too dry.

Dracaena sanderana
Ribbon-plant, sander's dracaena

Ribbon-plant will get tall in time, but it is usually sold as a small plant less than a foot tall. The leathery, narrow leaves have white stripes along the edges. It does well in a dish garden, terrarium, or dimly lit spot. If the plant gets too leggy or spindly, air-layer it and replant. Water and fertilize lightly if the plant is in low light. Keep it out of drafts to avoid leaf scorch.

Light: Will survive in low (reading-level) light.
Water: Let plant approach dryness before watering, then water thoroughly and discard drainage.
Humidity: Average indoor humidity levels.
Temperatures: 55° to 60° F at night, 70° to 75° F during the day.
Fertilization: Fertilize lightly throughout the growing season.
Propagation: Take stem cuttings at any time, or start new plants by air layering.
Grooming: Pick off yellowed leaves.
Repotting: Repot infrequently.
Problems: Leaves will scorch if plant is in a draft or dry air.

Dracaena surculosa
Golddust dracaena

The form of golddust dracaena and the shape of its leaves make it different from other dracaenas. Golddust dracaena is small and shrubby. It has fairly broad leaves, somewhat like those of an elm tree. They are brilliantly spotted with yellow or cream markings. Several

cultivars, such as 'Florida Beauty', are now available that are even more colorful than the species. Golddust dracaena must have good light and be kept constantly moist. It is slow growing and will rarely reach more than 2 feet tall, even in ample light.
Light: Place in a bright, indirectly lit south, east, or west window.
Water: Keep evenly moist. Water thoroughly and discard drainage.
Humidity: Average indoor humidity levels.
Temperatures: 55° to 60° F at night, 70° to 75° F during the day.
Fertilization: Fertilize lightly throughout the growing season.
Propagation: Take stem cuttings at any time.
Grooming: Keep to desired height and shape with light pruning or clipping at any time.
Repotting: Repot in winter or early spring as needed.
Problems: Leaves will scorch if plant is in a draft or dry air and will drop if soil is too wet or too dry.

Epipremnum aureum
Epipremnum, pothos, devil's-ivy

Epipremnum (also known as *Scindapsus*) is commonly used in commercial interiors as a vining ground cover or as a cascading accent plant, often in a hanging basket. Its heart-shaped, leathery leaves look somewhat like the heart-leaf philodendron's. The species is irregularly marbled yellow, with better color in good light. *E. aureum* 'Marble Queen' is more heavily mottled with white and gray-green. Pinch back stem tips occasionally to promote branching. Cut back old runners or vines when they get leggy or loop them over the pot and root them near their ends.
Light: Provide at least moderate light but no direct sunlight.
Water: Keep evenly moist. Water thoroughly and discard drainage.
Humidity: Average indoor humidity levels.
Temperatures: 50° to 55° F at night, 60° to 65° F during the day.
Fertilization: Fertilize lightly throughout the growing season.
Propagation: Take stem cuttings at any time.
Grooming: Pick off yellowed leaves. Keep to desired height and shape by

pinching back stem tips or with light pruning or clipping at any time.
Repotting: Repot at any time.
Problems: Poor drainage, too-frequent watering, or standing in water will cause root rot. Will get spindly and weak if light is too low.

Eriobotrya japonica
Japanese loquat

Japanese loquat is a small tree or shrub often used in southwestern landscapes as an informal hedge or an espaliered specimen plant. The 6- to 12-inch-long leaves are dark green on top and tan beneath. Clusters of small, fragrant, white flowers open in late fall or early winter. If given enough light, fertilizer, and warmth, small edible fruit will ripen in mid- to late spring. Loquats will grow well in a solarium or greenhouse. They can get quite large; prune them well in spring to maintain a comfortable size and proper shape.
Light: Provide 4 hours or more of direct sunlight from a south window. Does best in a greenhouse setting.
Water: Keep evenly moist. Water thoroughly and discard drainage.
Humidity: Average indoor humidity levels.
Temperatures: 55° to 60° F at night, 70° to 75° F during the day.
Fertilization: Use an acid-based fertilizer and add trace elements once in spring.
Propagation: Take cuttings from stems or shoots before they have hardened or matured.
Grooming: Prune in early spring, being careful not to cut off flower buds or young fruit.
Repotting: Repot infrequently.
Problems: Will not bloom if light is too low. If soil is too wet or too dry, leaves will drop.

Euonymus fortunei
Winter creeper

Winter creeper is often used outdoors in northern states as a semievergreen climbing plant. Indoors, it does best in a cool location, such as an entranceway. The trailing stems will climb and attach themselves to vertical surfaces, so it is best to train the plant onto a wall or post. The variegated form of this slow-growing plant, *E. fortunei* 'Aureo-variegata', is particularly popular.

Dracaena surculosa 'Florida Beauty'

Epipremnum aureum

Eriobotrya japonica

Euonymus fortunei 'Ivory Jade'

Euonymus japonica

× *Fatshedera lizei*

Indoors, it will grow to 2 feet or more. The all-green varieties are rarely grown indoors.

Light: Place in a bright, indirectly lit south, east, or west window.

Water: Keep evenly moist. Water thoroughly and discard drainage.

Humidity: Average indoor humidity levels.

Temperatures: 40° to 45° F at night, 60° to 65° F during the day.

Fertilization: Fertilize lightly throughout the growing season.

Propagation: Take cuttings from stems or shoots before they have hardened or matured.

Grooming: Keep to desired height and shape with light pruning or clipping at any time.

Repotting: Repot infrequently.

Problems: Subject to infestations of scale and mealybug.

Euonymus japonica
Evergreen euonymus

Many evergreen euonymus cultivars are used outdoors as semievergreen foundation plantings. Indoors, the woody, bushy plants do well if given ample light. The foliage is about ½ inch long, produced abundantly all along the stems and often variegated. Popular cultivars for indoor use include *E. japonica* 'Aureo-variegata', 'Microphyllus Variegatus', and 'Silver Queen'. Keep these plants constantly moist and do not allow them to become pot bound. Stress may make them susceptible to spider mites.

Light: Provide at least 4 hours of curtain-filtered sunlight from a bright south, east, or west window.

Water: Keep evenly moist. Water thoroughly and discard drainage.

Humidity: Average indoor humidity levels.

Temperatures: 40° to 45° F at night, 60° to 65° F during the day.

Fertilization: Fertilize lightly throughout the growing season.

Propagation: Take cuttings from stems or shoots before they have hardened or matured.

Grooming: Keep to desired height and shape with light pruning or clipping at any time.

Repotting: Repot infrequently.

Problems: Spider mites can be a problem, especially if air is too dry. Subject to crown rot in overly moist conditions. Leaves will drop if soil is too wet or too dry.

× *Fatshedera lizei*
Tree-ivy, aralia-ivy

Tree-ivy is a hybrid, a cross between English ivy and Japanese aralia. It is semierect, with a green, partially woody stem and leaves that are sometimes 10 inches across. Tree-ivy usually needs staking to keep it upright. The variegated cultivar, *F. lizei* 'Variegata', is particularly popular for indoor culture.

Light: In winter, keep in about 4 hours of direct sunlight. In summer, provide curtain-filtered sunlight from a south or west window.

Water: Keep evenly moist. Water thoroughly and discard drainage.

Humidity: Requires moist air. Use a humidifier for best results.

Temperatures: 40° to 45° F at night, 60° to 65° F during the day.

Fertilization: Fertilize lightly throughout the growing season.

Propagation: Take stem cuttings at any time, or start new plants by air layering.

Grooming: Prune in early spring. Give plant plenty of room.

Repotting: Repot in winter or early spring as needed.

Problems: Leaves will drop if soil is too wet or too dry.

Fatsia japonica
Japanese aralia

Japanese aralia is a handsome, evergreen plant with bold, lobed leaves of shiny green, occasionally variegated with white. In frost-free climates it can be grown outdoors, but it also makes an excellent contribution to indoor gardens. It's fast growing, durable, and tolerant of many environments. It is particularly easy to grow in a cool, well-ventilated location with bright light. Wash and mist the leaves regularly and feed every 2 weeks during the growing season, otherwise the leaves may yellow from lack of nitrogen. The plant needs to rest during winter, so move it to a cool spot and water much less frequently than usual. Remove any flower buds that emerge on the mature plant to prevent it from diverting its energies to reproduction. If it begins to look gangly or has misshapen leaves, trim it back to the stalk.

Light: Place in a bright, indirectly lit south, east, or west window.
Water: Keep evenly moist. Water thoroughly and discard drainage. In winter, keep almost dry, watering infrequently.
Humidity: Average indoor humidity levels.
Temperatures: 50° to 55° F at night, 60° to 65° F during the day.
Fertilization: Fertilize lightly throughout the growing season.
Propagation: Take cuttings from recently matured stems or shoots.
Grooming: Keep to desired height and shape with light pruning or clipping at any time.
Repotting: Repot infrequently, in winter or early spring when needed.
Problems: Poor drainage, too-frequent watering, or standing in water will cause root rot.

Ferns

Ferns, with the delicate composition of their spore-producing fronds, instill a room with a peaceful air. Ferns are among the oldest plants on earth; only the algae and the mosses are older. They come in a multitude of shapes and sizes, such as the small ribbon fern, with its ribbonlike fronds, or the large maidenhair fern, which has fan-shaped leaflets. Several types grouped together in entryways, patios, or conservatories can create a stunning design. They also work well displayed alone, in pots, or in hanging baskets.

The secret of success in growing ferns lies in your ability to match as nearly as possible their natural environment. The better you can imitate the moist, cool air and light shade of a tropical forest, the better your fern will grow. Since its natural habitat has only dappled light, avoid exposing your plant to the direct sunlight that strikes a windowsill. Hot, dry air is a problem for ferns. Both the air and the soil must always be moist. Provide humidity by placing the pot on a humidifying tray or in a larger pot of moist peat moss. Most ferns will grow well in average indoor temperatures during the day, with a drop in temperature at night.

The variety of ferns is enormous. Of the two thousand or so species to choose from, the following are some of the most popular types to grow indoors.

Adiantum
Maidenhair fern

Maidenhair ferns are found in northern states growing in damp, cool spots near mountain streams. Their fronds have striking black stems and leaflets that are broad but frilled. The leaflets tend to be borne horizontally and seem suspended in midair on a mature plant. Their main limitation indoors is that they require an extremely damp atmosphere. A lighted terrarium is ideal for growing maidenhair ferns. Give them plenty of room so they can mature properly. Common varieties include *A. hispidulum, A. raddianum,* and *A. tenerum.*
Light: Provide at least moderate light but no direct sunlight.
Water: Keep plant very moist, but do not allow to stand in water.
Humidity: Requires moist air. Use a humidifier for best results. Does best in a terrarium.
Temperatures: 50° to 55° F at night, 60° to 65° F during the day.
Fertilization: Fertilize lightly.
Propagation: Start new plants by dividing an old specimen.
Grooming: Cut back in early spring.
Repotting: Repot in winter or early spring, as needed.
Problems: Dry soil or a high level of soluble salts may damage roots, causing plant to die back. Leaves will scorch if plant is in a draft or dry air.

Asplenium bulbiferum
Mother fern

The mother fern has fronds that arch outward from the crown, like those of its cousin the bird's-nest fern. They are finely divided into extremely narrow leaflets and carry tiny plantlets that can be used for propagation, hence the common name of mother fern. *A. daucifolium* is similar in appearance, but more delicate.
Light: Provide at least moderate light but no direct sunlight.
Water: Keep evenly moist. Water thoroughly and discard drainage.
Humidity: Requires moist air. Use a humidifier for best results.
Temperatures: 50° to 55° F at night, 60° to 65° F during the day.
Fertilization: Fertilize twice a year, in early spring and midsummer.
Propagation: Remove plantlets or rooted side shoots as they form.

Fatsia japonica

Fern: *Adiantum*

Fern: *Asplenium bulbiferum*

Fern: *Asplenium nidus*

Fern: *Blechnum occidentale*

Grooming: Pick off yellowed fronds.
Repotting: Repot in winter or early spring, as needed.
Problems: Leaves will scorch if plant is in a draft or dry air.

Asplenium nidus
Bird's-nest fern, spleenwort

Bird's-nest fern will grow into a large plant in time. The graceful, arching fronds can reach 15 inches. They emerge from a dark crown that looks like a bird's nest. The plant is relatively easy to grow indoors, but be sure to give it plenty of room.
Light: Will survive in low (reading-level) light.
Water: Let plant approach dryness before watering, then water thoroughly and discard drainage.
Humidity: Average indoor humidity levels.
Temperatures: 48° to 45° F at night, 60° to 65° F during the day.
Fertilization: Fertilize lightly.
Propagation: Brush spores onto a clay pot and cover with a plastic bag to maintain dampness. Keep out of direct sunlight.
Grooming: Pick off yellowed fronds.
Repotting: Transplant young plants when they are large enough to put into soil. Repot mature plants in winter or early spring, as needed.
Problems: Leaves will scorch if plant is in a draft or dry air.

Blechnum gibbum

When young, blechnum forms a neat, ground-hugging rosette of deeply lobed fronds, reaching a diameter of 3 feet. As it ages, it forms a narrow, black trunk up to 3 feet tall. As one of the easiest tree ferns to grow, and also one of the least massive, it is ideal for homes and apartments. It is unfortunately rarely available in its adult form. Buy it as a young plant . . . and be patient!
Light: Place in a bright, indirectly lit south, east, or west window.
Water: Keep very moist at all times, but do not allow to stand in water.
Humidity: Requires moist air. Use a humidifier for best results.
Temperatures: 60° to 65° F at night, 75° to 80° F during the day.
Fertilization: Fertilize lightly throughout the growing season.

Propagation: Root the occasional offsets or grow from spores.
Grooming: Pick off yellowed fronds.
Repotting: Repot infrequently.
Problems: Leaves will scorch if plant is in a draft or dry air.

Cibotium chamissoi
Hawaiian tree fern, Mexican tree fern

Hawaiian tree ferns are suited only for spacious locations. They are magnificent plants in an indoor solarium, beside an indoor pool, or in a greenhouse. The fronds are finely divided and up to 6 feet long. The plants can be purchased with a trunk several feet high if desired. A related fern, *C. schiedei* (Mexican tree fern), usually has a "trunk" only a few inches high or no trunk at all.
Light: Provide at least 4 hours of curtain-filtered sunlight from a bright south, east, or west window.
Water: Keep evenly moist. Water thoroughly and discard drainage.
Humidity: Requires moist air. Use a humidifier for best results.
Temperatures: 55° to 60° F at night, 70° to 75° F during the day.
Fertilization: Fertilize lightly.
Propagation: Propagation is difficult but can be done from spores.
Grooming: Pick off yellowed fronds.
Repotting: Repot in winter or early spring, as needed.
Problems: Leaves will scorch if plant is in a draft or dry air.

Cyathea
Tree fern

Tree ferns become truly tree size outdoors in tropical environments. Indoors, they grow slowly, so they can make fine specimen plants for many years in a spacious area. The finely divided fronds, which emerge from the top of a 3- or 4-foot-high trunk, may reach 2 feet in length. Purchase a fairly large plant so that you can enjoy its tree stature without having to wait 10 years. Keep the soil wet. Place in a humid spot protected from drafts.
Light: Place in a bright, indirectly lit south, east, or west window.
Water: Keep very moist at all times, but do not allow to stand in water.
Humidity: Requires moist air. Use a humidifier for best results.
Temperatures: 50° to 55° F at night, 65° to 70° F during the day.

Fertilization: Fertilize lightly.
Propagation: Not generally attempted but can be done from spores.
Grooming: Pick off yellowed fronds.
Repotting: Repot infrequently, in winter or early spring when needed.
Problems: Leaves will scorch if plant is in a draft or dry air.

Cyrtomium falcatum
Holly fern

Of all the ferns, holly fern is perhaps the most tolerant of indoor environments. It is a slow-growing plant that may grow to 2 feet in time. The fronds are divided into fairly large leaflets 3 to 5 inches long and up to 1 or 2 inches wide. Like holly leaves, they are a glistening green. The cultivar 'Rochfordianum' is the most commonly grown holly fern.
Light: Will survive in low (reading-level) light.
Water: Keep evenly moist. Water thoroughly and discard drainage.
Humidity: Requires moist air. Use a humidifier for best results.
Temperatures: 40° to 45° F at night, 60° to 65° F during the day.
Fertilization: Fertilize lightly.
Propagation: Start new plants by dividing an old specimen.
Grooming: Pick off yellowed fronds.
Repotting: Repot in winter or early spring, as needed.
Problems: Leaves will scorch if plant is in a draft or dry air. Subject to crown rot in overly moist conditions.

Davallia
Deer's-foot fern, rabbit's-foot fern, squirrel's-foot fern

Like the polypody fern, ferns in the *Davallia* genus are noted for their furry rhizomes, which creep over and down the sides of the growing container and resemble animal feet. The plants become more interesting with age, so do not divide them often. They are attractive in a hanging basket; the "feet" cascade or creep downward. The fronds are usually finely divided and delicate. The most commonly available species include *D. mariesii*, *D. fejeensis* 'Plumosa', and *D. trichomanoides*.
Light: Provide at least moderate light but no direct sunlight.
Water: Keep evenly moist. Water thoroughly and discard drainage.

Fern: *Blechnum gibbum*

Fern: *Cyathea*

Fern: *Davallia mariesii*

Fern: *Cyrtomium falcatum*

Fern: *Nephrolepis exaltata* 'Bostoniensis'

Fern: *Pellaea rotundifolia*

Fern: *Platycerium bifurcatum*

Humidity: Requires moist air. Use a humidifier for best results.
Temperatures: 50° to 55° F at night, 65° to 70° F during the day.
Fertilization: Fertilize lightly throughout the growing season.
Propagation: Start new plants by dividing an old specimen.
Grooming: Pick off yellowed fronds.
Repotting: Repot infrequently.
Problems: Leaves will scorch if plant is in a draft or dry air.

Nephrolepis exaltata 'Bostoniensis'
Boston fern, sword fern, Dallas fern

Boston ferns are the most popular indoor ferns for good reason: They are striking and they tolerate a variety of indoor conditions. Their arching form makes them useful for hanging baskets. Many new cultivars are available. Some have particularly long fronds; others, such as 'Fluffy Ruffles', are small plants with more finely divided fronds than the older cultivars. *N. exaltata* 'Dallasii' (Dallas fern) is a particularly choice cultivar because of its ability to adapt to dry air. The similar *N. obliterata* 'Kimberley Queen' is a close relative of the Boston fern and is likewise especially tolerant of dry air. If plants begin to thin out and weaken, repot them and place them in better light.
Light: Provide at least moderate light but no direct sunlight.
Water: Let plant approach dryness before watering, then water thoroughly and discard drainage.
Humidity: Average indoor humidity levels.
Temperatures: 50° to 55° F at night, 65° to 70° F during the day.
Fertilization: Fertilize all year, more heavily in summer.
Propagation: Start new plants by dividing an old specimen, or root the tips of the runners.
Grooming: Pick off yellowed fronds. Keep to desired height and shape with light pruning or clipping at any time.
Repotting: Repot infrequently.
Problems: Poor drainage, too-frequent watering, or standing in water will cause root rot. Leaves will drop if plant is suddenly moved into low light. Plant will get spindly and weak if light is too low.

Pellaea rotundifolia
Button fern

The round, shiny leaflets of the button fern are borne on ground-hugging black stems, making the plant look more like a ground cover than a fern. Often sold in a small hanging basket, it is also a fine choice for terrariums and plant shelves.
Light: Place in a bright, indirectly lit south, east, or west window.
Water: Keep very moist at all times, but do not allow to stand in water.
Humidity: Requires moist air. Use a humidifier for best results.
Temperatures: 55° to 60° F at night, 70° to 75° F during the day.
Fertilization: Fertilize lightly throughout the growing season.
Propagation: Divide in spring, or grow from spores.
Grooming: Pick off yellowed fronds.
Repotting: Repot infrequently.
Problems: Leaves will scorch if plant is in a draft or dry air.

Platycerium bifurcatum
Staghorn fern

Staghorn ferns are epiphytes and grow on surfaces rather than in soil or potting media. They can be purchased on bark slabs, clumps of sphagnum moss, or cork boards. Growth is slow, but eventually they develop massive fronds that resemble the antlers of a large animal. A wall in a humid, brightly lit location is an ideal spot for hanging staghorn ferns. Plantlets will eventually form at the base of the parent plant and emerge between the large, flat basal fronds. Water staghorn ferns by attaching some moisture-holding material, such as sphagnum moss, to the growing surface at the base of the plant. Once a week take the plant down and soak it in a pail or sink.
Light: Provide at least 4 hours of curtain-filtered sunlight from a bright south, east, or west window.
Water: Keep evenly moist. Water thoroughly and discard drainage.
Humidity: Requires moist air. Use a humidifier for best results.
Temperatures: 50° to 55° F at night, 65° to 70° F during the day.
Fertilization: Fertilize lightly.
Propagation: Remove plantlets or rooted side shoots as they form.
Grooming: Pick off yellowed fronds.

Repotting: Replace or replenish the water-holding sphagnum when needed.
Problems: Leaves will scorch if plant is in a draft or dry air.

Polypodium
Bear's-paw fern, hare's-foot fern, golden polypody fern

Polypodium gained its common names from the furry rhizomes that grow along the surface of the soil and resemble animal feet. The rhizomes eventually creep over the sides of the pot. The tough fronds are divided into a few large lobes. As with most ferns, coolness, light fertilization, and infrequent repotting are best. Many indoor gardeners grow this fern on a bark slab, but they usually keep it in a terrarium, where high humidity can be maintained. The most popular cultivar is
P. aureum 'Mandaianum'. All are easy to grow.
Light: Provide at least 4 hours of curtain-filtered sunlight from a bright south, east, or west window.
Water: Let plant approach dryness before watering, then water thoroughly and discard drainage.
Humidity: Average indoor humidity levels.
Temperatures: 50° to 55° F at night, 60° to 65° F during the day.
Fertilization: Fertilize lightly.
Propagation: Start new plants by dividing an old specimen.
Grooming: Pick off yellowed fronds.
Repotting: Repot infrequently.
Problems: Leaves will scorch if plant is in a draft or dry air; leaves will drop if plant is suddenly moved into low light.

Polystichum tsus-simense
Dwarf leatherleaf fern

Dwarf leatherleaf fern is a slow-growing plant ideally suited to terrariums and dish gardens. When it grows too large for those spaces, transfer it to a hanging basket or individual pot. The shiny, deep green fronds are deeply cut and quite tolerant of dry air.
Light: Provide at least moderate light but no direct sunlight.
Water: Let plant approach dryness before watering, then water thoroughly and discard drainage.
Humidity: Requires moist air. Use a humidifier for best results.
Temperatures: 50° to 55° F at night, 60° to 65° F during the day.

Fertilization: Fertilize lightly.
Propagation: Start new plants by dividing an old specimen.
Grooming: Pick off yellowed fronds.
Repotting: Repot in late spring, if needed.
Problems: Leaves will drop if soil is too wet or too dry. Dry soil or a high level of soluble salts may damage roots, causing plant to die back.

Pteris
Table fern, brake fern, fan table fern, silverleaf fern

Table ferns are so named because they grow slowly indoors, remaining small and useful as a table centerpiece. The fronds are variously divided and variegated. *P. cretica* 'Albo-lineata' (variegated table fern), for example, bears a broad band of creamy white down each slightly wavy leaflet and the *P. ensiformis* 'Victoriae' (silverleaf fern) has finely divided fronds with a silver band down the middle. *P. cretica* 'Wilsonii' (fan table fern) has bright green, fan-shaped fronds with dense crests at the tips. There are many other choice varieties. Despite their name, do not keep these ferns permanently on a table in dim light. They require a little more humidity than is generally available indoors.
Light: Provide at least moderate light but no direct sunlight.
Water: Keep evenly moist. Water thoroughly and discard drainage.
Humidity: Requires moist air. Use a humidifier for best results.
Temperatures: 50° to 55° F at night, 60° to 65° F during the day.
Fertilization: Fertilize lightly throughout the growing season.
Propagation: Start new plants by dividing an old specimen.
Grooming: Pick off yellowed fronds.
Repotting: Repot at any time.
Problems: Leaves will scorch if plant is in a draft or dry air.

Sphaeropteris cooperi
Tree fern

Tree ferns are best suited for a solarium, indoor swimming pool area, or similar large indoor setting. The fronds are several feet long and have hairy stems. They generally grow from a crown at the end of a long trunk. Plants of this size are quite old, but can be purchased from a specialty store (they may still be sold under their old name, *Alsophila*).

Fern: *Polypodium aureum*

Fern: *Polystichum tsus-simense*

Fern: *Pteris cretica*

Ficus benjamina

Ficus deltoidea

Ficus elastica 'Variegata'

Keep the soil moist and the air humid and warm.

Light: Place in a bright, indirectly lit south, east, or west window.
Water: Keep very moist at all times, but do not allow to stand in water.
Humidity: Requires moist air. Use a humidifier for best results.
Temperatures: 65° to 70° F at night, 75° to 80° F during the day.
Fertilization: Fertilize lightly.
Propagation: Not generally attempted but can be done from spores.
Grooming: Pick off yellowed fronds.
Repotting: Repot infrequently.
Problems: Leaves will scorch if plant is in a draft or dry air.

Ficus
Fig

Fig is a large, diverse family of more than 800 tropical trees, shrubs, and vines. It includes not only *F. carica* (edible fig), but a number of ornamental plants for container gardening. Listed below are some indoor favorites.

Figs will do well if they have good light, rich soil kept evenly moist, and frequent feeding. Guard against overwatering, and protect against cold drafts, dry heat, and any sudden changes in environment.

Shrubby Figs

Some ficus naturally form compact shrubs. They normally don't become much larger than 3 or 4 feet in height and can be kept considerably smaller by judicious pruning.

Ficus deltoidea
Mistletoe fig

The mistletoe fig (also known as *F. diversifolia*) is an interesting indoor shrub. It bears spreading branches covered with small, rounded to wedge-shaped leaves and many tiny (but inedible) green figs that turn red in bright sun.

Ficus 'Green Island'
Green Island fig

A fig of purportedly hybrid origin, Green Island fig has thick branches that bear leaves resembling those of *F. benjamina* but less pointed and much

thicker. Although it is slow growing, it is particularly easy to grow.

Ficus triangularis
Triangleleaf fig

Triangleleaf fig resembles a large mistletoe fig, but it has larger leaves that have a distinctly triangular outline and rounded edges. Like the mistletoe fig, it produces numerous, tiny, but inedible, figs.

Tree-Sized Figs

The following figs are normally sold as indoor trees, from 3 to 8 feet or more in height. Some are sold with braided trunks, giving them extra support. The smaller-leaved varieties can be pruned and grown as indoor shrubs.

Ficus benjamina
Weeping fig

Ficus benjamina holds a prominent position among container plants because it is favored by so many designers. It has pale brown bark like birch bark and graceful, arching branches loaded with glossy, pointed leaves. It grows from 2 to 18 feet tall. Several variegated forms, with leaves speckled or splotched in white or yellow, are also available. This plant often loses most of its leaves when moved to a new location. It will need a period of adjustment, but with care it will flourish again.

Ficus elastica
Rubber plant

Ficus elastica and the larger-leaved *F. elastica* 'Decora' are old favorites commonly known as rubber plants. They have bold, deep green leaves on stems 2 to 10 feet tall. 'Variegata' has long, narrow leaves that make rippling patterns of grass green, metallic gray, and creamy yellow. When a rubber plant becomes too lanky, cut off the top and select a side branch to form a new main shoot, or air-layer the plant.

Ficus lyrata
Fiddleleaf fig

Ficus lyrata (also known as *F. pandurata*) is a striking container plant. It has durable, papery leaves of deep green in a fiddle shape. The plant grows 5 to 10 feet tall.

Ficus maclellandii 'Alii'

This fig is a recent introduction with long, narrow, pointed leaves, which give it a bamboo appearance. It makes a striking specimen plant and is more tolerant of being moved than *F. benjamina*.

Ficus retusa
Indian-laurel

Indian-laurel, often listed as *F. retusa nitida*, is one of the easiest evergreen trees to grow indoors. It is similar to *F. benjamina* (weeping fig), but has a slightly larger leaf and is more upright in its branching habit. Indian-laurels are commonly seen in commercial interiors. Grow as a single-stemmed shrub when it is small. As it grows, gradually prune it into a tree form.

Ficus stricta

Ficus stricta is similar to *F. benjamina*, but has larger, less pointed leaves. It is often listed as *F. benjamina* var. *nuda*.

Care of Tree-Sized and Shrubby Ficus

Light: Provide 3 to 4 hours of curtain-filtered sunlight from a bright south, east, or west window.
Water: Let plant approach dryness before watering, then water thoroughly and discard drainage.
Humidity: Average indoor humidity levels.
Temperatures: 50° to 55° F at night, 65° to 70° F during the day.
Fertilization: Fertilize all year, more heavily in summer.
Propagation: Take stem cuttings before they have hardened or matured or air-layer.
Grooming: Prune to desired form as plant matures.
Repotting: Repot infrequently.
Problems: Dry soil or a high level of soluble salts may damage roots, causing plant to die back. Leaves will drop if plant is suddenly moved into low light.

Climbing Figs

In outdoor settings climbing figs scale great heights into treetops and up walls and cliff faces. Indoors, unless they are in a humid greenhouse, they rarely produce the clinging aerial roots that would allow them to climb. However, they can be trained up trellises, used as ground covers, or grown as hanging plants. Their thin leaves are more sensitive to dry air than those of other figs.

Ficus pumila
Creeping fig

Creeping fig has tiny, heart-shaped leaves. It's a fast-growing trailer that looks especially attractive in a hanging basket or cascading from a shelf. It also makes an excellent ground cover for terrariums. Variegated and oakleaf versions are available. Variegated cultivars sometimes produce all-green branches, which should be removed.

Ficus sagittata 'Variegata'
Variegated rooting fig

Also sold as *F. radicans* 'Variegata', variegated rooting fig bears thin, pointed, 2- to 4-inch leaves heavily marked with creamy white. It makes an elegant hanging-basket plant. Brown patches in the variegated areas are due to too much cold or sun.

Care of Climbing Figs

Light: Place in a bright, indirectly lit south, east, or west window.
Water: Keep evenly moist. Water thoroughly and discard drainage.
Humidity: Require moist air. Use a humidifier for best results.
Temperatures: 60° to 65° F at night, 70° to 75° F during the day.
Fertilization: Fertilize only during late spring and summer.
Propagation: Take stem cuttings at any time.
Grooming: Pick off yellowed leaves. Pinch or prune plant regularly for a fuller shape.
Repotting: Repot infrequently.
Problems: Leaves will scorch if plants are in a draft or dry air.

Fittonia
Fittonia, nerveplant, mosaic-plant

The intricately veined, oval leaves of fittonia grow semiupright, then trail over the sides of the container.

Ficus lyrata

Ficus maclellandii 'Alii'

Ficus pumila

Fittonia verschaffeltii var. *argyroneura*

Gynura aurantiaca

Hedera canariensis

F. verschaffeltii var. *argyroneura* displays a mosaic pattern of white veins; *F. verschaffeltii* var. *argyroneura* 'Minima' bears small leaves. *F. verschaffeltii* var. *verschaffeltii* has deep red veins on paper-thin, olive green leaves. They all make striking hanging plants, and the small types work well in terrariums. Fittonias will thrive in most households.

Light: Provide at least moderate light but no direct sunlight from a north or east window.

Water: Water thoroughly, but allow to dry between waterings. Water lightly during winter.

Humidity: Requires moist air. Use a humidifier for best results.

Temperatures: 65° to 70° F at night, 75° to 80° F during the day. Move to a cool spot during the winter.

Fertilization: Fertilize lightly throughout the growing season.

Propagation: Take cuttings from recently matured stems or shoots.

Grooming: Keep to desired height and shape with light pruning or clipping at any time. As older plants become unattractive, start them over from cuttings.

Repotting: Repot in winter or early spring, as needed.

Problems: Subject to crown rot in overly moist conditions. Will get spindly and weak if light is too low.

Geogenanthus undatus
Seersucker-plant

On its short stems the seersucker-plant produces 2-inch leaves that have white stripes and a puckered texture. It will remain small. The plant grows well indoors if given warmth at night.

Light: Provide at least 4 hours of curtain-filtered sunlight from a bright south, east, or west window.

Water: Keep evenly moist. Water thoroughly and discard drainage.

Humidity: Requires moist air. Use a humidifier for best results.

Temperatures: 65° to 70° F at night, 75° to 80° F during the day.

Fertilization: Fertilize all year, more heavily in summer.

Propagation: Take stem cuttings at any time.

Grooming: Pick off yellowed leaves. As older plants become unattractive, start them over from cuttings.

Repotting: Repot at any time.

Problems: Leaves will scorch if plant is in a draft or dry air.

Gynura aurantiaca
Velvetplant, purple passionplant

A trailing plant, velvetplant has intensely purple leaves and stems with thick, reddish hairs covering all surfaces. It is easy to grow, and, if pruned, is attractive in a hanging basket. With enough light, the plant will produce clusters of tiny flowers with white petals and yellow centers. It is best to pick these off quickly, however, because they have an unpleasant aroma and will produce a mess of dropping petals and seedpods. The plant probably won't flower if it is grown in low light.

Light: Place in a bright, indirectly lit south, east, or west window.

Water: Keep evenly moist. Water thoroughly and discard drainage.

Humidity: Average indoor humidity levels.

Temperatures: 55° to 60° F at night, 70° to 75° F during the day.

Fertilization: Fertilize lightly throughout the growing season.

Propagation: Take stem cuttings at any time.

Grooming: Keep to desired height and shape with light pruning or clipping at any time.

Repotting: Repot at any time.

Problems: Dry soil or a high level of soluble salts may damage roots, causing plant to die back. Subject to infestations of whiteflies and aphids.

Hedera canariensis
Canary Island ivy, Algerian ivy

Canary Island ivy is a fast-growing plant with large leaves. It can be grown in a basket or trained on a trellis. The most popular cultivar, *H. canariensis* 'Variegata' (also known as 'Gloire-de-Marengo'), has green leaves with white variegation. Keep these ivies moist and warm when growing them indoors.

Light: Provide at least 4 hours of curtain-filtered sunlight from a bright south, east, or west window.

Water: Keep evenly moist. Water thoroughly and discard drainage.

Humidity: Average indoor humidity levels.

Temperatures: 65° to 70° F at night, 75° to 80° F during the day.

Fertilization: Fertilize all year, more heavily in summer.
Propagation: Take stem cuttings at any time.
Grooming: Keep to desired height and shape with light pruning or clipping at any time.
Repotting: Repot at any time.
Problems: Will get spindly and weak if light is too low.

Hedera helix
English ivy

Many plants are called ivy, but the most famous is *H. helix*, the English ivy. Countless varieties of this trailing and climbing plant are available. 'Merion Beauty' has small leaves in the characteristic English ivy shape. 'Itsy Bitsy' is a tiny variety. Others have leaves that are curled, waved, or crinkled. 'Curlilocks' is an example. Still others have color variegation, such as the yellow-gold 'Gold Dust'; 'Glacier' is one of the white-variegated cultivars. Many ivies send out aerial roots that will climb rough surfaces—a brick fireplace wall, for example. You can also use them in large planters as a ground cover. They are excellent in hanging baskets and can be trained on a trellis.

Protected from hot, dry air, English ivy will flourish as long as a few basics are followed: Place it in a cool, bright location, and keep the soil and air moist. During the growing season, feed every 2 weeks. Bathe the foliage occasionally. Plants rest in both fall and winter.
Light: Place in a bright, indirectly lit south, east, or west window.
Water: Keep evenly moist. Water thoroughly and discard drainage.
Humidity: Average indoor humidity levels.
Temperatures: 40° to 45° F at night, 60° to 65° F during the day.
Fertilization: Fertilize lightly throughout the growing season.
Propagation: Take stem cuttings at any time.
Grooming: Keep to desired height and shape with light pruning or clipping at any time.
Repotting: Repot at any time.
Problems: Spider mites can be a problem, especially if air is too dry. Small leaves and elongated stems indicate lack of light. Brown leaf tips result from dry air. Green leaves on variegated types result from too little light.

Hemigraphis
Red-ivy, red-flame ivy

Red-ivy is a weak-stemmed plant with oval to heart-shaped leaves that are an attractive combination of metallic violet above and wine red underneath. Short-lived but inconspicuous white flowers appear in summer. There are two common varieties: *H. alternata* (also known as *H. colorata*), with small, truly heart-shaped leaves, and *H.* 'Exotica', with larger, puckered leaves.
Light: Provide at least moderate light but no direct sunlight.
Water: Water thoroughly, but allow to dry between waterings.
Humidity: Requires moist air. Use a humidifier for best results.
Temperatures: 65° to 70° F at night, 75° to 80° F during the day.
Fertilization: Fertilize lightly throughout the growing season.
Propagation: Take stem cuttings at any time.
Grooming: Keep to desired shape with light pruning or pinching at any time during the year.
Repotting: Repot in winter or early spring as needed.
Problems: Subject to crown rot in overly moist conditions. Will get spindly, weak, and pale if light is too low.

Heptapleurum arboricola
Dwarf or miniature schefflera

Although its common names may suggest a diminutive stature, *H. arboricola* is only smaller that its cousin, the common schefflera (*Brassaia actinophylla*) in leaf size; it can reach over 6 feet in height and diameter. Fortunately, unlike the common schefflera, it branches readily and can be kept in check through regular pruning. The compound leaves are up to 7 inches across and deep green. There are several named cultivars, including some with yellow variegation and notched leaves. All are easy to grow.
Light: Provide 3 to 4 hours of curtain-filtered sunlight from a bright south, east, or west window.
Water: Let plant approach dryness before watering, then water thoroughly and discard drainage.
Humidity: Average indoor humidity levels.
Temperatures: 50° to 55° F at night, 65° to 70° F during the day.

Hedera helix 'Kolibri'

Heptapleurum arboricola

Homalomena wallisii

Hypoestes phyllostachya

Iresine herbstii

Fertilization: Fertilize only during late spring and summer.
Propagation: Take stem cuttings at any time, or air-layer.
Grooming: Pick off yellowed leaves. Pinch or prune regularly to maintain a fuller shape.
Repotting: Repot infrequently.
Problems: Will get spindly and weak if light is too low. Leaves will drop if soil is too wet or too dry.

Homalomena
Homalomena

The decorative potential of homalomenas are only just being discovered. Some, such as *H. wallisii,* with its thick, oblong, dark green leaves mottled with yellow, are grown for their variegation. Others, such as *H.* 'King of Spades' and *H.* 'Queen of Hearts', are grown for their dark, shiny foliage.
Light: Place in a bright, indirectly lit south, east, or west window. Will survive in poor light but growth is minimal.
Water: Water thoroughly, but allow to dry between waterings.
Humidity: Requires moist air. Use a humidifier for best results.
Temperatures: 65° to 70° F at night, 75° to 80° F during the day.
Fertilization: Fertilize lightly throughout the growing season.
Propagation: Propagate from cuttings or by division.
Grooming: Pick off yellowed leaves.
Repotting: Repot infrequently.
Problems: Leaves may die back or dry up in dry air.

Hypoestes phyllostachya
Hypoestes, pink-polka-dot, freckle-face

The common names for *Hypoestes* come from the unusual pink spots on its leaves (its botanical name formerly was *H. sanguinolenta*). It's a bushy, herbaceous plant that grows rapidly in good light. Keep it well branched and to a height of 12 inches by pruning it frequently. Many colorful hybrids are now available, including 'Pink Splash' and red or white spotted cultivars.
Light: Provide at least 4 hours of curtain-filtered sunlight from a bright south, east, or west window.
Water: Let plant approach dryness before watering, then water thoroughly and discard drainage.

Humidity: Requires moist air. Use a humidifier for best results.
Temperatures: 65° to 70° F at night, 75° to 80° F during the day.
Fertilization: Fertilize lightly throughout the growing season.
Propagation: Grows easily from seed, which is readily available. Take stem cuttings at any time.
Grooming: Start new plants to replace old specimens when they get weak. Keep to desired height and shape with light pruning or clipping at any time.
Repotting: Repot in winter or early spring, as needed.
Problems: Will get spindly and weak if light is too low.

Iresine herbstii
Beefsteak-plant, bloodleaf

The ornamental foliage of this plant is an intense, full-bodied red, as its common name bloodleaf suggests. *I. herbstii* has heart-shaped leaves with light red veins. *I. herbstii* 'Aureo-reticulata' produces green leaves tinted with red and lined with yellow veins. These small plants make brilliant accents in groupings of larger plants.
    They are easy to care for, but without a good deal of light, the leaves turn pale and the plant becomes leggy rather than bushy and compact. Water regularly and keep the air humid. In the summer, revive the plants with a vacation outdoors.
Light: Provide 4 hours or more of direct sunlight from a south window.
Water: Keep evenly moist. Water thoroughly and discard drainage.
Humidity: Requires moist air. Use a humidifier for best results.
Temperatures: 55° to 60° F at night, 70° to 75° F during the day.
Fertilization: Fertilize all year, more heavily in summer.
Propagation: Take cuttings from stems or shoots that have recently matured.
Grooming: Keep to desired height and shape with light pruning or clipping at any time.
Repotting: Repot in winter or early spring, as needed.
Problems: Will get spindly and weak if light is too low.

Laurus nobilis
Sweet bay, Grecian bay laurel

Sweet bay is seen in ancient artwork that depicts people wearing leafy crowns. The leaves are just as decorative today and are also used in cooking. As a houseplant sweet bay grows slowly, but eventually will become a 4-foot shrub. It prefers a well-lit, cool spot, such as an entranceway. Try to buy a large plant, since it will take several years to develop its bushy form.

Light: Provide 4 hours or more of direct sunlight from a south window.

Water: Let plant approach dryness before watering, then water thoroughly and discard drainage.

Humidity: Average indoor humidity levels.

Temperatures: 40° to 45° F at night, 60° to 65° F during the day.

Fertilization: Fertilize only during late spring and summer months.

Propagation: Take stem cuttings at any time.

Grooming: Keep to desired height and shape with light pruning or clipping at any time.

Repotting: Repot infrequently.

Problems: Poor drainage, too-frequent watering, or standing in water will cause root rot. Leaves will drop if soil is too wet or too dry.

Ledebouria socialis
Silver squill

Usually sold under its old name, *Scilla violacea*, silver squill is a small plant ideally suited for windowsills. It bears fleshy, pointed, olive green leaves splotched silvery gray with wine red undersides. The leaves are 2 to 4 inches long. The bulb grows above the soil and is purple in color. Clusters of tiny, green flowers are produced in spring but do not add much to the attractiveness of the plant.

Light: Provide at least 4 hours of curtain-filtered sunlight from a south, east, or west window.

Water: Water thoroughly, but allow to dry between waterings.

Humidity: Requires moist air. Use a humidifier for best results.

Temperatures: 55° to 60° F at night, 65° to 70° F during the day.

Fertilization: Fertilize lightly throughout the growing season.

Propagation: Pot bulblets that appear beside the parent bulb, or root plant after flowering.

Grooming: Pick off yellowed leaves and dried bulb tunics.

Repotting: Repot after flowering, setting the bulbs so that just the base is covered in potting mix.

Problems: Subject to crown rot if kept too moist. Will not bloom if light is too low.

Leea coccinea
West Indian holly

West Indian holly produces shiny, deep green compound leaves on an upright stem. Although it can reach 4 feet or more in height, it is generally kept pruned to 2 feet or less. There is also a purplish-leaved cultivar sold under the name *L. coccinea* 'Rubra'.

Light: Place in a bright, indirectly lit south, east, or west window.

Water: Water thoroughly, but allow to dry between waterings.

Humidity: Requires moist air. Use a humidifier for best results.

Temperatures: 65° to 70° F at night, 75° to 80° F during the day.

Fertilization: Fertilize lightly throughout the growing season.

Propagation: Take cuttings.

Grooming: Pick off faded leaves.

Repotting: Repot in winter or early spring, as needed.

Problems: Spots of black sap form on undersides of leaves. They are caused by a natural process called guttation and can be removed with a damp cloth.

Liriope
Liriope, lily-turf

Although well known in warmer parts of the country as a ground cover, lily-turf is only just beginning to be discovered as an attractive houseplant. It is grown for its graceful, grassy leaves and is popular in dish gardens and terrariums. Under very good conditions, it may bloom indoors, with clusters of dark blue to purple flowers. Dwarf and variegated cultivars, as well as those with dark, almost black leaves, are all suitable for indoor growing. The plants look fuller in a mass, so do not repot them often.

Light: Place in a bright, indirectly lit south, east, or west window.

Laurus nobilis

Ledebouria socialis

Liriope spicata 'Silver Dragon'

Maranta leuconeura var. erythroneura

Monstera deliciosa

Mimosa pudica

Water: Water thoroughly, but allow to dry between waterings. Water sparingly during the rest period.

Humidity: Average indoor humidity levels.

Temperatures: During the growing season, 65° to 70° F at night and 75° to 80° F during the day. During the winter rest period, 50° to 55° F at night, 65° to 70° F during the day.

Fertilization: Fertilize lightly throughout the growing season.

Propagation: Propagate from divisions in spring. Trim off brown leaf tips as necessary.

Grooming: Pick off yellowed leaves.

Repotting: Repot in spring as necessary.

Problems: Leaves may die back or dry up in dry air.

Maranta leuconeura
Prayer-plant

The name prayer-plant comes from the growth habit of *M. leuconeura* var. *kerchoviana*. In the daytime its satiny foliage lies flat, but at night the leaves turn upward, giving the appearance of praying hands. The plant reaches a height of about 8 inches. The two other main cultivars are *M. leuconeura* var. *leuconeura* and *M. leuconeura* var. *erythroneura*.

All three of these cultivars are fairly easy to grow. They grow best in a warm, humid environment with partial shade. Direct sunlight will cause the leaves to fade. Surround pots with peat moss or plant them in a grouping to improve humidity.

Light: Provide at least moderate light but no direct sunlight.

Water: Keep very moist during growth and flowering; at other times, allow to dry between waterings.

Humidity: Requires moist air. Use a humidifier for best results.

Temperatures: 55° to 60° F at night, 70° to 75° F during the day.

Fertilization: Fertilize lightly throughout the growing season.

Propagation: Start new plants by dividing an old specimen, or take stem cuttings at any time.

Grooming: Pick off yellowed leaves. Start new plants to replace old specimens when they get weak.

Repotting: Repot infrequently, in winter or early spring when needed.

Problems: Leaves will scorch if plant is in a draft or dry air. Poor drainage, too-frequent watering, or standing in water will cause root rot.

Mimosa pudica
Sensitive plant

When the finely divided leaflets of sensitive plant are touched, they immediately fold up. This habit makes the plant especially popular with children. It is a fast-growing plant easily started from seed. When the seedlings have several leaves, pinch back the stem tips to promote branching. Prune frequently to prevent legginess. Sensitive plant flowers readily, with small pink flowers. Keep it warm and in good light.

Light: Provide at least 4 hours of curtain-filtered sunlight from a bright south, east, or west window.

Water: Keep evenly moist. Water thoroughly and discard drainage.

Humidity: Average indoor humidity levels.

Temperatures: 65° to 70° F at night, 75° to 80° F during the day.

Fertilization: Fertilize lightly throughout the growing season.

Propagation: Start from seeds. Sow in a small pot and transplant seedlings as needed.

Grooming: Keep to desired height and shape with light pruning or clipping at any time. Prune seedlings only when several leaves have formed.

Repotting: Repot at any time.

Problems: Poor drainage, too-frequent watering, or standing in water will cause root rot. Will get spindly and weak if light is too low. Leaves will scorch if plant is in a draft or dry air. Plant will become unattractive with time, but can be started over with seeds at any season.

Monstera deliciosa
Monstera, split-leaf philodendron

Found in many homes, *Monstera deliciosa* climbs and sends out aerial roots that attach to supports or grow into the ground. Stems can reach 6 feet or more; they bear large, perforated, deeply cut leaves. *M. friedrichsthalii* is commonly available for use in hanging baskets. Its leaves are small, with wavy edges, and are perforated on either side of the midrib.

Monsteras are easy to grow as long as you provide a few essentials. Direct the aerial roots into the soil to give support to the weak stem. Keep soil barely moist in winter. Feed every 2 weeks during the growing season.

Light: Provide at least moderate light but no direct sunlight.

Water: During active growth water thoroughly, but allow to dry between waterings. Water sparingly in winter.

Humidity: Average indoor humidity levels.

Temperatures: 55° to 60° F at night, 70° to 75° F during the day.

Fertilization: Fertilize all year, more heavily in summer.

Propagation: Take stem cuttings or air-layer at any time.

Grooming: Wash mature leaves. Guide aerial roots into soil or onto a support. Cut tops of tall plants to limit their growth.

Repotting: Repot infrequently.

Problems: Waterlogged soil will cause leaves to weep around edges. Leaves with brown, brittle edges result from dry air. Brown edges and yellowed leaves are a symptom of overwatering or, less frequently, underfeeding. Dropping of lower leaves is normal. Serious leaf drop results from moving the plant or any other abrupt change. Young leaves often have no perforation. Low light may cause small, unperforated leaves to form.

Musa
Banana

The numerous plants in the genus *Musa* are all large, treelike, tropical plants best suited for greenhouses. Some species have attractive foliage and a semidwarf habit. Commercial container-plant growers are beginning to sell these smaller varieties, including the readily available *M. acuminata* 'Dwarf Cavendish', to florists, but even the smaller varieties grow large and need plenty of room. Banana plants require plenty of water and light. They are also very sensitive to cool temperatures at night. Do not expect them to flower and set fruit indoors unless they are in a greenhouse.

Light: Does best in a greenhouse setting.

Water: Keep very moist at all times, but do not allow to stand in water.

Humidity: Requires moist air. Use a humidifier for best results.

Temperatures: 65° to 70° F at night, 75° to 80° F during the day.

Fertilization: Fertilize all year, more heavily in summer.

Propagation: Take root cuttings at any time.

Grooming: Do not prune plant or cut it back. Give plenty of room.

Repotting: Repot at any time.

Problems: Leaves will scorch if plant is in a draft or dry air. Some species subject to spider mites in dry air.

Myrtus communis
True myrtle, Greek myrtle

True myrtle is commonly seen as a garden shrub in dry, warm climates; *M. communis* 'Microphylla', a small-leaved variety, is the most widely available. This cultivar is suitable for well-lit indoor gardens and is popular as an indoor bonsai specimen. It is a woody shrub that will grow 4 feet across if given enough room. The tiny leaves are aromatic and abundantly produced all along the stems. Myrtles have bright green leaves and attractive white flowers. Some cultivars have variegated foliage.

Light: In winter, keep in about 4 hours of direct sunlight. In summer, provide curtain-filtered sunlight from a south or west window.

Water: Let plant approach dryness before watering, then water thoroughly and discard drainage.

Humidity: Average indoor humidity levels.

Temperatures: 40° to 45° F at night, 60° to 65° F during the day.

Fertilization: Fertilize lightly throughout the growing season.

Propagation: Take cuttings from stems or shoots that have recently matured.

Grooming: Keep to desired height and shape with light pruning or clipping at any time.

Repotting: Repot in winter or early spring, as needed.

Problems: Spider mites can be a problem, especially if plant is too dry. Dry soil or a high level of soluble salts may damage roots, causing plant to die back. Leaves will scorch if plant is in a draft or dry air.

Musa ensete (Ensete ventricosum)

Myrtus communis 'Compacta'

Nandina domestica

Nicodemia diversifolia

Nandina domestica
Heavenly-bamboo

Heavenly-bamboo is a summer-flowering shrub, not a true bamboo. Indoors it needs plenty of sunlight and since it can grow to 8 feet, it is best suited for a greenhouse or solarium. It is also popular as a bonsai specimen. Keep heavenly-bamboo constantly wet and out of cold drafts.

Light: Provide 4 hours or more of direct sunlight from a south window. Does best in a greenhouse setting.

Water: Keep very moist at all times, but do not allow to stand in water.

Humidity: Requires moist air. Use a humidifier for best results.

Temperatures: 55° to 60° F at night, 70° to 75° F during the day.

Fertilization: Fertilize only when plant is growing actively.

Propagation: Start from seeds. Sow in a small pot and transplant seedlings as needed. Or divide a mature plant.

Grooming: Prune as needed.

Repotting: Prefers to be a little root bound. Cut back and repot as needed.

Problems: If plant is in a draft or dry air, leaves will scorch.

Nicodemia diversifolia
Nicodemia, indoor-oak

The true name for nicodemia is *Buddleia indica,* but it is never available under that name. A woody plant, it has small, shiny leaves shaped like those of an oak. With proper pruning, it will make an attractive indoor shrub about 1½ feet tall. Nicodemia grows slowly in summer and needs a moderate dormant period during winter. While it is resting, keep it warm, do not fertilize, and allow it to dry out between waterings.

Light: Provide at least 4 hours of curtain-filtered sunlight from a bright south, east, or west window.

Water: Let plant approach dryness before watering, then water thoroughly and discard drainage. Water less frequently during dormancy.

Humidity: Average indoor humidity levels.

Temperatures: 65° to 70° F at night, 75° to 80° F during the day.

Fertilization: Fertilize only when plant is growing actively.

Propagation: Take cuttings from stems or shoots before they have hardened or matured.

Grooming: Keep to desired height and shape with light pruning or clipping at any time. Prune in early spring.

Repotting: Repot in winter or early spring, as needed.

Problems: Dry soil or a high level of soluble salts may damage roots, causing plant to die back. Susceptible to spider mites.

Oplismenus hirtellus 'Variegatus'
Basketgrass

Basketgrass is one of the rare true grasses grown as a houseplant. The leaves are like those of lawn grasses but are striped green, white, and, in good light, pink. They hang down around the pot on long stems, making the plant ideal for hanging baskets. Fast growing and easy.

Light: Provide 2 to 3 hours of curtain-filtered sunlight in a south, east, or west window.

Water: Keep evenly moist. Water thoroughly and discard drainage.

Humidity: Average indoor humidity levels.

Temperatures: 60° to 65° F at night, 70° to 75° F during the day.

Fertilization: Fertilize lightly throughout the growing season.

Propagation: Take cuttings at any time.

Grooming: Pick off yellowed leaves. Cut back old stems to soil level to promote rejuvenation.

Repotting: Repot as necessary.

Problems: Leaves may die back or dry up in dry air. Growth may be stringy and color poor when light is too low.

Ornithogalum caudatum
Ornithogalum, pregnant-onion, false sea-onion

Although there are many ornithogalums that grow outdoors, only one is popular as a year-round houseplant. It derives its common name of pregnant-onion from the fact that its onionlike bulb, which is above ground, produces offsets just under its skin, causing it to bulge outward. Although grown mainly as a curiosity, it readily produces a tall, though weak-stemmed, flower stalk with numerous white, star-shaped flowers. The leaves are bright green and straplike, arching gracefully away from the bulb. The leaves, when crushed, are reputed to have a healing effect and have been used as a poultice for cuts.

Light: Keep in direct sunlight for at least 4 hours in winter. Provide curtain-filtered sunlight from a south, east, or west window in summer.

Water: Grows best if allowed to approach dryness before watering. Discard drainage.

Humidity: Average indoor humidity levels.

Temperatures: 60° to 65° F at night, 70° to 85° F during the day.

Fertilization: Fertilize only when plant is growing actively or flowering.

Propagation: Start new plants from the bulblets that develop beside the parent bulb.

Grooming: Remove old leaves as plant goes dormant.

Repotting: Repot after flowering, setting the bulb so that only its base is covered with potting mixture.

Problems: Grows weak and straggly if light is too low.

Osmanthus heterophyllus 'Variegatus'
False-holly, holly osmanthus

The shiny, spine-edged leaves of false-holly do indeed resemble those of the true holly. The variety most often grown has creamy white markings on the leaf edges, which may also be tinged with pink in bright light. The same plant may have both spiny leaves and leaves that are almost round. False-holly rarely blooms indoors.

Light: Provide about 4 hours of curtain-filtered sunlight from a bright south, east, or west window.

Water: Water thoroughly, but allow to dry between waterings.

Humidity: Requires moist air. Use a humidifier for best results.

Temperatures: 50° to 55° F both day and night. Place in a cool, even drafty spot in summer.

Fertilization: Fertilize lightly throughout the growing season.

Propagation: Take stem cuttings in spring; use a rooting hormone.

Grooming: Pinch regularly to obtain bushy growth.

Repotting: Repot infrequently.

Problems: Leaves may die back or dry up in dry air.

Palms

Palms are consistently popular as houseplants. Their graceful fans and rich green color can give even the coldest northern home a tropical air. The family is large and varied, but only a few are available as houseplants. Although they are among the most expensive plants, palms are well worth the investment. They are very tolerant and adapt well to the limited light and controlled temperatures of indoors. You can save money by purchasing small, young plants that will grow slowly into large trees. Some types will flourish for decades.

Most palms are easy to care for and have uniform growing requirements. During the spring and summer growing season, water plants heavily and feed them once a month. Reduce water and stop feeding them in winter. Protect palms from dry air and direct sunlight, especially if you move them outdoors. Do not prune palm trees unless a stem or frond dies. Unlike most plants, palms will produce new growth only from the tip of the stalk. Pinching back this tip or cutting off the newest frond below its point of attachment to the trunk will eliminate all new growth.

Caryota mitis
Fishtail palm

Fishtail palms become large. They have a thick trunk and many spreading fronds, each laden with fans of dark green leaflets. The ribbed texture of the leaflets and their wedged shape account for the common name. Fishtail palm is often used in commercial interiors because it grows relatively slowly and is easy to care for.

Chamaedorea elegans
Parlor palm, bamboo palm, reed palm

Parlor palm (also known as *Neanthe bella*) has handsome, light green fronds. Given enough light, it will bear clusters of yellow flowers among the lower leaves. It is a small palm, eventually

Osmanthus heterophyllus 'Variegatus'

Ornithogalum caudatum

Palm: *Caryota mitis*

Palm: *Chamaedorea elegans*

Palm: *Chamaerops humilis*

Palm: *Chrysalidocarpus lutescens*

Palm: *Howea forsterana*

Palm: *Phoenix roebelenii*

growing to a height of 6 feet, which makes it suitable for entryways and living rooms. *C. erumpens* (bamboo palm) bears clusters of drooping fronds. *C. seifrizii* (reed palm) has clusters of narrow, feathery fronds.

Chamaerops humilis
European fan palm

The European fan palm has fan-shaped leaves about 1 foot wide. The multiple trunks, reaching 4 feet high and taller, are rough and black and grow at an angle from the container.

Chrysalidocarpus lutescens
Areca palm, butterfly palm

The areca palm is a cluster of thin, yellow canes with arching fronds and strap-shaped, shiny green leaflets. It is a medium-sized palm and slow growing.

Howea forsterana
Kentia palm

Outdoors, the popular kentia palm grows to be a very large tree, but indoors it will rarely exceed 7 or 8 feet. Feather-shaped leaves arch outward from sturdy branches to create a full appearance. The leaves scorch easily, so take care to place this plant in the shade if you move it outdoors.

Livistona chinensis
Chinese fan palm

Chinese fan palms are large plants with deeply lobed, fan leaves up to 2 feet across. The plants will eventually grow to 10 feet if given enough room and a large enough container. They will tolerate bright, indirect light. Keep the soil very moist, but not soggy, and keep the plants warm at night.

Phoenix roebelenii
Pygmy date palm

Pygmy date palm is a dwarf, growing to a height of only 4 feet. A delicate-looking plant, its arching, narrow-leaved fronds branch to form a symmetrical shape. Like the other palms, it requires a minimum of attention.

Rhapis
Lady palm

Lady palm features 6- to 12-inch-wide fans of thick, shiny leaflets, 4 to 10 per fan. The fans grow at the ends of thin leafstalks that arch from a brown, hairy trunk. Popular varieties include *R. humilis* and *R. subtilis*; many variegated cultivars are also available.

Care of Palms

Light: Provide at least moderate light but no direct sunlight.
Water: Let plant approach dryness before watering, then water thoroughly and discard drainage.
Humidity: Average indoor humidity levels.
Temperatures: 50° to 55° F at night, 60° to 65° F during the day.
Fertilization: Fertilize all year, more heavily in summer.
Propagation: Start from seeds. Sow in a small pot and transplant seedlings as needed. Usually propagated only by professionals. Some palms can be divided.
Grooming: Pick off yellowed leaves. Wash leaves from time to time.
Repotting: Repot infrequently.
Problems: Poor drainage, too-frequent watering, or standing in water will cause root rot. Spider mites can be a problem, especially if air is too dry.

Pandanus
Screwpine

Screwpine owes its name to its leaves, which spiral upward, corkscrew fashion, in a compact rosette. The leaves resemble corn leaves, but they have prickly edges. Screwpine is a tough, yet graceful plant. Common varieties include *P. veitchii*, its cultivar 'Verde', and *P. utilis*. Some varieties have white, vertical stripes; others have burgundy edges. Aerial roots grow downward, searching for moist soil. This is an almost foolproof, pest-free specimen to add to an indoor plant collection. But be careful with this plant; its prickly leaves can injure both you and plants that are close to it.
Light: In winter, keep in about 4 hours of direct sunlight. In summer, provide curtain-filtered sunlight from a south or west window.

Water: Keep very moist during growth and flowering; at other times, allow to dry between waterings.
Humidity: Requires moist air. Use a humidifier for best results.
Temperatures: 55° to 60° F at night, 70° to 75° F during the day.
Fertilization: Fertilize lightly throughout the growing season.
Propagation: Remove plantlets or rooted side shoots as they form.
Grooming: Wash foliage from time to time. Train aerial roots into soil.
Repotting: Repot in winter or early spring, as needed.
Problems: Dry soil or a high level of soluble salts may damage roots, causing plant to die back.

Pellionia
Pellionia

Pellionias are trailing plants, suitable for small hanging baskets. They are also occasionally used as ground covers in terrariums or bed plantings, because the stems root wherever they contact the soil. The small leaves of most pellionias are borne closely along the stems. The two main species are *P. daveauana* and *P. pulchra*. Many variegated cultivars are available. Keep pellionias warm and out of drafts.
Light: Place in a bright, indirectly lit south, east, or west window.
Water: Keep evenly moist. Water thoroughly and discard drainage.
Humidity: Requires moist air. Use a humidifier for best results.
Temperatures: 55° to 60° F at night, 70° to 75° F during the day.
Fertilization: Fertilize lightly throughout the growing season.
Propagation: Take stem cuttings at any time.
Grooming: Keep to desired height and shape with light pruning or clipping at any time.
Repotting: Repot in winter or early spring, as needed.
Problems: Leaves will scorch if plant is in a draft or dry air. They will drop if soil is too wet or too dry.

Peperomia
Peperomia, baby rubber plant, creeping-buttons, false-philodendron, silverleaf peperomia, watermelon begonia

Peperomia is an extremely varied genus. It offers an astonishing variety of leaf forms, colors, and growth habits. Most

Palm: *Rhapis*

Pandanus veitchii

Pellionia pulchra

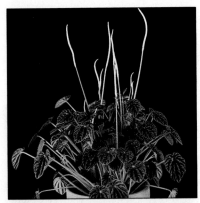

Peperomia caperata 'Emerald Ripple'

Peperomia obtusifolia (Upright)

Peperomia (Trailing)

Persea americana

peperomias are easy-to-grow, small plants ideally suited to windowsills and plant shelves. Under good conditions, they produce curious, if not necessarily striking, creamy white blooms the shape of mouse tails.

Clumping Peperomias

Clumping peperomias are a mass of leaves on short stems originating from the clump. *P. argyreia,* formerly known as *P. sandersii* (watermelon begonia), has thick, smooth, almost round leaves striped with green and silver. *P. caperata* 'Emerald Ripple' has small, dark, heart-shaped leaves with a deeply corrugated surface. This plant has many different cultivars, including dwarf types and variegates. *P. griseoargentea* (silverleaf peperomia) has a similarly corrugated surface but is silvery gray throughout. Another interesting one is *P. orba* 'Princess Astrid', a dwarf plant with spoon-shaped, apple green leaves covered with fine hairs. Generally speaking, clumping peperomias are more susceptible to crown rot than other peperomias.

Trailing Peperomias

Trailing peperomias have weak, pendant stems. The best known is *P. scandens* 'Variegata' (false-philodendron), which bears 2-inch, heart-shaped leaves with a broad cream edge on arching stems. It's indeed much like a variegated version of the heart-leaf philodendron. *P. rotundifolia* var. *pilosior* (creeping-buttons) is very different; it produces thin, weak, zigzagging stems and tiny, round, domed leaves with green and silver markings.

Upright Peperomias

Upright peperomias have visible stems and generally grow upward, although they become prostrate as the stems become heavier. Since they branch readily at the base, they are usually pruned back when they start to droop. The best known is *P. obtusifolia* (baby rubber plant), which bears thick stems and waxy, obtuse leaves of varying sizes. It has many cultivars with different forms of variegation, from light speckling to large zones of yellow or cream.

P. magnoliifolia is similar to *P. obtusifolia* but has larger leaves. Quite different is *P. verticillata*, with its shiny, sharply pointed leaves in whorls of 3 to 5 along an upright, reddish stem.

Care of Peperomias

Light: Place in a bright, indirectly lit south, east, or west window.
Water: Let plant dry slightly before watering, then water thoroughly and discard drainage.
Humidity: Requires moist air. Use a humidifier for best results.
Temperatures: 55° to 60° F at night, 70° to 75° F during the day.
Fertilization: Fertilize lightly throughout the growing season.
Propagation: Divide, or grow from stem cuttings. Many peperomias with thick leaves will also grow from leaf cuttings.
Grooming: Pick off yellowed leaves. Prune or pinch upright and trailing kinds as needed.
Repotting: Repot as needed.
Problems: Subject to crown rot in overly moist conditions. Will get spindly and weak if light is too low.

Persea americana
Avocado

Avocados are popular classroom plants because the seeds germinate so easily when partially submerged in water. They make attractive pot plants after several years of pinching back to encourage branching. Give them plenty of light so they do not get spindly. The plant may require staking. It will not flower or set fruit indoors.
Light: Provide 4 hours or more of direct sunlight from a south window.
Water: Keep evenly moist. Water thoroughly and discard drainage.
Humidity: Requires moist air. Use a humidifier for best results.
Temperatures: 55° to 60° F at night, 70° to 75° F during the day.
Fertilization: Fertilize all year, more heavily in summer.
Propagation: Put fruit pit halfway into water, at any time. When well rooted, place in a pot with soil, keeping half the pit above the soil.
Grooming: Pinch back stem tips routinely to encourage branching. Stake to keep plant upright.

Repotting: Repot at any time. Keep half of pit above soil.
Problems: Leaves will scorch if plant is in a draft or dry air.

Philodendrons

No other group of plants is as widely used indoors as philodendrons. The great variety of sizes and growth habits (vines, shrubs, and trees), as well as the uniquely shaped glossy leaves, give the indoor gardener many choices for almost any situation. And you don't have to worry about providing perfect growing conditions. Originally from South American tropical forests, philodendrons are strong, tolerant plants that don't need a lot of sunlight.

The 200 or so species are classified according to their growth habit, as either climbers or nonclimbers. The climbing species are the ones most commonly grown in the home. The name is a bit of a misnomer, though, since none of them climb well indoors. They must be tied to supports as they grow, and the aerial roots tied to the stem or directed to the ground for further support.

The nonclimbing philodendrons can become large plants 6 to 8 feet tall. Their leaves, of varying shapes, extend from self-supporting trunks. These plants are ideal for offices or for large rooms with high ceilings.

A few basic techniques will keep your philodendron healthy and thriving. It will do best in bright light, but it doesn't need direct sunlight. Water regularly to keep the soil moist, and wash the leaves about once a month. An undersized pot, low temperatures, or poor drainage will cause leaves to yellow and drop. However, it is natural for the climbing types to drop their lower leaves as they grow.

Philodendron bipinnatifidum
Twice-cut philodendron, fiddleleaf philodendron

The deeply cut, star-shaped leaves of twice-cut philodendron are large. It is a nonclimbing type, so it needs no support.

Philodendron hastatum
Spade-leaf philodendron

Spade-leaf philodendron is a lush, evergreen, climbing vine with aerial roots.

Deeply veined, bright green leaves take the shape of giant spearheads, 8 to 12 inches long.

Philodendron pertusum
See *Monstera deliciosa*

Philodendron 'Red Emerald'
Red Emerald philodendron

Red Emerald philodendron has red stems topped with bright green, yellow-veined, spear-shaped leaves. It's a climbing kind.

Philodendron scandens oxycardium
Heart-leaf philodendron

Heart-leaf philodendron, also known as *P. cordatum,* has many glossy, deep green leaves. It is the most popular philodendron grown in the United States. Since it's a vigorous climber, train it on a column, frame a window with it, or hang it from a beamed ceiling. This plant does fine in the shade.

Philodendron selloum
Lacy-tree philodendron

A nonclimbing, cut-leaf species, lacy-tree philodendron is often used to decorate offices. As it ages, the cuts deepen and cause the leaves to ruffle.

Care of Philodendrons

Light: Provide at least moderate light but no direct sunlight.
Water: Keep evenly moist. Water thoroughly and discard drainage.
Humidity: Average indoor humidity levels.
Temperatures: 50° to 55° F at night, 60° to 65° F during the day.
Fertilization: Fertilize all year, more heavily in summer.
Propagation: Take stem cuttings at any time, or air-layer climbing types.
Grooming: Keep climbing types to desired height and shape with light pruning or clipping at any time. Direct aerial roots to soil or remove them if they are unattractive. Clean the leaves from time to time.
Repotting: Repot in winter or early spring, as needed.
Problems: It is natural for climbing philodendrons to drop lower leaves.

Philodendron scandens oxycardium

Philodendron selloum

Philodendron hastatum

Philodendron 'Red Emerald'

Pilea cadierei

Pilea 'Moon Valley'

Pittosporum tobira

Pilea
Aluminum-plant, artillery plant, creeping-charlie, panamiga, friendship-plant

There are more than 200 widely varied species in the *Pilea* genus. Most of the ones that are suitable for indoor gardening are moderately sized herbaceous plants. They grow about a foot tall and have variegated leaves with depressed veins, giving them a quilted appearance. The dark green leaves of many species are tinged with red, silver, or copper. Others bear a resemblance to their wild cousins, the stinging nettles, but are harmless. Still others have a creeping or trailing habit that makes them particularly useful in hanging baskets. Some species produce inconspicuous flowers in summer.

P. cadierei (aluminum-plant) is one of the most popular species. Its wafered, green leaves look like they have been brushed with silver paint. *P. cadierei* 'Silver Tree' is similar, with bronze leaves. *P. involucrata* (panamiga or friendship-plant) is more compact, with thick clusters of broad leaves. They are yellow-green with a coppery sheen above, and they have a rich, velvety texture. *P. involucrata* 'Norfolk' is similar to *P. involucrata* but with larger leaves in deep bronze and bright silver markings. *P. nummulariifolia* (hairy creeping-charlie) is very different from the others, with its small, pale green, rounded leaves and creeping stems. It makes a good choice for hanging baskets. *P. depressa* (shiny creeping-charlie) resembles *P. nummulariifolia,* but has smaller leaves and a smooth, hairless surface. *P. microphylla* (artillery-plant) bears arching, upright, green stems and tiny, fleshy, apple green leaves. It gets its common name from the fact that its tiny flowers shoot out pollen within seconds after being watered. Pileas are most attractive when young and should be pruned back severely or started anew from cuttings on a regular basis.

Light: Place in a bright, indirectly lit south, east, or west window.
Water: Keep evenly moist. Water thoroughly and discard drainage.
Humidity: Requires moist air. Use a humidifier for best results. Small varieties do well in terrariums.
Temperatures: 65° to 70° F at night, 75° to 80° F during the day.
Fertilization: Fertilize lightly throughout the growing season.
Propagation: Take stem cuttings at any time.
Grooming: Start new plants to replace old specimens as they get weak. Keep to desired size and shape with pruning or clipping at any time.
Repotting: Repot each year in late spring.
Problems: Subject to crown rot in overly moist conditions. Very susceptible to cold drafts or cold irrigation water. Will get spindly and weak in low light.

Pittosporum tobira
Japanese pittosporum

Japanese pittosporums are widely used in commercial interiors because they are tolerant of moderate light and many diverse indoor environments. They are woody shrubs that eventually get quite large. Their glossy leaves somewhat resemble those of a rhododendron. In ample light, the plant may bloom in the spring; its flowers have a fragrance similar to that of orange blossoms. A variegated form is available, *P. tobira* 'Variegata'.

Light: Place in a bright, indirectly lit south, east, or west window.
Water: Let plant approach dryness before watering, then water thoroughly and discard drainage.
Humidity: Average indoor humidity levels.
Temperatures: 40° to 45° F at night, 60° to 65° F during the day.
Fertilization: Fertilize lightly throughout the growing season.
Propagation: Take cuttings from stems or shoots that have recently matured, or air-layer.
Grooming: Keep to desired height and shape with light pruning or clipping at any time.
Repotting: Repot infrequently, in winter or early spring when needed.
Problems: Will not bloom if light is too low. Subject to scale and mealybugs.

Plectranthus
Swedish ivy

Although commonly known as Swedish ivy, plectranthus is neither from Sweden nor an ivy. The name comes from its popularity in Scandinavia as a hanging and trailing plant. Spikes of white flowers appear occasionally. *P. australis* has waxy, leathery, bright green leaves and a trailing habit. *P. coleoides* 'Marginatus' is not as trailing as other species. Its leaves are green and grayish with cream edges. *P. oertendahlii* has leaves of silver and purple with scalloped edges.

These striking plants are fairly tolerant and require a minimum of care. Place them in bright light, and water regularly.

Light: Place in a bright, indirectly lit south, east, or west window.

Water: Keep evenly moist. Water thoroughly and discard drainage.

Humidity: Average indoor humidity levels.

Temperatures: 55° to 60° F at night, 70° to 75° F during the day.

Fertilization: Fertilize all year, more heavily in summer.

Propagation: Take cuttings from stems or shoots that have recently matured.

Grooming: Pinch back stem tips of young or regrowing plants to improve form, being careful not to remove flower buds. Start new plants to replace old specimens when they get weak.

Repotting: Repot at any time.

Problems: Poor drainage, too-frequent watering, or standing in water will cause root rot. Dry soil or a high level of soluble salts may damage roots, causing plant to die back.

Podocarpus macrophyllus var. 'Maki'
Podocarpus, Japanese yew

A more pleasing compact shrub than *P. macrophyllus* var. 'Maki' is hard to find. A group of branches supports spirals of thin green leaves, each 3 inches long. As the branches lengthen, they gradually arch downward. Some species grow to 10 feet.

In the right environment podocarpus will thrive for many years. It's a slow-growing, tolerant plant that does best in cool temperatures and bright, filtered light. Control its size by pinching back the tips; this will encourage branching and bushiness.

Light: Place in a bright, indirectly lit south, east, or west window.

Water: Let plant approach dryness before watering, then water thoroughly and discard drainage.

Humidity: Average indoor humidity levels.

Temperatures: 50° to 55° F at night, 60° to 65° F during the day.

Fertilization: Fertilize lightly throughout the growing season.

Propagation: Take cuttings from stems or shoots that have recently matured.

Grooming: Keep to desired height and shape with light pruning or clipping at any time.

Repotting: Repot in winter or early spring, as needed.

Problems: Leaves will scorch if plant is in a draft or dry air. Poor drainage, too-frequent watering, or standing in water will cause root rot.

Polyscias
Aralia, balfour aralia, ming aralia

Aralias are woody shrubs frequently grown indoors for their lacy, often variegated foliage. They grow large and bushy and are popular in commercial interiors. The leaves of some cultivars are aromatic when crushed or bruised. *P. fruticosa* (ming aralia) has finely divided leaves and can reach a height of 8 feet. Its cultivar 'Elegans' is smaller, with extremely dense foliage. *P. balfouriana* 'Marginata' has leaves edged with white. The leaves of *P. balfouriana* 'Pennockii' are white to light green with green spots. *P. guilfoylei* 'Victoriae' is compact, with deeply divided leaves edged in white. Give aralias plenty of room, and prune them frequently to achieve good form.

Light: Provide at least moderate light but no direct sunlight.

Water: Let plant approach dryness before watering, then water thoroughly and discard drainage.

Humidity: Requires moist air. Use a humidifier for best results.

Temperatures: 55° to 60° F at night, 70° to 75° F during the day.

Fertilization: Fertilize lightly throughout the growing season.

Propagation: Take stem cuttings.

Grooming: Keep to desired height and shape with light pruning or clipping at any time.

Repotting: Repot in winter or early spring, as needed.

Plectranthus australis

Podocarpus macrophyllus

Polyscias fruticosa 'Elegans'

Radermachera sinica

Saxifraga stolonifera

Scirpus cernuus

Problems: Will get spindly and weak if light is too low. Poor drainage, too-frequent watering, or standing in water will cause root rot. Susceptible to mites, scale, and mealybugs.

Radermachera sinica
China-doll

The shiny, bright green leaves of *R. sinica* are doubly compound, giving it a delicate, fern appearance, although its stems are woody. In the nursery, it is usually planted 3 to a pot for a fuller look, and treated with a growth retardant, which decreases the distance between the leaves, making the plant more compact. The effect of the retardant may last for over a year; as it wears off the plant will return to its more open natural growth habit.
Light: Provide 2 to 3 hours of curtain-filtered sunlight through a south, east, or west window.
Water: Keep evenly moist. Water thoroughly and discard drainage.
Humidity: Average indoor humidity levels.
Temperatures: 60° to 65° F at night, 70° to 75° F during the day.
Fertilization: Fertilize lightly throughout the growing season.
Propagation: Commercially, it is grown from seeds, but it can be started from cuttings.
Grooming: Pick off yellowed leaves. To keep it compact, pinch regularly when the effect of the growth hormone has worn off.
Repotting: Repot as necessary.
Problems: Leaves may dry up if soil dries out between waterings.

Saxifraga stolonifera
Strawberry-geranium, strawberry-begonia

Saxifraga stolonifera is neither a geranium nor a begonia; its names come from the shape, resembling geranium leaves, and colors of the foliage, resembling that of begonias. One variegated cultivar, *S. stolonifera* 'Tricolor', is available, but is not as easy to maintain as the species. Strawberry-geraniums are best suited for ground covers or hanging baskets. They divide quickly, sending out runners that form plantlets much as strawberries do. In summer, small, white flowers appear on long stalks

above the foliage. Many gardeners display these plants on a patio during the summer. If you take them outdoors, make sure they are pest free before you bring them back indoors.
Light: Place in a bright, indirectly lit south, east, or west window.
Water: Let plant approach dryness before watering, then water thoroughly and discard drainage.
Humidity: Average indoor humidity levels.
Temperatures: 50° to 55° F at night, 60° to 65° F during the day.
Fertilization: Fertilize lightly throughout the growing season.
Propagation: Start new plants by dividing an old specimen, or remove any plantlets or rooted side shoots as they form.
Grooming: Cut flower stalks if you wish.
Repotting: Repot each year. Cut back and repot when flowering stops.
Problems: Will get spindly and weak if light is too low. Dry soil or a high level of soluble salts may damage roots, causing plant to die back. Leaves will scorch if plant is in a draft or dry air.

Scindapsus aureus

See *Epipremnum aureum*

Scirpus cernuus
Miniature bulrush

Miniature bulrush is a graceful, grassy plant, whose thin, green stems arch over and hang downward as they grow, making it a good choice for a hanging basket. Each stem bears a tiny, cream flower at its tip, which, although it adds a little interest to the plant's appearance, is not showy enough for the plant to be considered as anything other than a foliage plant.
Light: Place in a bright, indirectly lit south, east, or west window.
Water: Keep thoroughly moist at all times; can stand in water permanently.
Humidity: Average indoor humidity levels.
Temperatures: 60° to 65° F at night, 70° to 75° F during the day.
Fertilization: Fertilize lightly throughout the growing season.
Propagation: Divide in spring.

Grooming: Pick off yellowed leaves.
Repotting: Repot in spring as necessary.
Problems: Leaves may die back or dry up in dry air. Plant will die if soil dries out.

Selaginella
Spike-moss, moss-fern, sweat-plant, spreading club-moss

Selaginella is a group of primitive, mossy plants that are actually more closely related to ferns than to true mosses. They are popular terrarium plants; they don't do well in the open air. Some species, such as *S. martensii,* grow upright for about half their height, then spread, making small forests of miniature trees. Others, such as *S. pallescens* (up to 1 foot) and *S. kraussiana* 'Brownii' (a true miniature at only 1 inch high) form soft mats. There are various variegated and golden-leaved cultivars.
Light: Place in a bright, indirectly lit south, east, or west window.
Water: Keep evenly moist. Water thoroughly and discard drainage.
Humidity: Needs extremely high humidity levels. Does poorly outside a terrarium.
Temperatures: 65° to 70° F at night, 75° to 80° F during the day.
Fertilization: Fertilize lightly throughout the growing season.
Propagation: Take stem cuttings in spring.
Grooming: Trim any overgrown sections.
Repotting: Repot in spring as necessary.
Problems: Leaves may die back or dry up in dry air.

Senecio
Waxvine, German ivy, parlor-ivy

Although the genus *Senecio* is a vast one, including both flowering annuals and succulents, the two houseplants mentioned here are similar hanging plants grown for their foliage. *S. macroglossus* is generally available only in one of its variegated forms: *S. macroglossus* 'Medio-picta', with a splotch of bright yellow in the center of each leaf, or *S. macroglossus* 'Variegatum', with a creamy yellow border to its leaves. The leaves are shiny with 3 to 5 pointed lobes and are borne on purple stems. In shape and size, they resemble those of true ivy. *S. mikanioides* is similar to *s. macroglossus* but has entirely green leaves with 5 to 7 lobes.
Light: Provide about 4 hours of curtain-filtered sunlight from a bright south, east, or west window.
Water: Water thoroughly, then allow to dry between waterings. Water sparingly during the rest period.
Humidity: Average indoor humidity levels.
Temperatures: During the growing season, 65° to 70° F at night, 75° to 80° F during the day. During the winter rest period, 50° to 55° F at night, 60° to 65° F during the day.
Fertilization: Fertilize lightly throughout the growing season.
Propagation: Take stem cuttings at any time.
Grooming: Pick off yellowed leaves and prune overly long stems.
Repotting: Repot in spring as necessary.
Problems: Subject to spider mites in dry air.

Soleirolia soleirolii
Baby's tears

Baby's tears, often sold as *Helxine soleirolii,* is a compact creeper that has tiny, delicate, rounded leaves on thin, trailing stems. It grows into a dense mat and makes a good terrarium ground cover. It thrives in high humidity.
Light: Place in a bright, indirectly lit south, east, or west window.
Water: Keep evenly moist. Water thoroughly and discard drainage.
Humidity: Requires moist air. Use a humidifier for best results.
Temperatures: 50° to 55° F at night, 60° to 65° F during the day.
Fertilization: Fertilize all year, more heavily in summer.
Propagation: Start new plants by dividing an old specimen, or grow easily from cuttings, pressing them into moist rooting mix.

Selaginella kraussiana

Senecio macroglossus 'Variegatum'

Senecio mikanioides

Soleirolia soleirolii

Rhoeo spathacea

Grooming: Keep to desired height and shape with light pruning or clipping at any time.

Repotting: Repot at any time.

Problems: Dry soil or a high level of soluble salts may damage roots, causing plant to die back.

Sonerila margeritacea
Sonerila

Sonerilas are small plants. They have fleshy stems and foliage that is silver on top and reddish on the underside. The plants are very sensitive to dry air and are best suited to a terrarium or other humid location. Given ample light, sonerilas occasionally produce clusters of small, lavender flowers.

Light: Place in a bright, indirectly lit south, east, or west window.

Water: Keep evenly moist. Water thoroughly and discard drainage.

Humidity: Requires moist air. Use a humidifier for best results.

Temperatures: 55° to 60° F at night, 70° to 75° F during the day.

Fertilization: Fertilize lightly throughout the growing season.

Propagation: Take stem cuttings at any time.

Grooming: Pinch back stem tips of young or regrowing plants to improve form, being careful not to remove flower buds.

Repotting: Repot in winter or early spring, as needed.

Problems: Leaves will scorch if plant is in a draft or dry air. Poor drainage, too-frequent watering, or standing in water will cause root rot.

Spiderworts

Wandering-Jew, inch-plant, spiderwort—these are all common names for the popular and easily grown houseplants in the *Commelinaceae*, or Spiderwort, family. They belong to the genera *Callisia, Gibasis, Setcreasea, Tradescantia,* and *Zebrina* and have such similar needs and growth habits they are often grouped together.

Spiderworts have boat-shaped leaves of varying lengths borne alternately along trailing stems. All of them flower seasonally, with small, three-sepaled blooms, but most are grown strictly for their colorful or variegated foliage. They are used as ground covers, in hanging baskets, or as trailing plants on shelves. Pinch back the stem tips and remove old, unattractive stems frequently to prevent legginess or a spindly appearance. Stems of the variegated spiderworts often revert to the nonvariegated form. These should be pinched out.

Callisia
Striped inch-plant

Callisia elegans is very similar to *Tradescantia* and shares the same common name. The leaves are olive green with white stripes.

Gibasis geniculata
Tahitian bridal-veil

The tiny-leaved Tahitian bridal-veil is the only spiderwort that blooms with any frequency. It bears delicate, white flowers on thin stalks in spring and summer. For more information, see the listing for *Gibasis* in the "Flowering Houseplants" section.

Rhoeo spathacea
Moses-in-the-cradle, boat-lily, oyster plant

The common names for *Rhoeo spathacea* (now known as *Tradescantia spathacea*) come from the odd way it bears flowers. At the base of the terminal leaves on the shoots, small, white blooms appear within cupped bracts. The foliage is striking: It is green on top and deep purple or maroon beneath. The cultivar *R. spathacea* 'Variegata' is especially noteworthy. The plant has cane stems that trail as they get older, so it is generally grown in a hanging basket. Fertilize lightly, and flush the soil occasionally to keep the older leaves from dropping. Unlike most spiderworts, Moses-in-the-cradle is not propogated by cuttings, but by division.

Setcreasea pallida
Purple-heart

Purple-heart (*Setcreasea pallida*, more correctly *Tradescantia pallida*) is slower growing than most spiderworts, requires less pinching, but it needs more light to bring out the attractive deep purple that gives it its name. The bright pink flowers are short-lived but nonetheless very attractive.

Tradescantia
Striped inch-plant, wandering-Jew

The most common *Tradescantia* varieties are variegated with white or cream bands. Among them are *T. albiflora* Albovittata, *T. blossfeldiana* 'Variegata', and *T. fluminensis* 'Variegata'. *T. sillamontana* differs from the other tradescantias in that it bears entirely green leaves, which are covered in woolly, white hair.

Zebrina pendula
Wandering-Jew

Zebrina pendula, now *Tradescantia zebrina*, has shiny green leaves with broad, iridescent silver bands and purple undersides. Among the various variegated forms, *Z. pendula* 'Quadricolor' is the most colorful; it's heavily striped with white and pink.

Care of Spiderworts

Light: Provide at least moderate light but no direct sunlight. *Setcreasea pallida* prefers some direct sunlight.
Water: Let plant approach dryness before watering, then water thoroughly and discard drainage.
Humidity: Average indoor humidity levels.
Temperatures: 50° to 55° F at night, 65° to 70° F during the day.
Fertilization: Fertilize all year, more heavily in summer.
Propagation: Take stem cuttings at any time.
Grooming: Cut back overly long stems to stimulate regrowth from base. Pinch stem tips frequently. Remove dried leaves.
Repotting: Repot at any time.

Zebrina pendula

Setcreasea pallida

Syngonium podophyllum

Synadenium grantii 'Rubra'

Strobilanthes dyeranus

Problems: Will get spindly and weak if light is too low. Dry soil or a high level of soluble salts may damage roots, causing plant to die back.

Strobilanthes dyeranus
Persian-shield

The narrow, lance-shaped, quilted leaves of Persian-shield are heavily marbled with rich purple and highlighted with iridescent blue markings. The underside of the leaf is deep wine red. Pale blue flowers are easily produced, but should be eliminated, as they weaken this fast-growing shrub.

Light: Place in a bright, indirectly lit south, east, or west window.

Water: Water thoroughly, then allow to dry between waterings. Water sparingly during the rest period.

Humidity: Requires moist air. Use a humidifier for best results.

Temperatures: 65° to 70° F at night, 75° to 80° F during the day.

Fertilization: Fertilize lightly throughout the growing season.

Propagation: Take stem cuttings in spring.

Grooming: Prune regularly to rejuvenate plant; it ages poorly.

Repotting: Repot in spring as necessary.

Problems: Leaves may die back or dry up in dry air.

Synadenium grantii 'Rubra'
African milkbush

A borderline succulent, the African milkbush makes an attractive, fast-growing indoor tree or shrub. The stem is thick, and the leaves are spoon-shaped, measuring 4 to 6 inches in length. They are irregularly splashed with dull red, sometimes to the point where the whole leaf is burgundy. This is an extremely adaptable plant; it will tolerate just about all indoor conditions.

Light: Place in a bright, indirectly lit south, east, or west window.

Water: Water thoroughly, then allow to dry between waterings.

Humidity: Average indoor humidity levels.

Temperatures: 65° to 70° F at night, 75° to 80° F during the day.

Fertilization: Fertilize lightly throughout the growing season.

Propagation: Take stem cuttings at any time.

Grooming: Pick off yellowed leaves. Prune as necessary to keep plant within bounds.

Repotting: Repot in spring as necessary.

Problems: Lower leaves may drop if plant dries out.

Syngonium podophyllum
Syngonium, arrowhead vine

Arrowhead vine closely resembles its relatives the climbing philodendrons in both appearance and care requirements. An unusual feature is the change that occurs in the leaf shape as the plant ages. Young leaves are 3 inches long, arrow-shaped, and borne at the ends of erect stalks. They are dark green and may have bold, silvery white variegation. With age, the leaves become lobed, and the stems begin to climb. Eventually the variegation disappears, and each leaf fans into several leaflets. Older leaves may have as many as 11 leaflets. All stages of leaf development occur together on mature plants.

Arrowhead vines do best in a warm, moist environment protected from direct sunlight. Older climbing stems require support; a moss stick works well. To retain the juvenile leaf form and variegation, prune the climbing stems and aerial roots as they appear. Popular cultivars include 'Emerald Gem', 'White Butterfly', and 'Pink Allusion'.

Light: Place in a bright, indirectly lit south, east, or west window.

Water: Keep very moist during growth; at other times, allow to dry between waterings.

Humidity: Requires moist air. Use a humidifier for best results.

Temperatures: 55° to 60° F at night, 70° to 75° F during the day.

Fertilization: Fertilize lightly throughout the growing season.

Propagation: Take cuttings from stems or shoots that have recently matured.

Grooming: Keep to desired height and shape with light pruning or clipping at any time.
Repotting: Repot in winter or early spring, as needed.
Problems: Poor drainage, too-frequent watering, or standing in water will cause root rot. Older climbing stems require support.

Tetrastigma voinieranum
Chestnut vine, lizard-plant

Chestnut-vine is a massive indoor vine suited to large spaces. Its leaves are composed of 4 to 6 (usually 5) coarsely toothed leaflets, each measuring 4 to 8 inches in length. The stems are thick and bear clinging tendrils that allow the plant to climb nearby objects.
Light: Place in a bright, indirectly lit south, east, or west window.
Water: Water thoroughly, then allow to dry between waterings.
Humidity: Average indoor humidity levels.
Temperatures: 65° to 70° F at night, 75° to 80° F during the day.
Fertilization: Fertilize lightly throughout the growing season.
Propagation: Take stem cuttings in spring.
Grooming: Pick off yellowed leaves.
Repotting: Repot in spring as necessary.
Problems: Entire sections often drop off for no apparent reason, but are quickly replaced.

Tolmiea menziesii
Piggyback plant

Piggyback plants are popular with indoor gardeners because of their plantlets, which sprout over the top of the foliage at the junctures of the leaf blades and petioles. Under proper conditions, the trailing stems will quickly produce a large plant suitable for a hanging basket or a pedestal. A variegated form (T. menziesii 'Variegata') is available. These plants must be kept cool at night, and constantly moist. They need only light fertilization and will not tolerate drafts or dry air.

Light: Place in a bright, indirectly lit south, east, or west window.
Water: Keep evenly moist. Water thoroughly and discard drainage.
Humidity: Requires moist air. Use a humidifier for best results.
Temperatures: 40° to 45° F at night, 60° to 65° F during the day.
Fertilization: Fertilize lightly throughout the growing season.
Propagation: Remove plantlets as they form.
Grooming: Keep to the desired height and shape with light pruning or clipping at any time.
Repotting: Repot each year.
Problems: Leaves will scorch if plant is in a draft or dry air. Dry soil or a high level of soluble salts may damage roots, causing plant to die back and making it prone to infestations of spider mites.

Xanthosoma lindenii
Indian kale, spoonflower

Strikingly beautiful, arrow-shaped leaves with ivory white veins characterize Indian kale, a relative of the philodendron. It grows from tubers, much like another close relative, the caladium, and like the latter, enters into a dormant state in winter. At that time, it requires only enough water to keep it from drying out entirely. Besides X. lindenii, there are several other species and hybrids that make suitable houseplants.
Light: Place in a bright, indirectly lit south, east, or west window.
Water: Water thoroughly during the growing season, allowing plant to dry slightly between waterings. Keep almost dry during dormancy.
Humidity: Requires moist air. Use a humidifier for best results.
Temperatures: 65° to 70° F at night, 75° to 80° F during the day.
Fertilization: Fertilize lightly throughout the growing season.
Propagation: Divide in spring, at the end of dormancy.
Grooming: Pick off yellowed leaves.
Repotting: Repot infrequently.
Problems: Subject to crown rot in overly moist conditions. Leaves will wilt or become damaged by dry air.

Tolmiea menziesii

Xanthosoma

Cactus: *Aporocactus flagelliformis*

Cactus: *Astrophytum myriostigma*

Cacti and Succulents

Over millions of years, cacti and succulents, stubborn individualists of the plant world, adapted to great climatic changes. Many stored water in their stems or leaves. Others abandoned the land and took to the trees as epiphytes, using their roots for gripping instead of taking nourishment. Some developed disproportionately thick rootstocks. Others adapted to rocky, frigid climates. In the course of developing such special talents, these plants evolved into unique and wonderful shapes, colors, and textures.

The apartment gardener who has only a sunny windowsill, the commuter who needs patient plants, the collector looking for the unusual—all will find succulents absorbing and satisfying plants. The variation in color, form, size, and drought resistance among the thousands of succulents is surprising to the uninitiated. It is entirely possible to get hooked on succulents without ever tangling with a prickly one. The richness of variety accounts for their wide appeal.

Succulents, of which cacti are a part, have mastered the art of water conservation. By reducing their leaf surface to cut down on water loss from transpiration and by storing water in their stems or leaves, succulents can control both the amount of water they need and the amount they use.

The following section describes some of the more popular species and gives general care information.

Cacti

The large family of cacti encompasses more than 2,000 plants, all of which are succulents. It is a common misconception that spines are the characteristic that distinguishes cacti from other succulents. Although most cacti have spines, some do not. The distinguishing characteristic is the presence of *areoles,* the small sunken or raised spots on cactus stems from which spines, flowers, and leaves grow. A few of the most popular cacti are described below. They are divided into two categories, desert cacti and epiphytic cacti, according to their cultural requirements.

Desert Cacti

Desert cacti are extremely tolerant plants, but they do need a very porous soil that drains well. Water them occasionally and feed them with a low-nitrogen fertilizer every 2 weeks during the growing season, from early spring to midautumn. Place them in a sunny window with warm daytime temperatures and nighttime temperatures around 10° to 15° F cooler. Most cacti need a cool, dry, dormant period in winter to bloom well the following spring or summer.

Aporocactus flagelliformis
Rattail cactus

Rattail cactus produces narrow stems ½ inch wide and up to 6 feet long. In the wild it has aerial roots that grip onto rockfaces. For indoor culture, place the plant in a hanging basket and occasionally remove the old, brown stems. The flowers are large and are borne all along the stems in summer.

Astrophytum
Bishop's-cap, star cactus

Bishop's-caps have thick, green stems. Their globular forms vary in shape, accounting for the common names. Most are small plants, but some grow to 3 feet. Yellow flowers appear on the top of the cactus. Many cultivars are spineless.

Cephalocereus senilis
Oldman cactus

An upright, cylindrical cactus, oldman cactus can reach a height of 10 feet and a diameter of 8 to 10 inches. Its gray-green body develops soft, furry spines while still immature. Rose, funnel-shaped flowers are borne atop the cactus when it is several years old. It grows slowly and is good on a windowsill when young.

Cereus
Peruvian apple, curiosity-plant

Cereus species have deeply ribbed, blue-green stems. Certain cultivars, such as *C. peruvianus* 'Monstrosus', are noted for the numerous deformed growths that cover the plant. They can reach a height of 20 feet. Large flowers, borne all along the stems in summer, open at night.

Chamaecereus
Peanut cactus

Chamaecereus, a popular genus sometimes sold as *Lobivia,* has short, clustering green stems that grow to 6 inches long. They are ribbed and covered with short, bristly spines. Vivid, scarlet red flowers appear in the summer all along the stems. These cacti do best in a shallow pot. Susceptible to mealy bugs.

Cleistocactus
Scarlet-bugler, silver-torch

The cylindrical, green, clustering stems of the cleistocactus can grow to a mature size of approximately 3 inches in diameter and 2 to 3 feet high. They have many ribs and spines, which vary from white to brown, dense to sparse. Scarlet or orange flowers are borne along the length of the stems during the summer.

Echinocactus grusonii
Golden barrel cactus

A popular globe-shaped cactus, golden barrel cactus has yellow spines prominently borne on its stem ribs. It grows slowly but can reach 3 feet in diameter. Yellow, bell-shaped flowers are borne on the top central ring in the summer. This plant will tolerate moderately lit locations, but will not grow or flower in them.

Cactus: *Cephalocereus senilis*

Cactus: *Cereus peruvianus*

Cactus: *Chamaecereus*

Cactus: *Cleistocactus*

Cactus: *Echinocactus grusonii*

Cactus: *Echinocereus pulchellus*

Cactus: *Echinocereus triglochidiatus*

Cactus: *Ferocactus latispinus*
Cactus: *Echinopsis silvestrii*

Cactus: *Gymnocalycium denudatus*

Echinocereus
Strawberry cactus

Strawberry cacti are generally upright, cylindrical plants that form self-branching clumps of stems. The various cultivars have differing spine arrangements and colors. The flowers, which are usually purple, appear near the tops of the stems in late spring or summer. Strawberry cactus is sensitive to salts and crown rot and is not recommended for beginners.

Echinopsis
Urchin cactus

The urchin cactus is best known for its abundant, large, long-lasting, funnel-shaped flowers, which range from white to pink and sometimes reach 8 inches in length. Its gray-green, globular to oval stems grow singly or in clusters. They are distinctly ribbed and have clusters of spines along the ribs. Urchin cactus is small and makes a good windowsill specimen.

Ferocactus
Blue barrel cactus, devil's-tongue, fishhook cactus

Ferocactus species can be globular or columnar and vary in color from blue-green to green. They have approximately 10 to 20 ribs, spines that range from yellow to red, and yellow to red-purple flowers that appear at the top of the plant in summer (once the plants are many years old).

F. echidne is a globular species with straight, yellow spines and yellow flowers. F. glaucescens (blue barrel cactus) is a distinctive glaucous green with pale yellow spines and yellow flowers. F. latispinus (devil's-tongue) is a depressed, globular plant with yellow radial spines, red central spines, and rose-colored flowers. F. macrodiscus is a depressed, glove shape with curved spines and purple flowers. F. wislizenii (fishhook cactus) is columnar, with white radial spines; red, brown, or gray, hooked central spines; and orange-red to yellow flowers.

Gymnocalycium
Chin cactus, spider cactus

The globular stems of chin cactus grow in clusters or singly, each stem 8 to 12 inches thick, depending on the species. They usually bear thick spines that vary in color and number from one species to the next. The bell-shaped, white to pale rose flowers are borne near the top of the plant in spring and summer. The most common chin cacti are *G. mihanovichii* and its red cultivar, 'Hibotan'.

Lobivia
Lobivia, cob cactus

Lobivias are small cacti often grown in clumps in a wide, flat container. They bloom more easily than many other cacti. The large, yellow, red, or purple flowers appear in spring and summer and generally last a long time.

Mammillaria
Pincushion cactus, snowball cactus, little candles cactus, silver cluster cactus, rose pincushion

The numerous and extremely diverse members of the *Mammillaria* genus include globular and cylindrical forms. They range from tiny, individual heads only a few inches wide to massive clumps. Unlike other cacti, whose flowers are borne on areoles, mammillaria blooms grow from the joints of tubercles, or nodules, forming a ring around the top of the plant. Flowering occurs from March to October.

M. bocasana 'Inermis' (snowball cactus) has hooked, yellowish spines and yellow, bell-shaped flowers. M. prolifera (little candles or silver cluster cactus) is a small, globe-shaped cactus with bristly, white spines and yellow flowers. M. zeilmanniana (rose pincushion) has a solitary stem topped with a ring of purple flowers.

Notocactus
Ball cactus

The dark green ball cacti have spines that may be white to yellowish white or reddish brown and bell-shaped flowers that are mostly yellow (though some are red-purple). N. leninghausii, one of the largest species, can reach 3 feet tall. This plant is a good choice for beginners.

Opuntia
Opuntia, bunny-ears

A flattened stem resembling a pad characterizes most of the *Opuntia* genus. Small tufts of spines create a dotted

Cactus: *Lobivia allegraiana*

Cactus: *Mammillaria bocasana*

Cactus: *Notocactus leninghausii*

Cactus: *Opuntia microdasys*

Cactus: *Rebutia minuscula*

Cactus: *Epicactus* 'Bella Vista'

pattern over the surface of the plant. *O. microdasys* (bunny-ears) has flat pads growing out of the top of large mature pads, creating the form that gave it its name. These cacti require minimal care once they are established. Most *Optunia* rarely bloom indoors, but *O. salmiana*, differing from other *Optunia* with its long, cylindrical stems, will produce snow-white flowers in summer.

Rebutia
Rebutia, fire-crown, red-crown, scarlet-crown

Rebutias are small, glove-shaped, shiny, light green to dark green cacti covered with small, warty tubercles. The short spines range from white to dark brown. Yellow, red, or purple flowers, which are long, thin, and large, open from the base of the plant during the summer, often obscuring the cactus itself.

Care of Desert Cacti

Light: Provide at least 4 hours of curtain-filtered sunlight from a bright south, east, or west window.
Water: During dormancy, water sparingly. At other times, water thoroughly, but allow to dry between waterings.
Humidity: Dry air is generally not harmful, but keep plant out of drafts.
Temperatures: To set flower buds, 40° to 45° F at night, 60° to 65° F during the day. At other times, 50° to 55° F at night, 65° to 70° F during the day.
Fertilization: Fertilize lightly during the spring and summer growing season with a low-nitrogen fertilizer.
Propagation: Start new plants by dividing an old specimen. Seeds are available, but can be more difficult than division.
Grooming: None usually needed.
Repotting: Repot infrequently, into a very porous soil mix.
Problems: Poor drainage, too-frequent watering, or standing in water will cause root rot. Will not bloom if light is too low.

Epiphytic Cacti

Epiphytic cacti are the jungle cacti, plants that adapted to their environment by using their aerial roots for clinging to trees rather than for seeking

nourishment. Epiphytic cacti often make spectacular hanging-basket plants; their long, spineless or lightly spined branches bear large, showy blooms in a wide range of colors. These cacti require filtered shade, frequent watering and feeding, and a soil that is rich in humus. Most need a cool, dry, dormant period in the winter to bloom well the following summer.

Epicactus
Orchid cactus

The orchid cactus is grown indoors in hanging baskets. Its branches are flat and arch outward from a central crown. It's grown primarily for its large, showy flowers, which appear anywhere on the stem in spring and early summer. Hybrids are available in reds, yellows, oranges, or white.

Rhipsalidopsis gaertneri
Easter cactus

Easter cactus (also known as *Schlumbergera gaertneri*) is often confused with *S. × buckleyi*, but it droops less, and its stems and joints bear scarlet, sharp-tipped, upright or horizontal flowers. It blooms at Eastertime, and sometimes again in early fall. Cultivars are available in shades of pink and red.

Rhipsalis
Chain cactus

The jointed, branching, leafless stems of the chain cactus cascade or climb in its native habitat, making them particularly suitable for hanging pots and baskets. They have aerial roots on their flattened or cylindrical green stems. Flower shape, color, and size vary greatly within the genus.

Schlumbergera
Holiday cactus, Christmas cactus, Thanksgiving cactus

Schlumbergeras are native to the tropical forests of South America, where they grow on trees. Their stems are unusual and the blossoms beautiful and timely. *S. × buckleyi* (Christmas cactus) has arching, drooping stems of bright green. The stems are spineless, but scalloped, and bear tubular flowers in a wide range of colors at Christmastime. *S. truncata* (Thanksgiving cactus) flowers earlier in winter. Its stem joints are longer and narrower than later-blooming schlumbergeras. The 3-inch-long flowers, borne at the ends of the stems, are shades of white and red.

Schlumbergeras require a rich, porous soil. Keep the soil moist but not soggy, and fertilize weekly when the plants are growing. They do well in front of a cool, bright window. During the summer you can move them outdoors into partial shade. Budding is brought on by the short days of October and November or by a cold shock. To promote flowering, place plants outdoors for a time during the fall. After plants flower, keep them drier and withhold fertilizer.

Care of Epiphytic Cacti

Light: Place in a bright but indirectly lit south, east, or west window.
Water: Keep very moist during growth and flowering; at other times, allow to dry between waterings.
Humidity: Average indoor humidity levels.
Temperatures: To set flower buds, 40° to 45° F at night, 60° to 65° F during the day. At other times 50° to 55° F at night, 65° to 70° F during the day.
Fertilization: Fertilize only when plant is growing actively or flowering.
Propagation: Take cuttings from recently matured stems or shoots when plant is not in flower.
Grooming: Prune after flowering if needed.
Repotting: Repot infrequently, into a humus-rich soil.
Problems: Dry soil or a high level of soluble salts may damage roots, causing dieback.

Succulents

Succulents are generally easy to care for and are a good starting point for beginning gardeners. Despite the many different types of succulent plants, they require the same basic care. To grow well they need a porous, fast-draining soil, plenty of sunlight, good air circulation, and plenty of water. During the winter they must go dormant in a cool, dry environment. Succulents need this rest time to bloom the following season. In summer, revitalize the plants by moving them outdoors.

Cactus: *Rhipsalidopsis rosea*

Cactus: *Schlumbergera bridgesii*

Cactus: *Rhipsalis cruciformis*

Cactus: *Rhipsalidopsis gaertneri*

Succulent: *Agave victoriae-reginae*

Succulent: *Adromischus mammillaris*

Succulent: *Adenium obesum*

Succulent: *Aeonium arboreum*

Adenium
Adenium, desert-rose

Adeniums take rather strange forms, each one creating its own sculptural design. The fleshy stem varies from gray to pale brown; the leaves are a shiny green, but they are not produced in any abundance. Flowers are brilliant red to pink with pale centers and appear in clusters at the branch tips during the summer. *A. obesum* (desert-rose) is a popular variety with pink flowers. To flourish, adeniums require more attention than most succulents. Keep them underpotted and in loose soil, and be patient: They take many years to grow to any size.

Adromischus
Adromischus, pretty-pebbles, sea-shells, plover-eggs, leopard's-spots, crinkleleaf

The many species of adromischus are stout-stemmed succulents that grow in clumps and look best in a shallow, broad container. Many have egg-shaped leaves with speckles or spots, giving rise to their unusual common names. Some species have crinkled leaves. The plants will grow in indirect light but develop better leaf color in bright light. Like most succulents, they can be allowed to dry out between waterings if they are not overfertilized. Many indoor gardeners use them in bonsai plantings.

Aeonium
Aeonium, pinwheel-plant

Variety is the word for aeoniums. Some grow into large bushes; others make just one large, flattened rosette, up to 16 inches wide. The leaves are glossy and vary from apple green to a deep maroon-tinged red. The flowers are usually small and yellow and bloom in profusion at the ends of long stems. Aeoniums need more water than most succulents to thrive and bloom, and they do best in large containers.

Agave
Agave, century plant

Agaves are large plants with thick, pointed leaves. Several of the smaller types, such as *A. victoriae-reginae* (painted century plant), are particularly suitable for indoor gardening, although

A. americana and its various variegated clones are also popular indoor plants, despite their size. Agaves grow very slowly but need good light. Keep them drier in winter to give them a moderate dormancy period. Repot very infrequently. After a plant matures it may produce a tall flower spike.

Aloe

Aloe, torch-plant, lace aloe, medicine-plant, burn aloe, tiger aloe

There is great diversity among the plants in the *Aloe* genus. *A. aristata* (torch-plant, lace aloe) is a dwarf species that has stemless rosettes edged with soft, white spines or teeth. In winter it bears orange-red flowers. *A. barbadensis* (also known as *A. vera*) is commonly called medicine-plant or burn aloe, since it is most widely known for the healing properties of its sap. Many people use the liquid from a broken leaf to treat minor burns. It is a stemless plant with green leaves and yellow flowers. *A. variegata* (tiger aloe) has white-spotted green leaves in triangular rosettes. Pink to dull red flower clusters appear intermittently throughout the year.

Beaucarnea recurvata

Elephantfoot tree, ponytail-palm

The common names of *Beaucarnea recurvata* come from its somewhat unusual appearance. Its trunk resembles that of a palm, and mature specimens have a greatly swollen base that resembles an elephant's foot. It has a cluster of long, narrow leaves that arch outward from the top. Although the plant can grow to more than 30 feet outdoors, it usually reaches only 6 or 8 feet indoors. This succulent stores water in its trunk, so it can go without water (and most other care) for long periods. Because it grows so slowly, purchase a large specimen for an indoor garden.

Ceropegia

Rosary vine, hearts-entangled

Rosary vine produces long, purple runners with tiny, heart-shaped leaves. The leaves, borne in pairs at regular intervals along the vine, are patterned with silver on top and purple beneath. Tiny tubers that form at the leaf joints as the plant matures can be removed and rooted to start new plants.

Succulent: *Beaucarnea recurvata*

Succulent: *Aloe barbadensis*

Succulent: *Ceropegia woodii*

Succulent: *Cotyledon undulata*

Succulent: *Crassula argentea*

Succulent: *Echeveria elegans*

Cotyledon
Silver-crown

Cotyledon is a large and diverse genus. The plants are shrubby, and their mature size ranges from a few inches to several feet. Most species grown by collectors have persistent, succulent leaves in varying colors from yellow-green to blue-gray, and bell-shaped, yellow to red flowers on long stems borne above the leaves during spring and summer. *C. orbiculata* is distinguished by red-margined leaves and red flowers. *C. undulata* is large, with wavy-edged leaves. Many of the deciduous species are available under the name *Tylecodon.*

Crassula
Airplane-plant, baby jade, jade plant, moss crassula, rattail crassula, rattlesnake, scarlet-paintbrush, silver jade plant

Crassulas form a widely diversified plant group, characterized by unusual and varied leaf forms, arrangements, and colors. *C. argentea* (jade plant, baby jade) is popular and easy to grow. A compact, treelike succulent, it has stout, branching limbs with oblong, fleshy leaves 1 to 2 inches long. In direct sunlight, the smooth, dark green leaves become tinged with red. Repot it infrequently, but prune occasionally to maintain its shape and size. *C. arborescens* (silver jade plant) has gray leaves with red margins and seldom flowers. *C. falcata* (scarlet-paintbrush, airplane-plant) is known for its long, sickle-shaped, gray-green leaves and clusters of scarlet flowers above the foliage. *C. lycopodioides* (moss crassula, rattail crassula) is good for hanging baskets; its slender stems bear tiny, green, scaly leaves. *C.* 'Morgan's Pink' has fragrant, salmon to rose flowers and small, clustering leaves. *C. teres* (rattlesnake) is a narrow, cylindrical plant with closely arranged, pale green leaves.

Echeveria
Echeveria, hen and chicks, pearl echeveria

All echeverias have in common a rosette form. Their greatly varied leaf color ranges from pale green through deep purple. Many are luminous pink in full sun. *E. elegans* (pearl echeveria) forms a tight rosette of small, whitish green leaves. Rose flowers tipped with yellow are borne on pink stems in spring or summer. *E.* 'Morning Light' is a hybrid that has rosettes of luminous pink foliage. Echeverias are ideal for dish gardens.

They generally do well with more water, more fertilizer, and richer soil than most succulents. Exposure to light has a direct effect on the intensity of foliage color. If stems become leggy, cut down the plant and root a cutting.

Euphorbia
African-milkbarrel, corkscrew, cow's-horn, crown-of-thorns, living-baseball

The genus *Euphorbia* is too diverse to allow more than a few generalizations. All species have a toxic, milky sap. Mature sizes range from a few inches to many feet. The leaves are generally insignificant and deciduous. Many species have spines, though unlike cacti spines, they do not grow out of areoles. The flowers are usually quite small, often yellow or greenish yellow. Euphorbias are propagated most easily from cuttings. The end must be immersed in cold water or powdered charcoal and allowed to form a callus before rooting. As a rule, euphorbias require a slightly richer soil than do most succulents. They are unbothered by low humidity indoors, but do need bright light.

E. flanaganii 'Cristata' has ribbed, spiny green stems. *E. grandicornis* (cow's-horn) has spiny, branching gray-green stems. *E. horrida* (African-milkbarrel) has many spiny, succulent ribs. *E. mammillaris hybridus* (corkscrew) is a dwarf euphorbia, with clusters of cylindrical stems. *E. milii* (crown-of-thorns) has twining, spiny stems with green leaves and bright pink to red bracts. *E. obesa*, with the intriguing common name of "living-baseball," is a spineless, ball-shaped succulent with gray and green markings. *E. pseudocactus* is spiny, ribbed, and columnar.

Faucaria
Tiger's-jaws

Tiger's-jaws, a popular, short-stemmed succulent, takes its name from its triangular leaves, which have small teeth along their margins. The leaves are often spotted and grow in small, low clumps, ranging in color from bluish

Succulent: *Euphorbia baioensis*

Succulent: *Euphorbia milii*

Succulent: *Euphorbia grandicornis cristata*

Succulent: *Euphorbia fulgens flava*

Succulent: *Euphorbia milii*

Succulent: *Faucaria*

Succulent: *Gasteria*

Succulent: *Graptopetalum saxifragoides*

Succulent: *Haworthia*

Succulent: *Kalanchoe blossfeldiana*

green to olive green. *F. tigrina* has gray-green stems with white dots. *F. tuberculosa* has dark green leaves with small white bumps on the upper side. In summer, both produce yellow to white flowers that resemble dandelion blossoms. This plant is a good choice for beginning gardeners.

Gasteria
Ox-tongue

The leaves of ox-tongues form rosettes, spiraling one on top of another. They are thick and usually dark green with variously colored dark or light spots. In summer, reddish orange flowers appear on a long stalk, which may dip or arch. These plants will tolerate a little less light than many other succulents.

Graptopetalum
Graptopetalum, ghost-plant, mother-of-pearl plant

Graptopetalums bear lovely rosettes of thick leaves on long stems. The leaves are a luminous white with pink-purple tones. Mature rosettes measure approximately 3 inches in diameter. The bell-shaped flowers are straw-colored with maroon markings. Graptopetalum is easy to grow and especially suited to hanging baskets.

Haworthia

There is wide variation among haworthias, but all are excellent indoors. Although they will grow in moderate light, bright indirect light will improve their foliage color and texture. The leaves of most species are thick and form rosettes on stemless plants. They flower at different times, depending on the species. The flowers are small and borne in clusters on long stems. After flowering, the plants may go dormant and will need repotting.

Kalanchoe
Kalanchoe, Christmas kalanchoe, felt-plant, flaming-katy, pandaplant

Kalanchoes are popular succulents grown for both their flowers and foliage. The leaves of *K. beharensis* (felt-plant) are large and triangular with curving, rippling edges. They are covered with brown hairs, which give them a felty appearance. Pink flowers appear in spring. *K. blossfeldiana* (Christmas kalanchoe, flaming-katy) produces heads of brilliant scarlet, orange, or yellow flowers on thin stems 15 inches high. Its shiny, green, oval leaves are tinged with red. *K. tomentosa* (pandaplant) grows to 15 inches. Plump leaves covered with silvery hairs branch from a central stem. The pointed leaves are tipped with rust brown bumps. *K. daigremontiana*, and some other species, has plantlets on its leaves, but rarely flowers indoors.

Living-stones

Living-stones are perhaps the most interesting of all succulents. As the name implies, this group of several genera with similar cultural requirements resembles small rocks, mimicking their natural environment. They can be particular in their cultural requirements and are not recommended for beginning gardeners. They need minimal watering during their nonflowering periods, which for some are our summer months. They are usually best propagated from seed.

Conophytum grows in stemless, clumping leaf pairs. Its round, thick foliage ranges in color from blue-green and gray-green to yellow-green. The leaves are often speckled and usually have "windows," or small slits, at the top, which form the division between the leaves. Each year the surface of the old leaf pair dries and splits to expose two new leaves. White to yellow flowers, like dandelions, appear from the slit, usually during winter.

Dinteranthus (flowering-stone) has thick, stemless, whitish leaf pairs that mimic the surrounding stones in their native habitat. It grows in clumps that rarely exceed 6 inches in diameter. Yellow, dandelionlike flowers appear in winter at the split between the leaf pair.

Fenestraria (window-plant, baby-toes) has thick, dull green, stemless leaves that clump to form a 2- to 2½-inch rosette. The leaves have "windows," or slits, at the top of each. The yellow or white daisy flowers, 2 to 3 inches in diameter, are borne on a short stem above the leaves in summer.

Lapidaria has smooth, stemless pairs of leaves that resemble very pale green stones. The daisylike flowers are yellow to creamy white, fading to pink as they age. They are 1½ to 2 inches across and appear in the summer.

Lithops is probably the most popular and well known of the living-stones. Its short leaves imitate both the shape and the coloring of rocks. It grows in stemless clumps of paired leaves approximately 1 to 2 inches in diameter. Yellow to white dandelionlike flowers emerge from between the leaves in November, December, and January. Lithops needs very-fast-draining soil.

Pleiospilos has thick, low-growing leaf pairs that are brown-gray with darker dots over the surface. They grow in stemless clumps from 1 to 5 inches in diameter. Yellow-orange dandelionlike flowers emerge from between the leaves in summer. Blossoms are usually 2 to 3 inches across.

Pachyphytum
Pachyphytum, thick-plant

The fat, rounded leaves of pachyphytum form attractive rosettes on long stems. Leaf color varies from a dusty gray-pink to a glaucous blue. Rosettes can be up to 8 inches across, depending on the species. Small, bell-shaped flowers range from white to orange to red or pink. Pachyphytums need plenty of bright but not too hot light to bring out their maximum foliar color. They are a good choice for hanging baskets.

Pachypodium
Pachypodium

A widely varied genus, *Pachypodium* includes plants that are shrubby and plants that are columnar and covered with thorns. Most species have long, thick, leathery, dark green foliage. The flowers range from white to yellow to red. The star-shaped blooms are borne at the tips of the branches in spring. Pachypodiums go through a leafless winter dormancy, when water should be withheld.

Succulent: *Lithops*

Succulent: *Pachyphytum*
Succulent: *Pachypodium lamerei*

Succulent: *Portulacaria*

Succulent: *Sansevieria trifasciata*

Portulacaria
Elephant-bush

Elephant-bush is a shrub with a reddish brown trunk and stems and small green leaves. Clusters of pale pink flowers are produced by very old specimens; younger plants do not flower. This plant is very easy to grow, and the attractive stems and shrubby habit make it ideal for bonsai gardens. *P. afra* 'Variegata' has light green and creamy white variegated foliage.

Sansevieria trifasciata
Sansevieria, snakeplant, mother-in-law's-tongue

One of the hardiest of all indoor plants is *Sansevieria*. Erect, dark green, lance-shaped leaves emerge from a central rosette. Golden yellow stripes along the margins and horizontal bands of grayish green create a striking pattern similar to the coloring of an exotic snake. *S. trifasciata* 'Laurentii' has wide, creamy yellow stripes along the leaf edges. Dwarf sansevierias include *S. trifasciata* 'Hahnii' and *S. trifasciata* 'Golden Hahnii'. A relative, *S. cylindrica,* has round leaves with pointed tips. Mature plants produce fragrant, pink or white blooms in spring.

Given proper care, sansevieria makes a showy accent for any indoor decor. Place it in a brightly lit, warm location, and water it regularly, as soon as the soil becomes dry. Overwatering will cause root rot. Fertilize every 2 or 3 months.

Sedum
Donkey's-tail, burro's-tail, jellybeans

S. morganianum (donkey's-tail, burro's-tail) is a trailing, slow-growing succulent. Its light gray to blue-green leaves are ½ to 1 inch long, oval, and plump. The 3- to 4-foot trailing stems, densely covered with these leaves, create a braid or rope effect. This plant is ideal for hanging containers. Place it where it won't be disturbed, because the leaves break off easily. Also, don't be alarmed by the powdery bluish dust covering the leaves; it's called bloom. *S. × rubrotinctum* (jellybeans) has rosy-tipped, bean-shaped leaves on upright stems and yellow flowers that appear in late winter.

Senecio
Cocoon-plant, gooseberry-kleinia, string-of-beads

Senecio is a large and widely varied genus that includes small succulents, hanging or climbing vines, and large shrubs. The stems of all the succulent species are spineless, supporting leaves that are spherical and thick or flat and elongated. The small daisy flowers come in yellows, whites, and reds, depending on the species. Some are petalless. They are borne at the ends of the stems in summer. *S. haworthii* (cocoon-plant) is a small shrub with soft, felty hairs on the leaves and yellow flowers. *S. herreianus* (gooseberry-kleinia) is an excellent hanging plant with elliptical green leaves. String-of-beads (*S. rowleyanus*) has hanging stems that bear unusual, ½-inch, spherical leaves. The leaves look like light green beads with pointed tips and have a single translucent band across them. Small, fragrant, white flowers appear in winter.

Stapelia
Carrion-flower, giant toadplant

Carrion-flowers have leafless, green stems and large, star-shaped flowers that are notable for their lurid colors, odor, and size. The flowers are generally in shades of yellow or red with maroon spotting and are borne along the stems in late summer and fall. Sometimes they have an extremely unpleasant scent, like decaying meat. Although it does serve to attract pollinating flies to the flowers, the odor is undesirable for most indoor gardens unless the plants are placed away from people. *S. gigantea* (giant toadplant) has flowers that are large even for the genus; they are yellow with red ridges and grow to 12 inches. *S. nobilis* has flowers of a darker yellow with a thick, purple pile. Carrion-flowers are susceptible to crown rot and mealybugs if the soil is too wet or too dry.

Yucca

Yucca

Yuccas are commonly grown outdoors as accent, or specimen, ornamentals. Because they are large and tolerate adverse conditions, they are also frequently used in commercial interiors. The thick, swordlike leaves have sharp tips that can puncture the skin. Mature plants have a canelike trunk with whorls of foliage at the end. Side shoots form occasionally. *Y. aloifolia* has sharp leaves to 2½ feet long and white flowers in dense, erect clusters. *Y. elephantipes* has wide, dark green leaves 4 feet long that are particularly effective for a dramatic setting; *Y. elephantipes* 'Variegata' is a variegated cultivar. Recently rooted canes taken from sections of large stock plants will produce a floor-sized specimen in very little time.

Care of Succulents

Light: Place in a bright, indirectly lit south, east, or west window.

Water: Water thoroughly when the soil ½ inch below the surface is dry. Discard drainage.

Humidity: Dry air generally does no harm.

Temperatures: 50° to 55° F at night, 65° to 70° F during the day.

Fertilization: Fertilize lightly with a low-nitrogen fertilizer in spring and summer. Continue fertilizing, though even more lightly, through fall and winter for succulents that grow actively the year around.

Propagation: Stem cuttings and off-sets root easily. Dry the offset or cutting for a few days until a callus forms, then plant in well-drained potting mix and keep barely moist. Many succulents can also be reproduced from leaf cuttings.

Grooming: Cut off flower stalks as the blooms age.

Repotting: Repot only every 3 or 4 years, when essential. Use a shallow pot and a very porous soil.

Problems: Root rot can result from soggy soil caused by poor drainage or excessive watering. Stem and leaf rot may be caused by cool, damp air. Leaves wilt and discolor from too much water, especially in winter. Brown dry spots are caused by underwatering.

Succulent: *Sedum morganianum*

Succulent: *Senecio rowleyanus*

Succulent: *Yucca pendula glauca*

Succulent: *Stapelia pulvinata*

Index of Common Names

If a plant's common and botanical names are the same, the plant name will not be on this list. For more detailed information, see the Index at the back of the book.

INDEX

Note: Page numbers in boldface type indicate principal references; page numbers in italic type indicate references to illustrations. Information for specific plants is indexed under the botanical name only. To determine the botanical name for a plant, please refer to the Index of Common Names on pages 308 to 311.

315

320

PHOTOGRAPHERS
Names of photographers are followed by the page numbers on which their work appears. R=right, C=center, L=left, T=top, B=bottom.

Front Cover
Kenneth Rice
Back Cover
Michael McKinley: Top left, bottom left, bottom right
Pam Peirce: Top right
Chapters 1 through 6
Bill Apton: 164
Max Badgley: 187B
M. Baker: 179
Laurie Black: 12, 15, 20, 22, 23, 26–27, 28, 32–33, 34–35, 37, 38, 41, 44, 46, 48–49, 51, 54–55, 61, 102T, 138, 139T, 139B, 146, 148, 181, 182
John Blaustein: 97, 120R
Allen Boger: 195B
Ralph Byther: 188T
Kristie Callan: 186T, 194C, 195C
Clyde Childress: 154–155
Richard Christman: 70BR
Cooperative Extension Association of Nassau County, N.Y.: 191T
Alan Copeland: 25, 63
Al Crozier: 189B
Spencer H. Davis: 194B
Douglas Evans: 175
W. E. Fletcher: 196B
R. Foothorap: 103R

David Goldberg: 68, 85BR, 91, 95TL, 95R, 101, 132, 134BR, 141, 156, 194T
Richard Henley: 188C
Saxon Holt: 80, 173, 177
R. K. Jones: 191B
M. Keith Kennedy: 187T
Michael Lamotte: 102B
Michael Landis: 85CR, 92R, 120L, 176
Fred Lyon: 72, 140
Michael McKinley: 79, 142
James McNair: 153
Wayne Moore: 192T
Jean Natter: 196T
Lester Nichols: 190T
Ortho Photo Library: 66T, 66C, 66B, 73, 88, 95BL, 116, 117, 124TL, 124TR, 124BL, 124BR, 125T, 125C, 125B, 130T, 130C, 130B, 131T, 131B, 134T, 134BL, 135T, 135B, 150, 152, 165, 166–167, 168
Pam Peirce: 89, 92L, 111T, 111B, 172, 174, 187C, 190B, 193T
Sandra Perry: 193B
Charles Powell: 186B, 191C, 192B, 301B
Kenneth Rice: 1, 2–3, 8–9, 10, 11, 14, 17, 19, 30, 43, 53, 56–57, 65, 70TL, 70TR, 70BL, 82, 83, 85TL, 85TR, 85CL, 85BL, 99T, 99C, 99B, 103L, 105, 107, 108, 114–115, 118–119, 129, 133T, 133B, 136–137, 143, 144, 157, 159, 161, 162–163, 169, 184–185
Malcolm Shurtleff: 197B
Michael D. Smith: 195T
Lauren Bonar Swezey: 196C, 197T
Tom Tracy: 104
Ron West: 188B, 189T

Chapter 7
All photos in this chapter are by Michael McKinley except for the following:
William H. Allen: 246B
Josephine Coatsworth: 212T
Richard W. Lighty: 224B
John A. Lynch: 289B
Robert E. Lyons: 277C
Tovah Martin: 214T, 231TL, 233B, 237CB, 244C, 249C, 280B, 281T, 289C, 292B, 300BL, 303CTR
Joe Mazrimas: 262T
Jack Napton: 208C, 215T, 235B, 247T, 259T, 307B
Ortho Photo Library: 210T, 233B, 237CB
Pam Peirce: 205C, 207B, 209T, 209C, 209B, 212B, 213T, 218T, 219T, 220T, 221B, 222B, 223TL, 223BL, 223TR, 225B, 226B, 227T, 230B, 231B, 232B, 234T, 234B, 235T, 236T, 236B, 237B, 238TL, 238TR, 239B, 240B, 241T, 243B, 244B, 245B, 248B, 249B, 250B, 252T, 252B, 253TL, 256T, 257C, 264B, 266T, 266C, 268B, 269TL, 269TR, 269BR, 271C, 273BR, 274B, 275T, 275B, 276T, 277B, 281C, 284CT, 284CB, 284B, 288T, 288B, 289T, 292C, 293B, 294B, 295TL, 295CL, 295CR, 296TL, 296TR, 296CL, 296B, 297TR, 297B, 298C, 299TL, 299BL, 299BR, 300BR, 302T, 303TL, 303TR, 303CBR, 304T, 304C, 305C, 305B, 306T
Rainbow Gardens: 228B, 298B
Kenneth Rice: 198–199
William Strode/Black Star: 203T, 220C

U.S. Measure and Metric Measure Conversion Chart

		Formulas for Exact Measures			**Rounded Measures for Quick Reference**		
	Symbol	**When you know:**	**Multiply by:**	**To find:**			
Mass (Weight)	oz	ounces	28.35	grams	1 oz		= 30 g
	lb	pounds	0.45	kilograms	4 oz		= 115 g
	g	grams	0.035	ounces	8 oz		= 225 g
	kg	kilograms	2.2	pounds	16 oz	= 1 lb	= 450 g
					32 oz	= 2 lb	= 900 g
					36 oz	= 2¼ lb	= 1000g (1 kg)
Volume	pt	pints	0.47	liters	1 c	= 8 oz	= 250 ml
	qt	quarts	0.95	liters	2 c (1 pt)	= 16 oz	= 500 ml
	gal	gallons	3.785	liters	4 c (1 qt)	= 32 oz	= 1 liter
	ml	milliliters	0.034	fluid ounces	4 qt (1 gal)	= 128 oz	= 3¾ liter
Length	in.	inches	2.54	centimeters	⅜ in.		= 1 cm
	ft	feet	30.48	centimeters	1 in.		= 2.5 cm
	yd	yards	0.9144	meters	2 in.		= 5 cm
	mi	miles	1.609	kilometers	2½ in.		= 6.5 cm
	km	kilometers	0.621	miles	12 in. (1 ft)		= 30 cm
	m	meters	1.094	yards	1 yd		= 90 cm
	cm	centimeters	0.39	inches	100 ft		= 30 m
					1 mi		= 1.6 km
Temperature	°F	Fahrenheit	⅝ (after subtracting 32)	Celsius	32° F		= 0° C
	°C	Celsius	⅝ (then add 32)	Fahrenheit	212° F		= 100° C
Area	in.²	square inches	6.452	square centimeters	1 in.²		= 6.5 cm²
	ft²	square feet	929.0	square centimeters	1 ft²		= 930 cm²
	yd²	square yards	8361.0	square centimeters	1 yd²		= 8360 cm²
	a.	acres	0.4047	hectares	1 a.		= 4050 m²